# The Resurrection of Rights in Poland

Jacek Kurczewski

CLARENDON PRESS · OXFORD
1993

*Oxford University Press, Walton Street, Oxford* OX2 6DP
*Oxford New York Toronto*
*Delhi Bombay Calcutta Madras Karachi*
*Kuala Lumpur Singapore Hong Kong Tokyo*
*Nairobi Dar es Salaam Cape Town*
*Melbourne Auckland Madrid*
*and associated companies in*
*Berlin Ibadan*

*Oxford is a trade mark of Oxford University Press*

*Published in the United States*
*by Oxford University Press Inc., New York*

*Some chapters of this book have previously appeared in Polish,*
*and the author is grateful to their publishers for granting permission*
*to reproduce them in this volume*

*British Library Cataloguing in Publication Data*
*Data available*

*Library of Congress Cataloging in Publication Data*
Kurczewski, Jacek.
The resurrection of rights in Poland / Jacek Kurczewski.
p. cm.
Includes index.
(alk. paper)
1. Poland—Social conditions—1945–  2. Poland—Politics and
government—1945–  3. NSZZ 'Solidarność' Labor organization)
I. Title.
HN539.5A2K87  1993  306'.09438—dc20  93–9237
ISBN 0–19–825685–X

*Set by Hope Services (Abingdon)Ltd.*
*Printed in Great Britain by*
*Bookcraft Ltd, Midsomer Norton, Bath*

To J., M., and M.

# Foreword

This book deals with the social, political, and normative changes of the last decades in Poland, and aims to synthesize the empirical evidence of the normative aspects, as reflected in attitudes and action, with a theoretical interpretation of this historic process. Under Post-Stalinism, as this particular version of Communist rule is called, new social movements were developing throughout Central Eastern Europe. The Polish peaceful revolution of Solidarity has been the object of analysis as a social movement and as a political project, but its normative meaning has been neglected. The question of whether the Polish experience is unique, or whether it has been an expression of processes in train throughout Communist Europe is of singular theoretical and also practical interest. Today, seeing this part of the world as cleansed from the imposed New Social Order, politicians tend either to over-stress the uniqueness of their particular country's experience and prospects or to underline the common features of the regional issues and problems. The political history of the region is, however, more difficult to elaborate due to the secrecy in which some of the major decisions were made. Overall similarity of political effect should not blind us to the variety of forces and circumstances. The question of the peculiarity of modern Polish history also offers a challenge to the social theories elaborated in the last decades in the West under the protective umbrella of the institutionalized Rule of Law within democracy. Was the revolution of the 1980s a living museum, a demonstration of antiquated social problems and ideas? Or was it rather a manifestation of common problems affecting all societies towards the end of the twentieth century? This book aims to help answer these questions.

The book uses different kinds of evidence. The historical political battles waged by Poles against the 'regime', and by Poles within the regime against 'society', are described. In addition, extensive use is made of empirical data collected by the author and his institute. This includes data from surveys of public opinion carried out in Warsaw during the 1980s, and from a nationally representative sample in 1988. The questionnaire used in the survey dealt extensively with views on various rights, and makes it possible to establish for the first time how widely and in what social milieux the idea of various rights was established in Polish society. This material is placed firmly in the context of the historical events through which these rights have been manifested. Data is available from the 1970s (a survey carried out in 1973 by the author with Krzysztof Kiciński of the attitudes of Polish youth, and studies of patterns of conflict management and dispute resolution amongst the inhabitants of Polish towns carried out in 1977 and 1978) to illuminate the historical analysis. This material has not previously been available to the Western reader. Some of this data was gathered as part of a comparative international research project, so the original data is also cited.

The first chapter sets forth the general theoretical perspective on the subject. 'Introduction' is thus to be understood in its literal sense, as a guide enabling one to enter the area under discussion. The function of the guide is to localize the general names. If someone is introduced as 'Mavis-the-friend' or 'Joanna-the-professor', the task is achieved through a combination of direct pointing out of an individual and reference to the general type. 'Solidarity-the-trade-union' might have been a proper example in our case if not for the fact that it might be taken as a misnomer at the beginning. This is why another approach is taken in which the bold attempt is made to look at Polish history prior to the 1989 dissolution of Communist power through sociological categories. This puts the major idea of the book to the fore, to make history intelligible in terms of social structures and, reciprocally, to make social structures intelligible as historical processes. It is not the chronology of the events which is of interest to us but the chronological structure of the process. The events are selected according to the general idea presented in this chapter, the idea of the gradual and painful labour undergone by a society that moved a repressed normative structure to the publicly communicated surface of its collective life. The greater part of the remaining chapters document this labour, but not the earlier ones, because the reader needs to know the context. The second chapter, 'Stalinism as Crime', sets out a typological reconstruction of the Communist regime in Poland as it took shape after 1945. The bloody terror of the early 1950s is held to represent, in its internal logic, the same basic elements of the system that were in effect in later decades after repression on a mass scale had ceased (until the martial-law period) and liberalization occurred. The view of law as purely instrumental did not change, because the social structure of power relations in society did not change at all. The peaceful oppression continued for the sake of the formally but secretly separate ruling class. The Leninist doctrine of State, Party, and Law was the official doctrine throughout the whole period, and provided the internal justification for the power of the ruling class. The basic rules of this system of government are made clear in the third chapter, 'After Stalin: Organized Injustice'.

The fourth chapter describes 'the rise of the new middle class' in Polish society, providing a sociological explanation for the growing resistance to the Communist *ancien régime* in Poland. The present author, since the early 1970s, has held the view that the real social structure in Poland is to be seen neither in terms of a simple rulers–ruled dichotomy, nor in terms of the Stalinist Holy Trinity of working intelligentsia/working class/peasantry, but rather in terms of a ruling élite backed by the organized support of *nomenklatura* membership (the list of positions reserved for the party to fill with its nominees), confronted by the active sectors of the society—the educated and white-collar workers and intellectuals—frustrated in their aspirations. This new middle class (or new middle classes) had a common interest in abolishing the barriers to their influence in their immediate environment of family life, career, and life after work.

In Chapters 5 and 6, the normativity of Polish culture is discussed through the focus of social conflict. Chapter 5 on 'Words and Deeds' deals first with the qualitative as well as the quantitative analysis of a particular source, the demands of Polish strikers made in 1970 and 1971. This analysis permits illustration of the characteristics of Polish culture made earlier in more abstract terms. For instance, it shows that a decade before the idea of 'Solidarity' was invented it had already existed as a normative project, not only in the hearts but also in the mouths of those representatives of the new middle class who were protesting. It also points to some contradictions in the normative structure, particularly a permanent tension between libertarian and egalitarian tendencies. The normative project, as it is understood here, does not limit itself to words but is expressed through deeds as well, and those deeds are analysed to point out that what was labelled as 'rioting' by the ruling élite was in fact the organized expression of both protest against power and solidarity among those oppressed. The words are unintelligible without the deeds that accompanied them, and vice versa; the normative is thus the closely interlinked combination of both conventionally divorced aspects of social action.

Not only words and deeds but other dualities also seem fundamental to social life, and in particular the distinction between ordinary and extraordinary events. Public conflict, such as the Baltic Coast events of December 1970, belong to the second category, while everyday life in the 1970s was in principle devoid of such dramatic events. One needs to remember this duality, which often shocks students of the dramatic periods of history when they encounter it in the depictions of the perennial dramas of birth, work, and death, and trivial memoirs of mundane affairs. This is why a piece of evidence about the style of articulation of 'daily conflicts' presented in Chapter 6 is necessary, and why it makes sense only within the context of the other degrees of awareness with which most of the book is concerned.

Chapter 7 and 8 continue to use sociological evidence to describe Polish normativity as revealed in the internal democracy that was so characteristic a feature of Solidarity in 1980 and 1981. The present author was personally responsible in those years for co-ordination of expertise on internal democracy within Solidarity. The historical facts as well as internal Union statutes, by-laws, and so on are used in Chapter 7 on 'Union Democracy' to point out how it was understood at the macro-sociological level by the participants in the great social project while in Chapter 8 on 'Union Democracy in Action', detailed transcripts of a top-level Solidarity meeting that took place in the first months of 1981 are used in order to point out that the distinction between micro- and macro-sociological levels is not necessarily of significance in the full-scale analysis of social events such as this book attempts to be. Despite all the accusations of an authoritarian style of decision-making, the internal life of Solidarity may serve as an illustration that not only in the American union (the ITU) studied by Seymour Lipset and his colleagues, but also the Polish union, without external regulation but with the conscious attempt to challenge external oppression, there are exceptions to the Iron Rule of Oligarchy. The tensions and the costs of this democracy are shown, as well as the direct democracy which may be linked with both the traditional political ethos and with the novelty of experiencing democracy in practice.

The two following chapters deal with the legacy that the 1980/1 Solidarity left for the martial-law period: formalized censorship and food rationing. This is a remarkably little-known aspect of the historical development of democracy in Poland, but in the context of the preceding description of organized injustice as a feature of the Communist administration of law it should not be surprising. In Chapter 9, on censorship, the history of the negotiations concerning the first legal regulation of administrative preventive censorship in a Communist country is narrated from the autopsy. The main point is that the paradoxical task was to delineate administrative discretion as much as possible, and thus it was necessary to curb freedom of expression in the wording of a statute to provide more room for freedom of expression in practice. Chapter 10 deals with another aspect of the Gdansk Agreements, rationing, which was also forced on the Communist authorities by strikers and then by Solidarity. The 1980s are the years of a complex and formalized system of food rationing, reminiscent of rationing in World War Two. This system, which might be taken as the culmination of the centralized command Communist economy, was in fact a self-defence of society against the Communist administration. This explains the stubborness with which the Communists resisted pressure to introduce it, pressure which Solidarity was applying in 1980/1. In both cases, the regulation was not aimed at introducing a limitation (of freedom of expression or of the market), but at formalizing the otherwise arbitrary Communist Rule of Power which gave the authorities full discretion in matters of political or economic liberties. The following two chapters are based on the more conventional sociological source of attitudinal surveys, with reference to the national survey of 1988, that is, the last year of Communist rule in Poland.

Chapters 11 and 12 represent an attempt to put the observations concerning the Polish case into a broader interpretative context. Chapter 11, 'Daily Bread and Liberation', points to the philosophical question of the norm and normalcy. What is normal in a society which is run contrary to the expectations of its members? Political oppression was too often absolved on the grounds of cultural differences, so it is necessary to realize that there are at least some cases when what from the outside may seem normal for those inside is contrary to their normative expectations. It is tempting to show that even if subjective expectations are put aside, there is a structure that defines the phenomenon in question, so the abnormality of the surface norms is self-evident. This is why I take the phenomenon of the queue as both particularly characteristic of Communist everyday life, and universal as human experience. 'The Constitution of the Heart' (Chapter 12) links the issue of rights and normative structures with some other perennial issues of comparative moral philosophy. Supposedly amoral tribal cultures are compared with Communist society. The potential normative structure that is interpreted through the notion of 'rights' is activated under friendly social circumstances and in this sense could be taken as universal. To take into account both the potentiality and actuality of human experience one needs to consider human life as social and social life as composed of a multitude of layers with different ontological characteristics.

The penultimate Chapter 13, 'Personal Freedoms', uses the other part of the questionnaire on rights used in the 1988 survey. The basic question is, given the development of the democratization of public life based upon political rights that privatize the political conscience, what happens in relation to the individual in his or her physical life concerning rights such as sexual freedom, the right to abortion, procreative decisions, and attitudes towards nakedness? The results show that, contrary to the stereotype, and although Poland is a widely Catholic society, the development of the new middle class movement for personal autonomy has helped also to sustain the principle of the moral autonomy of the individual in relation to the body and its functions. Though there is a vast reserve of traditional Catholic attitudes in this area, based on village life, among old people and those with little education, there is also a new trend towards both secularization and individual religion. The anti-abortion attitudes indicate the possibility of agreement between this new trend within public opinion and the official ideology of the Church, while attitudes on nudity or contraceptives illustrate the opposite case.

In the concluding chapter the author stresses that in Poland at the moment old problems coincide with new ones. People are still concerned with developing the political freedom which they have been deprived of for so long. The new constitution is in preparation, and very slowly the idea of the rule of law is trying to gain ground. To bring the reader up to date, some findings of the author's 1990 national survey on attitudes towards rights are cited. On the other hand, as the recent debate on abortion showed, there are new divisions and new political conflicts waiting at the door for the Polish people. The same problems are evidenced in other post-Communist countries of Europe. Polish tradition focuses on rights, as historical evidence both from the old Poland and from the nineteenth century prove. A specific combination of historical circumstances led to the crystallization of the ethos of rights based not upon legislation or case law but upon mutually contested, but at the same time universally accepted, individual rights. This is an ethos that is characterized by in-built opposition between the forces of individualism and sociability, egoism and solidarity, libertarianism and collective consensus. Communism may in fact have strengthened these traditional proclivities in Poland as well as elsewhere. The question remains open whether in this situation the new public culture will continue to be rights-centred, or whether the rule-of-law model will develop or, yet another possibility, whether another version of authoritarian rule will emerge to deal, at least temporarily, with the settlement of those tensions.

To describe present-day developments in Poland or in other countries leaving totalitarianism is another task and another book. Some observations, however, can be made at this point, summer 1992. Western observers express dissatisfaction with the reality of post-Communist Europe, pointing to the ethnic strife, xenophobia, anti-Semitism, disintegration of political élites, lack of political predictability, and the permanent danger of potentially anti-democratic mass movements. All this is not to be neglected. On the other hand, one needs to put things in a proper perspective. These societies, even if they knew of democracy before, were not able to practise it, and to begin real democracy is a painful task both for the politicians and for the ruled. Europe today should do its best to help its Eastern part to achieve this task in the quickest and least painful way possible. This is why, for instance, it is important to develop inter-parliamentary and supra-parliamentary, intergovernmental and supra-national fora where the new political class from the East can participate. Needless to say, it is even more important to take into account the necessity for the societies at large to participate in what has emerged in the last decades in the West, that is, the international civilization of democracy which is shared by inhabitants of the world from Vancouver through Oxford to Rome, but not yet in Vladivostok. Television here has a role that should not be underestimated. However limited the cultural competence of the newcomers from the East is, it does not seem to be critically below a threshold that can be passed quite quickly, and this is due to the educative influence of television. In this sense what we witness today is the accelerated adherence of the citizens of the former Communist empire to international middle-class culture. For them to assume an active role would, nevertheless, necessitate proper economic restructuring if those newly arrived are not to remain on the margins of the developed world, adding to the pockets of marginalized, culturally and destructured economically and politically dependent populations already existing in the West.

The stress on individual rights and freedoms, so evident in the unofficial currents of Polish history after the Second World War, has as it corollary distrust of central power, the State, and politicians. Fragmentation of the political class in a sense reflects the individualism that remains a pervasive feature of Polish society. The societies that had less of this component in their culture before were perhaps less resistant to Communism, but may have less problems with their readjustment to the political culture built upon free elections and the free market. It is, however, remarkable that problems which a few months ago may have been seen as peculiar to this or that post-Communist society touch the West (or rather the North) as a whole. Candidates for presidency who do unexpectedly well without support from any of the existing political machines; the triumphant entrance into the legislative bodies of organizations that only faintly resemble traditional political parties; sudden switches of the electorate's moods between national- and local-level elections; consumerism, beer-drinking, love-making, ecologism, and localism as the new bases for political identification—all these phenomena seem to demonstrate that, at the moment when we in the East are trying to accommodate ourselves to what are conceived of as the respectable norms of Western political life, the West is facing the problem of accommodating its traditional political institutions of democracy to some, not-yet clearly visible, social undercurrents of change that are affecting the East as well. One thing seems common to both situations, though I would not dare to take it as all-explanatory—the strain between representative and participatory democracy has become too strong. It seems that both in the West and in the East, in the reunited North and in the South, there is a need for new political ideas that would allow the human normative potential to be realized better. Let me hope that studying the past of one of the societies that put so great a stress on freedom may be of some use for those who attempt to work out the new ideas for the new generations.

# Acknowledgements

The Oxford University Centre for Socio-Legal Studies at Wolfson College is both the institution and group of people without whom the writing, editing, and publishing of this book would have been inconceivable. Over the years a close relationship has developed between the Centre and socio-legal scholars at the University of Warsaw. My teacher, the founder of sociology of law in Poland, Professor Adam Podgórecki was hosted by the Centre after he was deposed from his chair in Warsaw by the Communist authorities in the late 1970s. In what emerged from Podgórecki's former chair I was able, gradually, in the 1980s to establish a department of Sociology of Custom and Law, an old-fashioned name which covers a broad area of interests from black-market practices to laws on human reproduction. After martial law, the hospitality of the Centre was a respite. An Australian colleague recently recalled his view of Polish visitors from those years, with a 'Prisoner of War' look. As a POW on holiday leave, I was able to enjoy for some weeks the pleasure of the *Rose and Crown*, and quiet reading. Then my younger colleagues started to come over, and to enjoy British hospitality and the admirable mixture of intellectual rigour and the good way of life which Oxford epitomizes for so many people all over the world.

Visits to the other side of the planet followed. First Don Harris, director of the Centre arrived in Warsaw, his luggage full of powdered milk for the babies of our younger colleagues, in the midst of the Chernobyl disaster! I will never forget that terrifying summer night. We left behind the abandoned cars, and travelled South with Don and two other brave friends, the philosopher Brenda Almond and the late classic figure of sociology of law, Vilhelm Aubert. All of this was to allow a bunch of isolated Poles to have a feeling of being part of the normal academic international society, somewhere in a forgotten castle on the Polish-Slovak border. Mavis Maclean and Robert Dingwall visited us and lectured us later, offering the no-nonsense Oxford Centre view of the sociology of family law, and conversational analysis.

All this was done without any institutional agreements or multi-partite grants, at a time when living conditions in the decaying totalitarian system were at their worst, and only contacts like that established with the Oxford Centre could support our self-integrity amidst the prevailing atmosphere of pessimism and despair.

I wish to express gratitude for this adventure of friendship, not only on behalf of myself, but also on behalf of my colleagues who took part in it—at one time or another members of the Sociology of Custom and Law Centre in today's Institute of Applied Social Sciences (formerly in IPSIR) at the University of Warsaw—Beata Bugaj, Andrzej Czynczyk, Dr Małgorzata Fuszara, Dr Iwona Jakubowska, Dr Sergiusz Kowalski, and Joanna Smigielska, who all experienced the merits of friendship with the Centre.

Coming back to the book, let it suffice to reveal that my mature years have offered me both the excitement of the liberation of the society in which I live, and disenchantment with my own limitations. Neither has made me prone to set out upon such an enterprise. When we are young we struggle with our texts, and a sentence is thought to be decisive in our battles for truth and good. Then we see the new generation struggling with the same innocent zeal on matters that seemed to have been settled a thousand years ago, while others take up the same issues in new words. Dialectics, existentialism, positivism, anti-positivism, structuralism, post-modernism, and others follow one another in the unending string of discourses that, from a time perspective, seem rather to provide new fields for the same game of seeking prestige, rather than a road to deeper knowledge. Intellectual resistance against evil has its internal strength and gives meaning to one's life, while democracy certainly is not a paradise in itself. I did not expect it to be, but it is different to know it and to experience it. Enough to say that, if not for the stubbornness of my good friend Mavis Maclean whom I met in the Oxford Centre for Socio-Legal Studies, nothing would have been accomplished, as it was she who tried to make my broken English easier for the reader, and advised me on how to organize the material, keeping me under strict control. I must confess the whole work would not have been completed but for the memory of Mavis' smiling face, introducing me to the mysteries of punting on the Cherwell close to Wolfson College, with strawberries, champagne, and a contract to be signed with Oxford University Press.

I doubt if it would have been written without the help of others also.

Joanna Kurczewka and Małgorzata Fuszara offered me support in moments of doubt and discussed parts of the text. All the colleagues I have already mentioned from the University assisted me in my teaching and managing tasks, so that I could finish this book. I should mention also Professor Swida-Ziemba who shared the burden of various directorship and deanship tasks since 1980, as well as Professor Krzysztof Kiciński, Director of the new Institute of Applied Social Sciences. I would like to express my thanks to Professor Thomas Mathiesson of the Institute of the Sociology of Law, University of Oslo, and the Norwegian Council of Research for my stay in Oslo in 1990. Susan M. Smock, Dean of the College of Urban, Labor and Metropolitan Affairs at Wayne State University, Detroit, where I spent four quiet months in 1991, also deserves her due share of gratitude for tolerance towards a visitor busy with editing his book. Finally, I would like to thank the Delegates of the Oxford University Press for their willingness to invest in this unpredictable enterprise, during which the warm words of encouragement of Richard Hart and the careful work of editors were the final elements of the *sine qua non* for the product that follows. The responsibility however rests with me.

# Contents

# 1

# Introduction: The Old System and the Revolution

The sudden social movement which, in 1980, crushed the shell of the apparent calmness, passivity, and satisfaction of the Polish people, offered an exceptional opportunity for a review of the various conceptions and pseudo-conceptions which—in lieu of the prohibited sociological reflection—Polish sociologists produced for themselves and for others. Polish sociology, reborn after the liberalization of October 1956, soon lost its breath in the sphere of theories of Polish society. The sociologists' own opinions were camouflaged in the form of the various socio-vocational classifications that passed as the theory of social structure, cyclic models of disturbances that, instead of political theory, were carried out in terms of changing configurations of power within the ruling élite, and in the choice of problems for critical diagnoses of the various spheres of social life. Such a result was probably the goal of the official organizers of academic life: sociology was to be wedded to pseudo-Marxism, the language of official propaganda, so that critical diagnoses—which incidentally were less and less critical in view of the growing conformism of both the sociologists and their superiors—would serve as expert opinions in the sphere of social engineering, to be used by the political leadership which in turn preserved its monopoly of the theory of Polish society and its problems. Such a theory ultimately emerged in the mid-1970s when—to use Jan Strzelecki's formulation—the lyrical model of socialism became absolutely dominant.

That model was based on the following two assumptions: (i) Western societies and other societies within the orbit of the Western world are, as Polish pre-1939 society was, torn by class conflict in general and the daily conflicts of interests of the various social classes, strata, and groups. The Marxist model of social conflict is applied to countries which are not our allies. (ii)

Marxism is not applied to Polish society and to countries which are our allies. A new social theory was worked out, which in fact meant a clandestine adoption of the picture of Western societies as they were seen in Poland. The Polish version of that theory might be termed a patriotic organicism: it is claimed that Polish people in their mass form a homogeneous social organism, inter-connected by various functional relationships and based on the classical division, known from the very inception of the socialist system in Poland in 1945, into the leading functions exercised by the Communist party (first the Polish Workers' Party, and later the Polish United Workers' Party) and the executive functions exercised by the rest of the people, in fact by millions of non-party people and PUWP members, subordinated to 'the leader-ship'. In that model, a given citizen has the same interests as other citizens, and his or her supreme interest consists in the good of the mother country understood as the said organism with bipartite functions. For the good of the country he or she has cer-tain duties, and the leadership has the corresponding prerogatives of power. The goal of an organism consists in development, and hence we have not so much a welfare state as a development state, with the corresponding postponement of welfare some-where into the future. This has its counterpart in the doctrine of 'advanced socialism', propagated in the 1970s, and in non-inci-dental interest in system analysis, structural and functional approaches, and similar theoretical constructions which, even in those versions which do not tend toward social engineering, stress the 'scientific management of society' which was then so strongly favoured.

I claim that by wedding simplified Marxism, oriented out-wards, with an equally simple patriotic-organicism for home use, 'the leadership', after many years of striving in post-1945 Poland, finally achieved a success in the sphere of ideology. This was so because the fundamentals of the doctrine maintained for home use were in agreement with the basic features of the popular social teachings of the Church, which were in favour of social sol-idarity, and with the Polish national tradition which, as a result of the struggle for independence in the nineteenth and twentieth centuries, developed a culture of national unity in the face of an external enemy. This ultimately produced a strange conglomera-tion of opinions, one which, when we study the historical consciousness of the Poles, a historian must view with surprise. In that 'common consciousness' 'the Polish Committee of National Liberation, formed by Communists in 1944, emerges as a direct continuation of General Sikorski's government in exile in London; the Home Army and the People's Army—in fact political opponents—fought shoulder-to-shoulder against the Nazis during the occupation of Poland; Dzierżyński, who organized the Bolshevik political police in Russia after the 1917 revolution,and Piłsudski, who defended Polish independence against the Red Army, were the greatest Polish politicians of the twentieth century, the first to criticize the fatal Polish inclinations to anarchy and mismanagement. This criticism was later taken up by the PUWP Central Committee, and culminated in the benevolent stern regime of martial law introduced on 13 December 1981.

In the 1970s it seemed, then, that Polish society had returned to the stagnation of a monocentric order. Stanisław Ossowski, the most important Polish sociologist after the war, says that under such a system there is no use for sociology. If social order is based on the carrying out by the masses of orders given by the authorities, there is no point in studying individual attitudes and group intentions. Instead of analysing the configuration of social forces, it suffices to analyse the configuration of power in the leadership and, in the perfect case, to analyse the personality of the leader. The sociology of such a society is reduced to cybernetics and political science, the latter being confined to the study of the élite. In such a system the *ancien régime* courtesans are replaced by experts, and the contacts between Professor Paweł Bożyk, Gierek's ill-famed principal economic adviser, and the First Secretary of the PUWP are as important as the contacts between Madame de Montespan and Louis XIV.[1]

The critical attitude toward the recent past manifested itself in the adoption of two ready-made formulas which were abused in the description of social conditions in Poland: unofficial references were made to an authoritarian system and to a totalitarian state. But in fact that system was neither authoritarian not totalitarian, although it strove to become both. The authority and the will of the leader never reached a peak since the time of Stalin,

---

[1] On experts see J. Kurczewski, 'Power and Wisdom: The Expert as Mediating Figure in Contemporary Polish History', in: I. Maclean, A. Montefiore, and P. Winch, *The Political Responsibility of Intellectuals* (Cambridge, 1990).

whose death was deplored by millions of people who in everyday life had suffered under his rule.

The mono-party suffers from a political disease, known in some other systems, which consists in the vagueness of succession. As in the Roman Empire and in traditional African monarchies, there are neither legal not traditional rules that define the way of appointing the successor. This is why the leading group is never in a position fully to accept the actual leader, and this results in a permanent nuclear opposition within the broader and the narrower élite. On the other hand, those groups view with alarm the possibility of a change of leader and try to postpone it until the moment when each member of the group separately, and the group as a whole, become maximally influential. Thus the leader is constantly threatened by resistance on the part of potential successors, each of whom in turn tries to annihilate the chances of his rivals. When the leader gains an almost absolute power, that power is already almost totally reduced to appearances. The leader tours the country visiting steel plants and state animal farms tidied up in his honour, hails the applauding activists, and in turn is fed by them with faked data on the economic development of the country. The individual performances may differ, as widely as the rather benevolent Edward Gierek's rule over Poland through 1970s and the malicious tyranny of Nicolae Ceauşescu in Romania from the 1960s until 1989, but the basic mechanisms are the same.

The authoritarian and totalitarian systems make sense only if directives issued at the top are transmitted downward in an unmodified form, and if true information is passed in the reverse direction. The first part can more easily be put into practice than the second. An effectively functioning monocentric order requires terror to have its instructions carried out, and a secret machinery of supervision of the functioning of the authorities at various levels, which cannot be replaced by supervision by millions of low-level executors of orders. After Stalin's death the use of terror *vis-à-vis* the lower authorities was abandoned with relief for the latter, but the general model of functioning of the social order was preserved. Such a system, however, cannot function well in view of its inner contradiction.

As Max Weber said, authority can be based on law, on tradition, and on individual charisma. Charisma is not subject to rules, and it can never be that each First Secretary enjoys it. Tradition states merely that the First Secretary is chosen by the Political Bureau, but nothing more. The law, as is the rule of such systems, is even more reticent on the subject.

The leader is accordingly chosen on *ad hoc* principles. Dramatic circumstances which make succession necessary account for the fact that, in a dangerous situation, more or less indefinite social hopes are connected with his person: he is to bring the policy of the leadership closer to the aspirations of all, which is an impossible task. At the same time he is handicapped by a lack of legitimation of his personal position, and depends on the élite which has chosen him. Treated with incessant suspicion by the inner élite and made the object of vague hopes by the masses, he is doomed to failure from the very beginning. The arbitrary nature of his selection results in his authority too becoming not so much authoritarian as arbitrary. Such at least has been the political history of post-1945 Poland.

Nor was that system totalitarian: totalitarianism assumes effective control by the state authorities of all spheres of life of the citizens, who are turned into subjects. But the belief that this was so in Poland persisted at the highest level, which explains the strange arbitrariness in the sphere of economic decisions, typical of its whole post-1945 history. It is interesting to note that illusions about the omnipotence of the state persevere longest with reference to industrial administration. It cannot be denied that this is due to the adoption of certain dogmas of vulgar Marxism, or rather to a reversal of Marx's ideas: people want to control economic life in detail by resorting to the law, as if something which is supposedly a reflection of social consciousness could determine relationships in the economic base. If we approach the issue from the historical point of view we note immediately that economic despotism was most efficient in plundering people engaged in private enterprise, and least efficient in direct productive action. The striving for totalitarianism under the system of nationalized economy implies that any functioning of that economy must refute totalitarianism, which becomes merely apparent in the same way that the state was only apparently in a position to control economic activity in the post-1945 system. The managers do what they want, they store illicitly excessive quantities of raw materials and goods, and submit false reports. Their economic inefficiency is due not to their disobeying instructions from the higher authorities, but to their disobedience taking place within an artificial economic system created by the party in power.

That organizational inefficiency of the monocentric order, combined with such typical defects as the idea of representatives of authority who are not subject to any supervision, has become even clearer after the reform of the administrative division of the country. This followed the French model, and eliminated the earlier vestiges of self-government and local government which masked the arbitrariness of the decisions made by a small group of people.

The concept of 'relative deprivation' helps us to recognize one of the parties in the conflict. Popular theories of revolutions are of two kinds. According to the first, revolutions are fomented by external agitators; according to the second, they are rebellions of the most deprived. Historically, both theories are usually wrong. Agitators, if they exist at all, often work in a vacuum. What survives are the memories of romantic heroes and reports in police records. Those who are deprived of everything usually take part in acts of violence if such occur during a given outburst, but they neither initiate nor lead the revolutionary movement. In the case of Poland too, both theories fail. There is, however, a third theory which is quite common and which refers to the first and states that the working class is one of the principal parties of the conflict. I must say that I do not agree with this, although I have to add that I do not use the term 'class' in its narrow, Marxist sense.

As early as December 1970, government propaganda stressed the relatively high earnings of the shipyard workers who went on strike. In August 1980, too, the strikers included the highest-paid groups of workers, which is not to say that other groups did not strike. Is a member of the intelligentsia who helps a worker an agitator, or is he merely involved in the conflict? Can simple formulas of the alliance between workers and part of the intelligentsia adequately explain the participation in strikes of people employed in design offices, nurses, physicians, taxi drivers? We might speak about a solidarity that crosses class divisions, but would it not be simpler and more in accordance with sociological tradition to say that, if there is a common denominator for the groups, persons, and strata on one side of a conflict on a societal scale, then we are dealing with a 'class' even though we had earlier failed to notice the existence of such a class? Such a class, so active in Poland in the summer of 1980, did not comprise, as we shall see later on, all Poles (hence it was not a nation); nor all and only non-party people (hence the conflict was not one between non-party people and the PUWP); nor all those subject to the authorities, for it did not embrace private enterprise, the peasants, or the peasant-workers.

I think that the best way forward is to assume that in the summer of 1980 the struggle was taken up by a new middle class, consisting of people directly subordinate to the authorities in the institutions and factories run by those authorities, people who were more educated or had higher earnings as compared with the truly proletarianized social strata and classes. Perhaps the real social achievement of post-1945 Poland was the blurring of differences between white-collar and blue-collar workers, which made assigning any worker to one or other category purely a matter of statistical convention. The cultural and economic promotion of millions of working people resulted in the emergence of a new middle class, whose further promotion was blocked, on the one hand, by the closed nature of the ruling class, and on the other, by the hampering of social development due to the incompetence of the rulers, that incompetence being linked to the essential features of the system as a whole.

Who, then, formed the other party in the conflict? The generalized theory of social conflicts states simply that it was 'the ruling class'; not any 'new bourgeoisie', 'new capitalists', or 'bureaucracy', but the ruling apparatus for all those spheres of life which are subject to interference by state authorities. In the class conflicts which Marx wrote about, the industrial workers, and the capitalists who were the owners of the factories and ran them, were the opposed parties. It was not a conflict with the ruling class in the state, if that class did not take the side of the capitalists. In the twentieth century the ruling class finally learned to strive for impartiality in such cases. In Polish society, though, since the state took over the management of various spheres of life which had previously been in the hands of private or public (but non-state) enterprise, the apparatus of power *qua* the ruling class became a potential party in any conflicts that might emerge. That class included politicians, the apparatus of the PUWP, the civil service, managers of state-owned enterprises, heads of cultural, educational, and scientific institutions, and so on. Within that class there developed the governing élite and the small group consisting of the leaders of the country. There is nothing discreditable in the existence of a ruling class as such; the embarrassing point is that the ways in which the members of the class were recruited and given prizes and privileges were kept secret.

Standing apart from the conflict were other, lower, classes—which is not to say that these would not join the actively revolutionary class if a given conflict were to develop. In the first place we have the peasants who, as a result of the discriminatory policy of the ruling class, still largely retained the nature of an estate which was underprivileged from the legal, economic, and cultural points of view. A separate category consisted of peasant-workers, who lived in two systems of reference and hence could not develop a clear sense of their own social identity. I shall just mention here the masses of low-skilled manual and clerical workers, the urban lumpenproletariat, the socially isolated categories of poor pensioners, and the small private entrepreneurs. In those social categories the traditional sociological divisions still retained their meaning and the sense of the various distinct interests seemed to be still strong. This is not to say that this structure is eternal, although I think that any change must be preceded by profound changes in the entire social organization.

Let it be added that the difficulty of identifying the real meaning of the demands made and actions which were undertaken has become an almost definitional characteristic of the revolutionary situation in which Polish people have found themselves. This is so because the situation was fluid. New opportunities were emerging; dormant needs were awakened, and these in turn bred new ones. If I am right in claiming that this includes the frustrated aspirations of the new middle class, then such aspirations are very difficult to formulate because that class still did not exist as a class for itself in the 1970s. The trade-union movement initiated as 'Solidarity' organized that class and its consciousness, but that movement was constantly being joined by new social elements. Solidarity caused changes in the social situation from day to day, and this in turn was changing the strivings and aspirations of the class which it was organizing. In this light it became clear that there were immense problems connected with the need of this movement to find its own language, that would be in contrast to that used by the ruling class. The language of that class, in conformity with the doctrine of patriotic organicism, had appropriated and distorted most terms traditionally valued in Polish culture, such as patriotism, self-government, and socialism.[2]

Alexis de Tocqueville wrote that a revolution does not always break out when those who had it bad begin to have it still worse. It occurs most often when those people who, without complaint and as if indifferently, have tolerated the harshest laws, reject them violently when their burden becomes a little less severe. The system which is abolished by a revolution is almost always better than that which immediately preceded it, and experience shows that the most dangerous moment for a bad government usually comes when it begins to introduce reforms. The evil which people used to suffer patiently as something inevitable begins to seem intolerable to them at the moment when they develop the idea that it can be evaded. The modern sociology of revolutions seems to support that view by making use of the concept of 'relative deprivation'. The most popular model of revolutions, formulated by James Davies, refers to de Tocqueville and treats the suddenly growing hiatus between the rising level of aspirations and the improvement of actual living conditions to be one of their necessary prerequisites. It is in periods of development, after 'a great leap', as Waldemar Kuczyński called it, that people come to realize better that they are handicapped in comparison with their expectations, and this leads to an outburst of accumulated social energy.

As long as the unwieldy system functioned on the principle of programmed economic stagnation under Władysław Gomułka, its defectiveness was irritating but did not lead to any violent counteraction. But when aspirations were aroused (note the propaganda of 'renewal' and 'egalitarianism' after the conflict between the authorities and the intellectuals in March 1968), the sudden increase of prices in December 1970 resulted in the outburst of violence. Increases in meat prices in 1976 and 1980 played the same role with respect to the both dynamic and incompetent

[2] It is of noteworthy symbolism that, as the *Black Book of Censorship*, edited abroad in 1970s, evidences, Communist censorship had not allowed my wife Joanna Kurczewska to publish an article on 'The Patriotic Socialism of Bronisław Limanowski' to be published in the 1970s in independent Catholic monthly *Więź*, edited by T. Mazowiecki, with the underlying assumption that this would suggest that there are patriotic and unpatriotic brands of socialism.

economic policy pursued by Edward Gierek's team. Those crises were also stimulated by the general political conception of the development of the state, which must in principle be continuous so that social aspirations are incessantly stimulated. Hence any serious price increases repeat the classical paradigm, and demonstrate the handicapped position of the masses in the light of development announced as permanent, so creating a potentially revolutionary situation. Cycles of explosions correspond to the cycles of upward business trends and increased aspirations, which are later dramatically confronted (because the public is systematically misinformed about the economic conditions of the country) with facts, namely with a worsening of the economic situation.

Thus, Poland has been changed, not by a rebellion of people in despair, but by a revolution of those whose hopes remained unfulfilled.

The post-1945 political history of Poland can be in the first approximation described as a cyclical process in which the dominant apparatus of power moved towards and away from legitimation based on public approval. That process, in a system which directly combined political and economic power, coincided with a process of cyclical economic ups and downs.

The rise of a new political system is usually dubious from the legal point of view, and the approval of the public is usually a fiction imposed upon it by the victorious section of society. The beginnings of People's Poland are not anomalous in that respect, and there is no point in recalling them. Much more important is what happens later. Does the ruling team succeed in winning the support of an important social group, and can it rule with the atleast tacit approval of the country, or must it oscillate between threats of force and promises of abandoning its use? It seems now that the new configuration in Poland had on several occasions at least a good chance of becoming permanently legitimate in the eyes of the public, but that it lost the chance each time. Though the nation did not want to accept the alien system of rule imposed by Stalin, civil war in the first post-1945 years was rejected by the majority in favour of reconstruction of homes for the people and of the country as the home for all. The resulting animation of the country encountered the second period of reprisals in the form of Stalinist terror and the Stalinist political system. Then again, I would venture to claim, the basic social groups were probably ready to pay that price in exchange for the fulfillment of the promises of social justice and economic prosperity, promises which the Stalinist system was so willing to make. The collapse of the Six-Year Plan (1950–5), preceded by some years of growth, gave way to historically the first movement striving for a change, which found its culmination in October 1956. Władysław Gomułka with his team again gained the confidence of a country tired of Stalinism, only to lose that confidence in the late 1960s. History repeated itself under the rule of Edward Gierek, but more quickly, so that (as I observed in 1980), if nothing changed we expected that the time of rule for the various teams would ultimately be reduced to a decent four-year term of office.

There were some events in the 1970s which visibly led to a weakening of the authorities. First there were the chaotically introduced and immediately recalled price increases in 1976. People saw that the economic decisions of the authorities could be changed, though one had to pay for that with the humiliation of one's human dignity. On the eve of the New Year of 1979 came the disastrous snowstorm followed by the authorities making a staggering public display of incompetence, and people saw that they could save themselves only by taking matters into their own hands. This totally unpolitical event might have had decisive political implications, as the implicit basic duty of any government, however tyrannical, seems to be at least to provide its subjects with the personal security in which public order resides. The Pope's pilgrimage to Poland in 1979 was in turn an opportunity for the millions of Polish Roman Catholics to regain their sense of dignity, as well as to demonstrate suddenly their strength and alternative organizational efficiency. It was somewhere between bargaining over prices, coping with snow and floods, and the Pope's visit that the weakness of Communism and the strength of the masses were revealed; that strength soon, in the summer of 1980, took on the form of a growing movement of solidarity and resistance to the authorities, which were deprived not so much of their means of coercion and violence, as of their legitimacy in the eyes of the ruled.

The introduction of martial law by Prime Minister and First Secretary, General Wojciech Jaruzelski on 13 December 1981 by no means put an end to all this. We don't know his intentions; those stated publicly were addressed both against the developing revolution and the prospect of direct intervention by the Warsaw Treaty forces which served as the military instrument of power of the supranational ruling Communist élite. Judging from a historical distance one may say that it was a wise and costly postponement of a finally inevitable outcome. From this point of view even the narrow national perspective is instructive. The main value of studying Polish post-1945 history for comparative reasons is that it shows, since 1956, the insurmountable limitations of even the most liberal and far-reaching internal reforms within the frame of Communist system of government. Throughout most of the 1980s General Jaruzelski was attempting what later became known as the Soviet project of *perestroika*, that is, fundamental reform without challenging the sacred principle of ultimate political power residing in the Communist party. The question of the development of civil society rapidly became the subject of political debate in Poland. More and more legal institutions were introduced by the Communist government, but still the current state of political life, state, law, and justice was widely held to be unsatisfactory. One may introduce, as Polish Communists did under the anaesthesia of martial law, a Constitutional Court, a Tribunal of the Republic, Ombudsmanship, and so on and still the results will be felt to be unsatisfactory, because the public knows by experience that the invisible 'leading role' of the Party is of a decisive character. The construction of a 'legal state', *Rechtsstaat*, or *pravovoye gosudarstvo* is possible, but since for Communists this means limitation of legality to the state, which remains under their unchallenged political control, the result is even more damaging as the discrepancy between the public concept of the polity and the Communist one becomes more clearly visible.

The resurrection of the language of rights that occurred in the middle of 1970s under the influence of the Helsinki Agreements and the inspiration these gave to the various small but influential political opposition groups, such as the Movement for Defence of Human and Civic Rights, or the Committee for Defence of Workers, and later simply Helsinki Watch could be considered to indicate a recent change in ways of thinking. If this is so, Solidarity then appears as the product of these years, perhaps even of very concrete political circumstances and the personal policies of people like President Jimmy Carter. One can see, however, all these changes as being a manifestation of the deep normative structure that permeates Polish culture and that comes to the surface whenever opportunities appear. That this is the case is, in fact, the main thrust of this book. In this sense it can be said that 'Solidarity' has existed in effect since 1945, when the Communists took power. The same could be said of the struggle for other rights also, not only the fight for freedom of association.

Sociology, with its concern for societal norms, may be employed to study the underlying normative structure. The sociologist is also interested in learning what social conditions favour the emergence of this structure on the surface of institutionalized life. A key social factor here is the development of a strong middle class. This view has been held since Aristotelian times and forms the core of standard theory concerning democracy today. The concept of the middle class is bound inextricably with the market economy, whether in ancient or modern times. The author has maintained since 1980, however, that Solidarity is both a manifestation of and the organization for the new middle class coming into existence within Communist society. This new middle class linked skilled shipyard workers and university professors, who both remained outside the barrier of *nomenklatura*. This class, therefore, united those who had been left outside the sphere of real decision-making, but at the same time were skilled enough to feel legitimate aspirations to such decision-making when it concerned their home, work, living conditions, and the state of society. The problem is that this new middle class lacked sufficient economic power to counterbalance the power of *nomenklatura* that controlled the state. Such economic power seems necessary to secure real freedom of association and the rule of law, and to secure the actualization of the normative structure already in existence.

There seems to be sufficient agreement among social scientists that the normative order represents both collective creation and permanent process, so that I may refrain from quoting the relevant authorities. Instead, I prefer to apply this concept of the normative order to the reality of contemporary Poland. As a guide-line I quote Barrington Moore, Jr. describing the contractual insight into the social sphere:

What takes place, however, is a continual probing on the part of rulers and subjects to find out what they can get away with, to test and discover the limits of obedience and disobedience. No one knows exactly where the limits are until he finds one by experience, although both parties may have reasonably accurate anticipations beforehand . . . Some limit is always there. Otherwise there would be no society. In this sense the terms of the social contract are always being renegotiated.[3]

At first glance the above quotation could have served very well as a summary of the history of Poland since 1945, if it were not for the fact that this history is still in the making. There is, I suggest a striking dissimilarity between social process in Poland prior to the Second World War and after 1945, a difference that forces me to feel that this image of a social contract under permanent renegotiation fits socialist better than capitalist Poland. It reflects, I think, the fact that the very distinction into subjects and rulers is more acute under Communism, while in capitalist democracy power is monopolized to a lesser degree and active support for the ruling group is more widespread among the general population.

Let me move now to the more important issue, that is, to the process of collective discovery of the limits of obedience and disobedience. The simplest application of this idea can be demonstrated by pointing out dramatic moments in Polish history as crucial test cases. After the Second World War the new Communist party (the old one having been exterminated by Stalin) had been installed by the Red Army as the ruling party. This rule was of a *de facto* character, as the Soviet political police and military units were the armed instrument of the Communist authorities, executing directions received from the Soviet Union. The Polish government in exile remained in London, forgotten by the Western allies, with its armies in the West demobilized and its Home Army persecuted by the Red Army and the Communist regime. Toward the end of 1940s the process of monopolization of political, economic, and cultural domination following the Stalinist model was completed. Independent political, cultural, or professional associations were either banned or changed into servile instruments for extending central control over all aspects of life. Trade unions were organized in a single congress, and the right

---

[3] Barrington Moore, Jr., *Injustice* (1978), 17–18.

to strike fell into disuse as a result of the system of terror that embraced factories as well as forcibly collectivized farms, schools and universities, nationalized grocery shops, and the mass media. The terror was both physical and psychological: some people were kept for years in prisons where they were tortured without being brought to trial. Citizens were always at risk of losing their jobs and related food coupons.

In 1956, with the weakening of Soviet Stalinism, Polish society started to contest this social structure. The Catholic Church was liberated, collective farms were reprivatized, and political discourse became much more open. The party counter-reacted in 1957, but a return of the police terror of the early 1950s seemed impossible, even though in 1956 and in 1957 street riots were controlled by force. A long period of stagnation followed, interrupted in 1966 when the already tense relations between the Catholic Church and the party reached a critical point, and Catholics were attacked by police on the streets. In 1968, in reaction to demands for political freedom from the students, the party, under the cover of a campaign of anti-'Zionism' and an anti-Semitic purge within its ranks, curtailed the limited freedom of expression that had developed in the universities and intellectual milieux. In 1970 workers from the Baltic coast who had remained quiet until then went on to the streets after increased food prices had unexpectedly been announced. Violent suppression with the help of tanks followed. The government changed and the promises of development and liberalization were renewed in the early 1970s, but in 1976 the strikes and pacification occurred again. Then the peaceful revolution of Solidarity started in the summer of 1980, and developed until the coup and introduction of martial law on 13 December 1981. The following years saw the development of permanent resistance from a variety of sources: underground organizations, cultural and scientific life, alternative press and literary works, and soon in 1988 strikes again opened the new chapter, with a surprise coup against the party *apparatchiki* made by the general who had taken the position of party leader before the 13 December 1981 only to renounce his power as the civilian President of Poland in 1990.

All these events in the dramatic history of Communist Poland might be interpreted as action and reaction, thesis and antithesis, movement and countermovement, following the mechanically

applied dialectical scheme. Taken together, however, they constitute what could otherwise have been described as eternally dis-
equilibrated equilibrium. But in fact what is permanent is the
struggle, not so much over the limits of obedience and disobedience, as over the degree to which basic rights are to be enjoyed in
life by the people. Through reference to these basic rights we may
put this both spasmodic and regular history into some sort of
order. If history—that is, unfolding collective human action—
is to be understood at all, reference to the normative structure
that makes the action comprehensible is at least one of the
possible ways of understanding. This structure, which, following
the philosopher of Enlightment, Rousseau, and the nineteenth-
century Polish poet of Romanticism, Adam Mickiewicz, we might
call the 'hidden constitution of the heart', need not be treated as
a collection of separate, well-defined, and enforceable rights and
duties. More often the historical process consists in conflicts over
the degree to which a given right may be enjoyed. Various rights
and duties are differently understood in different contexts, and
the standards against which tolerance is assessed vary according
to the context.

Let us take for illustration religious freedom. The Stalinist
Constitution of the Polish People's Republic, enacted in 1952, in
article 70 (article 82 after revisions made in 1976), guaranteed
freedom of conscience and religion, freedom to perform religious
functions by the Catholic Church and other denominations, and
freedom to take part in religious practices and rituals or to
abstain from them, thus separating Church from State. Until
1976, however, it warned that 'abuse of freedom of conscience
and religion for purposes harmful to the interests of Polish People's Republic is to be punished'.

Though the Roman Catholic Church before the war was not a
landlord in possession of large estates, it was often associated
with the political right and therefore criticized by the democratic
left and liberals. At the same time, part of the clergy and lay
Catholics were involved in support for workers' rights, and these
groups welcomed the social reforms instituted in the aftermath of
the Second World War. The Church was attempting a historical
compromise with the new regime, which started by hiding its bel-
ligerent atheism under the disguise of approval for the patriotic
role of organized Catholicism in Poland. The attempt could not

succeed for very long, though, and the situation deteriorated very quickly with the strengthening of Communist rule toward the end of the 1940s. Finally, in the early 1950s, all the Church's benevolent institutions were closed, and some clergy were exemplarily sentenced for alleged co-operation with the alleged Fascist (that is, anti-Communist) underground. The architect of the conciliatory policy, Primate Stefan Wyszyński, archbishop of Gniezno, was interned, and of all lay Catholic organizations only one, unrecognized by the Church, was allowed to function. This was the association PAX, led by one of the numerically marginal but, because of their anti-Semitic excesses, highly visible pre-war fascists, Bolesław Piasecki. PAX was allowed to run its private enterprises, a Catholic publishing house and a press that was deliberating on the possibility of a 'socially progressive Catholic movement'. Finally religion was banned from schools and theology from the universities, and was relegated to official non-existence, so that even Christmas was celebrated as a secular holiday, and the Christmas tree and Santa Claus were changed in schools and the media to a New Year tree and the Soviet *Dyadya Moroz*. The year 1956 brought a relaxation of all these measures, symbolized by the return of the Primate to Warsaw from his internment in the mountains of South-East Poland. Religion was reintroduced in schools, and PAX was left by independent-minded Catholic politicians who were trying to form their own political groups, like Tadeusz Mazowiecki who organized the monthly *Więź* of Personalist (French liberal Catholic) persuasion and influenced the formation of the Warsaw Catholic Intelligentsia Club, attempting a dialogue with Marxists. In Cracow the Catholic intellectual weekly *Tygodnik Powszechny* was given back to Jerzy Turowicz and his group. But this marked the limit of the concessions made by the Communists to the Catholic majority. Again the clergy came under attack from the government-controlled press, while the otherwise government-censored Catholic press was administratively kept at a very limited level of circulation. Religion was taken out of schools again after two years and crosses taken down against the will of the parents. In the Seym, the Polish parliament, a few seats were allotted to representatives of PAX, to another tiny collaborative group, the Christian Social Association run by Count Morawski, and to the independent 'Znak' Catholic intelligentsia group that included Tadeusz

Mazowiecki. After a letter from Polish bishops to German bishops urging reconciliation, a letter which was welcomed with surprise and silence by intellectuals, Gomułka launched the fierce anti-Church campaign that culminated in the police harassment following Catholic gatherings to commemorate the millennium of Christianity in Poland in 1966. Primate Wyszyński was not allowed to leave Poland to visit the Vatican, and the Pope was not invited to come to Poland, against his expressed wishes. In some areas of employment, such as education, the open admission that one was a practising Catholic limited the chances of getting a better job and put promotion under threat. In all areas of party-state dominated society Catholics were banned from the top positions through the strict and secret rule of *nomenklatura* that, until 1989, ensured that all senior posts were filled with the approval of the relevant party authorities. Believers were put into a kind of backward sector made up of second-class citizens by the party officials, mass media, and the educational system. At the same time, public-opinion polls were showing continually that more than 90 per cent of the population were believers, including many within the ranks of the Communist party. All this resulted, among other things, in widespread conflicts of conscience, the more so the higher one stood in the social hierarchy.

It is in this context that one must read the demand for public broadcasting of the Sunday mass that figures on the list of the most important demands made by the Inter-Factory Strike Committee in August 1980. The message here was also to force the state to recognize not only the existence of the Church as an organization with its own hierarchy—something the party's hierarchy found easy to understand though not to accept—but also to recognize the existence of the Catholic majority in society. The proceedings of the lengthy negotiations between the Strike Committee and the government included several pages of referring to the general situation of believers. Strikers mentioned cases of people being fired from their jobs because of their strong religious convictions, and attacked the very limited circulation of Catholic publications then allowed by the government. This time the impact of the right wing was more, shall we say, positive, in the sense that it served as the base for taking something away from the rulers. In the 1950s the question at issue was more often the need to defend something against erosion by the ruling power of the already established structure of social life. Now the reverse process was beginning. In this context it is important to note that during the martial law period after 13 December 1981, the effects of this reverse process were not erased. On the contrary, the political position of the Church was elevated while representatives of social organizations were proscribed. This led to a new interpretation of the right wing. This time discussion focused on direct political representation, and a solution to the problem of securing the institutionalized participation of Catholics in public life was to be found. The government during martial law always included some non-party members who identified themselves as Catholics; but now the possibility of a new, Catholic party being allowed to participate in political life was publicly discussed; independent Catholic figures and groups were invited to join mushrooming bodies of a consultative character created by the government.

All this ought to make us aware of the fact that rights and duties do not only exist as sharply delineated entities, and that normative reality is much more multi-faceted than is supposed in everyday parlance. Different standards appear with different degrees of clarity in social thought and social action. If we accept that they also differ in the degree to which they are put into effect in social life, then we may say that instead of a sharp division into the earth of the 'is' and the heaven of the 'ought', there is a Jacob's ladder on which people may move up and down.

All this is well illustrated by case of 'Solidarity'. On the one hand, we have the demand for free and independent unions already high on the list of priorities at the beginning of the 1980 summer strikes, but then raised to the *sine qua non* condition by Walesa and his followers in Gdansk in the second half of August. This had been the demand 'of a political character' with which Communist party propaganda had reproached the strikers, and the demand around which internal debate had evolved within the ruling élite of the country as well as of the whole Soviet bloc. After agreement was made, not only the workers from the coast but people from the whole country manifested their interest in the issue, and this included not only workers but teachers, university professors, taxi-drivers, private farmers, engineers, office staff, and others as well. In October 1980 the idea of the nation-wide independent and self-managing trade union, Solidarity, organized not according to branches of trade and industry but along territorial lines, was already institutionalized. Those who could find organizational security under the trade-union formula as farmers or private taxi-drivers decided to form their own Solidarnosc trade unions on the special statutory base. Such was the beginning.

One can, however, look at this from another perspective. We have already mentioned the labour unrest in December 1970 that was crushed with tanks in the same Baltic Coast cities that gave rise to Solidarity ten years later. Several independent analysts have studied the documents of December 1970 as well as the demands made in January 1971 by the workers in Szczecin and Gdansk. Though the drastic increase in food prices made without warning just before the week of Christmas shopping had been the event that triggered the strikes and public protest, it would be misleading to attribute the events to economic unrest or to describe them as food riots, if we look into the content of the demands then made. Though a detailed analysis will be undertaken in Chapter 5, let me mention as an example that on the lists of demands made by the strikers in Szczecin in December 1970 the ten most frequent were, in order: (1) abolition of the increase in food prices; (2) a wage increase; (3) the independence of trade unions; (4) immediate withdrawal of the decree authorizing the use of firearms against civilians; (5) punishment of those responsible for issuing the order to shoot civilians; (6) withdrawal of military units surrounding the works; (7) safeguards for strikers and demonstrators, especially for members of strike committees and representatives of the workers; (8) withdrawal of the army from cities; (9) freeing of detained demonstrators; (10) punishment of those responsible for the economic crisis in the country. This list also documents the climate of life, or rather the direct threat to life that was felt at the time. Written under the possibility of police and military forces using firearms to disperse the population and arrest active participants in the protest, these demands pass the most restrictive tests of reliability, and show very clearly the importance of the wider, political interests of the strikers. It has been observed, indeed, that the demand for free trade unions was made more often then than in the summer of 1980, before the final list of twenty-one demands of the Inter-Factory Strike Committee in Gdansk and the similar one in

Szczecin was decided. It remains a sociological puzzle why neither sociologists nor intellectuals opposing the existing regime were able to recognize the significance of this demand a decade after the self-nominated experts to the Gdansk Committee had discovered with surprise the stubborness of the strikers on the issue, and had had to follow it as they became the advisors acknowledged by the Committee itself. Sometimes the simplest explanation is the best, and one is inclined to guess that the lack of relevance of the factories and shipyards to the intellectuals themselves is the key fact here. Although those engaged in the so-called professions were mostly assumed in the Communist state to be employed by a kind of state-supported employer, or needed to prove that they were members of a professional organization, still their real world was arranged according to channels of personal influence and not formal relations. This is why the otherwise openly dissident intellectuals remained, in almost all cases, members of state-appointed trade unions or their professional equivalents.

Coming back to our main point here, however, the question to be raised is whether the right to independent trade-unionism was less relevant in 1970 than in 1980, as the stress put on it by activists was less? The revocation of the increase in food prices, linked with the preceding pacification by force and subsequent change in the top leadership of the Polish United Workers Party, ended the unrest. Does this mean that the increase in food prices was 'really' at stake then, in contrast with 1980, when the increase in food prices that had again been the precipitating event soon ceased to be the main point, and freedom of association became the *sine qua non* of a peaceful end to the conflict? Or had the standard remained the same, being in both cases the freedom of the trade union, while the configuration of power among the major elements in the conflict had changed?

In other words, the 'discovery of limits' of which Barrington Moore, Jr. speaks is the action itself, and like any action it results from many forces of accident, luck, will, and wisdom. Though the naively behaviouristic stance would force us to accept the overt result as an explanation, in contrast to the methodologically more humane and politically more prudent approach that looks for standards as standards, even if not fulfilled—even if never overtly expressed—the latter standpoint seems to be the only one that could help us to understand what happens in history. And I am by no means inclined to believe that this methodological principle of understanding by reference to the deep structure of events applies to Polish society alone.

If, then, we accept the emergence of self-managing trade-unionism as historically permanent (that is, permanent within the time brackets we are dealing with here) as a standard against which the workshop as well as the national polity is judged, we are perhaps obliged to accept that the underlying order of higher-level normative standards—freedom of association and expression, political democracy, and rule of law and social justice—did exist in the sense of having generated the more concrete, more detailed, and more practical demands. Let me remark here that the demand for an independent trade union was seen until 1980 as less damaging to the ruling party jealous of its monopoly of power than the higher-order demands for rights and values. It was seen as something that people presenting themselves under the name of the working class could legitimately demand without transgressing the rules of language of the Communist state. Only after the summer of 1980 did it become clear that even trade-unionism was a politically hot issue (though it had been previously treated as hot in practice; the persecution of small groups of free trade unionists in the late 1970s shows this clearly). After 13 December 1981, even in the official language of the system, however, the call for free trade unions became an offence, while in law even the wearing of badges of the banned trade unions became a criminal act. It did not prevent Solidarity from existing, although in a different social form than in the sixteen months between summer 1980 and the beginning of martial law. This leads us also to re-emphasize what was said earlier—that 'Solidarity' was not invented or discovered in 1980. It had already existed as a normative project in 1970; and, possibly, other institutions of political democracy had existed in the form of a normative project not only since 1980 or even 1970, but perhaps since 1945, if not longer. We will return to the historical question later.

To say that a normative structure exists from which manifestations such as the above spring does not mean, however, that this structure determines the conduct of people and that it is unchangeable. As to the latter aspect, one might say that the process of the continuous interpretation of the rights at issue is the best proof of the fluidity and impermanence of the structure in question. One may doubt even whether the supposed structure really influences the people's conduct at all. In view of the commonly expressed critical assessment of moral behaviour in Poland since the war, the widely shared opinion on brutalization of manners, the development of the dual economy, the corruption of officials, and so on, one may ask why this was so marked if the normative structure was so strong? If such is the social performance, why assume the normative structure to be so ideal?

Let me address the question again from the surface of social reality. Both the above questions, in order to be legitimate, assume some degree of discrepancy between social values and social behaviour. People sometimes urge freedom of expression, while sometimes they silently put their ballot paper, without opening its envelope, into the box in front of the monitoring commission without even attempting to use the booth. They condemn others for misappropriation of public funds, while doing the same thing themselves. Sometimes they support revolutionary leaders, sometimes they criticize them for lack of realism. This is what happens at the surface. Our conviction is, however, that it is reasonable in sociological interpretation to speak of the heart (*il cuore*) or of the conscience, the content of which is not necessarily known to the individual but which is felt as a pressure, more or less clearly recognized. Durkheim with his interpretation of society as individual personality, Parsons with his reinterpretation of the Freudian concept of super-ego, and Petrażycki with his idea of the motivating force of ethical impulses that push people toward this or another action are all relevant here.

Nobody needs to follow strictly the pressure mentioned above, as some other pressure may be a stronger influence at the moment. Thus, what is in the heart may not be in the reason, and what is in the reason may not be in the action. Questionnaires, observations, experiments, interviews—all these techniques for codifying human action deal only with the most superficial aspect of social reality if taken literally. But we rarely do so. One need not be an ethnomethodologist to realize that these technical instruments serve only as reference points in the process of interpreting human action. In this process we inevitably assume much more than the technique *per se* permits. We assume, for example, sincerity, and this means that we assume at least two layers of personality, an exterior and an inner self. We assume, for example, seriousness of intent, and this means that we distinguish between the layer of mere verbal or behavioural manifestations, and the layer of the permanent, even if mutable, self.

Of course, one is free to accept the variability of the surface as the only certain fact and to remain with this certainty. One is free, however, also to say that our duty is to offer interpretations that go beyond mere observation. Some would even say that mere observation is impossible. Interpretation must be made through reference to various structures inferred from the reality we know. These structures are of different kinds, of which one is the normative. One can imagine, though, that individuals participate in various structures and in various normative structures as well. In the preceding section we have dealt with what might be termed the *nomos* of freedom. In the ethos of Polish society, however, the *nomos* of equality could be discerned as well, and if allowed to manifest themselves in action these two *nomoi* inevitably conflict. But all the time we have also assumed that in Polish society the structure of terror or of fear was present; the structure that manifested itself in various political arrangements that achieved their peak of logical consistency in Stalin's days but were also felt in the pressures of everyday life that prevented people from following the forces of the normative structures of freedom or equality.

Solid and permanent does not mean immutable. Social life consists in discovering structures through the conflicts one enters into by following the contradictory pressures they exert. This permanent process of life is what we have referred to earlier as the process of permanent interpretation. The social scientist is in only a slightly better position to make such an interpretation. It will always remain hypothetical. The partial, situational, individual interpretations remain for him or her the base for their own interpretation. Structures are, then, as permanent as the social action itself; structures are like the social action, also undergoing permanent change. One need not, nevertheless, identify mutability of structures with variability of action. The latter is of another degree as it results from the interaction of structures in social life.

With this in mind let me go back to the point of departure again and ask if any 'discovery' is possible in the perpetual process of renegotiation of the normative order as social contract?

If we are to speak of discovery, a map ought to be envisaged on which, step by step, the blank spots disappear and the details emerge until the whole investigated area is thoroughly known. The discovery model, when applied to the normative order, is seemingly of approximate value only, particularly in the case of Polish society. As to the general case, let it suffice to say that there is no real society in which once-discovered limits do not change over time, and even the seemingly eternal individual freedoms and liberties of Western democracy might very soon be restricted as a result of public-health exigencies. Still, so far as the Polish case is concerned, one cannot refrain from making at least one reference to the way in which the legal system used to work until lately.

The deficiency I would like to mention in this context as the most important one is the incapacity of the legal system for cumulative development. As the rule of law is based, among other things, on the conceptual autonomy of the legal domain, the lack of such autonomy is not surprising in a society that was not yet able to leave behind the relics of Stalinist social design. One needs to remember that until the 1970s the basic relationship between citizens and the public institutions of the State had been exempted from any judicial control and review, and had been subject to purely arbitrary administrative procedures. There was no room for test cases to be decided by an independent judiciary and thereafter publicised through the mass media, as is the common and thus often undervalued practice of modern democracy. The normative structure in its development is dependent upon the technology of justice that deals with it at the social surface. The machinery of justice in countries which, while ridiculing the rule of law, still practise it secures the accumulation of the affects achieved through individual or 'class' actions, and within the generated micro-paradigm, like, for example, the concept of positive discrimination or of deregulation, and the normative structures become gradually more precise and richer in substance. During this process the knowledge of rights and duties becomes more and more widespread and stereotyped while these rights are more widely enjoyed, forcing those interested in the goods and services at stake either to become accustomed to the respective claims or to initiate a reaction against the tide. Finally,

normative change may occur that would lead to further development in the reverse or, at least, a different direction.

This technology has been inaccessible in post-war Poland as in
any other Communist country. The practical goal of those dealing with the ever-burgeoning administration was to remain individual gain. The vagueness of publicly stated reasoning, the
privacy of proceedings, the autonomy of the administration, the
secrecy of decrees and regulations—all these worked towards this
goal. Only since 1979, when the supreme Administrative Tribunal was re-established, has the process that makes possible the
institutional arrangements that are necessary, though not sufficient, for the rule of law been started, with the introduction of
various top-level courts, judicial review, ombudsman's office, and
so on, though all this, as I have already stressed took place within
the frame of the Communist party's rule.

Against this background I hope it is clearer how the strikes of
1980 culminated around the negotiation of the Gdansk agreement. It is obvious that the agreements were attempted in order
to impose the binding obligations of the state and the party that
ruled it on to society in general, as represented by the Inter-
Factory Strike Committee. With the help of these agreements the
oppressive fluidity of the law was to be overcome, and there was
not so much a 'discovery' as a 'construction' of the limits so
effected. The next battle concerning the official registration of
Solidarity was of equally decisive normative significance, as it was
the test case for the validity and enforceability of the agreements
conceived of as providing both the specification and the safeguards for basic rights. The notion of 'rights' is important here,
where one might suspect that we have extended the discourse of
rights beyond its proper area of use. Looking back at the normative expressions used in the documents I have already referred to,
that is, the demands formulated by the striking workers and all
staff of the Baltic Coast enterprises in 1970 and 1971, we see
there the language of claims being used. The legal language of
claims, based upon assumed rights, could be contrasted with two
other types of discourse that were in use in Polish official pronouncements. One is the moral language of various individual
duties towards the state, society, the nation, and God. This language of individual duties towards external authorities has been
used in official education, by state and party speakers, and in the

traditional discourse of the Church before the language of human dignity and rights became dominant in the Church of today. Finally, there was the normative discourse of planning that is used in the day-to-day administration of the Communist state. In the demands made by the strikers and protestors we also find the very clear conviction that the rulers were responsible for the crises in the economy as well as for the bloodshed resulting from police and military pacification of the public protest following these crises. The very notion of such responsibility assumes hierarchically organized power with clearly delineated responsibilities, that is, a conception of public power contrary to the organization of the Communist Party State where until recently the lack of clearly defined competence and responsibilities was the rule.

More conventional sociological evidence could be added to this historical evidence. In 1987 and 1988 I was able to conduct surveys of public opinion, first in Warsaw and later on a nation-wide random sample of people aged 16 years and more. Detailed analysis of the latter survey is provided in the two last chapters of the book. It is important to note here, however, that from all these surveys it has emerged that in the political area the *nomos* of freedom was accepted by the majority of the subjects. To give just one illustration, at the beginning of October 1988 only 20 per cent of a national sample of 926 people supported the official refusal to re-legalize Solidarity, while 63 per cent were openly against the government's policy. The percentages of those who supported the use of force by the police against the anti-government public demonstrations were even smaller. Between 14 and 26 per cent supported the various limitations imposed by the government on the civil rights listed in the questionnaire. The only exception was the politically motivated refusal to serve in the army, and in this case the majority was against such a right. The open ethos of freedom, not to speak of the hidden *nomos*, seemed to prevail especially amongst the skilled and better-educated workers, and among the intelligentsia defined as people with university education. These two categories belong to the 'new middle class', composed of those who are skilled and educated enough to feel able to shape their own as well their national situation, and who feel blocked in these aspirations by the members of *nomenklatura*, that is, the holders of top positions of power strictly defined by secret, or at least unpublished, rules. These hidden barriers controlled access to the ruling political class that was self-recruited by the ruling group of the Communist party leadership and bureaucracy, and prevented wider social circles from direct or even indirect political self-determination. Thus, at both ends of the social-stratification ladder we find a preference for law understood as public order. For the underdogs it means compensation for their social and psychological inferiority and insecurity; for the top-dogs it is the way to remain in control of the society, control being the basic reward if we take into account the fact that it gives, at best, access to the more concealed pleasures of power, and at worst, that it is better than being subject to that power.

The analysis until now has supported the static description. This is what I have alluded to when describing the permanence of the normative structure and the resulting permanence of political tensions that arise from the lack of corresponding objectivizations and institutionalizations. This is valid, I think, so far as the very lack of objective institutionalization of the normative structure makes it impossible to specify the expectations and to bring the resulting inconsistencies and gaps to the surface. Once the mode of social existence is changed, as it was in summer 1980, and collective expression became possible, those processes of interpretation of the normative core begin which make for the sometimes revolutionary dynamics of change. Let me illustrate with the case (to be elaborated further in Chapter 9) of the law on censorship that was passed in 1981 following pressure from Solidarity. In the Gdansk Agreements a provision was secured by the strikers seeking to restrict censorship by law to cases where amongst others, the 'interests of the security of State' were affected, and this was seen as a clear victory. When, with others, I took part in the preparation of the independent draft of this law, we were already working in a changed context and found the above formulation too vague and allowing too much discretionary power to the administration. Therefore, we put in our draft a list of very specific clauses describing where censorship is allowed, as well as a long list of the absolute exemptions, such as scientific publications, all publications of no more than one hundred copies, and so on. As winter 1980/1 approached this draft came under attack more and more from those who (like us, to tell the truth) were against all censorship. Solidarity stood behind us, though an exemption was added at the last minute that made all publications intended for the use of the members of organizations free from censorship. But after the law was passed in May 1981, Solidarity was unable to control the 'external' publications that, bearing its name, were freely abusing all other clauses of the negotiated law. All this illustrates well how easily the freshly constructed limits are trespassed under the conditions of basic existential change. It illustrates also the truth of the more static character of the whole change, which can be taken to represent a movement toward the full enjoyment of one of the basic rights, freedom of expression, as guaranteed not only by human nature but also by the United Nations Declaration of Human Rights of 1948 and by the Constitution of the Polish People's Republic of 1952.

The dynamics of the Polish case offer a rare opportunity to study the basic processes through which society is composed. Here the change became institutionalized in organized social action, that is in the social movement Solidarity. To conclude, let me deal with this aspect of the whole story. As the sociology of the normative must inevitably deal with normative questions, we are inevitably asked what are the merits and demerits of the social movement as action that tends to express the normative structure, and change its hidden elements into objectified and institutionalized ones. The sociologist is straining to look behind the veil of the normal, typical, and repetitive, in order to watch the growth of innovation. There is an almost instinctive bias on her or his part to appreciate so-called spontaneity, especially when it is collectively produced. Social movements are the paradigm of collective creativity, though under close scrutiny one is forced to recognize common elements, albeit in new configurations or in new contexts.

Solidarity is a good example of the dialectics of the old and new that is inherent in social innovation. How was it new? It was a trade union that cut across the barriers not only of trade but also of social class, unless one accepts that this may be, in itself, a sign of the emergence of the new social class I have described above. Solidarity not only expressed the interests of this new class but also served as its symbol and its organization. Social movements that include both workers and intellectuals, cleaners and directors are, however, not rare. It is not heterogeneity that is unusual but rather the trade-union form. It was a trade union with a political aim. But this is even less unusual. It was a truly independent and self-managing mass organization in Communist society. That was the most novel aspect, though both things happen in disjunction. Less well understood was another unusual element: the profound democracy not only of goals, but also of the internal organization of Solidarity. Democracy and independent trade-unionism coexisting within a Communist state—a combination abusing the criteria of the functional elegance of societal design.

With all its novelty, Solidarity was the product of 'real socialism'. The merits of the movement resulted from the weaknesses of the political system. The wide, almost universal, clientele reflected the mass character of the society in which the lack of differentiation by economic role prevails, making the managers of the industry as subject to administrative arbitrariness as the lowest clerk in the office. The totality of the scope of interest of the movement—from political institutions to educational policy and the issue of abortion—resulted from the totality of the interests of the ruling organization. Stress upon procedural democracy at the expense of discipline was meant as opposition to the altogether contrary practice in official public life. In this sense, the liberalizing effects of Solidarity were possible only in so far as it coexisted with the Communist party and its state. But all this also shows the historical vocation of the movement: once the form is removed the positive goals cease to be valid. One then is tempted to think that the significance of a social movement like this one is symptomatic for the malfunctioning of the society in question. This holds for any society, feudal, democratic, or communist. Freedom of association is sometimes used as a measure of the goodness of political systems. Philosophically, however, a more sound measure would be how often it is really needed in civic life. Pacifist or not, the militant social movements have in common the tendency to dehumanize through the total involvement they expect from individuals and the total experience they reward them with. Thus it seems that the more human issues can be settled by human beings in close personal co-operation, the better a society is. The last of the merits of Solidarity that may be listed here is that it aimed at this ideal in social relationships.

# 2

# *Stalinism as Crime*

## INTRODUCTION

The political organization set up for Poles by Stalin in the aftermath of the Second World War lacked not only legal continuity—that remained with the Polish government in exile in London, tolerated by its old wartime ally though kept outside the frame of international diplomacy—but also its legitimate borders. Red Army field-maps at the time showed a strange state of affairs. The border with Germany in the north and west dated from 1918, while the eastern frontier, based on the 1939 German–Soviet partition, reduced Poland to half its pre-war size. Eastern territories were lost, resettlement from today's Vilnius and Lvov was beginning, while many Polish citizens were still waiting to be allowed to 'return' from Siberia and Kazakhstan where they had been forced to live after 1939. The process officially ended in 1957, but some were never let out. The 'Polish question' was soon to be settled by Stalin, who generously decided that Poles should be offered some statehood and compensated with large German territories east of the Oder and Neisse rivers. The forced resettlement of Germans followed in its turn. All this resulted in large-scale human suffering and misery, though Poles were of the opinion that the Germans should pay the price for the war their leaders had started, which had cost Poland loss of sovereignty, the extermination of about three million of its Jewish population, the death of another estimated three million ethnic Poles, the deliberate destruction of the capital, and the loss of one-third of its territory. To this account the imminent arrival of victorious Communist rule under Stalin was soon to be added.

Russian rule in part of Poland was not new. Russians have influenced Polish politics since the time of Peter the Great, whose very greatness derived from his turning the tide against the Swedes, Poles, and Turks who had until then isolated Russia from the rest of the civilized world. Then, at the end of the eighteenth century, Poland as a great European power disappeared, partitioned between the neighbouring absolute monarchies of Russia, Prussia, and Austria. The remnants of Polish self-government were dismantled after the insurrection of 1863, after which Warsaw became just a Russian provincial garrison town. This is how it was until the First World War. Communist rule in part of Poland was not new either. In 1920 Red armies reached the outskirts of Warsaw, to be defeated on 15 August. The short-lived episode of rule by the Bolshevik revolutionary committees left vivid memories for both sides. On 17 September 1939 the Red Army entered Poland again, without declaring war, and this time was unopposed by Polish military detachments who were then engaged in fighting the German army that had invaded Poland on 1 September. When the Soviet–German partition of Poland was agreed, Molotov hailed the event with a tirade against the 'bastard of Versailles' as the Polish state was called. Following the Red Army, a second internal NKVD army invaded. Soon the forced resettlement of a million Poles to the north and south of the Soviet Union began, and the annexation was effected which lasted until the arrival of the German armies in 1941.[1]

These experiences determined the Polish people's response to the advent of Communism. It came from abroad, and had not emerged from within the country. It was brought by alien, Russian-speaking soldiers, interrogators, and officials, so that it was difficult to say whether it was Russian or Communist, and what the difference was, if any. If it had been simply another Russian episode in Poland's history it might have meant simply a change in occupation from German to Russian. The German occupation of 1939–45 was, in its absolute lack of concern for human rights, an exercise in totalitarian nihilism, but it was above all an occupation. National Socialism was above all national; Jews and gypsies, therefore, were to be exterminated, and ethnic Poles were to be deprived of their civic status and for all practical purposes enslaved as an unskilled work-force. Soviet arrival meant liberation from national oppression and subjugation, but only to be followed by another form of oppression: Communist social organization. Nazi rule over Poland was experienced first and

[1] Jan Gross, *Revolution from Abroad: The Soviet Conquest of Poland, Western Ukraine and Western Byelorussia* (Princeton, NJ, 1988).

foremost as German rule, while Russian rule was above all felt as Communist. This does not imply that the terror of the former was not to be explained by the totalitarian nature of its regime, or that Communism did not bring limitation of sovereignty. The Polish Communist state was a puppet state, particularly in the early days when party officials in Warsaw could not resist directions from Moscow. Poland was ordered to refuse the offer of the Marshall Plan, to resist from seeking further war reparations from the German Democratic Republic, to sever relations with Titoist Yugoslavia, to help North Korea, and finally, to join the Warsaw Treaty which led to the institutionalization of all such orders, directions, offers, and invitations. Stalin ruled by division. The Central European satellites were never allowed to deal directly with each other. It took years after his death for Comecon to emerge. Just as the Warsaw Treaty was a response to NATO, so Comecon was a response to Western European integration—but it was too late. The Soviet centre never regained its efficiency in controlling the empire.

The introduction of Communism from abroad may be an important factor in explaining the resistance later manifested by Polish society. Certainly the new order was not based upon the native intellectual an organizational work of Polish socialists, who had played an important part in the political life of the country since the beginning of the century. The local Communist movement was numerically small, and its reputation was always tainted with a strong suspicion of betrayal of national aspirations. After all, how else could a political party be regarded that supported an invading alien army and opposed the national state re-established after 123 years of foreign domination? And not least, Stalin, for still unknown reasons, not only purged the Polish Communist party militants when they were seeking refuge in the Soviet Union before the war, but also simply disbanded the whole organization on suspicion of Polish police infiltration. The local Communist tradition was bound, therefore, to be held in contempt by Moscow, while socialists were regarded as enemies and the few who remained after the war were ordered to merge with the newly created Communist movement to form the Polish United Workers Party (1949–90). The Polish Communist state was, in view of all these events, an outgrowth of the Stalinist Soviet organization, with Communism (that is, Socialism,

Marxism, and Leninism) filtered through the Stalinist experience and interpretation. It seems that, despite the variation in local conditions, the same situation pertained throughout Eastern and Central Europe, even where the Communist take-over was effected by the local political forces, as in Albania, Yugoslavia, and Czechoslovakia in the absence of the Red Army. Those who took power had already been shaped by the Stalinist experience before the war. By the early 1930s there was no form of Communism other than the totalitarian form, and one cannot underestimate the importance of the totalitarian nature of the movement as it developed to that point. Independence from Moscow could have been an interesting asset, since the national economy could have been relieved of the burden of forced unequal exchange with the USSR, as well as from the point of view of the West attempting to limit the global influence of the Soviet Union; but in no way could it have changed the basic features of the social organization. Titoism was a local variety of Stalinism, very Yugoslav in its nature but also very totalitarian. This explains why Stalinism, even today, is worshipped in practice if not in words in some parts of the world. Stalinism was able to develop in Russia as a result of the particular combination of elements present there—the post-revolutionary social vacuum, the great power of the state if recreated, the history of absolute rule, and the lack of a middle class combined with massive expectation of social advancement. Later it could be implanted wherever local society had been destroyed, either from outside or from within, in civilized Germany, democratic Czechoslovakia, nomadic Mongolia, Confucianist China, or feudal Ethiopia—the historical peculiarities were irrelevant.

What, after all, was the nature of this system which embraced Polish society in 1944, and provided the practical as well as the theoretical resources necessary to create a new order? Robert Daniels observed that:

In the history of Soviet intellectual life and social policy the novelty of Stalinism stands out in sharp contrast to the original direction of the Revolution. Stalin turned the Soviet state into a unique structure serving rapid development and national power and gearing the individual to these overriding governmental objectives.[2]

---

[2] R. V. Daniels, *The Conscience of the Revolution* (Cambridge, Mass., 1964).

There were several features of this unique political organization of society that were of decisive importance to its development and continuity over time. Towards the end of this chapter
an attempt is made to present some of these features in summary
form. But before this we need to point out that, whereas the history of post-revolutionary Russia cannot be reduced to Stalinism—there were the different periods of civil war, terror, and
later on the New Economic Policy and the social, artistic, and
moral experimentation that preceded it, as well as the waves of
chaotic thaw and stagnant bureaucracy that followed—in
Poland, and in the other satellite countries, there was no starting-point other than Communism in its Stalinist form. The
changes after Stalin's death were immense and led many to write
about the end of totalitarianism in the Soviet Union. The retreat
from the use of terror after decades of slaughter need not, however, change the character of the system in question. Imagine a
Nazi Germany after all racially 'unclean' people had been killed.
Would it mean that the Nazi system is not based upon terror?
The fact that it is no longer used doesn't alter the fact that the
present state has been shaped by its bloody past. A Russia without capitalists, peasants, and liberal professions could have been
ruled without any reference to terror, but this would be an altogether different Russia. The classical question remains as to
where a given society ends and a new one begins. One could not
detect in the atmosphere of post-Stalinist Russia any change in
the quality of the system, which was based upon the total power
of the authorities over everybody and everything. Unlimited state
power is the defining feature of totalitarianism.

### STALINIST RULE

The general statement (see above) by Robert Daniels on the
nature of Stalinism needs to be supplemented by some details.
The Polish student of Stalinism, Zdzisław Albin Ziemba[3] lists no

---

[3] Zdzisław Albin, Ziemba, 'Prawo karne Polski Ludowej w latach 1944–1956'
(Penal law of People's Poland 1944–1956), in J. Kurczewski (ed.), *Stalinizm*
(Stalinism) (Warsaw, 1989), 97–163.

less than fifteen characteristics of Stalinist rule in Poland since 1944:

What constituted the rule of terror? Such a list cannot pretend to be complete but one may mention the following factors:

(1) Numerous rules in force that prescribe the death penalty for politically motivated deeds and frequent application of capital punishment of such deeds;

(2) punishment for all actions independent from the authority, for example, the creation of political parties other than those licensed by the state;

(3) control of all licensed association; no freedom of association;

(4) control of the media, preventive censorship and punishment for communication of uncensored information;

(5) inviting, rewarding and even making obligatory the provision of information about opposition activities, as well as punishment for failure to perform such a duty;

(6) isolation of citizens from the democratic world through the prevention of travel to democratic countries, prohibition of importation of foreign publication, jamming foreign broadcasts, etc.;

(7) collective family responsibility for opposition activities;

(8) dependence of citizens on authorities through the maximum limitation on gaining a livelihood independent from the authorities through the abolition of private commerce, artisanry, free professions, small family farms etc.;

(9) extended uncontrolled and punishment-exempt apparatus of secret political policy permanently controlling all citizens, even those in the power élite;

(10) diversion of political trials to military courts;

(11) summary procedure for trial;

(12) investigation in political cases by political police;

(13) abolition of the independence of the judiciary;

(14) no regard even for the rules in force by state organs with reference to action against those who manifest opposition to he state rulers, and impunity for those responsible for these actions;

(15) withholding some criminal cases from the courts' jurisdiction and passing them to extra-judicial bodies.[4]

Ziemba illustrates the changes that were introduced in law in order to construct the system of terror with several telling examples. First, the judiciary was to be held at bay, and the new order abolished some conditions that used to be required to be met to

---

[4] Ziemba, 97–8.

become a judge. Practically no education or qualifications were necessary. Furthermore, the minister of justice was allowed to cancel the requirement for legal training, and there was no legal specification concerning the education required to become a judge. The Communist authorities established a special law school, named after a well-known pre-war advocate who had defended Communists in political trials. The training was short and summary, and one could complete the necessary courses in a few months. Promising young, politically loyal, officers or security-forces functionaries were selected and sent for this training, after which they were appointed to the judiciary by the Minister of Justice. The training was based on Soviet textbooks. The Soviet handbook of criminal law, translated into Polish in 1952, was preceded by a clause saying:

Warsaw, 25 June 1952.
I advise the use in military courts and in the military School of law of this handbook, Criminal Law. The General Part, by Prof. A. Gercenzon. Signed by Colonel Oskar Karliner, Commander-in-Chief of Military Courts.[5]

It should be remembered that the military courts, in which the summarily educated judiciary were expected to judge according to the Soviet textbook, handled all criminal cases which were of a political nature, while investigation in those cases was to remain in the hands of the secret political police through the Office of Public Security. The competence of those tribunals can be seen more clearly if we note that fact that a strict definition of political crimes has never been introduced into the penal law. The military jurisprudence of the late 1940s and early 1950s used the concept of counter-revolutionary crime, which defines a crime in relation to the object against which an act is performed rather than by the act itself: 'The object of counter-revolutionary crime is the Polish People's Republic—the state of the people's democracy as the form of proletarian dictatorship, the political and socio-economic system, the people's power, the economic foundations of the People's Poland, its independence and security.'[6]

---

[5] Directions issued by the Meeting of Judges of the Supreme Military Court on 19 December 1952, cited in Ziemba, 100–1.
[6] Ziemba, 100.

To this development of the military branch of Communist justice, serious changes in the civil branch were added. Although the independence of judges was confirmed by the letter of the law, the confirmation took a rather strange direction, as one may read in the law on the judiciary as modified in 1950:

Art. 76: the judge (lay assessor) has a duty to serve faithfully the People's Poland, to abide by the principles of the people's legality, to administer justice in a non-partisan way, according to the interests of the people's Poland, to willingly and conscientiously fulfil his duties, to keep official secrets, and permanently increase his own level of social consciousness and of professional knowledge.

The clause concerning keeping official secrets did not appear by accident, as in 1950 the Ministry of Justice had established the secret tribunals about which very little is known even now. This Secret Section of the Warsaw Court continued to function until 1954. Three professional judges acted there (among whom were some who later achieved wide renown as professors of law, such as Igor Andrejew and Mieczysław Szerer), or teams composed of one professional judge and two lay assessors, the list of whom was prepared in co-operation with the Public Security Office and approved by the local Warsaw Communist party authorities. The secret trials took place in the notorious Mokotów Prison. The defence lawyers were also mostly *ex officio*, allocated from the small list of those whose loyalty was beyond doubt. The defence contacted the defendants under strict surveillance by the security department. Case files could be examined *in situ* and no notes were allowed. The defence usually pleaded for leniency and refrained from examining the witnesses. Public prosecutors were organized in the autonomous state agency of *prokuratura* and co-operated with security in collecting the evidence. The investigation usually involved torture, for example, beating, psychological harassment, humiliation, sleep deprivation, keeping the subject naked in a cell without heating or in water, and so on. Medical services in prisons were poor, inadequate, and designed to serve the 'interests of the People's Poland' rather than those of the imprisoned. Appeal was allowed, but in any case judged by the secret tribunal behind closed doors the appeal had to be made not under the normal procedure but by the special team working in the Ministry of Justice.

Ziemba illustrates the court's proceedings with the case of General Józef Kuropieska, who was sentenced to death in 1952:

In 1954, almost two years after General Kuropieska appealed against the death penalty pronounced by the court of the First Instance, when in the Tatatar Affair more and more of the sentenced were revoking their testimony, Colonel Wilhelm Swiatkowski, president of the Supreme Military Tribunal (recalled in 1954 to USSR) made a memo that was attached to the files of Gen Kuropieska's case: 'Comrade Radkiewicz [then Minister of Public Security] communicated that there is a decision of the Party's leadership that the verdict is to be recalled and the case heard anew.'[7]

So the case was heard anew and the judges again served the interests of the People's Poland as defined by the functionaries sent from the Soviet metropolis.

General Kuropieska's case, one among thousands, needs explanation. One of the first acts of the Communists in 1944 was to undermine the independence of the judiciary. A decree of 4 November 1944 allowed the transfer of a judge from one court to another without his consent. Another decree of 27 December 1944 stated that for a year the authorities may change the posting, put on the retired list, or dismiss any public functionary, and this included judges. Before the war the law on the judiciary stated that a candidate for the judiciary should have completed a university education in law, an apprenticeship in court, and should have passed a special examination. There were courts of First Instance where appointments were made by the Minister of Justice; and for the District, Appeal, and Supreme courts there were annual elections, but the administration nominated three candidates out of those who applied once there was a vacancy, and these were candidates favoured by the administrative body of the upper-level court. The president of the Appeal or Supreme Court was finally nominated by the Minister of Justice. The final selection was made by the President of the Republic. The Minister of Justice was authorized to pinpoint other candidates fulfilling the statutory criteria, but the number of nominations made in this way could not exceed one-tenth of the average nominations in the preceding three years, or one-tenth of the Supreme Court's number. This complex process for selecting the judiciary, which

---

[7] Ziemba, 149.

was immovable and in principle irrevocable, was now abruptly put aside.

The decree of 14 March 1945 abolished the pre-war prohibition on membership of political parties for the judiciary, with the intention of introducing Communists into the tribunals. But what was more important for the future was the party discipline imposed on a misbehaving judge by the secretary of the party's cell, either in the court or above, at the level of the ministry or in the regional party's committee. Through the introduction of an apparently innocent freedom of civic activity, or the understandable introduction of a politically new kind of judge, the judiciary's independence was abolished. Apart from the existing hierarchy in the administration of justice, a new line of dependence and control was created that involved the judges in the political machine. Only a few were recruited who were not party members. This mechanism remained most important after the official days of Stalinism had passed with Stalin's death, when Communism 'with a human face', that is, without direct reference to the use of physical terror, had established itself in the country, and continued right through until the end of the 1980s. At the beginning, however, quick decisions were necessary and the decrees cited above were supplemented by on from 22 January 1946 to the effect that anybody

who, due to personal qualities and scholarly, professional, social, or political activity and adequate legal knowledge acquired either through professional work or through education in the law schools [of the type already mentioned] recognized by the Minister of Justice could guarantee proper fulfillment of the judge's or prosecutor's duties

might be nominated for those posts by the minister without all due examinations, degrees, and years of apprenticeship. No wonder, then, that the judiciary was soon filled with politically safe though professionally unprepared judges who were accompanied in their primarily political task by willing accomplices from the proper judiciary of the old days, if such could be found. One of these, Judge Wacław Barcikowski, who presided over the Supreme Court from 1944 to 1956, published his memoirs in 1988 and wrote afterwards that:

The burden of responsibility was maliciously put on me for the rascally tricks of others, such as holding courts in prisons, the kangaroo courts that were illegal, issuing secret verdicts in the Ministry of Justice rooms, and verdicts made by courts composed of the Ministry's officials who received the title of judge but had not either fulfilled the criteria for a judge nor had the right to judge, especially in the Supreme Court. The Ministry fiercely fought against the pre-war judges. The reasoning behind this was quite schematic, without deeper insight, and it was held that they were 'conservatives' without political credit, with the label of anti-Semite attached. Until 1952 there were difficulties in filling the posts. The situation was greatly ameliorated by help from the party in breaking down obstacles to getting in new people. In the lower-degree courts there was a shortage of the old cadres who had been fired from the judiciary, and the young ones were not fulfilling the criteria for members of the Supreme Court. As to the Public Security, its arbitrariness already went too far, as shown by both the composition of the judging team as well as the verdicts dictated.[8]

As Andrzej Rzepliński shows in his study,[9] this lack of independence in the judiciary was maintained throughout the post-war period. As the best example of the subtler ways of influencing decisions, one may cite the binding force of directives issued by the Supreme Court (the Polish legal system is not based upon precedents), the training sessions for judges arranged by the Ministry, the allocation of cases to individual judges and teams of judges by the president of the court, and the ever-present threat of lack of advancement, postponement in advancement, relocation to another city, or finally dismissal from the judiciary. All these mechanisms worked well, even after proper standards of legal education and apprenticeship had been partially reintroduced in 1956.

To this description of the dispensation of justice one needs to add another aspect, the very doctrine itself of socialist legality or the people's legality which has already been mentioned. 'Legality' was the term that gained visibility in the media in 1956, the year marking the end of Stalinism, though all this was before Soviet tanks rolled into the streets of Budapest. The brutal acts of the security forces were revealed to the public and a short trial of the people in charge of the former Ministry of Public Security was staged, followed by a silent purge which took over-zealous functionaries into other jobs, some into academic life, and others into

[8] Cited in Ziemba, 148–9.
[9] Andrzej Rzepliński, *Sądownictwo w Polsce Ludowej* (Judiciary in the People's Poland) (Warsaw, 1989).

the private taxi business. Inquiry into the crimes of the past was made for the sake of the newly recovered legality. All this came to an abrupt end very soon, as the new Ministry of Interior Affairs began to develop its own cadre of security functionaries. The sentences were short and lenient, censorship stopped independent journalism from reporting the cases, a line was kept in textbooks on 'cases of serious abuse of the principles of legality', and legality was again to be prefixed with the qualification of 'socialist' or 'people's'.

In fact, legality (although the socialist kind was not invented until after his death), was one of Stalin's contributions to the language of Communist politics:

In line with his reinterpretation of Communist Party theory, Stalin heavily emphasized state authority and individual responsibility. Law, in both its theoretical and practical aspects, was rehabilitated as a permanent foundation of the Communist State. Criminology paralleled the purges by shifting the burden of guilt from the corrupt society to the rotten individual. The permissive attitude to relations between the sexes was repudiated as 'bourgeois' and replaced by a rigid divorce code and a stifling public puritanism. Education was revamped to end the progressive approach of democratic self-expression and returned to the old disciplinary methods of authoritarian instruction and grading. For the sake of industrial productivity, labour relations were recognized, to stress individual responsibility and material incentives.[10]

When Stalin put Andrei Vyshinsky in charge of Soviet legal life, the latter developed the whole doctrine out of totalitarian premisses. Vyshinsky was a trained lawyer himself of a quite traditional character, and this could explain his disdain for the preceding revolutionary doctrines such as the one concerning the intuitive sense of justice expressed spontaneously by workers or soldiers. This doctrine was developed by N. Reysner, following the pre-revolutionary teaching of Leon Petrażycki. This great thinker escape the revolution and was offered a chair in the Law Faculty of Warsaw University, while Reysner found in the concept of intuitive law a legitimation of the revolutionary chaos that persisted and was to achieve its full expression during the withering away of the state, a process which Stalin was, both in theory and in practice, postponing into the more-distant future. In the

---

[10] Daniels, *Conscience of the Revolution*, 157.

intuitive-law doctrine, the new order was to be created through the institutionalization of a centralized hierarchy of command which was equated with the legal order. The embodiment of this creation lay in quickly recreated law, Stalin's Constitution that gave his political organization the appearances of legality and doctrine.

As to the doctrine itself, the basic textbooks were produced in cheap editions in the series called 'Library of the Association of Polish Lawyers'. These included the Soviet *Theory of State and Law*, edited by M. P. Karyeva (1951) and *Problems of Theory of State and Law* by Academician A. J. Vyshinsky (1952), translated into Polish as well as into other languages and distributed throughout the empire. These were the templates to which the local product was compared. The first impression a reader gains from these books is that of the self-idolatry of the Soviet system, where everything is best. The second is the normative foundation of the terror that reigned during those years. The new doctrine stated above all that there is no one legality, but different ones which are related to different social structures, so that one has a feudal legality which differs from bourgeois legality, which in turn differs from the socialist legality which is the one of highest value. The legality of Stalin's rule could not be defined in terms of the rule of law, therefore this point of reference was to be eliminated. What *was* good, no longer *is* good. Bourgeois legality had a positive quality at its beginning when the bourgeoisie was fighting against feudalism, but only then. In its later stages bourgeois legality is misused against the working classes, and finally against the vanguard Communist movement. The various abuses were carefully collected and presented as the only view of the reality of the rule of law in the capitalist countries of the West.

On the other hand, this historical relativism helped to preserve early writings by Marx and Engels in which several rights of man and citizen were vindicated. To preserve, however, does not mean to disseminate. The attacks by Marx on Prussian censorship were not well publicized by the Communist censors a century later. Marxism was of instrumental value, but was not subjected to real independent academic analysis. Its basic tenets were formulated in popular booklets by Stalin and lesser writers, and in carefully edited excerpts for the public. But even these selections could not fully eliminate the revolutionary and democratic fervour of some for the classics of Marxism. Russian patriotism was also to be reinforced by pointing to the proper, that is the progressive, elements in pre-revolutionary thought, and this included writers who were defending the rights of the citizen against Tsarist absolutism. In this way elements of another stream of thinking were entering public knowledge; one cannot, however, exclude the possibility that this was a quite deliberate attempt to surround Stalinist socialism with a legitimating aura derived from previous generations of freedom-fighters. This was never taken too far though, in order to avoid the slightest idea that some rights might well be worthy of vindication in the present as well.

The new legality is the 'specific method of the proletarian dictatorship'. The relationship between this 'legality' and the 'rule of law' is best explained by Vyshinsky himself: 'Proletarian dictatorship is power that is not limited by any laws. But proletarian dictatorship doesn't mean anarchy and chaos; on the contrary, it means rigid order and strong power.' This is not only a new type of legality but also a new type of democracy, 'proletarian democracy, that is, the proletarian dictatorship'. The legality of a system in which power is not bound by laws correlates with a democracy based upon the dictatorship of the proletariat. One is worthy of the other, as might be discovered in the theory of how the state works. As Vyshinsky wrote, the Soviet state, as it is the state, 'cannot refrain from violence, state force and throttling'. It cannot refrain from 'throttling' because here it leads to throttling 'the exploiters of the people and oppressors of all kinds'. 'Democracy', on the other hand, is expressed by the fact that 'This process of throttling is brought about by the masses themselves, it is organically linked with the activity of the masses, and with the education of the masses'. There is also a second method. Sometimes 'in preference to the method of throttling, the administrative method may be selected, that is the method of coercion linked with education'. At one time one educates the masses for throttling, at another one throttles in order to educate. The Communist system of statecraft relies, then, on 'properly pairing methods of coercion with methods of persuasion'. This dialectical statecraft was so democratic and internationalist in its application that the process of its realization involved killing not only old Russian capitalists, Tsarist functionaries and politicians, and thousands of Polish officers, but also more than twenty million ordinary Soviet citizens who were shot or died during the deliberately created famine or in the labour camps of the Gulag.

The Stalinist doctrine of socialist legality did not hide those difficult questions of method, though the scope was hidden as were the details, such as when and where mass executions took place. This can be illustrated by information about the forced collectivization, for which the Soviet peasantry paid with millions of victims, the abolition of household property, and mass deportations—events to be repeated later on throughout Central Europe, though on a much more limited scale. Vyshinsky recollects Lenin saying that one needs 'to fight culturally for legality, though never forgetting the limits of legality during the revolution'. According to Vyshinsky, the enemies and falsifiers of Marxism thought that 'legality has allegedly to limit the proletarian dictatorship'. This is, according to him, a 'brutal and evident diversion from Marxism', as severe revolutionary legality needs to be linked to the application of extraordinary measures 'in some circumstances' against the enemies of revolution.

Some Communist theoreticians make a distinction between administrative orders (for instance, those orders issued by a military command under martial law) and legal orders. Stalin, 'in a masterly way had settled a quite complex issue in the theory of administrative law' by saying that the administrative orders in question are based upon the law and therefore are fully legal. If some still harbour doubts about the essence of the doctrine of socialist legality, these might be fully removed as a result of another quotation from the most authoritative sources, Vyshinsky himself:

Comrade Stalin has revealed the very essence of Marxist politics when, in unmasking the right, he urged that in some historical conditions extraordinary measures be applied skilfully ('the Ural-Siberian method') that, as Comrade Stalin said, led once to the comic laments on behalf of the Bukharinites and Rykovites.

Then Vyshinsky adds what one may take as the last and most telling sentence on the issue of socialist legality: 'If the law lags behind life it needs to be changed, or as Comrade Stalin has expressed it, to be put aside.' In saying this Vyshinsky well remembered that he personally had been responsible for the victorious purge in 1938 of the 'Bukharinites' and 'Rykovites', who were arrested under fictitious charges, interrogated with torture, forced into making a guilty plea, and sentenced to death or to forced labour under a summary procedure and without proper defence.

The message of his theory is that the party, since the days of Lenin, has never expressed itself against the application of extraordinary measures. 'Extraordinary measures', including the killing or resettlement by force of families who were dispossessed of all property and belongings (the so-called 'kulaks', that is, peasants with some arable land), were in no case to be taken as 'abuses'. 'The creative fervour of the poor', expressed itself in the administrative orders that 'put aside' the anachronistic laws of property, land tenure, privacy, and so on. The administrative order addressed, in the case of the kulaks, to the local and regional organs of the party, state administration, Red Army, and NKVD has not been preserved, but it was simple and could very well have been oral, as were so many orders of this kind: 'Go and expel them!' In this way the landed peasantry, the potential resistance to the state's power and economy, was abolished in the USSR. Then came the academic handbook on the 'theory of state and law' edited by M. P. Karyeyeva, which rather hypocritically defines socialist legality as: 'a method of putting in practice the dictatorship of the working class, and the construction of socialism that consists of safeguarding strict and uncompromising adherence to Soviet laws by all organs of the Soviet state, public functionaries, and citizens.'

Since in Stalin's state everything is based upon the vaguely formulated Constitution, everything is legal. That legality, based upon arbitrariness and deliberate unpredictability of state action, evidently contradicts the idea of law as such, law as something regular and predictable. But the essence of Stalin's system cannot be reduced to chaos. The so-called Stalinist revolution was bringing back some order into life. Can order be based upon unpredictability and arbitrariness? Yes. This is exactly the essence of the revolutionary doctrine and practice of Communism: to create an order in which any arbitrary decision by authority is legal, while any reference made to law that runs contrary to the authorities' wish is illegal.

## STALINISM AND STATEHOOD

One can doubt whether this is law; one can also doubt whether there is a state. Hobbes may be the best philosopher to whom Joseph Stalin might have turned for an argument to repudiate such doubts. In Chapter XII of his *Leviathan*, 'Of the Liberty of Subjects', Hobbes attempts to overcome the conflict between the principle of unlimited sovereignty and that of the basic rights of the people. The sovereign has the right to shape the law according to his will, but nevertheless this does not rule out the possibility of legitimate resistance in certain cases. Hobbes is of the opinion that the unlimited power of the sovereign results from the agreement that it is better to have any authority than to risk the state of war. But some rights of the people are irremovable, and these cannot be passed on to the sovereign even if such an agreement was actually made in history. 'If the sovereign command a man (though justly condemned), to kill, wound, or maim himself; or not to resist those that assault him; or to abstain from the use of food, air, medicine, or any other thing, without which he cannot live; yet hath that man the liberty to disobey.'[11] And then Hobbes adds something clearly connected with political trials before the various tribunals established by sovereigns, though naturally he does not have enough imagination to fantasize about what will happen one day before the tribunals of Moscow or Warsaw: 'If a man be interrogated by the sovereign, or his authority, concerning a crime done by himself, he is not bound (without assurance of pardon), to confess it: because no man (as I have shown in the same chapter), can be obliged by covenant to accuse himself.'[12]

'As for other liberties, they depend on the silence of law', says Hobbes a little further on. 'In cases where the sovereign has prescribed no rule, there the subject hath the liberty to do, or forbear, according to his own discretion.' The most important limitation of the duties towards the sovereign is expressed further by cautious reference to the commonly held view that: 'The obligation of subjects to the sovereign, is understood to last as long, and no longer, than the power lasteth, by which he is able to protect them. For the right men have by nature to protect

---

[11] Thomas Hobbes, *Leviathan*, II. 21 (Harmondsworth, 1985), 209–10.
[12] Ibid. 210.

themselves, when none else can protect them, can by no covenant be relinquished.'

A Sovereignty, thus, is unlimited in so far as it is efficient in the provision of protection to its subjects. The basic question that even a theoretician of the omnipotence of the state's power must ask is whether Communism or Stalinism gives such protection to its subjects, or, on the contrary, does it threaten the people? The answer is in Hobbes, who justifies the state as 'the only way to erect such a common power, as may be able to defend [the people] from the invasion of foreigners, and the injuries of one another, and thereby to secure them in such sort, as that by their own industry, and by the fruits of the earth, they may nourish themselves and live contentedly'.[13]

Had Stalinism such power? To answer this question, we need to investigate two points. First, one may ask what is the output of Stalinism in the 'ultimate instance', that is, after making a thorough calculation of the various costs and benefits. The answer will differ, perhaps, with the point in history to which the calculation refers. Of course the Stalinist revolution brought an element of stability, though a perverse one, into the lives of people tired of revolutionary chaos and post-revolutionary experimentation. It very often happens in history that people from their own will, sometimes even expressed in a free referendum or ballot, reject unpredictable freedom and surrender their liberties to the arbitrary will of one man. Stalin's case, though in theory it might have resembled this description, in practice does not as he did not achieve his position by consent, but by fraud and murder. The industrialization he accelerated brought effects that were judged differently in 1930, in 1960, and in the 1990s. No ultimate judgement on this can be made. Hitler's highways and people's cars were as good as Stalin's electricity and canals. One does not make a sound judgement of a system based on such partial achievements; nor can the character of a person be judged by such achievements—character cannot be judged by the beauty of the profile. Stalin possibly brought back, at most, the hope of the rule of law, but clearly not the rule of law itself. This hope, reinforced by the Constitution and by the reintroduction of the full legal machinery, statutes, courts, and the doctrine of legality,

[13] Thomas Hobbes, *Leviathan*, 176.

could give temporary relief. In speaking of the Stalinist revolution, too much attention is paid to the institutional disguise and too little to the expectations that most probably helped him by making his opponents passive and resistance non-existent. It was a counter-revolution in that the utopia of the classless and stateless society was to be postponed into the future, but it was also counter-revolution betrayed, as the hopes Stalinism was raising with its rhetoric and propaganda were not fulfilled. Stalinism has neither defended Soviet people from invasion by foreigners, nor from injuries inflicted by one another. Stalinism has not offered people the protection that would make them secure to nourish themselves and to live contentedly. In other words, Stalinism has accumulated power over people, but has not included the power to fulfil the nature of power. Stalinism was contrary to the nature of power, as it was not able to fulfil the minimum duties of a sovereign power while being in possession of all of its external attributes. What can be demonstrated with a theory of the sovereign, such as that of Hobbes, will remain true in more citizen-orientated theoretical contexts.

The above argument may be used to show that Stalinism is in direct contradiction of basic human rights. Is not the right to good government one of these, even if we only allow ourselves an interpretation as narrow as that made in *Leviathan*? But Stalinism was trespassing on every human right as defined in today's pacts and covenants. In this, Stalinism not only was not a state, it was also a crime.

There are those who would call this view an exaggeration, and who would prefer to speak of crimes committed by Stalin and his men instead of defining the whole system as criminal. One may wish to point to the exigencies of revolution. The answer to this argument is that, if revolutionaries commit crimes there is nothing strange in calling the deeds by their proper name. It might even be advisable to do so in order to escape the complicity that results whenever a revolutionary power is, out of sympathy with its aims, exempted from moral judgement, only to discover too late that the promised land has changed into the killing fields. There was never anything stranger than the view of foreigners from democratic societies who were convinced that all the obvious rights they enjoyed need not be enjoyed by the citizens of another country, the rulers of which had endeavoured to follow the path of social progress with the obvious price to be paid for that, consisting of the death, or at least loss of identity, of those falling in servile loyalty to the ruling élite. On the other hand, if one defines as a crime something that, under closer scrutiny, does not merit this name—a defensible and justifiable act or, as in case of the limitation of political liberties, a precaution, legitimate under certain circumstances—nothing really harmful has been done either to the system or to the cause in question. The price to be paid this time is simply the necessity to launch into an independent and reliable investigation, that usually brings better conditions of living, or conditions for detention, and so on.

The second point is that the Stalinism with which we deal here cannot be identified with the revolution of 1917, even if Stalin took part in that. Those who are sympathetic to the Bolshevik cause should therefore consider the plight of the old Bolsheviks, the majority of whom were simply exterminated by Stalin himself. Of course, one may take the Stalinist revolution—or counter-revolution—as the point of departure, and take it as the cause to be defended at any price, but this rarely happens. More usually, however, one has heard the argument that the construction of socialism was a cause of such merits that some necessary—or even unnecessary—acts of violence had to be committed to bring it about. In response, it has not once been said that the cause is doubtful, the necessity never proved, and the achievements contrary to the advertisement.

The Jacobin terror is often compared with the Bolshevik one, and may not only give rise to comparison but may have acted as a model as well. When Lenin himself drafted the law on the Red Terror, he relied on the Jacobin experience. Terror for Lenin was never more than the instrument, but do we infer that the altruistic butcher is in a morally better position than the sadistic one? Lenin planned to overcome the deficiencies of Jacobinism. The Boleshevik revolution stopped before devouring its own children. One may think that this was Lenin's plan, to apply terror against the counter-revolutionaries only, or at least against suspects. But the *loi de suspects* is the paradigm of terror, and its internal logic. Once embarked on the course of terror one cannot stop. The suspects are those who, on the balance of probabilities, might be expected to be counter-revolutionaries when the circumstances demand it, even against their subjective identities and convictions. A fundamental revolution like that which began in Russia in February 1917 puts people into unprecedented positions, and poses dilemmas as part of everyday experience as described, though trivialized, in novels such as *Doctor Zhivago*. One can expect disloyalty even from one's own brother when politics come into play. The leaders of the revolution were, in most cases, the uprooted members of the intelligentsia who, from their own experience, knew that they could not trust anybody. The social origin of a child was certain to determine its future unconscious allegiances. It is not surprising, therefore, that for Marxists social class was the key to future political behaviour. Moreover, there was a simple and sincere belief that working people were better, and therefore more worthy of life, a belief that led to a substantial reduction in the life expectancy of people from the old, pre-revolutionary social categories. All of them were suspect and therefore to be shot on sight if the political order had any reason to feel unstable. Their future, if they survived was not peculiarly well planned for by the authorities. But, once shot, are people no longer alive because they have committed a deed, or because Marxist sociology says that they are most likely to commit it in the future? The spiral of terror had started, and could not be stopped.

Sociology is not a precise enough science to calculate probabilities exactly. The very principle that you exterminate potential enemies endangers life for everyone, as nobody knows whether, for some unknown reason, he or she may not be taken on suspicion as well. The defence of the weak is to denounce others. This broadens the circles of the suspected; the main element in the spiral of terror is that there is no way to test suspicions, and therefore you need to shoot. The basic distrust for each other is what makes the exterminations, denouncements, and suspicions so intolerable. One cannot trust one's superiors, the army, the police, the state, neighbours, colleagues, family . . . 'Denounce or die' is the ruling wisdom of the day, and denouncing a suspect because you suspect that he might denounce you solves the problem only for a short time.

A period of terror is characterized by a dramatic increase in appetite for the pleasures of life; people know that nothing should be postponed until later. But in the hunger-stricken Russia of the post-revolutionary years, pleasures too were rather limited, and decadence was not widely accepted but rationed as the privilege of the Communist cadres. Social stabilization under Stalin at the same time brought a new wave of terror that entered the ruling party as well. But the analogy with the Jacobin terror is again misleading. The Jacobins killed the royal couple in the open, and with pride, while the killing of the Tsar and his family was arranged in secret. This was the symbolic start of the differences. The revolutionary justice with which the intellectual often sympathizes is performed on public squares and in the open to satisfy the cruel passion of justice. Here, from the very beginning, revolutionary justice was effected by specialized professionals in isolated camps and prisons. The Cheka was, from its beginning, a bureaucratic organization without revolutionary fervour but with military discipline. Dzierżyński was not the leader of an outraged mob of Russian proletarians but the very efficient manager and chief of a bureaucratic super-machine, in fact the director of the specific Communist invention, the bureaucracy that has the authority to kill people. It was no accident that it was he who, as chief of security forces, brought back order and discipline into the state railways, and arranged for the solution of the problem of large numbers of juvenile-delinquent vagabonds, whose gangs were shot. The security forces remained not only the secret political police, as developed in any authoritarian and absolutist state, but it became the *super-administration*, acting totally outside the law, above the law, and against the law, whenever the rationale of the system required it. It is not accidental that this organization was running labour camps for millions of people who constructed the system of canals, railroads, and roads through Siberia; who were employed to run the factories; who worked in the mines and quarries, and even in the design bureaus too. Efficient labour under a non-market state's economy was possible only if it was militarized, and labour strongly supervised. Terror, with its arbitrariness, not only served to paralyze the people by conditioned reflex—out of political loyalty I. Pavlov was acknowledged, against his personal convictions, as the idol of Soviet materialist reflexology and thus the founder of scientific sociotechnics—it was also instrumental in recruiting millions of people into forced-labour gangs which were not only efficient but also cheap. Until the 1980s, when physical terror in the classical sense was a thing of the past, there continued the terror resulting from a vagueness

of the laws which, when trespassed, led to penal labour sentences
—the Marxist educational slogan states that work educates and
re-socializes!—or to prison and from there to work again.[14] As
late as the 1980s, after the introduction of martial law, the Communist authorities in Poland felt strong enough, and weak
enough at the same time, to introduce the law making permanent
employment in the state's economy or in an officially recognized
private business obligatory. Such laws against social parasites
were in existence long before in all other Communist countries,
and forced labour was, of course, the sanction. In 1990, during
the debate on the future of the Ministry of Internal Affairs in
Poland, the functionaries of this office who had been responsible
for security since the Communist regime, upholding the traditions of Dzierżyński, demonstrated to Solidarity representatives
the usefulness of their work. This consisted above all in the
defence of the interests of the national economy. Control over the
national economy was, in fact, one of their major concerns.

While the Leninist stage of Communist society might be characterized by unsuccessful attempts to develop a modern society
organized like a factory, following various hints from Marxism as
well as from nineteenth-century socialist thought, of which the
Paris Commune of 1871 provides the most developed example,
Stalinism seems to be a mature version that had ejected any
doubts and romantic biases of the early period. Where Lenin
instituted terror as the instrument of the defence of the revolution, Stalin had mastered it as the basic technology of social life.
Where Lenin was attempting to control, but at the same time to
mobilize workers to politically motivated activity, Stalin introduced individual motivation and group control, abolished all
remaining possibilities for working-class self-organization, as well
as the privileges afforded to the proletariat after the revolution,
and changed slave-labour from being a by-product and extraordinary measure into the basic instrument of modernization. So,
whatever the motives behind Lenin's actions, he began the development of institutions and patterns of action which Stalin took to
their most extreme forms. This is the reason why one cannot
avoid the judgement that Stalinism is enclosed within Leninism—
and thus within Marxism—as a nut inside a shell.

[14] Cf. Paweł Moczydłowski, *Drugie Życie Więzienia* (Second Life in Prison)
(Warsaw, 1991).

Finally, with Stalinism, full supra-human collectivism is achieved, and one is left to speculate as to the other possibilities hidden within the Marxist socialist legacy. Were there any other nuts in that shell? Now all human rights have been abused, it means that in the apparently normal course of life the normal course of human action is abused. It is not permitted to pronounce judgement on what the authorities are doing unless that judgement has been approved by the authorities. Even in the privacy of the home one cannot tell a joke about the present regime. One cannot joke about the public functionaries, or about people of whom the public media speak well. One cannot speak well about persons, countries, and institutions whom the state-controlled media criticize. One is not allowed not to condemn somebody or something that is condemned by the authorities. It is forbidden to talk about one's job with people who are not from the same work-place, and one is not allowed to speak with a foreigner without proper notification. One should not, without proper permission, meet with other people even in order to talk, far less in order to do something together. At home, or rather in the officially allotted room space, one can only live with those who are registered officially as the inhabitants. One can only move from one place to another with proper permission and identity papers. One can live in a given town only by permission of the administration. One is forbidden to wear clothes or to have a haircut deviating from the one approved by the authorities. No unconditional and exclusive ownership rights are secured except, vaguely, for ill-defined personal property. The flat may be turned over to other people at the order of the housing authorities. A flat, as well as one's own person, must be offered for search at any moment by day or night if the authority wishes. Whether the functionaries are in uniform or in civilian dress, whether they have a written warrant or not, one must surrender personal freedom on demand. No safeguards exist except the good will of the authority against the execution of any penalty, and while in prison or another institution that limits the freedom—but what is freedom here?—no rights can be enforced against the functionaries and the managing staff. The body of a relative killed by the authorities, who died when under their direct supervision, cannot be taken home. No religious services can be held without administrative permission. One is expected to prove innocence if accused, and to make self-accusation when guilty. The good son is one who has denounced his father, the counter-revolutionary, and the husband is requested to expose the crimes of his spouse. If the interrogating authorities for the public good expect one to accept responsibility for having committed a criminal act, this must be done. One cannot freely choose school or college, subject or course. One cannot freely choose a job, or whether to hire or to fire somebody, or whether to leave a job. One cannot also choose simply to stay at home, or even to die of hunger. One is punished for attempted suicide and for abortion.

One is not allowed not to have children if one can, and one cannot have children if the authorities do not think it desirable. If children are at home they might be taken away by the authorities, who may also compel divorce. One cannot give children names that are not accepted by the authorities, and one cannot speak publicly in a language that has not been approved. Letters are read by the authorities if they wish, and telephone conversations are listened to. One cannot buy items that have not been put on sale by the authorities, nor items that have been put on sale only for officials and others who have the documents for privileged access to special shops and the specific items. One cannot possess gold except for wedding rings for the married, and one is forbidden to possess foreign currency. One is forbidden not only to trade in gold and dollars—even if there are shops that accept dollars only for rare goods such as canned sardines, colourful textiles, and whisky—but to trade in general. One can be imprisoned for applying for emigration abroad and one cannot leave the country without permission; and a passport is issued for the occasion only, even if the reason for travel is to go to a family funeral, or to visit socialist countries as a tourist. One is forbidden to celebrate historical anniversaries that are not recognized by the state, and one is obliged to take part in official assemblies and anniversaries if told to do so. No press other than the one edited by the authorities, or at least controlled by them, is allowed, and libraries are regularly purged of books that are on the blacklist, or not on the white one.

Of course, there are historical and regional differences in the scope of those restrictions. After Stalin's death, in some of the socialist countries (as they started to commence to call themselves) there was some relaxation in practice. There are cases like

Romania or Czechoslovakia where most of this regulation continued until recently, and like China, Albania, and Cuba where it is
still in effect. However liberal Polish Communism seemed to be,
not only in the eyes of Western visitors but also to those who
were comparing it with the situation in Russia or Poland in the
early 1950s, until 1989 most of the above rules were still in place,
with martial law reintroducing the thrill of possible terror in the
full meaning of the term. But in order to have terror in practice
one needs as a prerequisite a terrorized or pacified society, but
this time this was not the case.

Everyday life as presented above had as its distinctive feature
the fact that, apart from the heights and depths which are linked
with the human condition as such and are possible in any imagin-
able social activity, it was an inhumane life; that is, a life inconsistent with human nature. This is what constitutes the criminal
character of this form of social organization, and the criminal
responsibility of those who created this organization and helped it
continue to exist. The responsibility remains even if, firstly,
nobody has yet construed Stalinism as the crime, and secondly, if
nobody has yet been made responsible for the crime of Stalinism
before any court. If one imagines an international trial before the
allies, like the one in Nuremberg, the verdict is easy to predict,
bearing in mind the sheer number of victims. Of course a positivist lawyer would face some difficulty in making the accusation.
The atrocities of the NKVC, Cheka, or Public Security were carried out by specially created agencies of the sovereign political
power which was treated as the state, and according to the spirit,
if not the letter, of the laws of the country. How can we deal with
crime which has been legitimated by the law, crime which was
planned by the government of the state, executed by state functionaries, and legitimated by official state doctrine? One might
think it to be the greatest triumph of Stalinism, and of Stalin himself, if in this case positivism would lead the judges to say that,
apart from those cases where the written laws have been abused,
the remaining crime (and that was the main bulk of it) was perfectly legal. This would simply mean support for the Stalinist doctrine, for Communism, according to which the world is divided
into two blocs that aim to annihilate each other, where there is not
universal good or evil, and each individual is predetermined to
chose between loyalty to one bloc or the other. Relativization of

good and evil is the fundamental principle of Stalinism. Legal positivism could neatly surrender to that. But, as after the fall of National Socialism, it is once again necessary to choose between relativism and positivism on the one hand, and the doctrine of the universality of human rights which were abused here permanently, systematically, deliberately, and across the board. Which is the crime that takes precedence over local laws, written or not?

Stalinism fixes the social structure by introducing two apparently complementary principles for creating order out of the chaos of post-revolutionary social relationships. The first of these two principles is the functional one. When Stalin speaks of workers and kolkhoz farmers, adding the intelligentsia and the working intelligentsia, he introduces into post-revolutionary society, by an act of grace, the same principle of structuring that has helped to keep societies together since time immemorial. As between various *varnas*, to use the Indian term, so between those three classes of Soviet society no conflict occurs. Once private property—the foundation for all social differentiation, or at least class differentiation in society—is abolished, the contradiction of interests vanishes. No private property: no class conflicts. But there are some classes of a non-antagonistic character, resulting from differences in the character of work. Some people work physically in factories, some work physically on a kolkhoz, others are occupied with mental work which, as a result of its lack of productivity as understood from a materialist perspective, continues to carry a negative connotation decades after the revolution. Society is based upon the division of labour between those two main and the third, ancillary, social classes, who exchange products. There are no other classes, though there are still representatives of former classes against whom a permanent campaign is fought, mitigated from time to time by substituting re-socialization for annihilation or prevention.

The functional scheme of justification for social structure helps to combine the achievement of two divergent goals. People are made different, so now everybody knows to which social class people belong. The obvious differences in social position are explained in terms of a tripartite scheme; every individual comes from the working class, peasantry, or the working intelligentsia. This social background must be declared on every possible occasion, and in this way imprinted in the social ego. On the other hand, the proclaimed abolition of exploitation and the introduction of the functional division into classes helps to preserve equality as the great fulfilled objective of the revolution. Equality is not absolute, as the workers, immortalized by Karl Marx and Friedrich Engels, play the symbolic role of the finest and best group within society. Everything working class is good and beyond discussion, while the customs and beliefs of the intelligentsia are always subject to the control and censorship of the guardians of the revolution. Revolutionary rhetoric is preserved, and one hears permanent invocations to the dictatorship which, in addition, help to attach a positive connotation to the concept of dictatorship as such. Real democracy is for the proletariat—the people's democracies, as the satellites were called after the Second World War. The proletarian dictatorship thus became the most democratic form of the political regime. All this despite the fact that strikes were being put down with the iron fist of the special police troops, and the state take-over of trade unions and slave labour law was developing to a point where, according to the latest estimates, about 30 per cent of the population was involved. The proletariat cannot rule itself, it is therefore self-evident that someone needs to rule in its name. This is the Party, but that too needs a representative at the top. This is Stalin himself. Stalin does not rule because of his extraordinary personal gifts or capacities. Those simply make him the best possible representative of the interests of the proletariat in the name of which he is ruling. This notion opens the way for the second organizing principle of Soviet society, the principle of authority. The official doctrine subtly reminds us of an article on the functional principle of leadership by Friedrich Engels. Marxism provides both the theory of equality and the theory of authority. Although power has been achieved in the natural way, through murdering or banishing opponents, Stalin does not justify his position by reference to the will of the party that ostensibly put him in power due to his gifts and achievements.

This is why it is difficult to classify Stalinism as totalitarianism or authoritarianism, if those two categories are mutually exclusive. In fact, Stalinism is both of these. Stalinism is the total organization of human life with the help of violence, executed hierarchically, depending upon personal authority. Professor Barbara Skarga writes:

Kołakowski wrote that Stalinist society is composed of slaves without masters. I cannot agree with him. When I lived in Russia I had an impression of being surrounded by a whole hierarchy of lesser and greater little chiefs. Everybody there trembles before a superior, but feels a mastery over subordinates and from this power takes benefit and satisfaction. Stalin symbolizes the supreme power, but the cult of power begins at the very bottom. Common people bow before the secretary of the regional committee, he bows before the secretary of the provincial committee, the secretary of the republic is idolized and feared, let alone those from Moscow. 'V Moskve lutshe znayut, Moskva rozbyerotsiya' (In Moscow they know better, Moscow will get to the heart of the matter). It is delightful to rule people, especially those who often know better and are respected but still they need to obey and even the right to criticize is not afforded to them. Power is untouchable.[15]

The logic of the system excludes the possibility of collective decision-making. Whenever there is a breakdown in the political stability of the system the principle of 'collective leadership' is invoked, as after the death of Stalin, the failure of Khrushchev, and the death of Brezhnev. But the names listed remind us that this 'collective leadership' survived for only a short period the competition between the candidates for ultimate power, until one of them succeeded in the contest. There is nothing more remote from this political regime than the model of a parliament in which everybody has an equal vote in collective decision-making. The very idea of such a political process is conceptually alien to those raised under Communism. The best voting is in the open and is unanimous. Although a far cry from the outrages of Stalinism, I remember personally the freezing coolness with which Communist professors Adam Krukowski and Jerzy Bafia, then Minister of Justice, once greeted my plea for a secret ballot at faculty meetings on personal matters at the end of 1970s. The function of the collective is to approve necessary decisions taken unilaterally by a leader. This retroactive legitimization has been well known since Roman times, but found new popularity under Communism. The very fact that the 'leading role' of the Communist party was constitutionally acknowledged towards the end of the regime may serve as a good illustration here. To those accustomed to parliamentary democracy, the real anger produced by those few votes of dissent at various moments in the parliamentary history of the

[15] Barbara Skarga, in J. Kurczewski (ed.), *Stalinizm*, 5.

Polish People's Republic—of which the dissent by five deputies from the Catholic Circle 'Znak', who were unwilling to condemn students in 1968, was the most remarkable case—will not be understandable at all. But the leader knows better than the leadership, and the collective representation knows respectively less. After all, Leninism is the theory of the vanguard élite that efficiently rules the people and the world. The technocratic image of social order, which is inherent in Lenin's revolutionary program, excludes real collective decision-making. The latter is also excluded by the typically Darwinian concept of power as a struggle that is at the base of Communist theory and practice. If the scientifically organized society is the great factory, then a hierarchy of foremen is needed, directed by one manager. If this scientific project needs to be achieved through a struggle then the society needs to be organized in detachments under the command of the officers, topped by a marshal. Stalin indeed is the marshal, and later the generalissimo also, as well as the Great Designer and Helmsman, as he liked to be called in the mass media.

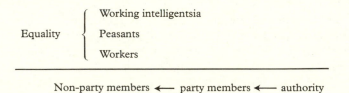

Fig. 2.1. The social structure of Stalinism

A diagram (Fig. 2.1) illustrates the coincidence and coexistence of equality and authority. The social classes are equal to each other, but all are subject to the authority of the top as well as of the lower levels. The hierarchy of authority is the hierarchy of dependence and power. In this coexistence, Stalinism expresses the synthesis of totalitarianism and authoritarianism which it has achieved. Totalitarianism is manifested in putting everybody into three all-embracing social categories on an equal standing; authoritarianism, by putting everybody into a state of dependency leading towards the top of the society, beyond the

tri-class structure, where the supreme authority resides surrounded by the ruling élite.


## THE COMMUNIST PARTY

This is the proper point at which to introduce the Communist
party. The historical starting-point for the development of a revolutionary party into a 'new type' comes when its role changes
from an organization taking part in competition for influencing
power into the organization of power itself. As the power relations are all-embracing, so the party also becomes the organization of the social structure. Independent of the tripartite division
in the frame for the functional division of classes, a basic division
into non-party members and party members develops. Membership of the Communist party does not offer power in itself but
offers another valuable element of ascendancy over those who do
not belong. Well-controlled membership of the party, that with
time oscillates around 10 per cent of the adult population, makes
mobilization of members possible. Party members are better, so
those who want to be better aspire to membership of the party
and, once in, are afraid of being expelled. Membership of the
party is a motivating force in comparison with membership of one
of the three social classes, which on the contrary are organized in
such way as to create equality. This is why, with the help of various, apparently absurd, economic measures, the material incentives to social-class mobility in the model case disappear, and the
wages of a worker may equal if not exceed those of the former
professions. It is unimportant whether one becomes an artist or a
skilled worker, but it is very important whether or not one
belongs to the party. The latter distinction is the key one. Membership of the party means new obligations, above all, the duty to
passively obey commands, and one is expected actively to support
the new regime and authority. The higher social position of the
members, together with hidden advantages and opportunities, is
well known to the general population.

The very existence of the party, which can mobilize millions of
active participants within the power structure, might, however,
prove dangerous for the authority of the supreme leader and his
élite of followers. The party could function as a reserve supply of

alternative élites and leaders. From the very beginning of the Bol-shevik movement this danger was felt by Lenin, who countered it in all possible ways. Once the Bolsheviks took power, the veterans started to compete with each other and a physical struggle devel-oped until Stalin won and exterminated the old élite, replacing it with new and personally loyal people. Stalin, however, had to solve the problem of the permanent danger from the lower ranks of the mass party machine he developed. Within such a system no leader could allow himself a moment of rest in the face of any potential threat. Thus the permanent purges and the symbolic fall of figures from the top of the political hierarchy made it clear that nobody could be secure in his or her position, and that privilege once achieved can always be lost. This adds an element of equal-ity to Communism, and makes ordinary people feel the symbolic equality of their position with those who are high above in Moscow, but who may sooner or later, as experience shows, fall to at best an ordinary position. One should not underestimate this feeling of equality, which helps everyone to survive their daily frustrations and to develop strong feelings of satisfaction with the new Communist regime. On the one hand, there is the hierarchy of power and authority Barbara Skarga describes so well. On the other hand, a new member joining the party in order to achieve power quickly discovers that the real power is elsewhere. One may move upwards through the concentric circles of power, up to the Kremlin itself, in order to discover that even the allegedly omnipotent minister Vyacheslav Molotov, deciding on the date of nations, is obliged to dance to gramophone music at a party while his wife is imprisoned by Stalin in a labour camp. The positions of power in this regime are not autonomous. The sovereign authority—as in the days of Hobbes—resides at the top in a single individual, and all else is delegated from above, revokable at any moment in response to a particular state of affairs. The supreme power in Stalinism is thus absolute and unlimited. There are masters and there are serfs, though the master of today may be the serf of tomorrow. Nobody is a citizen.

In the light of the preceding discussion it may be said that Stal-inism is Utopia realized. Stalinism, in contrast to the preceding revolutionary stage of Communism, and to the Communist design for a new, prosperous society of equals that is to flourish in the future, has been able to prepare the social construction of reality in such way that it introduced into reality something which was thought to be only in the design. The core element in this manipulation and persuasion was that something that was really just manufactured was credited with the label of design, while something which was designed and propagated as design was postponed for consideration in the distant future.

This may be illustrated by the principle of equality. Those in power stress nothing so often as the equality introduced by the revolution. Those who are interested may discover that several privileges of the former higher social classes were eliminated, élite private schools were closed, free education was offered to everybody, and so on. In pre-revolutionary society there had been thousands of children who could not get the education they or their parents wanted. This was undeniable, as was the fact that the new regime had even introduced preferential treatment for those who were coming from the working-class milieu. In this case an analogy can be made with Hitler being bad as a dictator but good as introducing otherwise very useful highways. I do not think that a real assessment of the system can or should be based upon assessment of an isolated element, made in reference to the values of another culture. Hitler developed highways not for the convenience of the citizens but for military transportation: he was thinking of the convenience of the citizens only as an instrument to preserve and to develop his power; thinking not of the citizens but of the Aryan Germanic Master Race. A highway in Hitler's Germany, therefore, though physically similar, is totally different from a highway in England or in the democratic Germany of today. There is no such thing in the social life of mankind as the value-neutral highway, knife, or education. Stalin's education was addressed towards achieving conformity of ideologically motivated masses, and he made it more widespread in order to monopolize the mind, to control and to exclude the Church, foreign influences, and the family. The equality he introduced was not, therefore, the one of which the romantic socialists dreamt. Moreover, mass education meant lowering its quality. Those better-suited in the social hierarchy of power press for better education for their offspring. In effect, under the cover of equal and mass free education, a complex hidden hierarchy of better and worse schools developed, and eventually the offspring of new Stalins in the 1960s and 1970s were sent for a proper education to the good capitalist schools of England, France, Switzerland, and United States. Stalinism, in contrast to the stratified systems of the past, is legitimized by equality and therefore the various privileges of rank and position are hidden to such a degree that until 1980, even in Poland, which was far from the ideal of the Stalinist society, the regulations concerning old-age pension for *nomenklatura* people and their extended families remained unpublished in order to support the construction of Utopia.

The efficiency of Stalinism will remain a deep mystery unless it is accepted that both good and evil are the property of the system. The longer the practical inequalities mentioned above are kept hidden, the stronger will be the criticism of the inequality that has been eliminated, or that had never developed in the Stalinist country or elsewhere. But to make the contrast more strongly, this inequality must be permanently castigated. Stalinism as a system needs for its legitimacy the permanent presence of the dialectical contrast that only evil can provide. It might be said, therefore, that even if capitalism did not exist it would be necessary to invent it, in the same way as consecutive waves of internal enemies were created in order to paralyze any potential resistance within the disintegrated and atomized ruling class. Some topics repeated *ad nauseam* have resulted in something that would be said to resemble a conditioned response of approval for the system. As an instance of such a topic, colonial exploitation by Western powers and racial discrimination in the United States might be used. For someone coming from the intelligentsia and brought up with respect for the emancipatory struggle of all the underprivileged, this topic soon started to be effective in producing automatic approval for the new regime. Whatever the economic, organizational, or political problems in Russia or Poland had been, all this was a mere trifle in the face of the safeguards the new regime offered against colonialism or racism. The respective arguments were provided by everyday support in the official media and sometimes in practice to the nations fighting for liberation from powers opposed to 'our regime', as well as by the lack of discrimination in Russia or Poland. Against a background of permanent information concerning the physical harassment of black people in the United States, the physical harassment of Poles in Poland becomes meaningless. More important is the fact that black people are not harassed in Poland. In this syllogism the actual absence of black people in Poland is irrelevant. In a similar way the support for liberation movements in Asia, Africa, and Latin America offered by the Soviet Union erases from the memory its annexation of the Transcaucasion republics and the Islamic states of Chiwa and Bukhara, its annexation of the Baltic states, of Tuva between Siberia and Mongolia, of eastern Finland, eastern Poland, eastern Czechoslovakia, and eastern Romania, not to mention the fate of the aborigines of Siberia and the Crimean Tartars. Any mention of all this is taboo, while the otherwise-just fight for independence and equal rights in the enemy's world is amplified in the media, in education, and in officially organized political activity. This struggle for independence and for equal rights is so legitimate that it might serve as the higher value that legitimizes the violation of others, such as peace and personal safety. If there were no black people in the United States, it would be necessary to invent another group suffering discrimination. If there were no women in Soviet Russia, sexism and the unequal treatment of women in the United States would have been given the same attention in Communist propaganda. Totalitarian society strives for economic self-sufficiency and autarchy—nothing is to be imported and nothing sent for export—so as to be immune from the danger of developing dependency. On the other hand, totalitarian society is open to the outside world and greedily collects all available information on the evils of the outside world. The outside serves as an external defensive shield on to which the axiological evil is projected. 'They' have exploitation, wars, poverty, unemployment, crime, hunger, and pornography. The evils of the West are related to some values that are paradoxically reinforced by the Communists in the course of their permanent critique of the West. Unwittingly, Stalinism reinforces in this way values such as equality, freedom, justice, and human rights. Used by the new regime as instruments of the critique of the evil West, those values will return later on in protest against the demystified reality of Socialism.

## SUMMARY

1. Stalinism is the deliberately introduced new social world evil, unconditionally an intentional crime against all innate

human rights; a crime organized by a group of people who define themselves as the leadership of a political party, and who rule in practice due to the realization of unlimited power and authority; a crime institutionalized in the shape of a new regime that continues for decades and is an imitation of a state upheld by a *de facto* monopoly of power, and is accepted as a state in international relations and by those subject to it.

2. Stalinism divides the world into mutually exclusive forces of good and evil that remain in permanent Manichean conflict. Good consists in the perpetuation of the new regime and extending it to the whole of mankind, while evil consists in the countervailing actions. All conflicts encountered in life can be expressed in these terms. Moreover, no situation and no person may remain neutral in the face of this basic conflict, which attaches a positive or negative value to everything in life, and directs lifes' actions.

3. Stalinism as a social order divides the world into two complementary spheres of base and superstructure which adjust to each other. The base serves the social technology of terror and produces maximum obedience at minimum expense; while as superstructure there is the idea of progress towards the fulfilment of fundamental human values. The base secures the efficacy of the new design for society through obedience, while the superstructure provides it through legitimation. Terror is legitimized through belief in progress accomplished, while belief is spread around with the help of terror.

# 3

# *After Stalinism: Organized Injustice*

The Communist party held *de facto* power in the Polish state from 1944, but until the passage of the Judiciary Act of 1950 the Communists made changes in the legal system in a piecemeal way. 'The Party in Poland did not need to fight against a long judicial tradition based on case law, as in the Anglo-Saxon systems, or against court powers of judicial review as specifically in the American system.'[1] The pre-war Polish legal order was based on statutory laws which, once properly promulgated, were binding in the courts. It was thus a typical Continental European system which, after French, Prussian, Austrian, and Russian impositions during the 125 years since Poland lost its independence and its native common law, had been wisely unified and modernized in the form of the statutory codification that took place after the First World War, when Poland regained its independence in 1918. The decisions of higher courts were binding on the lower ones in specific cases, not generally. Enactments of legislative and presidential decrees were not subject to judicial veto. On the other hand, the independence and impartiality of the courts were constitutionally safeguarded. The appointments, promotions, and transfers of judges required the nominations and the consent of the judges themselves with action by the Minister of Justice. As set out by the Judiciary Act of 1928, judges could be appointed only from among those meeting stringent legal-professional requirements; their decisions were not subject to review or veto by an non-judicial organs. They could not be removed from office except on conviction by the courts. The remuneration and control of the judiciary were carried on

---

[1] Alexander J. Groth, *People's Poland: Government and Politics* (San Francisco, 1972), 41. The following description of the introduction of the Communist rule over law is based upon his summary.

separately from those for all other administrative personnel of the state, with legal safeguards carefully spelled out and substantial self-government by the judges themselves. The judges were forbidden to affiliate with political parties or publicly take part in partisan politics. The police and the public prosecutor's office were legally barred from any control over the court. Protection against bureaucratic abuses was given by the Supreme Administrative Tribunal established in 1922. The constitutional liability of the senior officials of the government was established in the form of the special Tribunal of State to which impeachment cases were transferred by Parliament. Pre-war administration of justice was given a surprisingly good assessment by contemporaries, except for obviously controversial trials against the subversive extreme right (Fascists) and left (Communists) and the separationist organizations of ethnic minorities (Byelorussians and Ukrainians). Due process was nevertheless observed in those cases, and the political trial staged at Brzesc against some politicians from the parliamentary opposition became a *cause célèbre* and the symbol of the authoritarian tendencies that appeared in Polish political life since the unconstitutional coup brought Józef Pilsudski to power in 1926.

In 1939 Poland was invaded and then divided between the German, Soviet, and Lithuanian administrations. Of the latter nothing special can be said, since early in 1940 it gave way to the Soviet one, with what amounted to the imposition of the Soviet legal system supplemented with extra-legal Stalinist terror with no respect for previous institutions and habits. 'People's legality' meant mass executions and even more massive deportation by the KGB internal military units of Polish ethnic elements, and of the upper classes with no respect to ethnic origin to the penal labour camps in the north, Siberia, and Central Asia. This continued until the Germans started war with the Soviet Union in 1941, and began again once the victorious Red Army re-entered former Polish territories in 1944, of which half were annexed to the Soviet Union. The Germans for their part either annexed their share into the National Socialist Reich, or established a little general government modelled directly after the native reservation system but under direct German rule down to the county level. German security forces, along with the subjugated local police, were engaged in the clandestine—the decision was never made public by Hitler and his authorities—annihilation of millions of the Jewish and gypsy population, while Polish and other Slavic elements were without civic rights such as political representation, a free press, education above elementary level, and free choice of labour, though the lower-level administration of justice in the native language continued. While Jews and gypsies were subject to total annihilation by the Nazi authorities, for the Gentile Poles the situation under German rule was by no means good. Apart from the lack of national institutions, and the economic hardships, the systematic bloody terror in which hundreds of thousands were finally killed was organized by the German occupation administration, and the Polish intelligentsia especially was persecuted through exemplary executions, deportations to concentration camps, and forced labour.

The Communist government imposed by the Soviet military administration in the aftermath of the war gradually overturned and subverted the pre-war system of justice to its own purposes. In the late 1940s many pre-war laws were simply ruled null and void by the courts. The Communist party was openly giving directives to the courts on matters of judicial policy and conduct. Legal periodicals discussed speeches by Communist politicians and established the ways in which the courts ought to apply them. Those speeches and interpretive articles were discussed at judicial conferences. Government administration issued orders for the enforcement of the resolutions passed by the Party that became *extra legem* sources of the law, following the principles of the 'people's legality' and the 'social interpretation' of statutes.

The independence of the judiciary and security of tenure were destroyed by a variety of methods. One was the creation of the special tribunals, including military ones, which tried certain types of cases, 'offences against public security and public order' .and 'offences against the economic interests of the state'. The whole proceedings and the identity of the courts that freely used the death penalty remained secret.

The Judiciary Act of 1950 codified the various informal practices applied by the Communist administration until then. Judges were obliged by law to show political bias as 'revolutionary constructors of a socialist society'. On the other hand, the Minister of Justice was empowered to waive all legal and educational criteria in appointing them to the office. Although the later 1952 Constitution made provision for the popular election of judges, no legislation or administrative action implemented it, so the judicial office, except the Supreme Court named by the Council of State, remained the gift of the Minister of Justice. Protection of judicial tenure, revocable only upon legal conviction, was set aside. The Minister could remove, demote, or transfer judges as easily as any other state bureaucrats. Judicial salaries at a rather low level enjoyed no statutory protection against government manipulation.

Of 3,109 judges appointed before 1939, over 30 per cent were exterminated or died in the war. Of the remainder, the Communists hired more than half (1,346) almost immediately on taking power, and by February 1946 the Minister of Justice qualified others to serve on a temporary basis, after a speeded-up and ideologically loaded training in the basics of law from the security forces, political military apparatus, and so on. In 1950, judges appointed before the war still made up 59.3 per cent of the bench; in 1954, 26 per cent; and in 1956, 17.8 per cent.

Another way of subordinating the judiciary to control was through the rapid introduction of selected lay assessors. Prior to the war, in Polish procedure lay assessors were involved only as jurors in criminal proceedings, or in special labour or commercial courts when appointed by private associations. In 1950, in all courts, lay assessors were introduced with the same powers as a judge, so decisions could be made by a majority of two lay assessors against the professional judge. Officially elected by the local council, in practice the assessors were selected by the Communist five-person Board of the Council, from among people felt to be useful by the party. Legal and educational criteria were de-emphasized, while 'devotion to the construction of socialism' was stressed.

One should take into consideration that all these changes were occurring within the context of the legally unrestricted terror which, from 1944 onwards, was organized by the Communist party under the direct control of Soviet KGB experts and under supervision from Moscow, while the Red Army was present in military bases on Polish territory. There was no freedom of the press and no procedure against the administration except by expressing grievances to the upper levels of the administrative hierarchy or to the Communist Procuracy Office, while various uniformed or secret internal policing forces were in control of the prisons but under no judicial control at all, and were practising torture at will. To this day the number of victims of the post-war decade of Stalinism has not been established due to the secrecy of arrests, imprisonments, executions, and burial. Stalin's death in 1954 slowed down the vortex of terror that was finally officially condemned in 1956.

The liberalization that occurred around 1956 did not bring about an end to the Communist system of justice, even if the excesses of the Stalinism were stopped, because this was not in the interest of the members of the ruling *nomenklatura*, that is, the élite of the 'inner party'. From the late 1950s to the end of the 1970s a socialist 'people's legality' was the rule, more benevolent, though by no means less totalitarian and anti-democratic in form.

One can sketch the Polish, Soviet, or any other developed Communist system of administration of justice in a simple way for direct comparability with its American, British, or Western European counterparts. In the Polish case one deals with a hierarchy of low-level district courts and higher, regional courts that serve as appellate courts in cases dealt with in the first-level courts, or serve as the courts of first instance in some categories of cases. Superficial familiarity will be developed further if one adds to this a Supreme Court that may review cases dealt with in the lower-level courts, or may serve itself as a court of appeal in cases where the regional courts are of the first instance. There is a judge who puts on a gown, and who is obliged to be impartial and is therefore granted independence of judgement. In the courtroom one sees the national coat of arms, the defendant bench, a gallery for the public. There is a gowned professional who represents the public interest and accuses in criminal cases, and other gowned professionals will appear to represent the defendant, plaintiff, accused, and other parties. If there is a witness, he or she will be called in from the corridor. Finally, the judges withdraw from the courtroom to make their judgement and come back in order to pronounce the decision while the court bailiff urges everybody to stand up. The judgement, which must be accompanied with reasons, is delivered in writing later on.[2]

---

[2] There were national varieties of this external pattern. I have not been in the Soviet court that was described by American scholars, but in a Hungarian court in Pecs in 1981 I was struck not so much by the lack of gowns—even Polish lawyers do not wear wigs—but by the internal television-monitoring system that was proudly demonstrated by the president of the court who could watch what was going on in the courtroom. On what is going on among the judges when they are

To understand this system it is not enough to know the details of the organization of the administration of justice. One needs to keep in mind that about two-thirds of Polish families were directly employed by the state, while the remaining one-third was under direct economic control by the government in the pursuance of their family, usually farming, business; that the government was not elected but nominated by the ruling group of the Communist party; that all administrative agencies, officially recognized associations, industrial establishments, and the military and police were subordinated by force, by doctrine, and by law, if there was a law at all, to the Communist party ruling bodies; that all the banking, medical, and social services were part of the government itself. The direct dependance of the atomized individual in all life functions upon the centralized and unresponsible government is the basic fact of social life under this type of social, economic, and political organization.

To this we may add some details on how the administration of Communist justice—it is always argued by Communist jurisprudence that there is no such thing as an abstract justice, but that there is always a class- or system-bound one—worked in such a way that since the mid-1950s the level of direct terror could be held at an almost unrealizable minimum level while the level of conformity was at a maximum. It is difficult to obtain in practice such a measurable optimum; nevertheless, except for a few outbursts, the system did work in this way until 1989. In this chapter I would like to focus on the organization of the system of administration that helped to domesticate the Communist party's dictatorship, and prolonged it beyond the mass terror of Stalin's days. This might be understood now as a return to the Leninist concept of rule, by no means less dictatorial but of a much less exuberant variety. The return to the ideas of Leninism, a slogan so popular in the aftermath of Stalin's personal rule, meant in fact the stabilization of the power structure, and securing the rule of the Communist party over its state and society. While Lenin's occasional diatribes against the bureaucracy were often cited, in

left for themselves, see Leszek Kubicki, 'Udział ławników w orzekaniu', in S. Zawadzki and L. Kubicki (eds.), *Udział ławników w postępowaniu karnym* (Warsaw, 1970) and Małgorzata Fuszara, 'The Judges' Room', in J. Kurczewski and A. A. Czynczyk (eds.), *Family, Gender and Body in Law and Society Today* (Warsaw, 1990), 169–90.

fact his name was invoked to build up this most unappealing form of 'real socialism', as it was branded by the Communist sociologists, that is, bureaucratic Communism. Bureaucratic Communism is by no means to be equated with bureaucratic rule. Sometimes this feature was raised by those who wished, under the banner of Leninism, to rejuvenate the ideas of revolutionary socialism, especially the direct participation of the masses taking control over matters formerly reserved for the professional administration. The inevitable disasters that befell those enthusiasts and their projects were, in themselves, the sign of Leninism in practice. The truth about Lenin's criticism of the bureaucracy is that for him bureaucracy was wrong whenever it was inefficient, too formalistic, or too autonomous. The new Party State was to be devoid of any autonomous organizations, including bureaucracy as an independent estate. The new system is thus not a bureaucratic state but a special type of organization in which bureaucracy serves an important role, but where Max Weber's model of bureaucratic or legalistic rule (including such principles as the clear-cut division of tasks and responsibilities, advancement according to seniority and merits, or the prevalence of the general rule over the particulars of a case) do not apply.

Trying to discover the main features of the new organization that settled in Poland and in other Communist countries one should point out that the apparent contradiction between bureaucracy and efficiency was settled in the Leninist model with the help of institutionalized duality. The principle of duality, which is already expressed in the notion of the Party State, is the key element that manifests itself in the new Communist form of political organization as well as in its particular aspect, that is, in the administration of justice. The study of the Communist state from this point of view is justified further if we take into cognizance one of the basic precepts of the Marxist theory of the state, that is, the concept of state as the *monopoly* of coercive power. Western Marxists have, perhaps, not realized how the active theory of Marxism transforms this theoretical statement into political practice. In fact, as we have already observed in the preceding chapter, Communism is theory put into practice. Whatever the doubts concerning the validity of the theoretical statement on the essence of the state, the Communist state overcomes it and fulfills the theoretical statement to the maximum. In the end, even if the bourgeois state does not enjoy the full monopoly of coercive power and cannot be fully reduced to it, the Communist state, which is built upon this theory, attempts deliberately to fulfil it and to obtain the full monopoly. From this follows the contempt for the division of powers and checks on government. The administration of justice is seen as one of the branches of the Party State, and the essential one, as in the monopoly of coercive power is actualized. It is, then, of interest to learn how institutionalized dualism has been implemented within such a monopoly structure.

One illustration has been given already in the preceding chapter when discussing the role of the special and military courts. Kirchheimer makes a correct distinction between the role of ordinary and extraordinary justice,[3] even if, as I will try to show later, he mistakenly opposes National Socialist and Communist regimes in holding that only in the former was terror left mainly in the hands of the special courts, while the regular administration of justice was basically left intact. Certainly in Poland the introduction of Communism was effected with the help of the second branch of 'justice', the military courts, summary verdicts by the internal political police administration, and by the special courts of various types. If Kirchheimer had not recognized this duality in East Germany this could be due to either the lack of documentation or, as I rather suspect, to the neglect on his part of the role of the Soviet military occupation authorities who directly handled the political terror that most probably started with de-Nazification and then went beyond its original goal. So, at the start there was already a duality involved, that by no means totally disappeared during the relatively peaceful stage of domesticated Communism between 1956 and 1989.

One of the key factors in the Communist administration was the development of the special type of public prosecution called *Prokuratura* both in Russian and in Polish.[4] The procuracy operated independently of administrative supervision—in this it was, together with the political police, the only institution independent from the administration—and had broadly defined functions that

[3] Otto Kirchheimer, *Political Justice: The Use of Legal Procedure for Political Ends* (Westport, Conn., 1980), 299–303.

[4] In describing the *Prokuratura* and the Supreme Court I follow the characterization given in Barbara P. McCrea, Jack C. Plano, and George Klein, *The Soviet and East European Political Dictionary* (Santa Barbara, Calif., 1984).

ran from supervision over every government action and involvement in every stage of the judicial process, to the investigation of grievances by citizens dissatisfied with the administration. Not surprisingly, in the common lore of communist societies the procurator served as the symbolic figure of the Last Judgement, and in colloquial wisdom the omnipotence of the procuracy was recorded, while court, judiciary, and defence attorneys appeared as second-rank auxiliary elements of justice. In the courtroom, the procurator functioned as a prosecuting attorney, with greatly expanded powers. Procurators were empowered to detain, arrest, conduct pre-trial investigations, determine cause, indict, initiate trial, transfer a case, release the accused, recommend sentences, appeal decisions, and supervise detention. If the procurator decided that a civil case involved state interests, he might enter the case. If at any stage of the judicial process the procurator became convinced of the innocence of the accused, he was able to inform the judiciary that the case had been halted. The interest of the state was the ultimate reference point for a procurator; his duty to defend the citizens' interests was understood as also being the state interest, and therefore, in practice, he worked in the state's interest. The key to understanding the role of the procuracy in the socialist system lies, in turn, in the hierarchical organization of this all-powerful institution. At the top was the Procurator General named by the Council of State, who nominated his deputies, among whom the most important was the Chief Military Procurator. The procuracy was divided into several departments, such as military, general supervision, bureau of investigation, supervision of penal institutions, criminal and civil supervision, criminological research, statistics, finance, and administration. The same structure was repeated in the lower ranks of the nation-wide centralized organization that, due to its structural similarity and patterns of the close co-operation crossed national boundaries in a way similar to the international alliance of the Communist parties of the Soviet bloc. Lenin, who in 1922 re-established the absolutist institution introduced by Peter the Great in 1722 in order to control the bureaucracy, put great stress on the role of the Procuracy as the arm of the party. When faced with the uncontrolled and omnipotent procurator the judge seems really a pale figure. The occupational dependency of the procurator outweighs in that context the constitutionally acknowledged independence of the judge in court. The procurator is the explicitly political element in the structure of the proceedings and represents the will of the Communist Party State. The judge is, of course, independent but: (1) is limited by statute; (2) has only one out of three votes on the verdict;[5] (3) depends upon superiors for material advances. The case is allotted to a judge not on a random basis but by a knowledgeable president of the court. Political convictions will thus be taken into account, as well as the degree of personal integrity. A decision that is against the opinion of the directly political *Procuratura* will be appealed against to the upper court, and subjected to the same process of selection in case something went wrong earlier. By this process we arrive at the Supreme Court.

As any book in English on the subject warns, the Supreme Court in Poland as well as in any other Communist country should not be mistaken for its homonym in the United States. The Supreme Court was divided into four panels: civil, labour and social welfare, criminal, and military affairs, and was presided over by a chairman and vice-chairman. Members were appointed for five-year terms by the Council of State. The Supreme Court had no power of judicial review over legislative or executive actions; it exercised supervision over the judiciary, reviewing cases emanating from the district and regional courts. It also served as the court of cassation in cases of extraordinary appeal when a protest was brought by the Procurator General or the Minister of Justice. One should keep in mind that the decision in all those cases was valid for the particular case only, though was cited as of an auxiliary interpretive value in later cases. The Polish legal system, based upon the continental principles of Roman law, does not operate on the principle of judicial review and judicial precedent. Here the important role of the Supreme Court was, however, to issue general instructions, interpretations of laws, and applications that were legally binding. In this way, the Supreme Court was quasi-legislative, since those general instructions carried the force of law and were frequently used to instruct the courts as to how relevant legislation should be interpreted and applied. Through its power to issue binding

---

[5] On this the study by L. Kubicki (n. 2 above) documents the basic complacency of the lay assessors when it comes to the establishment of guilt and influence on the penalty pronounced.

instructions, the Supreme Court assured uniformity in judicial practice and served as the arm of the Ministry of Justice supervising the actions of all courts. The role of the Supreme Court was thus openly political, and followed the main principles of the Communist Party State with its centralization and hierarchical subordination. It was not political in the American sense, as the Supreme Court was not empowered to rule on the constitutionality of executive and legislative acts. As not only the Minister of Justice but also the General Procurator had privileged access to the Supreme Court through the extraordinary appellation, one should consider the Supreme Court as a co-operative element in the context of this branch of justice too.

The Communist system in its organizational aspect is characterized by a duality that corresponds to the ambiguity of the normative system. The official law textbooks would not mention the directives and instructions issued by party officials as the source of law, but the Constitution, since the 1976 amendments, acknowledged in the preamble 'the leading role' of the party. The organization of society is dual: first, there is the open state; then there is the party, confined to its members but ruling the whole state as its instrument of power. This duality makes it impossible to trace responsibility for political decisions. Not surprisingly, the Tribunal of State when re-established in 1982 could not discuss the constitutional responsibility of the most responsible of all, that is, of the former First Secretary of the Communist party, but only of his subordinates such as the former prime minister and members of the Cabinet. Such obsessive duality may be explained as a deliberate attempt to get rid of individual and institutional responsibility, and is evidenced in the case of the administration of justice as such. First, there is in fact the duality of justice, 'political' and 'mundane', to which we shall return later; secondly, there is the duality of the 'profane' Ministry of Justice that embraces the judiciary from the bottom up to the Supreme Court, and the 'sacred' and secret Procuracy that is above the 'secular' administration. In a sense this division is corroborated by the official information on salaries of those two sectors published in the 1990 *Statistical Yearbook for 1989*, the last year of the old system.[6] According to that information, there were

---

[6] *Mały Rocznik Statystyczny 1990* (Warsaw, 1990), 58.

in Poland altogether 5,530 professional judges (69,400 assessor judges) and 4,286 procurors. The average monthly income of the lower- and middle-level procurators was 416,000 zlotys; of the judiciary, 392,203 zlotys; in the General Procuracy 660,775 zlotys; and in the Supreme Court, 589,991 zlotys. Those figures show the difference in the social status between the two professions.

It would be difficult to answer the seemingly simplest question of all: was Polish society dissatisfied with the workings of such a system of justice? The question would be meaningless in the late 1940s and early 1950s, when there was no room for sociological investigations. Since the liberalization of 1956 the public-opinion survey became domesticated, and though its value will, of course, remain open to debate, it cannot be easily dismissed as its interviews were conducted in anonymity, answers were voluntary, elaboration of the results was professional, and the questions sometimes allowed subjects to air criticisms. One of the most striking examples of research of this kind comes from April 1986, when a nation-wide sample of 1,498 people was asked by the governmental Centre for Social Opinion Research on behalf of the General Procuracy their opinions and assessments of the judiciary and the procuracy. I will dwell on this questionnaire as the study itself is as telling as the results. Here we have one of the most powerful institutions of the Communist regime, that helped to manage martial law and to subdue the Solidarity's popular non-violent resistance with thousands of investigations and cases brought before the courts asking, a few months after the vestiges of the martial law had been abolished, about its image in the society. The overt re-politicization of the administration of justice that occurred since summer 1980 resulted in widened criticism of the functioning of the system. The barrier between special political justice and everyday justice for all had been taken down, since under the rule of martial law the common courts were burdened with politically controversial cases. The Decree on Martial Law established new summary procedures and extended the existing ones over innumerable types of acts contravening the martial-law regulations. The real figures for politically motivated criminal prosecutions do not exist; the fact is that any accusation might have been used against a person defined as a political opponent, and any action could be interpreted as resumption of suspended union activities, an act made illegal and criminal under the martial-law system.

Not surprisingly, in a social situation such as the 1980s in Poland the simplest question becomes ambiguous due to its political controversiality. Thus, the Centre asked if, in Poland, authorities and citizens in general abide by the law. One feels the educative instinct in that, as the interviewed citizens are reminded that socialist legality means that everybody—private citizens and government agencies—is bound by the law. It could mean, also, that the government applies the law on behalf of the citizens, while those who resist the law do so contrary to their real beliefs and interests. The answer to the ambiguous question is ambiguous as well: we learn that legality decreases from central government to local government, to state administration of enterprises, to the citizens themselves. This is why, perhaps, of those asked a majority of 61.7 per cent thought that Poland in 1986 could definitely be called a legalistic state, and only 26.4 per cent were of the opposite opinion; while 45.8 per cent were for major changes in the political system of the country and 38.9 per cent for some changes. The high opinion of the legality of the system did not prevent a majority of 64.8 per cent from answering that there were, in Poland, some persons or groups who were above the law.

Opinions about the administration of justice were twofold. On the one hand, there was a large positive assessment. For instance, selecting from sixteen negative and positive traits of professional judges, the latter were the most popular. If we take the top five traits we learn that judges were thought highly skilled (85.3 per cent), respected in society (76 per cent), of high culture (68.6 per cent) reliable (65.7 per cent), and materially prosperous (65.5 per cent). Next came objectivity (63.4 per cent) and fairness (62.2 per cent), while corruption (25.8 per cent), pleasing their superiors with verdicts (28.5 per cent), and openess to influences from above (44.1 per cent) were listed by a minority. Positive assessments prevailed also in the case of the procurators. One should take into account the personal experience with the administration of justice of those surveyed. Of the sample, 52.3 per cent had been in court themselves at least once, and 55 per cent of these had on the whole positive feelings about it as opposed to

38.7 per cent who did not; 21.8 per cent had been at least once in the procurator's office, and of those 47 per cent had positive feelings as opposed to 44 per cent who had not. The life situations to which those experiences were related could be of totally different kinds: a civil suit, divorce proceedings, criminal victimization, and a criminal act, participation in an illegal strike, or gossiping about political leaders. The heterogeneity of those experiences makes for the basic ambivalence towards the administration of justice as the basic factor behind those answers. The same ambivalence may be found in the empirical data collected in the earlier, most peaceful, period in the history of Communist Poland, that is, in the early 1970s. On the one hand, an overall favourable assessment of legality in the country was found,[7] while the administration of justice was significantly described by people as biased, especially by the administrative colleges for misdemeanours and in labour-management disputes.[8]

What is new in the 1980s is the explicit politicization of this ambivalence, achieved through public expression of discontent and overt counter-reaction by the threatened Communist élite. In the 1960s and 1970s the clash was implicit rather than experienced. As a kind of public self-criticism that would fit the present context,[9] let me cite *in extenso* the summary of sociological research on the Communist legal system which I attempted towards the end of that period.

First, patterns created in the empowered agencies of power are next modified in the process of their transmission to the particularly characterized addressees through the subsequent levels of hierarchically ordered organization or by mass communication media that inform the generally characterized addressee about the patterns. In this modification the content of the pattern becomes simplified and interpreted as much as possible according to the particular interests of each of the links in the chain of transmission. This is most simply manifested in the stress put upon the duties of the addressees and linked with the neglect of their rights against public agencies and their outposts.

---

[7] Adam Podgórecki and Andrzej Kojder, *Ewolucja świadomości prawnej i postaw moralnych społeczeństwa polskiego* (Warsaw, 1975).

[8] Maria Borucka-Actowa (ed.), *Poglądy społeczeństwa polskiego na stosowanie prawa* (Wrocław, 1978).

[9] The apparent absurdity of ritual Communist public self-criticism as an instrument of control wanes if we realize that through it publicity is created and not only the guilty but the judges as well are left with their private judgements that remain powerful though esoteric knowledge.

Secondly, the overwhelming majority of addressees have a generalized readiness to accept the patterns that arise if those are issued by the state legislative agencies and are not contradictory to the patterns already accepted in a degree that motivates directly the corresponding actions. In case a contradiction appears it will be resolved in such a way that, on the one hand, the deprivation that could result from the controlling and correcting actions by the state apparatus of the execution of law will be minimalized, while on the other hand, the deprecation resulting from abuse of one's own identity and self-evaluation will be minimized. In practice it results in the emergence of the sui generis legal niches in which apparent conformism and tolerant interpretation of the patterns arise mutually from the state lawmaking agencies as well as from the small family, peer, and acquaintance groups. The higher the social position, the less often the dissonance will be felt. This may result either from concordance between the ethical beliefs and interest or from identification with the interest of state.

Thirdly, in the relations between individuals and groups there exists a generalized readiness to appeal to the state apparatus of execution of law in order to eliminate behaviour that deviates from the patterns, or to resolve the mutual conflict. This readiness is relatively rarely realized, but it serves as an active factor that motivates in the direction of conformity and compromise through threat. In effect the basic pattern of reaction to the deviant behaviour of others is the threat that, in the case of inefficiency, is followed by withdrawal, or by putting the matter in the hands of the representatives of the official agencies of the state legal order. Legal self-help in defence of the officially binding patterns is rare, even if permitted. This is accompanied by the tendency to transmit all difficult cases that border on deviance to the official agencies. In interpersonal conflicts the compromise, flexibility, and mediation function is the ideal, while the direct negotiations between parties give way not to unofficial mediation and arbitration but above all to intervention on the part of the authorities. Here one should list, apart from the regular judicial avenue, appeals to the representatives of power and transformation, whenever possible, of all the official or state-protected institutions into an instrument for the punishment of the opponent in the dispute. The concilliatory institutions that are created are under permanent pressure of such expectations on behalf of those who are unwilling to risk the anger of the opponent, and aim at punishment as the necessary precondition for mutual agreement and reconciliation. This is accompanied by the permanently felt discrepancy between the ideal of communality of interests, and actually experience of the discrepancy between private and collective interests.

In effect we arrive at a scheme of the legal system in which the lawmaking bodies emit patterns that are modified step by step, while the individualized masses of the participants in the system construct expectations of settlement of their mutual differences, conflicts, and other transgressions of rights and duties by the agencies of execution of law. The more detailed the legal control and regulation of behaviour on the part of the state agencies of the legal order becomes, the more detailed are the expectations addressed by the citizens to those agencies. With increasing detailedness the likelihood increases that the patterns will conflict with those accepted by the addressees.[10]

The sudden politicization in the 1980s is best expressed in answers to one of the questions from the 1986 survey that was most directly addressed to the political aspect of the administration of justice. Twelve social positions were listed and it was asked whether a judgement by a Polish court would be the same if the same crime was committed by a person with a given standing. The list reveals the social differentiation in Communist Poland. On the one hand, there are several authority-related specialized statuses such as functionaries of party, government, army, and the police listed separately. Opposed to these are representatives of three major socio-economic categories: workers, private farmers, and private businessmen listed without any further specification. Finally, there is a list that includes some traditionally semi-independent or independent professions such as actor, barrister (denoted by his son, with the assumption of family influence), and priest, which are outside the formal circle of power and authority. The university professor is missing, but the 1980s added the new category of 'former Solidarity activist', who might be taken for an independent political activist, a direct counterpart of the party functionary. In Table 3.1 answers are given to the question of who is likely to receive the least severe, and who the least lenient judgement. Only 19.3 per cent answered that the judgement would be the same independent of the social position of the defendant, and the clear majority was of the opinion that judgement would be biased favourably towards people close to the power (and to the public notoriety enjoyed by the actor), and disfavourably against the common people, and especially against the Solidarity activist. This table sums up the history of a Communism that began with slogans about equal justice for all, if not preferential treatment for working people, and

[10] Jacek Kurczewski, *O badaniu prawa w naukach społecznych* (Warsaw, 1977), 130–2.

TABLE 3.1. *Opinions on the degree of sentence for a given crime which would be received by defendants in different professions* (%)

| Defendant's profession | (a) Most severe sentence | (b) Most lenient sentence | (c) Joint rank* |
|---|---|---|---|
| Manager of enterprise | 4.0 | 11.6 | 7 |
| Well-known actor | 0.4 | 6.l6 | 8 |
| Son of a barrister | 0.4 | 24.3 | 12 |
| Worker | 53.0 | 2.4 | 2 |
| Priest | 16.2 | 9.7 | 5 |
| Party activist | 1.5 | 32.5 | 10 |
| Private businessperson | 22.9 | 3.7 | 4 |
| Police functionary | 5.7 | 35.7 | 9 |
| Farmer | 25.1 | 3.0 | 3 |
| Army officer | 5.9 | 8.8 | 6 |
| Former Solidarity activist | 61.5 | 1.7 | 1 |
| Government minister | 2.0 | 59.6 | 11 |

*Note*: *The figures which serve as the basis for the joint rank were calculated by $C = (a-b)/(a+b)$.
*Source*: Unpublished survey, *Opinie o wymiarze sprawiedliwości i prokuraturze*, CBOS (survey organization), April 1986.

ended up with repressive justice discriminating against workers, peasants, small businessmen, priests, and trade unionists all together.

We can now list all the dualisms involved in the functioning of the Communist state in its advanced outpost, the administration of justice. First, there was the collection of special courts that survived in two basic forms:[11] (a) the military justice that was empowered to judge cases of civilians affecting national defence and the stability of the state, with the possibility of putting any serious political accusation under the special branch of the procuracy and judiciary; (b) the petty justice that was dispensed by

[11] In fact, as a third basic form the compulsory arbitration of all disputes involving a socialized, state, or co-operative company should be mentioned. Under this system almost the whole economy except for the private (both legal and hidden) one, was ruled by special procedure, with specialized arbitrators (read: administrative economic judiciary) and a separate body of law. Whatever the reasons, the fact remains that in this way the independent judge was kept far from the sacrosanct area of the Party-State economy, where the general interest of the socialist economy was supposed to serve as the ultimate good and measure of justice against the interests of the socialist companies in conflict. The 'arbitrator' dictated to companies the terms of contract as were thought proper by him, but no principle of independence and autonomy of judgement was envisaged here, so the 'arbitrator's' dictate might as well have been that of his superiors.

the local colleges for misdemeanours, which were composed of persons appointed by the local authorities, with the local clerk in control, and were empowered to jail or fine for many trivial, but usually ill-defined, misdemeanours which were left, therefore, to discretionary application, with legal defence barred and rules of evidence relaxed. The bias of those colleges was evident in that only one in ten of the defendants who felt overwhelmed by the informal procedure and the priority given to one police witness appealed. Throughout the whole history of Communist Poland these colleges were used not only to punish drunken drivers and noisy drunks but also to harass people who were notorious for their political dissent. In martial law, thousands of demonstrators and leaflet distributors were punished by the colleges. The normal work of the judiciary took place somewhere in between the few and exemplary cases of high treason dealt with by the military justice and the tens of thousands of cases dealt with by administrators putting the code of misdemeanours into practice.

Secondly, as already mentioned, bias in justice could have been displayed even though the principle of the independence of the judicary seemed to be guaranteed, not only in the letter but also in practice. This was secured above all by the complicity of the presidents of the courts, who were in control of the case-load and who would allocate cases according to the merits of a judge. In the Polish system the judge is a specialized judge. One tries either civil or criminal cases. Within this context, where stress is put on specialization, the further step is taken that some judges specialize in some cases within the given area of law; so some deal with divorce, others with illicit seizure of nationalized property. It is quite logical that in this context special cases of political significance are allotted to specially selected judges. The conscience of the judiciary will not be abused, and the efficient president of the court would rather assign a touchy case to a sensitive judge. Remember, however, that each individual judge is independent, and that she or he usually belongs to the party and thus to a local court's party cell that may be run by a court clerk who is at the same time the party secretary. Within the hierarchical structure of the party itself there is no procedure to refuse the party order. It is even impossible to leave the party at one's own request, as was sometimes discovered with astonishment by those who decided to put an end to their collaboration with the Communism. In such an atmosphere those who might still have some doubts about the legitimacy of political expedience as the reason behind an accusation will be simply grateful to the president of the court who will assign such a case to a more willing and better convinced colleague. The majority get on with the proper job of granting divorces, issuing execution orders against debts to the public-services agency, settling neighbourhood disputes, punishing evident trespass on the nationalized Party State's property, and putting troublesome juveniles on probation.

As the third, best institutionalized, dualism one can list the development of the procuracy, which was given priority over the system of administration, including the administration of justice. But the key to all three lies in the basic dualism of the Party-State organization that enables it to control both the citizen and the administration that controls the citizen, without being held responsible. As we have seen, when, in 1982, the Tribunal of State was re-established to deal with the constitutional responsibility of the top public functionaries of the country, it had to surrender its jurisdiction when the case of the previous First Secretary of the Communist party, Edward Gierek, was brought to the attention of the special Parliamentary Commission. The Communist party might have been afforded the constitutional 'leading role' by party legislators and jurisconsults in order to legitimize the highest position of First Secretary in the chain of command, but it proved itself insufficient to put the burden of individual responsibility on the incumbent of the position. The liability of the Prime Minister and his ministers was then debated by the Tribunal, but the general amnesty benevolently closed the case, so that in the end the lesser officials were punished while their superiors escaped unharmed.

The dualistic organization of society is well known at its pre-state level of development. Any reader of anthropology is familiar with the ingenious way in which, through the ceremonial or matrimonial display of dualism, the stateless society is able to achieve ordered institutional co-operation above the level of households. Here, in Communist society, one may admire another type of dualist structure that enables a ruler to assume complete power without any corresponding responsibility. Dualism brings to mind the legacy of Durkheim, and thus, nothing is more appropriate than to introduce the concepts 'sacred' and 'profane' into the picture. Although in traditional, pre-state dualist structures duality is often expressed in terms of 'sacred' and 'profane', it seems to underline those aspects of social relations where asymmetry is involved, as may be case with relations between male and female. Basically, the pre-state dualism is of a symmetrical character, a situation best expressed by a society in which everybody is either Smith or Kowalski, with Smith's daughters allowed to marry only Kowalskis and vice versa, and an annual ceremonial football game in which all the Kowalskis play against all the Smiths. The reason for such a structure we find in the mutual dependency and interrelatedness of both sibs: no Kowalski can see his valuable name survive without the procreative assistance of a Smith of opposite gender. In Communist society the principle of dualism is exploited in another, asymmetric way. Each sphere of social life is put under the authority of a form of public government that is visible and open even if difficult to confront, and which therefore may be called 'secular'. Each sphere of social life is also, however, under the hidden, esoteric power of what in democracy is called private government within a private association which the Communist party formally is. The workings of this government are open, understandably, only to the members of the party. Less understandably, but in accordance with the principle of the autonomy of private associations, the internal government of the party, that at the same time is imposed upon the whole society organized into a state, is invisible to the lower ranks of the party membership. The party government is thus a metagovernment; it is metapolitical as it rules the government as well. The ministers, being only public government functionaries, are of less importance than the chiefs of the relevant Central Committee administration departments, and each ministry has its corresponding department of commerce, industry, health, education, and so on, which is left unmentioned both in the written constitution of the country and in the more specific laws. At the same time, the Central Committee issues the directions that are binding for the party's public government, the same with the central committee administrative departments and the party's public government ministries. Professor Józef Chałasiński, an outstanding Polish sociologist, was punished with the refusal of a permit to travel abroad when, at a sociological congress in Stresa in 1957, in the presence of party sociologists he suggested that at least for reasons of parsimony this dualism should be suppressed. It wasn't; it flourished in subsequent decades, with symbolic manifestations such as military honours paid to the First Secretary as first in the rank order, high public functionaries' retirement pensions paid to party functionaries and their relatives, and so on. In this society Citizen Kowalski is opposed to the Smith who is not only a citizen but also a comrade. Dualism is peculiarly asymmetric. The more exclusive embraces in this way the more inclusive. What is in the other context the wider, universal category of citizenship, here becomes the more limited one. The dualism is dialectic: the particular comradeship is more general than the universal. Party government—General or First Secretary plus the Political Bureau surrounded by the Central Committee and the heads of its administrative departments—is the visible but secret government, exempted from the law simply because not mentioned in the law at all, and not subject to the expectations that were addressed to the public government either on grounds of the pre-Communist tradition or contemporary practice of non-Communist states. The well-guarded secrecy and the esoteric knowledge about its inner functioning, all those defining aspects of the party government, fully justify using the term 'sacred' in its Durkheimian and sociological meaning. The party was to be treated with awe, the feature Otto ascribed to the 'holy'; the party did not like to be inspected by the profane non-party eye; party rule was beyond criticism and the penal laws of the country applied by the secular government stood on guard for this exclusiveness.

In the light of this reconstruction some previously mentioned facets of the Communist legal system might be brought up for reinterpretation. The idea of 'socialist legality' on which so much has been written will be misunderstood if the strange context of what is 'public' in this system is not grasped. Let us take, for example, a notorious passage in one of the A. J. Vyshinsky's diatribes, where he writes:

At the foundations of Soviet law, and especially of Soviet civil law, lies not so much Roman law based upon the private property of the instruments and means of production that supports the law and legal systems of a society dependent on exploitation and elevating it to the dignity of the ruling legal principle, but the principle of public law. This principle was expressed in the 1923 Code of Civil Procedure of the Russian

Federal Socialist Soviet Republic and in the codes of other Union republics. The Code provides that the procurator has the right to initiate a [civil] case as well as join it at any stage of the proceedings, independent of the will and declarations of the interested parties if, according to the procurator, this is necessitated by the interest of the state or of the working masses . . . This principle of public law is also expressed in another law included in the same article, according to which the waiving by the interested party of its legitimate rights and the judicial protection of these rights does not decide the matter as it is up to the court to recognize this waiver or not.[12]

Though Vyshinsky and his theories were officially condemned, the principle was unchanged as it is the principle of the Communist system independent of whether Lenin, Stalin, or Gomułka rules. The condemnation itself is subject to the metaprinciple of dualism, the public law theory is condemned in the official, that is, publicly pronounced theory, but what remains is the secret, esoteric, not necessarily printed theory of party rule, passed on more as the hints, obvious banalities, and remarks behind the stage.[13] The principle of public law which he presents is in fact the principle of the preponderance of the 'sacred' over the 'secular' in the public sphere. The judge represents the classical model of rational decision-making, but the procurator acts as a legal prophet bearing witness to the supreme interest of the 'state and the working masses', a conjunction incomprehensible if the metapolitical character of the Rule of Power is not taken into consideration, as according to Leninism it is exactly the party itself that transcends the working masses and knows their interests to which the state is subordinated and, at the same time, of which the state is an instrument.

The secondary role of the judiciary in this Party-State system is the direct consequence of the secondary role of the state as the instrument of party power. We find the technical aspects of this best expressed in the protocols of the Round Table Agreements of 1989, where the issue of the administration of justice was per-

---

[12] A. J. Wyszyński (Vyshinsky), *Zagadnienia teorii państwa i prawa* (Warsaw, 1952), 140.

[13] I cannot refrain from observing that both political sectors of Communist society, the rulers and the ruled, a duality that sociologically explains the dualism of the superstructures, make use of verbal communication with Aesopic understatements and esoteric knowledge, guarded against the opposite sector of society by simultaneously developed deliberately false communication in public.

haps the most debated one, and where in fact agreement was not reached, as one can see looking into the documents signed on 5 April 1989.[14]

On the one hand, there is a lengthy list of points on which both sides, the Communists led by Łukasz Balcer and Solidarity led by today's President of the Supreme Court, Professor Adam Strzembosz, agreed. This included:

(1)   a need for constitutional guarantees for the immovability of judges with statutory definition of the exceptions such as health, disciplinary sentence by the peers, judicial verdict prohibiting performance of the judicial or procuracy profession;

(2)   abolition of art. 61, para. 1 of the Constitution, in which the terms for serving on the Supreme Court were introduced;

(3)   abolition of the prospect of 'proper fulfilling of judicial duties' as a condition in appointing and removing judges;

(4)   introduction into the Constitution of the National Council of the Judiciary where representatives of the judiciary, legislature, and the executive would meet in order to make personal decisions, especially to recommend candidates for judges;

(5)   introduction of the judiciary's influence on the nomination of the president of the court by the minister of justice, so the presidents of district courts are nominated from the candidates presented by the judiciary themselves and presidents of the regional judiciary from those whose candidatures have been accepted by the judges;

(6)   election of the full membership of the administrative board of the regional court by the judiciary;

(7)   introduction of the immovability of the thus-appointed presidents of the courts and of the two-terms four-years rule;

(8)   modification of the institution of the Supreme Court's directions so it would not transgress the principle of the judge being bound only by the statutes;

(9)   empowering all courts in session to ask the Constitutional Court questions on the concordance of the normative acts with Constitution;

(10)   enlargement of the scope of the courts by putting new

---

[14] *Porozumienia okrągłego stołu: Warszawa 6 luty–5 kwietnia 1989* ('Round Table' agreements: Warsaw 6 Feb.–5 Apr. 1989), Subcommission on the Reform of Law and the Judiciary.

kinds of cases like freedom of association, economic disputes until then under mandatory state arbitration, and administrative decisions under the jurisdiction of the courts;

(11)   elevation of the position of lay assessors 'which would probably necessitate the general election' of these;

(12)   introduction into the courts' by-laws of a detailed impartial regulation on the allocation of cases and transfer of the cases that would be known to the pubic;

(13)   elevation of salaries according to the 'high social position' of judges, making them contingent only upon functions and length of service.

The list substantiates our earlier remarks on the organizational ways in which the 'innocence' of the judiciary was secured if extraordinary circumstances surrounded the case. We see that especially well in those apparently technical aspects: the president of the court is appointed from above in the hierarchy that ends in the minister of justice, himself or herself appointed on behalf of the Communist party. The president of the court allocates the cases to individual judges according to his or her discretion; also a judge can be removed from the case he or she presides over. The lay assessors who are meant to represent the general public are in fact carefully selected from among the more loyal sectors of the population, retired members of the political security service, the police, or of the paramilitary voluntary police service being the best pools of candidates. The judge is always faced with the threat that his or her credentials will be removed because of the sudden loss of 'prospects of proper fulfillment of the judicial duties'; short of that, she or he may be moved to another district or miss an expected promotion. This is the organizational framework that makes the administration of justice within the system of written statutory law subservient to the higher authority of political power that, in accordance with the principle of duality, permeates this small world of the judiciary with the help of party cells and responsibilities transcends the judiciary as such, the courts, and links these with the administration of justice and of the country in general.

Our general description is further substantiated by the fact that, though remarkable agreement had been achieved on the institutional changes necessary to introduce the independence of the judiciary, there was also remarkable disagreement on other points that makes it clear that those changes would not have been sufficient to that purpose. On the one hand, the Communist side that included the Procurator General Lucjan Czubiński was totally unwilling to surrender party control over the judiciary and control of society by the procuracy for the sake of these changes. On this the protocol of the Round Table Agreements reads as follows.

Questions that were transferred to the decisions by the Commission on Political Reforms:
(1) Issue of the active participation of judges in political organizations while functioning as a judiciary. According to the Solidarity opposition side, judges for the period of their professional activity should suspend their membership in the political organisations to which they belong. According to the government-coalition side, a judge should remain a member of the political party.
(2) Issue of the position of the procuracy within the system of the state agencies. According to the Solidarity opposition side, it is necessary to subordinate the procuracy to the minister of justice as a consequence of the tripartition of powers. According to the government-coalition side, this issue should be considered during the reform of the organization of state.[15]

Apart from its resistance to the organizational changes, the Communist 'government-coalition side' was also very unwilling to change the substance of the law itself, a fact that led to the insertion of the following statement by Solidarity representatives in the final document:

The Solidarity opposition side states that almost all the most important proposals that it presented concerning changes in the penal law, law of

---

[15] *Porozumienia okrągłego stołu: Warszawa 6 luty–5 kwietnia 1989.* The third point of full disagreement was the issue of capital punishment is listed of which the Solidarity opposition side wished the immediate abolition. From my personal experience as member of the Solidarity negotiating team—that included Mr Strzembosz and was presided over by Zbigniew Bujak—on law and administration of justice in May 1981, I recollect that basically the same demands were met with similar resistance. The independence of the judiciary was then agreed in talks with the Ministry of Justice to be discussed further, while during the single meeting with the procuracy it became clear that no negotiations at all were possible. From those days I keep in mind a visual memory of the almost total physical difference between the Communist procurators and the Ministry of Justice people, and us. They were oversized and square-shaped both in body and face, only waiting for their Daumier to be immortalized as types. The late Brezhnev seemed to represent the same physical type, not frequent among Poles.

criminal procedure, law of misdemeanours, and law on the Ministry of Interior with its administrative specifications have not been approved by the government-coalition side. In such circumstances the joint initiative to change the widely understood penal law becomes impossible. Such partial reform would leave the penal legislation unchanged, in conflict with the International Covenants of Human and Citizens Rights, would not fulfill expectations, and, moreover, would lead to misinterpretation on the part of public opinion.[16]

At this point it seems necessary to remember the continental European style of legal structure that the Communist party exploited in building up its own system of government. In this system, as we have heard, the judge is subject to the statutes and to the statutes only. In particular cases this is supplemented by various other sources of law, but the Communist system, not surprisingly, stressed the role of the statute once it got full control over both the administration and the legislature. Vyshinsky might look, to an uninformed reader, like a defendant of old-fashioned, almost bourgeois-like legality when he fought against Reysner and his Petrazyckian doctrine of the 'revolutionary conscience' as the sole source of intuitive Bolshevik law, but one should note that in lieu of that the statutes introduced are in fact administrative commands, even if taking the form of parliamentary statutes. Communist rule of power is rule by commands that may take the form of parliamentary enactments. Those enactments might be in conflict with the Constitution, and the administration of justice will decide what is given priority; or they may be in conflict with the administrative decisions, and in that case it is for the political administration to decide what is to be given priority.

The stress on the penal law 'widely understood' in the above-quoted Round Table disagreements brings us back to some details of the institutionalized dualism as a characteristic feature of the Communist Party State in general, and the administration of law in particular. It does not seem to be an accident that the penal law plays so important a role in this system as it is public by nature, one is tempted to say, by definition. After all, is not a crime a wrong that needs to be compensated to the public? The publicization of private law in Communism is evidenced not only by Vyshinsky's teachings but also by (1) leaving any civil case open to the intervention of the procurator on behalf of the public interest; and (2) by putting most of the legally acknowledged (one should here bear in mind that with nationalization and state control of the economy a lot of private transactions became illicit *de jure* or *de facto*) economic transactions under the special administrative procedure called state arbitration. It even went so far that some criminal matters, at least in Poland, remained within the scope of private accusation, so the public procuracy need not bother with cases like insult, libel, slander, or minor bodily injury unless the local police wish to put the case before the administrative colleges for misdemeanours, or the wronged person herself or himself opens up proceedings before the court. The widely understood public law is thus of the utmost interest for the Communist administrator, and the 'public' is perceived as being subject to direct political intervention. Finally, nothing in the public sphere is left to be politically neutral, and therefore the politically proper shaping of everything in this sphere remains the main task of the Party State. 'Public' is, in the sphere of law, opposed not to law of torts or civil law, but to such aspects of interpersonal relations as the individual will, the drunken brawl, or the unpaid debt, which are insignificant from the point of the centralized political and economic system. If one would ask whether all these matters might be of some public interest, the answer is yes, and precisely because of that the public procurator may choose to intervene on behalf of the system at any time.

The penal law is the paramount case of both the public interest and impartial justice as expected by the public remaining alien to the esoteric administration of the system. The judge's judgement is to depend only upon the statute, so there is a need to make the statutes fit the interests of the Party State. This has been described briefly by Małgorzata Fuszara in her study of the developments that took place in this area since the introduction of martial law.[17]

The key point in Fuszara's analysis is in the title, as the author struggles with the normalcy and special status of various penal regulations that were introduced throughout the legal history of the Communist period. She mentions the beginning, when the

---

[17] Małgorzata Fuszara, 'The Law—A Special Or Normal State?', *Tidskrift for Rättssociologi*, 2 (1988), 133–48.

pre-war penal code of 1932 and the penal procedure code of 1928 were retained but supplemented with three important sets of regulations: (1) the decree on offences which are especially dangerous in a period of state restoration (decree of 13 June 1946, valid with modifications) which extended the pre-war code by adding several provisions on espionage, sabotage, and so on, to be met with the most severe penalties; (2) laws controlling profiteering; and (3) provisions concerning the heightened protection of nationalized property, which was guarded with the help of more severe criminal liability than private property. The criminal procedure was adjusted through a 1945 decree on summary procedure in listed cases of political and political-economic importance, when a case was to be heard within twenty-four hours from the time the indictment was made and the accused, independent of, say, the prospect of capital punishment, was allowed three days to present evidence, the verdict to be given within twenty-four hours of the hearing. All those measures that were publicly justified as necessary in the period of post-war reconstruction were in force until . . . 1970, when the series of new codes was promulgated that took into account a part of the political interest behind those supplementary and temporary measures. In the 1970s the political system was felt to be stable enough to allow some liberalization. Abolition of the special procedures and statutes was effected, the penal policy liberalized, and the idea of 'resocialization' given priority over 'prevention' in the doctrine. This was still a far cry from real liberalization; in later years the period was described as follows:

As early as the second half of 1980 both the mass media and specialized publications began to denounce the goals and methods pursued by the penal policy. The blow was aimed at the allegedly too-frequent imposition of the penalty of imprisonment and excessively high fines. The administration of justice was blamed for having become fiscalized. It was pointed out that the Polish legal system was strikingly repressive—both in its legislative measures and in their practical application. Comparisons were made between Polish penal policy and that pursued in socialist countries and in Western Europe. The resultant thesis was that Polish penal policy was unduly punitive.[18] So wrote the official lawyers in 1985, even though—as compared with the years preceding the 1980s—the

---

[18] See esp. Jerzy Jasiński, 'Punitywność systemów prawnych', *Studia Prawnicze* (1973), 35.

number of persons sentenced to imprisonment had dropped, from 48,413 in 1978 to 32,053 in 1981. It was the first time in ten years that the fine figures dropped, both in real terms and in terms of average wage. At the same time, the percentage of conditional suspended prison sentences showed a considerable rise—up to 63.8 per cent (53.1 in 1979). The penal policy adopted, as well as the widespread practice of conditional release from serving the full sentence, was responsible for the fall in the number of the imprisoned down to 51,436 (80,451 in 1979).[19]

On 12 December 1981 the decree was issued, the constitutionality of which was in 1990 undermined by the expertise of the constitutional lawyers but which could not, typically for the system we deal with here, be declared as constitutional because of the lack of relevant procedure. The decree on martial law signed by the Council of State, which voted in favour (except for the leader of PAX, Ryszard Reiff, removed afterwards), already included a lot of penal provisions. These were penalties for participation in associations and unions whose activity had been suspended; for those who organized, presided over, or participated in a strike; and for those who acted to the benefit of the unspecified 'enemy' or to the detriment of 'security of defence readiness'. The already vague clauses giving ground to general insecurity were strengthened by penalties for spreading false information, which might cause 'public unrest and riots', and very specific 'martial-law crimes', such as changing one's place of residence without administrative permit, disobeying prohibitions on the use of motor vehicles, or disobeying the duty to carry an identity document in public places, and so on, with penalties varying from a fine to imprisonment for up to ten years. This was accompanied by a decree on the special procedure to be applied in cases of crimes and offences committed during the martial law period. The most severe punishments, such as the death penalty and twenty-four years imprisonment, could have been adjudicated in cases where the uppermost punishment according to the 'normal' penal code had been eight years of punishment. This 'translation code' was to be applied by the judiciary to not less than eighty articles of the penal code, to which some other offences as defined by the law on civil defence, the national law on statistical

---

[19] Z. Jankowski and J. Michalski, *Ustawa z 10 maja 1985 r. o szczególnej odpowiedzialności karnej, Komentarz* (Warsaw, 1985), cited after Fuszara, 'The Law—A Special or Normal State?' (n. 17 above), 146–7.

information, or fiscal law were added. No appeal could be lodged against the sentence, which had to follow promptly, allowing no more than fifteen days for preparation of the case and five days for bringing the case before the court. In the light of our preceding discussion it is hardly surprising that the initiative to start a summary procedure of this kind was left with the procurator, although once started the decision to continue it was with the court. Regional courts of three professional judges were to be involved.

Ending martial law was not a simple process either. The decree of 18 December 1982 on 'special regulation in the period of suspended martial law' restricted the summary procedure to some dozen serious offences under the penal code as well as three offences under the fiscal law. On 26 September 1982 the law on evading work that for decades had been resisted by public opinion was passed, introducing mandatory registration of 'social parasites' to be offered work under quasi-penal sanctions. After martial law was formally abolished in July 1983, another law of 21 July 1983 was passed by parliament on 'special regulation for the period of overcoming socio-political crisis and on changing some statutes' that eased the (state) employer's situation against employees' rights and limited academic freedom. Under the declared new 'stabilization', the 'incidental' (that is, valid for the specified period of time, until 1988) law of 10 May 1985 was passed on 'special criminal liability' which restricted temporarily, that is until 1988, the use of suspended sentences, conditional release, and of mitigating circumstances. The law of 10 May 1985 on 'changing some provisions of the penal code and misdemeanours code' increased the level of economic repression and introduced two special procedures, one for indictments made by the police, the other for speeding up proceedings by approval of the oral notice by police, one judge on the bench, and a three-day deadline for issuing a written verdict to parties to be appealed within another seven days.

Fuszara observes that in the context of the Decree on Martial Law of 12 December 1981, and the supplementary special legislation, this already controversial 'liberalization' remained from the formal point of view the only period when normal law was attempted in practice. She concludes her review of Communist legal history:

It is worth remembering that about the only period when 'special' legislation was not in use and the need for liberalization was propounded, was the 1970s. After the true liberalization in the years 1980–1, in December 1981 the situation in Poland was again regarded as special, and thus calling for legal solutions that differ from those adopted in times of stability. Hence enhancement of repression in the penal law and resumption of the severe repression thesis.[20]

The thesis is then, that Polish Communism underwent a swing from the unrestricted severity of the Stalinism of early 1950s to the highly formalized system of repression under the martial law of the 1980s. One could think that the 'normal' state of the system is to be found in the 1970s, but that would limit the 'normal' stage to ten out of forty-five years. Moreover, there are further extremes to be mentioned, the liberalization of 1956 and of 1980–1 when the Communists, independent of their reformative or conservative notions, realized that events were dangerously close to escaping their control. Memories of those short periods of liberation help those who feel oppressed to survive the period of the real 'normalcy' which, in this inverse world, is exactly what one might consider as 'special'.

The meaning of all this is, then, that the real theory of Communist administration of law needs to be grounded in all those 'irregularities', 'special' cases, provisions, and procedures, without which the Party-State administrators feel unable to survive. This is why we need, in conclusion, to come to the already sketched theory of institutionalized dualism as making possible organized injustice and perseverance of the division into rulers and the ruled under the disguise of law and order. This is a good exercise in what could be called political semiotics as it turns out that the Communist government, though starting through acts of sheer physical coercion—revolution, civil war, coup, invasion or, as in case of Poland after the Second World War, liberation from another occupying power, is sooner or later domesticated with the help of converted meanings. The way this is done has been abundantly illustrated throughout this chapter. The opposition between the public and the private emerges as the most important dividing line that opposes two mutually related aspects of social organization. This opposition, however, needs to be made

[20] Fuszara, 'The Law', 147.

twice in order to make sense out of Communist reality. On the one hand we have the traditional area of the private affairs of citizens regarded as private persons in which the state does not intervene unless asked, and even if asked may not be willing to accede. Legal theory holds that such are, for example, matters of family life, or of relations between neighbours. In fact, the totalitarian ambition of the project results in the fact that the border of this 'private' zone is not strictly demarcated, as the 'public' surrounds the 'private'. The Communist activist may convoke the work collective to discuss publicly the marital infidelity of an employee or the persistent quarrels between two farmers, and in case the 'public interest' is endangered, the public procurator may enter any case that is related to those issues. In this way the conventional opposition of 'public' versus 'private' becomes superficial, as conditional upon the discretion of the authorities. Behind this there is, however, another opposition which is of more significance, between what is made 'public' for the general public and what is restricted for the discretion of those initiated into the esoteric knowledge and power. The decrees are signed by the constitutional Council of State but the decisions are made in secret, in private, but this 'private' is of decisive public implications. In contrast to the pure authoritarian system, this publicly invisible sphere of political decision-making is ordered and organized, and not left to the individual taste of the leader. The rules are perhaps largely unwritten, but the agencies are delineated. The by-laws of the Communist party may not be followed to the letter, but the decisions are to be issued on behalf of the party by the First Secretary in the Political Bureau, empowered by the Central Committee, as composed of people who have been approved by the Congress. In longer periods of time this becomes to a large degree inconsequential, but the party open only to its members continues to serve as the legitimation-base of the power enjoyed by the ruling élite and its leader. This invisible and impenetrable government whose proceedings are never publicly transmitted nor recorded (with one or two minor exceptions such as, for example, the famous transcripts of the Eighth Plenary Meeting of the Central Committee of the PUWP held in October 1956) runs the country and decides on the course of action to be taken by the lower-level 'public' government of the state, with its ministries, or by the procuracy which is to control that government. 'Public' retains its name but ceases to be public in any other sense than open to the public. The façade of the Council of State, the Council of Ministers, and Parliament hides not political bargaining between political parties, pressure groups, and politicians, but the hierarchically organized and sacrosanct political hierarchy to which 'public', 'civil', or 'secular' branches of government, including the judiciary or legislature, need to pay reverence and obedience.

A side-effect of this is the strange deconstruction of the normative that develops under Communism as the distinction between the 'ought' and the 'is' loses its ontological primordiality and self-evidence. An acute gap between the normative and actual reality seems to be an absolute attribute of reality. In Communism, however, the distinction ceases to make sense. The law is far from reality not because it is a normative text but because it is the public text and, thus, not from the sphere of real political significance such as decisions made by party bureaucrats. To compare law and social reality under such circumstances is a futile enterprise; everybody knows (though the knowledge is not 'public') that this does not matter. The normative that involves the 'ought' is to be found somewhere else, that is, behind what is publicly communicated. So in this system it is not what is 'on the books' which opposes the practice but what is to be reconstructed from hints and intentions. Vyshinsky's sin lay not so much in his theory but in the fact that the theory was exposed publicly almost in full. The next decades witnessed the development of the strange art of interpretation of the normative through reconstructing it out of political practice.

# 4

# *Polish Society: The Rise of the New Middle Class*

What happened between 1970 and 1980 cannot be left to the arcana of the political game within the top levels of the party bureaucracy nor to the permanent undermining of the system by the professional scepticism and defiance on the part of intellectuals. External forces, from both East and West, were creating the frame that shaped the history of the whole region, and not only in Poland. The Polish evolution was important not because it was metaphysically unique but because here the social process, potentially universal, came to the fore with full force much earlier, and influenced thus both Polish history and the further developments in the region. Countries and nations differ, but at least some of those differences may be interpreted not in terms of their innate characteristics or local predicaments but rather as the more or less clear manifestations of some currents of universal character. This is why sociologically interpreted history needs to aim at such interpretation of the particulars that would render the hidden structure of the events more visible. We have already suggested that this is to be found in the currents that slowly undermined Communist society and that resulted in the public emergence of the new middle class in the form of Solidarity in 1980. This means that we need to look at society in its historical movement.

The society that emerged out of the Second World War was divided into the pauperized remains of urban upper classes, intelligentsia, and workers and the peasantry that survived the war and was still full of the potential for advancement. In 1946 only 32.8 per cent of the population inhabited cities, and 70 per cent of the gross national product came from agriculture. The social, political, and cultural divisions that separated cities and the countryside were sharp prior to the war, and the sufferings of the urban population might give rise to some degree of *Schadenfreude* among the previously despised peasants. The older generation in the countryside was often illiterate, but the younger one equally often was educated not only in the elementary schools but also in the strong agrarian movement that was opposing the government. Under German occupation everybody was looking for hide-outs in the countryside—guerilla units of the Home Army and of the People's Army, Jews escaping the fate waiting for them in ghettos hastily organized by the German authorities, the Gentile population of Warsaw, forcibly removed from the city by the Germans after the abortive insurrection of 1944. War is a many-sided phenomenon and all this gave the countryside an opportunity to exploit the situation of the urban population; ransom was often taken from those in flight and, though drastically persecuted by the Germans, the black market in food for the cities was a financially worthwhile adventure. The crisis of the early 1930s had been overcome by deliberately putting the burden on the shoulders of the peasantry, whereas the German authorities supplied the peasants with artificial manure in exchange for the mandatory supply of food. The commercial middlemen in pre-war Poland were often Jews, now annihilated. Another ethnic component traditionally engaged in commercial capitalism, Germans, compromised by collaboration with the occupying forces, were forced to leave the old territories, and soon also the newly conquered ones that Poland acquired in the West in compensation for heavy territorial losses to the Soviet Union in the East.

Into this context one needs to insert the politics of industrialization that Communists have pursued since the beginning. The love affair of Communism with industry, especially with heavy industry, has its own mysteries. Communism, after all, developed out of the realization of the development of the new working class that accompanied industrialization. Where there was not enough of industry and of workers, victorious Communists were busy building it at any cost. To give due credit to history one should, of course, note that Communism developed out of a belief in the Messianic role of the working class and became the military dictatorship of the true believers, who soon discovered that they know the future better than those on whose behalf they acted. The history of Communism may perhaps be better understood in terms of the industrial organization of work in society than in terms of the mission of the proletariat. The dispossession of the capitalists meant that someone new was needed to run industry, and the task was assumed by the party. Industry became the paradigm of modern social organization, so that everybody was to be put into the Utopian mega-factory as intellectuals were accustomed to envisage it according to the theory and the few available actual cases.

This meant, above all, the need to turn peasants into workers. The task was accomplished in the early 1950s when the percentage of those employed in agriculture dropped from 60.3 per cent in 1950 to 42.3 per cent in 1955, while the share of industry in the gross national product increased much more slowly, from 24.3 per cent to 28.6 per cent. The industrialization of Poland was already estimated by Communist economists as following the most expensive model. This was due to the fact that it happened in the years when Soviet orthodoxy reached its peak, the Korean War was under way, and earlier the Marshall Plan offer of post-war reconstruction had been rejected on Soviet orders. Nevertheless, the plans were fulfilled, in that the ratio of industry's to agriculture's share in GNP changed from 0.31 in 1946 and 0.40 in 1950 to 1.00 in 1960 and 1.31 in 1965. At the same time the share of the labour force engaged in agriculture continued to decrease. Poland became an industrial-agricultural country, though it paid a heavy price for the way this was achieved. Masses of people migrated to the summarily reconstructed and constructed cheap housing estates, were given basic education and invited to enter higher education, and were offered free health and other social services. The upper class was stripped of its prestige as well as of political and economic power, while the intelligentsia was included as the engineering corps necessary to service the industrial organization of society. If not for the outburst of social unrest in 1956 one would expect growing satisfaction among the majority of the population with all these undoubtedly significant achievements. The price that was paid, however, meant that the increase in consumption lagged permanently behind the increase in production. This might be illustrated by the fact that between 1950 and 1970 the average consumption of meat per capita rose from 36.5 kilos to 53 kilos, that is 1.45 times, while the production of coal rose 1.37 times, of electricity 5.22 times, and of steel 3.59 times. It is not our task to summarize the economy of Communism here, but the postponement of consumption seemed to be the major factor that explained the material side of dissatisfaction with the system. A systematic presentation of the social history of Poland is not intended here, so let us now move to the final stages of Communist Poland in order to discover the main features of the social structure. This should give a clue to the major movement that happened in the meantime.

## POLISH SOCIETY

Chapters 10 and 11 present data from the survey that was conducted in October 1988 on a national random sample of 1,000 subjects over 16 years old. As the data from the statistical yearbook and censuses are quite limited, the view of Polish society revealed by the background information collected for this survey may be of value in providing the necessary frame of reference for the social attitudes studied in 1988, and in addition to giving a basic introduction to the sociology of Polish society in the 1980s.

The standard opinion of sociologists is that the social position of the individual in Polish society is dependent upon education above all other factors. The Constitution granted all citizens the right to free education through the general state educational system, with only a few secondary private schools run by the Catholic orders and organizations, and only one private university, the Catholic University of Lublin. Education was made obligatory between the ages of 7 and 18, and some children had pre-school experience in state-run nurseries and kindergartens for working mothers. The system was changing, but towards the end it consisted of a unified system of elementary schools, followed by a division into the vocational schools which did not work towards the matriculation certificate, and two types of more academic secondary schools, one providing technical and one general education. After completing secondary school and passing the French-style leaving-certificate examinations, the *matura*, a young person could either apply to take the entrance examinations for one of the university-level higher schools, leading to a degree, or go to one of the post-secondary schools for a shorter course. Competition for entry to the higher schools, army and police academies, medical schools, and musical and fine arts schools took place each year, with the numbers to be accepted or the qualifications needed for entry being set by the government. The socialist character of the higher-education system, apart from its being free of charge, was assured by the use of a highly developed scheme for positive discrimination established annually by the Ministry of Higher Education aimed at candidates of working-class origin, who were offered extra points. The children of private farmers were also included, if the income from the farm did not exceed the level specified by the regulations. To these were added also children of teachers in the countryside, of army officers in provincial garrisons, and of the police, as well as the extremely gifted winners of national competitions in physics, mathematics, and some other subjects. While some faculties, such as physics, have always had difficulty in filling the number of places allotted by the ministry (note that the number of staff was indirectly based on this number), others have often had more than three candidates for one place, of whom one in two might be entitled to the various extra preference points. It was quite frustrating to see good candidates from an intelligentsia or non-manual worker family giving way to weaker candidates who were successful as a result of their social origin. The system was generally held in contempt by academic teachers. The average working-class family, according to various sociological studies, in contrast to the intelligentsia and the farmers, was still not interested in academic education for their children, preferring them to achieve financial independence as soon as possible.

In the 1988 sample, the relatively low level of education in Polish society is demonstrated by the fact that less than one third had received the *matura* certificate of education issued after the final examinations at the end of secondary school. Only 6.7 per cent of the sample had completed university education, while 7.1 per cent had not completed elementary education. This result reveals a legacy from the war and pre-war days, when only four grades of school were obligatory in the countryside.

In 1918 Poland inherited different educational systems from the alien administration, with quality ranging from quite good in the former Prussian areas to very low in the former Russian parts. It is not surprising that in some parts of the country adult illiteracy continued until after the Second World War, when it was eliminated by the mass-education campaign organized by the Communist authorities. At the beginning of the Stalinist period education was held to be less important than 'proper class- (that is, political) consciousness', giving rise to the notorious slogan, 'it is not the school but free will which makes one into an officer' (*nie matura lecz chęć szczera zrobi z ciebie oficera*). Nevertheless, illiteracy was wiped out and skilled cadres of professionals—doctors, engineers, and so on—were educated to fill the need created by accelerated industrialization, the losses of the war, and the elimination of the politically suspect intelligentsia of the previous generation. The curriculum was devoid of religious education, obligatory until the end of secondary school, and supplemented by Communist ideological education. This involved the addition of ideological content to otherwise quite usual subjects. Even the school maths textbook would include exercises about two competing brigades of socialist workers, rather than two trains coming from opposite directions. In addition, there were special subjects such as civic education in schools, and obligatory courses in Marxist philosophy, sociology, and political economy in all university faculties, ranging from theology and fine art to medicine and engineering. One cannot deny the usefulness of those courses for the would-be participants in the Party State. In fact, the textbooks on philosophy by Adam Schaff and Władysław Krajewski, on sociology by Jerzy J. Wiatr, and on political economy by Oskar Lange and Włodzimierz Brus, were required reading for both students and political officers in the army, for military officers of the army, as well as for the whole host of party and state officials. Official doctrine was elaborated in full, and this continued, with some names changing from purge to purge, until the end of the 1980s. In its diluted form it was propagated through the state press and media, and through general education on the lower levels. It could not fail to have an effect, first, because for the majority of people it could have been opposed only by a personal message in church, at work, or at home, and secondly, because such total doctrines are convincing by the very totality of their explanatory promise and the elements of truth that are involved. Total doctrines are never false in the sense of being, in total, a sum of false elements. Their falsehood lies rather in the totality of truth promised, to which particular misinformations and misinterpretations are added. On the other hand this is why, having failed on one point, they fail as a whole. Since 1956 few people were inclined to believe this doctrine, but many took for granted that at least some parts concerning education were grounded in reality.

Having said this, we will now look more closely at the basic sociology of education in Poland in the 1980s. Looking at educational level by place of residence, there is a great discrepancy between the countryside, where only 2.5 per cent of inhabitants continued in education beyond secondary school and more than half had elementary education at best, and towns with over 20,000 inhabitants, where the rates for elementary education only fell to 28 per cent and the rate for higher education was about 12 per cent, rising to about one-fifth of the population in the large cities with over 100,000 inhabitants.

Level of education is also related to occupation. Moving from the self-employed, who are mostly farmers, to white-collar workers, we found an increase in the proportion who had completed higher levels of education. Of the self-employed, of whom in the Polish case 95 per cent were farmers, 72.9 per cent had no more than elementary education, compared with 45.8 per cent of manual workers and 7.6 per cent of white-collar workers. For university-level education the figures are respectively 4 per cent (self-employed); 1 per cent (manual workers); and 32.2 per cent (white-collar workers) a dramatic difference indeed. On the other hand, it is a sign of modernization that in fact 9.6 per cent of manual workers had completed secondary education. This figure would have been much higher were it not for the fact that in Gierek's years the vocational schools were used to strengthen the less skilled work-force in given organizations, and were given financial reinforcement in order to divide the incoming age-groups into an unskilled work-force and a skilled one. We found that 44.6 per cent of workers finished vocational school, compared with only 16.5 per cent of the self-employed, mainly small farmers (in order to inherit rights to a farm, the successor needed to have the agricultural training diploma), and 9.1 per cent of white-collar workers. To summarize, elementary education was for the farmer, vocational training for the worker, and secondary education for the white-collar worker. Before the Second World War, the *matura* certificate was still considered to constitute entrance to the intelligentsia, entitling the holder to the honorary rights of a gentleman (such as the informal right to duel). But with the accelerated creation of university-level schools in the

1950s and also in the 1970s, the definition underwent a change. The master's degree became the new symbol of the literate class.

The relationship of education to social position (though possibly indirectly, through the occupation it leads to), is illustrated by Table 4.1 on the relationship between education and class self-ascription.

TABLE 4.1.    *Education and social class in the 1988 survey* (%, n = 926)

| Self-ascribed social class | Highest educational level reached | | | |
|---|---|---|---|---|
| | Elementary (100% = 369) | Vocational (100% = 266) | Secondary (100% = 192) | Higher (100% = 98) |
| Upper | 4.6 | 1.5 | 1.6 | 6.1 |
| Middle | 66.9 | 76.3 | 85.4 | 86.7 |
| Lower | 28.2 | 21.8 | 12.0 | 6.1 |
| Don't know | 0.7 | 0.4 | 1.0 | 1.1 |

The fact that among those with elementary education the percentage of those who felt that they belonged to the upper class is second to that of the group with higher education can be explained in terms of the wealth which some of the farmers may have acquired. The percentage of those who felt themselves to be of the lower class decreases linearly with level of education. These figures will be compared below with data on social class and occupation. At this point we can observe that of the self-ascribed lower class, 54 per cent had at best elementary education, 30.4 per cent had attended vocational school, 12 per cent had secondary education, and 3 per cent higher education, while for the middle class the respective figures are 35.3 per cent, 29 per cent, 23.4 per cent, and 12.1 per cent. In terms of self-identity, 'middle' here seems to mean the 'average' or 'mean' position and standard of living. The worse educated were more likely to feel themselves to be on the bottom of the social class ladder. But the sheer numerical prevalence of the worse-educated categories leads to their presence amongst the middle and the upper classes as well. In terms of self-identification, social classes in Poland do differ by education, with an increase in the likelihood of better education when moving from the lower to the middle class, but there is no qualitative opposition between those two. Though it may seem to result from the numbers, from the relative novelty of the threefold scheme offered for self-identification to respondents, and from the lower level of education, one needs to underline that with all this it would still be possible to have, for instance, secondary education being dominant among the middle, and higher education amongst the upper strata. If it is not so, it means that education does not form the basis for class-identification in a scheme that takes into account the results of the various forms of distinction in social life. To this analysis, of course, the effects of the occupational division into three classes—self-employed (meaning basically farmers), workers, and white-collars workers—need to be added.

If occupational class is related to self-ascribed social class, the picture resembles that of the relationship between education and social class. The upper class is numerically so small that conclusions must be tentative, but still it is represented in all major occupational groups, the main distinction being that between the middle class, to which 76 per cent of the sample have attached themselves, and the lower class, which includes 21 per cent of the sample. From self-employed to workers to white-collar workers, the rate of middle-class self-ascription increases, and perceived membership of the lower class decreases. Workers constitute 51 per cent of the total sample, 46.7 per cent of the upper class, 50.2 per cent of the middle, and 58.1 per cent of the lower class, while white-collar workers constitute not more than 32.1 per cent of the middle class, but 15.7 per cent of the lower class, with 26.7 per cent of the upper class. The division into upper, middle, and lower classes in Poland in the 1980s did not, therefore, correspond to the division into the three major occupational categories.

If both education and occupation were taken into consideration the analysis is restricted, as some categories like higher-educated self-employed, or elementary-educated white-collar workers contained too few cases, but it is clear that both education and occupation are related to class self-identification. From left to right of Table 4.2 the percentage of those who feel themselves to be in the middle class rises, the workers with elementary education feeling themselves to be middle class more often than the self-employed with elementary education. White-collar workers with secondary education identified themselves as middle

TABLE 4.2.   *Social class by occupation and education* (%, n = 926)

| Self-ascribed social class | Self-employed (farmers) (n = 170) | | Workers (n = 480) | | | | White-collar workers (n = 264) | | |
|---|---|---|---|---|---|---|---|---|---|
| | Total (n = 170) | El. (n = 124) | Total (n = 480) | El. (n = 220) | Voc. (n = 214) | Sec. (n = 41) | Total (n = 264) | Sec. (n = 154) | High (n = 85) |
| Upper | 4.1 | 4.8 | 2.9 | 5.0 | 1.4 | — | 3.0 | 1.5 | 5.9 |
| Middle | 67.6 | 64.5 | 73.1 | 66.8 | 76.6 | 85.4 | 85.2 | 88.1 | 87.1 |
| Lower | 28.2 | 30.6 | 23.1 | 27.7 | 21.5 | 9.8 | 11.4 | 10.5 | 5.9 |

*Note:* El. = elementary education only; Voc. = vocational training; Sec. = secondary education; High. = higher education.

class more often than workers with the same level of education. On the other hand, three qualifications need to be made which show how this picture of social structure and the perception of it differ from the one encountered in the capitalist society of Western Europe. First, we find workers with elementary education and the self-employed in the upper class of the stratification scheme as often as white-collar workers with higher education. This can be explained by reference to the relative material well-being which some of them enjoy, which is independent from the classical ladder of social prestige. Secondly, the difference between the occupational and educational composition of the classes is still a difference of degree, as Polish society in the 1980s seems to be a working-class society in that this is the most numerous category of the population. This suggests that Poland also has to be characterized as an industrial society at its peak before the development of the tertiary stage with the expansion of services and the information industry of the post-industries stage present in the West. One cannot, therefore, dispute the self-identification of the classes on the grounds of their occupational characteristics. Thirdly, the difference between the better-educated workers who had completed secondary school and the white-collar workers of varying levels of education is so negligible that it seems more justifiable to speak of them together, as compared with people with no more than elementary education, and the specific category of workers with vocational education behind them. This might be summed up by saying that education proved itself to be of greater significance when explaining the different propensities for self-identification with reference to the threefold scheme of social stratification, and that a more sophisticated approach to the issue of social class rather than simply an attempt to reduce them to social strata by levels of education or classes of occupation is needed.

Other important background characteristics are gender and age. The gender differences in patterns of education are reflected in that women are represented in both marginal categories, that is among people with elementary education only and among those who had at least begun a university-level education, while among those with the vocational education meant for the working class, men were predominant. In this context it is remarkable that the number of women who stay at home while the men work was low, and comprised only 8 per cent of all females in the sample, excluding women employed on the family farm as well as pensioners. The gender structure of the work-force will be clearer when we look at Table 4.3.

TABLE 4.3.    *Work-force by gender* (%, n = 926)

| Occupation | Male (n = 431) | Female (n = 495) |
| --- | --- | --- |
| Gainfully employed | 77.3 | 51.3 |
| Housewives | — | 8.0 |
| Pensioners | 19.5 | 20.0 |
| Students | 4.97 | 0.9 |
| Unemployed | 0.7 | 5.1 |

Again, women are over-represented in the more traditional and the more developed sectors of employment. If housewives are added to the larger group of unemployed, this group will then include women who stay at home with their parents, those who have not entered education or work, and those who do some auxiliary work in the household and prepare themselves for further studies. Their brothers and male peers are usually in the army at that time. The proportion of women attending colleges is larger than for men. Polish women, as is typical in a Communist society, do not stay at home, but are burdened with child-care and care for the household and usually perform two jobs—one inside the home and one outside. This needs, however, to be related to the situation of men, who are also expected to do two jobs as the earnings from one would not suffice. A man has a basic job as his official main occupation in official work hours, usually eight hours per day, then afterwards he is expected to work in paid overtime on the same job or to take up some better-paid 'black' job, which is often performed with resources and tools from the official job. Of course, this extra job is non-taxable as it is, at best, semi-legal. No taxes are, in practice, levied either on work done at home or on service such as changing small amounts of hard currency on the black market into substantial earnings. The economy of the household, to which only a brief reference is made here, is complex. By the end of the 1970s it was estimated that at least 20 per cent of the family income came from unregistered economic activity, and in the 1970s, as in the 1980s, the family depended upon four jobs being performed at home and outside by the couple. This seems to be the reason for the apparent lack of interest in women's rights and feminist issues.[1] The Polish family under Communism was cemented by the equal concern which both partners needed to show for the household's welfare. Even for the mere survival of the family, the average earnings of the male would not be sufficient. In the process of accelerated industrialization, the Communists mobilized a massive work-force, not only by uprooting farmers from the countryside and using the slave labour of prisoners, which remained of importance in some areas until the 1980s and was the basic element in mining in the early 1950s, but also through making it necessary for ordinary women to take a job outside the household. And for a household to advance beyond a mere subsistence level, to buy a flat, a car, a colour television, or to pay for holidays abroad, someone needed to take up a third paid job, and this was usually the man's responsibility.

On the other hand, young women have more often been allowed to pursue their own educational advancement in a social milieu different from that of the traditional intelligentsia. A girl could go to university, while a boy was expected to find a good job as soon as possible. This over-supply of female candidates on the educational market might explain the gender quotas that have been instituted in some, mostly medical, schools a practice that was found unconstitutional by the Constitutional Tribunal in 1987. The results of this difference in expectations are manifest in the data presented above, as well as in the fact that more men are engaged in menial jobs while women are more likely than men to be in the white-collar group.

The same licence which enabled girls to depend upon their parents and enter higher educational establishments, seems to be behind the much lower percentage of women belonging to official political organizations. While in the total sample studied 10 per cent declared themselves members of the Communist (Polish United Workers) party, this was the case for only 3.8 per cent of women. In total, 89.1 per cent of women as against 74 per cent of men declared that they did not belong to any of the official political organizations. This results from the greater freedom

[1] M. Fuszara, in M. Maclean and D. Groves (eds.) *Women's Issues in Social Policy* (London, 1991).

granted to women in exchange for less responsibility, and not from their lower level of involvement in work and the public sphere indicated by their rate of membership in trade unions. In 1988 it was felt proper to ask in the survey about trade unions in general and not about legal trade unions or the illegal Solidarity specifically. Membership was found to be almost the same for both genders, 28.3 per cent of men and 25.4 per cent of women.

Finally, the age distribution. Figure 4.1 attempts to link the sample (divided arbitrarily into four age-groups: 201 people aged 16 to 29 years at the time of survey, 326 aged 30 to 45, 213 aged 46 to 59, and 186 aged 60 years and more) with the political history of the country. The age-groups differ in that the eldest one, group D, was educated mainly—if at all—during or before the Second World War. This is the generation that knew Communism from its beginnings, knew the Nazi occupation also, and can make comparisons with the post-war reconstruction of the country from its ruins as well as with the backwardness associated with the period of independence before the war. Generation C attended school at the height of the Stalinist period, experienced the worst form of totalitarian education, and was deprived of the value of comparisons with other political arrangements, but was also able to watch the first discrediting of Communism after the death of Stalin. It saw the Poznań riots in June 1956 pacified by tanks and security forces, and the sudden liberalization of political life in October 1956, the year when Władysław Gomułka, a Communist imprisoned in the early 1950s, was brought back to power warmly welcomed by the whole nation who expected an end to the oppression. Those hopes vanished in the 1960s. The next age-group, group B, was, nevertheless, in school during a period of comparative relaxation, and witnessed the stagnation of Gomułka's later years in power overturned when, after the suppression of the riots on the Baltic coast in December 1970, Edward Gierek came to power. Then began the seven fat years of prosperity, behind which corruption was increasing, based on mis-invested Western credit, soon to be revealed in the worst economic crisis to strike Poland under Communism. This generation knew only Communism throughout its life, from the stagnation of Gomułka through the miracle of prosperity offered by Gierek, to the rebellion of summer 1980 and the construction of Solidarity. Though Wałęsa and Kuroń, Mazowiecki and Geremek

Generations

| | A | B | C | D |
|---|---|---|---|---|
| 1990 | 18–31 | 32–47 | 48–61 | 62– |
| 1988 survey | 16–29 | 30–45 | 46–59 | 60– |
| | | | | |
| 1981 martial law | 9–22 | 23–38 | 39–52 | 53– |
| 1980 Solidarity | 8–21 | 22–37 | 38–51 | 52– |
| 1976 food riots | 4–17 | 18–33 | 34–47 | 48– |
| | | | | |
| 1970 coast riots | –11 | 12–27 | 28–41 | 42– |
| 1968 Students riots, | –9 | 10–25 | 26–39 | 41– |
| Czechoslovakia and purge | | | | |
| of Christianity in Poland | | | | |
| 1966 millenium | –7 | 8–23 | 24–37 | 39– |
| 1960 | –1 | 2–17 | 18–31 | 32– |
| 1956 Poznań riots and | | –13 | 14–27 | 28– |
| October thaw | | | | |
| 1953 Stalian dies | | –10 | 11–24 | 25– |
| 1950 Korean War | | –7 | 8–21 | 22– |
| 1944 Red Army re-enters | | –1 | 2–15 | 16– |
| 1940 | | | –11 | 12– |
| 1939 Nazi and Red Armies invade | | | –10 | 11– |
| 1930 | | | –1 | 2– |
| 1929 | | | | 1– |

1926 Piłusdski's coup

1920 Red Army overcome
1918 Independence of Poland

Fig. 4.1. Age-groups of the 1988 survey in terms of their political biography.

belong to the older generation, group B is the generation of Solidarity as it has developed. Then comes a new generation, group A, of people who witnessed the failures of their older brothers and sisters and who were in school and university when martial law was introduced. General Jaruzelski has made more of a mark on the experience of this youthful generation than Gierek, under whom they were born and mainly educated. Of course, it is not possible to link the individual to the political biography of the nation completely, but it is important to consider these basic relationships before going in detail into the study of social attitudes. Age—due to the direction of time—is related to traditionalism among the younger groups. Poland, like all countries undergoing a steady process of modernization, experiences its historical meanders, and the differences between age-groups in the population are most easily explained by reference to different experiences. But one cannot eliminate the difference in life experiences that cannot be termed progress. In the case of education, the age-groups differ so much that it seems that age has assumed the role of an indicator of level of education: among the oldest category, group D, 72.6 per cent had no more than elementary education as compared with 6.5 per cent with more than elementary education, and among group C, now aged 45 to 59 years, 55.4 per cent have only elementary education and 8.9 per cent higher; among group B, aged 30 to 45 years, the figures are 21.2 per cent compared with 15.3 per cent. It is only when we come to the young generation, the under-thirties, that the line changes into a curve, as here 23.4 per cent have only elementary education and 8.5 per cent have started higher education. This might have been seen as a result of the young being still in pursuit of their education, though the effects of the economic hardships of the 1980s pressing the administration to cut education funding and families' need to send their offspring out to paid work can not be ignored. In practical terms it means that the differences between the two younger out of the four age-groups are not due to differences in the level of education. One should stress, however, in this context that for some unknown reason the youngest category includes many more (46.3 per cent) village dwellers, and fewer inhabitants of large cities of over 100,000 people, than the older age-groups (between 32.8 per cent and 43.6 per cent, and 31.3 per cent and 34.7 per cent respectively). This cannot be attributed simply to different fertility rates but also perhaps to some bias behind the sampling procedures for which we have no explanation, having used the otherwise reliable Public Opinion Research Centre at PRTV, who conducted the poll for us in 1988. We are, therefore, cautious whenever age-differences are being considered. For instance, religiosity is distinctively lower in the B age-group than in the youngest. This cannot be attributed either to the difference in institutionalized socialization in schools in different periods, nor to age-differences understood as biological maturation, but rather to the direct influence of rural culture with its personal control, reliance on face-to-face contact, and the strong role of the local priest and parish in the community.

But at this point let us look back, and summarize the basic characteristics of Polish society as it was towards the end of Communism in 1988. With health standards among the lowest in Europe, people lived into their sixties and seventies after retirement at 65 years of age for men and 60 for women. The birthrate was modest but still high by European standards, the introduction of martial law having provoked the latest wave of increased reproductivity. The countryside remained the place of residence for almost 39.1 per cent of the sample, although agriculture was less significant in the economy. Only 16.3 per cent of the population worked on farms, compared with 51.8 per cent as unskilled workers and 28.5 per cent as white-collar workers. This was, therefore, not only a working society, but also a workers' society to a large extent. Roughly one-third of the adult population were in non-manual employment, and almost one-third had also completed secondary education. The majority read newspapers and watched television, but the good sermon on Sunday and a book read in school remained the main source of intellectual inspiration independent of homogenized mass propaganda. The family remained the basic arena of private life, the ultimate value in life, and second only to a circle of good friends whom one could depend on in economic transactions at the edge of legality, free political speech, and for mutual support in times of duress. The family links extended, due to the lack of housing and the economic situation, to three generations. In age-group C (46 to 59 years), 27.5 per cent still had dependent children. Grandmothers were not exempt from family duties, so the dependence of a child was mentioned by 4.3 per cent of those over retirement age. In the youngest age-group, 56.7 per cent were single, and thereafter the proportion falls to about 5 per cent plus about 3 per cent divorced and not remarried, while in the whole sample there were 71 per cent married for first time and 3 per cent for the second. With all the deprivation as compared with the Western standard of living, the majority counted themselves as middle class, including the workers. More significantly, in 1988 a similar majority of 74 per cent declared themselves as, in general, satisfied with their life.

## THE MIDDLE CLASS

A reader who vainly attempts to make a meaningful whole out of the macabre pieces of information on the crimes committed during the Stalinist era, and the old documentary newsreels showing the enthusiasm of the constructors of the great industrial complexes, would be shocked to find himself or herself in a Warsaw street, say towards evening on a New Year's Eve in the early 1950s. The dark street would be weakly lit in yellow by widely spaced lamps that help little in making one's way through the silent old buildings and the new red-brick apartment houses in the direction of the city. A carefully dressed couple, who hasten their steps when passing one of the many prisons hidden behind brightly lit walls, arrive at a large public building with a marble entrance where the guests show their pass-cards. The host is not awaiting them there, but is somewhere within. Tomorrow the newspaper will carry his picture, showing him in the midst of the Stakhanovites, the heroes of labour. Behind him is a row of silent generals, and behind them a row of gentlemen looking sadly and very carefully at those gathered. But in front are the heroes of socialist labour, the statues—the worker with an axe, the milkmaid mopping her forehead after her heavy work, a writer with pen and manuscript—which are found decorating the palaces and parks of culture and science and represented on the postage stamps. This Holy Trinity of Communist society—working class, farmers, and working intelligentsia—will survive the host of the New Year's ball for decades, immortalized by propaganda as well as by the handbooks of sociology. Whatever the social role of this trichotomy used to be, it is time to dispose of it now, as social reality disposed of it much earlier.

As long ago as 1980, while commenting on the events of August, I expressed the opinion that a new class started the fight, a class composed of people who directly confronted the authorities in companies, offices, and institutions run by them. This new middle class consists of the best-educated and most highly paid people in comparison with the lower, truly proletarianized classes. I took as the real social effect of Communism in Poland the fact that the actual differences between workers and intelligentsia, or between those who do mental and menial labour, have been obliterated and the distinction has become a statistical convention. The cultural and economic advancement of millions of people led to the situation in which a new middle class was formed, blocked in its aspirations on the one hand by the closed borders of the ruling class, and on the other by the misgovernment of the country and its economy.

The concept of a new middle class, of which Solidarity was the organizational as well as the ideological manifestation, did not find acceptance. In fact it was warmly welcomed only by *Rzeczywistość*, the anti-Solidarity weekly of the *apparatchiks*, trying to play on the populist mood in the country. This lack of acceptance will not surprise sociologists who, since Stanisław Ossowski's remarks on the role of dichotomy in the days of political struggle, know very well that in a period of conflict such as the 1980s, no schemes that try to make the picture of society more complex than the bipartite division into 'goodies' and 'baddies' will be accepted. Independent writers in the martial law period referred, however, from time to time to my idea while debating in the underground press about the causes of failure. It was criticized by serious students of social structure in Poland, such as Krzysztof Zagórski,[2] while some researchers from the team making regular surveys of Polish public opinion, known as 'the Poles', came slowly to support this opinion more strongly.[3] Of course there were various extra-scientific reasons for this reserve, apart from direct political ones. After all, the term 'middle class' on the continent suggests Philistine narrow-mindedness and preoccupation with small business, the burghers' virtues that for centuries were held in contempt by the gentry in Poland. This patronizing attitude was inherited by the Polish intelligentsia. On the other hand, the Left in the West resembles sociologically the Central European intelligentsia in their almost instinctive repugnance for power, as well as in their aversion to the middle class. Concern about the alleged disappearance of the working class among the

---

[2] K. Zagórski, 'Society, Economy and Class Relations', in R. F. Miller (ed.), *Poland in the Eighties: Social Revolution against Real Socialism* (Canberra, 1984).
[3] See e.g. A. Rychard, 'Granice reform' (Limits of Reform), *Odra*, 11 (1988).

middle classes in the West illustrates these attitudes well. What if the processes I observed in Poland and those long before diagnosed in the West are similar? And what, in fact, is wrong with it? Disciplines such as, for instance, the theory of the party or historical materialism, and the role of normal academicians since the days of Ivan Pavlov, add some glamour to those creatures. The 'working class' comprises an extraordinary range of people from the shipyard electrician to the milkman, but the 'working intelligentsia' also includes the honest poet smuggling her verses into the state-controlled press, and the director of the Institute of Marxism Leninism at the Central Committee of the Communist party. The situations, the experiences, and the aspirations of each of these are different. The allegedly homogeneous class of the intelligentsia in fact includes very different class positions, while the invisible barrier of *nomenklatura* very sharply determines the borders of the ruling class, and its potential for control of the other classes through the allocation of conditional, ever-to-be-withdrawn privileges.

One may doubt here the propriety of the usage of the term 'class'. When speaking of social classes I have in mind those large social categories of people who enter major conflicts and join in the 'solidarity' of the day on the same side. One might, therefore, understand social class as a category imposed upon the historical process as it develops, and not as a static social fact as such. Imagine iron filings on a sheet of paper. The closer we approach with a magnet from below the more evident is the pattern. Similarly with social classes; but do we need to say that those classes exist, or rather that they are manifested through the forces of conflict and solidarity?

The more classificatory approach however is not without value. Irena Nowakowa in the 1960s and Wacław Makarczyk in the 1970s have amply documented in their research the socially marginalized status of unskilled workers who are traditionally counted as part of the working class in general. But the marginal position of unskilled workers, as compared to other social categories of occupation such as farmers, skilled workers, white-collar workers without university education, and the intelligentsia proper (that is, with some university education), makes the very idea of including them in the same category as the skilled workers absurd.

This is very well illustrated by Makarczyk's survey,[4] carried out in 1975, with a nation-wide sample of 2,472 people. The most surprising result of this survey into cultural and material needs was that on almost each of Makarczyk's questions the unskilled workers ranked lowest in comparison with the other categories. This can be seen in the following summary of the results, where the percentages of those who declared deprivation is given: unskilled workers came first, followed by the next most-deprived category, and thirdly those who were the least dissatisfied with the state of affairs under consideration.

Unskilled workers most often declared low and very low incomes from the work they did (37 per cent), as compared with farmers (29.6 per cent) who were closest to them, and skilled workers (21.2 per cent), who were the least often dissatisfied with their wages. Unskilled workers most often thought that their income was much too low when compared with their needs (41.5 per cent), while white-collar workers without university education came next (but next means 27.6 per cent!), and the least dissatisfied were white-collar workers with university education (22.9 per cent). Unskilled workers most often felt that their nourishment was unsatisfactory (20 per cent, as against 10.7 per cent of skilled workers and 1.4 per cent of white-collar workers with university education); that their clothes were not adequate (51.9 per cent, as against 36.7 per cent of skilled workers and 18.2 per cent of farmers); that their basic needs were not satisfied so they could not cope (6.5 per cent, as against 4.3 per cent of skilled workers and none of the white-collar workers with university education). Housing conditions were reported as bad or very bad by 30.8 per cent of unskilled workers as against 29.1 per cent of skilled workers and 20.8 per cent of white-collar workers with university education), and more of them lived in overcrowded apartments with more than two persons to a room (23.4 per cent, as against 22.1 per cent of farmers and none of the white-collar workers with university education).

Material deprivation coincided with deprivation in human interaction. Unskilled workers most often said that their family life was bad or mediocre (22.3 per cent, as against 21.1 per cent

---

[4] W. Makarczyk, *Struktura społeczna a warunki życiowe* (Social structure and living conditions) (Warsaw, 1978).

of farmers and 7.2 per cent of white collar workers with university education); more did not have even a single friend (39.7 per cent, as against 36.2 per cent of farmers and 4.8 per cent of university-educated white-collar workers); more of them had nobody on whom they could rely in case of serious troubles (38.9 per cent, as against 28.2 per cent of skilled workers and 13.3 per cent of white-collar workers with university education); more of them had no contacts with anyone outside the close family (26.5 per cent, as against 18.8 per cent of farmers and 2.4 per cent of white-collar workers with university education); and more of them did not take part in social meetings outside the home (73.5 per cent, as against 69.4 per cent of farmers and 15.7 per cent of white-collar workers with university education).

The picture brightens somewhat when one moves to the work-place. Here the unskilled workers most often of all the categories assessed their relationships with their superiors as very good or good (85.7 per cent, as against 82 per cent of white-collar workers without university education and 79.6 per cent of skilled workers). This may in fact result from the inferiority felt by the unskilled worker toward his or her superior, so that he might be less likely to put his own interests forward and engage in conflict.

The position of unskilled workers compared with other occupational categories helps us to see the conventional character of the borders between the remaining groups. Even if in some ways the university-educated white-collar workers fare best, firstly this is not a uniform pattern, and secondly, the latter category includes people in widely divergent positions, such as an office clerk who has just started work and a world-famous composer. In the light of all this, the repeated pattern of unskilled workers' lack of satisfaction is striking. It is as if the differences between them and skilled workers were greater than, for instance, between the latter and the intelligentsia. But why not, after all? Why does one need to stick to the old ways in which the milkman and the vocationally trained electrician, welder, or miner who, as a result of education and material well-being, have higher aspirations to participate in modern standards of cultural and material consumption, are to be put in the same social category, and separated from a brother in the office and a sister in the university? In 1981 the Gdansk weekly *Czas* published a compelling letter by a young shipbuilder, who was assuring the editor and the public that the only thing he and his colleagues wanted was simply to be normal like other people in the world, and to be able to go freely to Greece and see the Acropolis. The futility of the traditional classification made according to occupation became more and more evident over the years, but August 1980 offered, with the Solidarity movement that evolved out of it, the best proof of what the real lines of conflict and solidarity in Polish society are. The language used at the beginning was that of the working class, which revolted against its Communist masters with the help of the intellectuals. This was epitomized by the letter of fifty-four intellectuals and the development of an emergency team of experts in the Gdansk Shipyard from the messengers who organized and brought that letter. On the one hand the electrician, Lech Wałęsa; on the other the professor, Bronisław Geremek, and the journalist, Tadeusz Mazowiecki. This symbolic group provokes thoughts of an alliance between workers and intellectuals, and was interpreted in such a way by Solidarity partisans.

It would be good, however, to remind the reader of some sociological features of Solidarity at its climax in 1981. Membership was roughly proportionate by gender, the preponderance of men resulting from their prevalence in the labour force. Solidarity was most popular among people aged 20 to 29 yeas, and least popular amongst those pensioners who could enter the new trade union only at the price of leaving the old one to which they had belonged while employed. Membership was higher among townspeople, though 20 per cent of villagers employed outside farming belonged as well. The average level of education in Solidarity was higher than in the total labour force. The survey findings vary, but between 42 per cent and 58 per cent of members were skilled workers, followed by white-collar workers without university education, who made up between 23 per cent and 29 per cent of membership. It was representative of the national labour force, while membership in Solidarity was relatively more rare, on the one hand, amongst unskilled workers, and on the other, among white-collar workers with university education, a fact easily explained if we take into account that the latter group includes not only the bulk of the ruling élite but also people directly subordinated in the bureaucracy of the Party State.

I asked about class self-identification in two regional chapters of Solidarity, in a survey based upon random samples of members. A complex picture emerged from the answers: 84 per cent of manual workers and 16 per cent of white-collar workers said that they belonged to the 'working class', while none of the workers identified themselves as members of the 'intelligentsia', in contrast to 77 per cent of white-collar workers. The division was made in principle according to occupation and education, except for the fact that some intelligentsia people preferred to identify themselves with the 'working class'. This is symptomatic, as normally we assume that it is the upper class to which lower-class people aspire when ascribing class-membership to themselves. I do not think that this scheme worked in the case described, but certainly it counters the arguments about the continuing existence of the sharp division between the classes, with the assumed superiority of the better-educated. Let me add to this the important observation that within the leadership of the strikers, as well as later on within the leadership of the new trade union, very often those who were identified as workers (and certainly many of those who were criticizing 'intellectuals') were white-collar workers with university education themselves. Of the two authors of the left manifesto of the mid-1960s, Professor Karol Modzelewski was elevated to the highest ranks of trade-union leadership, while the activist Jacek Kuroń served as the 'egghead' and union adviser. Solidarity language quickly adapted to sociological reality with reference to terms such as 'labour' rather than 'workers'. The internal organization of Solidarity, within which not only industries and trades but also universities and ministries were represented on a territorial basis, enabled the better-educated to move upward through the elections. On the other hand, was this not a manifestation rather than a cause? Was is not the feeling of solidarity that made people ready to accept organization on a territorial basis instead of by trade and industries, and to elect people according to their perceived merits instead of their sociological characteristics? And in fact the 'labour' consisted of 'enterprises', economically autonomous units such as a factory, or steel-mill, a shipyard, or a research institute as well. Though some of these were financed from the budget while others were supposed to earn money on their own, the economic system blurred the distinction, as it was the state who owned almost all of the independent enterprises of this kind, and it was the state that dictated the economy of those enterprises either directly through budget allocations, or through setting prices and establishing obligatory tasks and partners in production. The solidarity between the units of this state economy was rooted in the similarity of their economic situation. The major divisions within enterprises were made according to power: management versus staff, administration versus others. It follows that thousands of engineers were on the same side as the technicians and less-skilled employees in the non-administrative sector. The engineers and workers were often in the same strike committees, and though this micro-sociological study of the strikes of 1980 was never completed, it was here, as I suppose, that the solidarity of what is called here the new middle class developed.

There are other, less direct, arguments which support the picture I drew of the social structure of Poland. In winter 1984/4, for instance, interviews were carried out with 195 randomly selected households from Warsaw, and the issue of social differentiation was raised, as we were interested in whether the respondents thought of themselves as being below, above, or at the national average standard of living. Of those interviewed the majority, 57 per cent (and this is in line with other similar surveys) thought their standard of living was average, while 25 per cent described their conditions as below and 17 per cent as above average. When comparing the results with 180 interviews carried out in the countryside of Eastern Poland in the summer of 1983, the underprivileged position of the farmers as felt by them was clearly shown. Here only 32 per cent of the sample found their situation to be average, and 45 per cent thought themselves below average. These differences reflect the lack of many goods in village households, as described by the respondents.

The next question was: 'What kinds of people have the best standard of living?' There was little difference between the answers given in the city and in the country. In the city, people involved in private business of various kinds were most often (48 per cent) mentioned, then those who occupy the top positions of power (31 per cent), and profiteers of different types who technically might be added to the first category, though emotionally they were placed closer to the second (14 per cent). Of the traditional social categories, all three classes were mentioned—workers (5 per cent), farmers 94 per cent), and the intelligentsia (4 per cent). Village-dwellers characteristically put the power élite in the first place (39 per cent), men successful in business on their own account (12 per cent) and profiteers (11 per cent) less often. They also pointed to the farmers themselves (8 per cent), the intelligentsia (8 per cent), clerical staff (8 per cent), and city-dwellers (6 per cent) in general.

When asked: 'Who has the worst standard of living?', the majority of Warsaw people (55 per cent) identified pensioners as underprivileged and also families with many children (13 per cent), young couples (10 per cent), single mothers (6 per cent), and single people in general (3 per cent). Using traditional social categories, 10 per cent said that workers lived worst, 7 per cent the intelligentsia, and 3 per cent the clerical staff. Here the pattern of answers given in the countryside was markedly different, as the category most often described as underprivileged was that of the farmers themselves (37 per cent), and then the workers (12 per cent). The different climate of attitudes towards life among self-employed farmers in the countryside is reflected also in the fact that 14 per cent of respondents pointed to those who do not want to work as those who live worst. In the country one may presuppose, then, two categories of people—farmers promoting entrepreneurship and full of contempt for the lack of work ethic, and the peasants in the old style, feeling oppressed and frustrated by city-dwellers.

The data just quoted are relevant here because it is evident that in open-ended questions, posed in a relatively unstructured interview, the traditional social classes have been relatively rarely mentioned (though the position of farmers or peasants remains unclear, as it is unclear in reality). In fact, one may suggest that the peasantry as well as the unskilled workers were retaining their traditional social status inherited from the past, while the more modernized sector of these employed in agriculture took on the status of farmers. Politically more conservative, the countryside remained torn between the general anti-Communism of Polish society and the interest in peace and order that the strong government of General Jaruzelski seemed to guarantee. Farmers resemble much more closely the middle class of the traditional type, that is, the small- to medium-size private entrepreneur. On the other hand, two sectors were felt to be above the troubles of everyday life—the private businessman (different from the traditional peasant family household economy), and the Communist power élite with its auxilliaries.

# 5

# *Words and Deeds: Demands and Events*

If the ultimate sanction of execution always existed, the glue that kept the regime in place was what Dionisio Ridruejo, the repentant Falangist poet, once characterized to me as 'administrative coercion'. Everything from a driving licence to a job depended on acceptance—at least in foro externo—of the regime. Those who live in democratic societies cannot understand the efficacy of this mechanism when it pervades a whole society. It takes a brave man to risk his prospects of promotion and the livelihood of his family for his convictions. Most ordinary citizens conform in order to survive; even university professors do not relish losing their chairs. In an authoritarian regime self-censorship become a conditioned reflex for weary intellectuals.[1]

Substitute 'Communist' for 'authoritarian' and the words describe surprisingly well the condition of Polish society under Władysław Gomułka. The ultimate sanction of execution seemingly ceased to exist with the bygone days and nights of Stalinism at its height. This, however, was only an appearance, as the bloody pacification of food price riots on the Baltic sea-coast in December 1970 proved. In daily life, and well up to 1989, the mechanism of administrative coercion ruled. '*Everything from a driving licence to a job depended on acceptance—at least* in foro externo—*of the regime.*' In this depressing landscape there were, however, from time to time some changes. On one occasion it was flash of the festive joy of liberation that, with all its fears and threats, characterized the strike on the sea-coast in the summer of 1980. On another occasion the taste of freedom was much more bitter, when it resulted from acts of ultimate determination in confrontation with armed force, the howling of ambulances, the noise of tank caterpillars, and the smoke of tear-gas. Such was the liberation of December 1970, and nobody was full of joy then.

[1] Raymond Carr, *New York Review of Books* (4 Feb. 1988).

'We are stuck fast in the mud—but this is the party that put us in it', argued a worker at the open meeting of the party organization in the Gdansk Lenin Shipyard in 1971.

Non-party members do not have freedom of speech. In these events you, as the minority, instead of coming to us, have demanded that we, as the majority, should come making representation to you. We demanded that you should come to us. Now we have come to you as you wished. What will happen now that you did not come to us in the shipyard?

The approach of the majority to the minority the worker referred to took place in Gdansk, Gdynia, and Szczecin, major cities on the Polish sea-coast in December 1970. It is worth recalling the story here.

## EVENTS

On 11 December 1970, the Politburo of the Central Committee of the Polish United Workers Party debated the draft of the Council of Ministers' decree on the change in retail prices, exemplified by the increase in meat prices. The *Calendar of December 1970 Events*, prepared by the party-related research group directed by Stanisław Bucholc,[2] states that only one member, an experienced Communist economist politician, Stefan Jędrychowski, doubted the reasonableness of the whole operation. The idea of timing the increase in food prices to coincide with the beginning of the massive shopping for food that precedes Christmas came from another experienced Communist politician, a former Socialist, prime minister Józef Cyrankiewicz. The man who was soon to emerge as the only winner out of the crisis, as a moderate leader capable of appeasing the bewildered population, the long-standing 'crown prince' waiting for his turn in supreme power, Edward Gierek, when asked by Gomułka what the attitude of the working class would be, responded with servile support typical of courtly atmosphere throughout all ages: 'It will be difficult but we shall manage.' And he did. The Politburo approved the draft, as well as the letter sent in its name to all PUWP cells in the country clarifying the need for price increases.

Three comments are appropriate here. First, the collective

---

[2] Stanisław Bucholc (ed.), *Grudzień 1970* (Dec. 1970) (Gdansk, 1989).

decision-making was not just a token effort; it really took place. The responsibility of the ruling élite for the events of the 1970s was discussed in the sceptical parliamentary committee and in the Tribunal of State during the 1980s, until the benevolent act of amnesty put an end to it. This was not unwise if we remember that the amnesty was signed by General Jaruzelski himself, whereas the responsibility for the bloodshed of 1970 followed no such legitimating act; if it were, it seems that possibly all members of the Politburo, except one, would be held responsible for the bloodshed of 1970, as Gomulka could rightly point to the fact that he had requested advice, and simply followed the advice given.

Secondly, it is important to note that the whole affair tells us how the Constitution was functioning in practice in the country at that time; before the amendments to the Constitution of 1976, granting the PUWP the 'leading role in the country's life', drafts of the Council of Ministers' decrees needed to be presented first to the Politburo for approval, then debated, and if approved were issued by the Council. The politburo, the executive organ of the supreme elected body of a political party, serves here as the highest and sovereign political institution in the country.

Thirdly, the secrecy with which this debate was held made it possible for the actors to play up or down individual responsibilities afterwards, according to the outcome of events and political expediency. Jaruzelski emerged (as usual) as innocent; while Gierek, who reinforced Gomulka in the latter's wrong assessment of social attitudes, was elected First Secretary on 20 Sunday December 1970, and Gomulka was deposed, together with his former associates. Natural suspicion of the staged coup and provocation cannot be dismissed under such circumstances, even through the Gierek's memoirs, published in 1990, exclude this interpretation. But one should point to the fact that Gierek's views were sought, as party boss of the heavily industrialized region of Upper Silesia, where mining and steelworking has been concentrated since the last century and where the working class remained disciplined until the summer of 1980. Moreover, his subsequent election by the Central Committee represents a clear exploitation of the secrecy of political decision-making; he could assume not only innocence but even independence from the Gomulka policies, and so ask for and receive help from the sea-coast labour force as he did in January 1971, even though he was in fact a member of the same ruling establishment that had been responsible for all the previous political decisions.

Gomułka was the leader but not an absolute ruler. If he should fail to secure the continuance in power of the unnamed sector of the party's apparatus, both elected and appointed, he would be removed and exchanged for another representative (whose superiority was limited to the fact of his being a different person). In this, Communist rule in Poland after Stalin's death was different from the previous purer type of individual authority, but it was more stable. Through that mechanism, continuity of power by the ruling class was secured even if the ruling individuals were removed. One could say the same, perhaps, about Stalin, Trotsky, and other competitors for ultimate power in the Soviet Union from the 1920s into the 1930s. The difference is that, while the character and even the personal composition of the ruling class would certainly have remained the same independent of whether or not Stalin was in power, he was personally invincible, exactly as it said in the songs that praised his exceptional qualities. While in post-Stalinist Stalinism the individual leader, whatever he might think of his power, was hostage to the immediate circle of decision-makers, as the experience of Novotny, Gomułka, Gierek, Khrushchev, and even Zhivkov has shown. This set of names can be contrasted with another that starts with Lenin and is followed by Stalin, Mao Zedong, Kim Il-Sung, Ceauşescu, and Hoxha who can be removed from power only by natural or unnatural death. The despotic and more collegiate variants of Communist rule show some similarity with the history of Oriental political organizations, but these parallels will not be developed here. However, it seems that the prevalence of this or another version may tell us something about the relative strength of the ruling class; the stronger it is, the more self-confident it becomes and the more ready to adjust leaders to itself and not vice versa.

The fateful Politburo meeting was held on Friday, 12 December 1970. On Saturday the party cells in all factories, offices, and institutions of the country met to listen to the words of the Politburo letter addressed to the ruling class at large—the party membership. On television and radio Gomułka informed society about the decisions of the Council of Ministers. The timing was symbolic—the public was informed at 8 p.m. when shops were closed and people were back from work—and so was the person—Gomułka was simply the First Secretary of the Central Committee of the Polish United Workers Party, and had nothing to do with the Council of Ministers as such. But the lesson of hierarchy and authority is clear.

What followed belongs to the sociology of terror, riots, and revolutions. In a few days a calm country came to the brink of civil war. Bucholc's research group later arranged for detailed, minute-by-minute recording of what took place in the Gdansk area. To these events, those taking place in another seaport, the Szczecin area, should be added. The group tried to answer two questions: first, why did the events take place at all?'. and second, 'Why did they occur in the Baltic Coast region?' The answer they gave to the latter question seem of more importance. According to them, ten factors could be listed:[3]

1.   conflict of interests between the population of the region and the central power, due to the latter's diminishing interest in the sea and coastal economy dating back to the late 1960s;

2.   the above-average increase in the number of workers, exceeding the infrastructure, making the workers feel uprooted and insecure;

3.   a 'better-than-average' level of education of those employed in the nationalized economy had increased the level of aspirations of the young workers, most of whom had completed vocational schools and often further education. Social aspirations and the level of consciousness was high.

The calendar of events on the Gdansk coast make it possible to understand the process through which action and counter-reaction develop. The events of Gdansk were replicated on a smaller scale in Szczecin, another Polish Baltic port to the West of the country. Szczecin is a smaller port, and its link with the open seaport of Swinoujscie is less close, a few hours' drive. In the case of the Gdansk-Sopot-Gdynia agglomeration, there is a rail-link and a highway on which people travel to and from work through the wide belt of cities and townships along the seashore. The events in the centre of this belt cut communication between

[3] Bucholc, 6.

the two ends. Szczecin though, apart from its smaller size, also has the traditional European city pattern, with port and shipyard on the banks of the Odra river and a city centre planned by Haussmann inland. This pattern is important for the developments that took place in the Gdansk area in December 1970, when at the crucial moment masses of workers arrived by train from both ends of the belt going to the industrial centre. When the army started shooting there was nowhere to go. Any movement of the masses out of there would be seen as a demonstration that would again be suppressed by the armed forces, a pattern well known to students of police anti-riot behaviour: on dispersal, the police force the people to form a crowd to be dispersed again, in a kind of spiralling process.

We shall focus on developments in Gdansk as they are both better described and of more political influence than those elsewhere. The starting moment was a meeting staged by the party itself. The PUWP openly held thousands of meetings across the country, to which anybody interested might come, and at which attendance was sometimes even obligatory. The key meeting was held in one of the crucial departments, K-3, in the Gdansk Shipyard. It was so crucial to the party—the great industrial working class was expected to support its vanguard organization—that a member of the PUWP Central Committee, Stanisław Kociołek, was a local member, following good Bolshevik tradition that top politicians remain still with their party constituency. Kociołek, an economist by education, a member of the politburo, and Deputy Prime Minister, announced the price increases in person. This was met with shouts of protest from the floor where about 3,000 people congregated. Kocioek replied sharply—as an economist he was convinced of the necessity for changing prices after years of freeze—but the tumult rose up again, and the night-shift did not begin work. At 20.00 hours Gomułka informed society through television about the price increases, but this could only arouse the strikers further. At night some of the dock workers joined them in the strike. This was simply a strike by absence, and nothing peculiar is recorded for Sunday, 13 December, except that the press was full of arguments supporting the price increases, shops were open, and the public for whom Christmas shopping had already started had to buy food at the new prices. The atmosphere was warming up in the face of contact with the new economic reality, and not surprisingly on Monday at 5.00 in the morning activists of various sorts were called upon to meet in the shipyard in order to discuss the situation. The direction was issued that the activists should try to reduce the tension of party members and non-members, as both categories alike were stirred up. When the day-shift appeared at 7.00 two departments, S-4 and W-3, had not started work. Instead, discussion developed among the workers and people from W-3 gathered outside the management office. At 9.00 the Gdansk PUWP committee was informed about the 'break in work' of the S-4 department by the shipyard PUWP committee; at 9.10 the Central Committee in Warsaw was informed. The next report was passed to Warsaw at 9.30. The structure of events was thus reversed: until Monday actions and information were passing downwards, as is the usual pattern in Communist social organization, from the First Secretary to the workers via the party hierarchy. Now society took its revenge: the workers approached their management, while information on their movements was passed up the levels of the party hierarchy. By 9.45 about 3,000 people had already gathered in front of the management office. The director, Stanisław Zaczek, appeared. The employees requested withdrawal of the price increases and regulation of the system of wages, especially the distribution of bonuses, a topic that will emerge more clearly during further discussion of the demands. Political demands were made from the beginning, as people shouted the names of the ruling élite members—Władysław Gomułka, Józef Cyrankiewicz, Mieczysław Moczar, and Stanisław Kociołek—urging their removal from power. The director of the shipyard answered that he felt impotent in the face of such demands, and in fact he was, even with respect to the wage system, as this is decided at ministry level, not to speak of the political demands and the food prices. This illustrates well the nature of strikes in the Communist system. The conflict between employees and management is spurious in the sense that all conflict is between the management as such, on a nation-wide if not on the Soviet-bloc level. The people are not naive. They knew from the beginning that the exchange with director Zaczek could serve only as a stage in communication with those in power. He could only bring information about something that had been done; for instance, that price increases had been revoked. The exchange legitimized the protest: the grievances had been presented to the legal authority, that is, the management in the work-place.

The People's Republic is a country where the working masses rule, and in their name the state authorities act as monitored by their vanguard, the party. This is the simplest constitutional formulation of the regime, and therefore people appear as the 'working masses' at the work-place making use of their work-force in the argument. Moreover, the exchange also sends the message of the community to the rulers. There is, let us remember, no other way of doing that. Individual letters will disappear without result. As parliamentary elections in which almost everybody participates are seen as a sham, there is no attempt to mobilize the parliamentarians. The only thing that is left, therefore, is to press the management to inform *their* management that the situation was found to be intolerable by the people.

The temperature was rising, and there was a demand for the appearance of the first secretary of the Gdansk regional party committee, Alojzy Karkoszka, who, however, was in Warsaw at the plenary meeting of the Central Committee of the PUWP. The lack of response provoked a thousand participants in the meeting to make a third decisive move, after stopping work and meeting with the work-place management: at 11.05 a demonstration left the famous Gate 2 of the shipyard and walked towards the regional PUWP Committee building. In the meantime, in Warsaw, secretary Karkoszka had been informed about the work stoppage in the S-4 and S-3 departments of the shipyard, and the decision was made to form a team that would include, apart from Karkoszka and Kociołek, Babiuch and two other party officials. Kociołek, in telephone conversation with Zaczek, learned the details of the situation in the shipyard. The party resumed the initiative; the team informed Gomulka at 11.00 about the idea of leaving the plenary meeting and going to Gdansk.

Some time after 11.00 the demonstration arrived at regional party headquarters. Passers-by surrounded the demonstrators in work-clothes and helmets. The majority were silent, the minority sang the Communist Internationale and militant partisan songs. In the absence of Karkoszka, organizational secretary Jundzill appeared, but his words were barely audible and he was whistled out. A delegation of workers entered the office for talks. The crowd outside had no information about what was going on inside, and the message was soon passed round that the delegation had been arrested. The police ambulance that had approached the crowd was taken over, and through its loudspeakers the demonstrators demanded the release of the delegation. The tension resulted from the fact that, in an atmosphere of total distrust, once the delegation had passed through the door of the office there was no further contact between the demonstrators and their representatives. The gathering declared that the next day would be a general strike, and announced that a demonstration would take place at 16.00 in front of the party headquarters.

While all this was happening in Gdansk, news was passed to the presidium of the plenary meeting, but not to the Central Committee as such. At 12.00 the emergency team that had appointed itself without any authorization or directions from the top leadership began its flight to Gdansk, and discussed a possible course of action on the way. Two of the team were to go from the Gdansk airport directly to the shipyard, while Kociołek, Karkoszka, and Stażewski went to the regional party office. During their flight the fifth step—the demonstration in front of the PUWP office being the fourth—was taken by the demonstrators who, due to their work-clothes and helmets, were able to identify each other and distinguish themselves from any suspicious bystanders who would have liked to infiltrate their ranks as they began to march back towards the shipyard. At the front of the march the police ambulance was being pushed by the people. The march arrived at the gates of the Northern Shipyard, whose employees were invited through the loudspeakers to stop work, to join the meeting scheduled for 16.00, and to strike on the following day. At 13.00 the two members of the Central Committee arrived at the Gdansk Shipyard to meet the directors, the secretaries of the shipyard's party committee, the chairman of the Workers Council (the employees self-management body established in 1956 and then slowly and methodically relegated, under Gomulka's control, to token importance), and the chairman of the trade-union shop and of the shipyard's organization of the Union of Socialist Youth. At 13.15 some demonstrators broke down the gate of the Northern Shipyard, but only a few from this work-place joined the march. This moment is dramaturgically important as the two streams of action, that of the employees and that of the party politicians, began to mingle in time and space:

the party arrived at the shipyard, while the workers visited their neighbours. At 14.10 the demonstrators broke down the gate of the Gdansk Polytechnic where they were met by the rector and the school's party secretary. A few hundred of the demonstrators appealed to the students to join the march but in vain. This symbolic moment has been taken up in several stories, books, and above all in *Man of Iron*, the film by Andrzej Wajda. The lack of response on the part of the student body can be explained by reference to the participation of workers in the anti-student and anti-Semitic meetings organized in March 1968 by the PUWP throughout the country, Gdansk included. In March 1968 students demonstrating in the University of Warsaw courtyard against the relegation of Adam Michnik, their colleague, were chanting: 'No bread without freedom!' But the working class had remained indifferent, though sympathetic to the victims of police violence. It took eight years, from 1968 to 1976, for the intelligentsia and the workers to make contact once the Committee for the Defence of Workers (KOR) had been created by Jan Józef Lipski and others in order to organize aid to victims of repressions against the food riots in Radom and Ursus. The forced entry into the Gdansk Polytechnic marked a new direction for the demonstrators, who now travelled through the city trying to raise popular support and to achieve some tangible goals. The Northern Shipyard gave almost no response and the Polytechnic answered with official speeches and student silence, so the crowd moved towards the student dormitories where it got no response either, while a group of about 300 demonstrators arrived at Gdansk Wrzeszcz radio station. The time was about 15.00. The crowd wandered through the city and its further aims are unknown. Meanwhile, the security forces in the Gdansk area had been put under the direct command of General Henryk Słabczyk, who arrived in town (the security forces had a special hierarchy of officers and generals). The demonstrators at the radio station threatened to destroy the broadcasting facilities if their appeal to the workers of the country was not transmitted, but the local manager persuaded them against it. This incident may serve as an argument in favour of the rationality of rioting crowd behaviour. Support is something the demonstrators fight for. They understand that the only chance of success lies in solidarity: therefore they appeal for solidarity with other shipyard employees, stu-

dents, and finally, if this does not succeed, for solidarity throughout the country.

Frustrated in these attempts the demonstration started to move
back to the centre of Gdansk, this time not focusing on getting
support from the designated collectivities, work-place staff, or
student bodies (who, it had been assumed a priori, would be
thinking and feeling the same way as the initiators of protest), but
on collecting any volunteers on the route of the march. This was
a marked change: from a self-identified and organized detachment of rebellious working people to a crowd as such. With this
change, which can be seen as a decision forced on them by the
failure of their previous strategy, it was events in the open public
space which turned the work-place action into a public disorder.
At 15.30 when this march started to move from the broadcasting
buildings, the city streets were filled with young people coming
home from school. This youthful element is enterprising, but free
of assumptions about adult life, tactics, and politics. Close to a
bridge, at 15.55, the first confrontation with the police took place
when several thousand people did not disperse in response to
police requests, and the blockade which had been prepared for a
much smaller demonstration was forced to give way to a crowd
which had increased dramatically in size on the way there during
the last hour. In this confrontation stones were thrown by the
crowd, which was confident of its strength and advancing in the
direction of party headquarters, not so much to hold the planned
assembly but rather to attack the centre of authority. The decision to use batons and means of defence was made at 16.00 by
the commandos of the forces of order. Support for the demonstration was slowly growing, however, as at 16.20 a group of
about 200 port workers left work and moved to the city. At 17.15
the House of the Press was attacked, with the slogan 'The Press is
dying!' for the first time since March 1968. Police dispersed the
crowd there with water cannons. The scattering crowd returned
to the party office, where it attacked again at 17.40 and dispersed
anew. Some of those dispersed started to loot the shops (the
state's property, one needs to remember at this point). Between
17.40 and 18.15 the successful dispersal prevented the demonstration from being held where it had been planned. In the surrounding area the dispersed groups mingled with newcomers and
bystanders, and perhaps—who can tell?—the newly formed

groups may have included some *agents provocateurs* and criminals serving as police agents, engaging on their own account, but on behalf of the police, in various activities: demonstrating, looting, and attacking windows in offices and public vehicles.

At 18.15 the attack on the PUWP building was renewed. As the official research group wrote in their *Calendar*:

> Twice a group of young men attempted to set the building on fire. They succeeded in burning the printing facilities. Detachments of police and army arrived to defend the building of the Regional Committee. The crowd moved to the square in front of the railway station breaking windows in the Monopolowa café on its way. Calls for dispersal made by the forces of order had no effect, and the use of tear-gas and thunder-flashes did not help either. The demonstrators attacked further on. At the crossing of Hevelius Street and Rajska Street there was a great fire. From the direction of the Gdansk Shipyard a fire engine arrived. A group of young people took it over and set the fire engine on fire. The petrol tank blew up, feeding the fire. Two buses parked close to the Monopol Hotel were set on fire. In front of the main Gdansk railway station the 'Ruch' kiosk was broken, close to the railwaymen's health-service centre, and then set on fire. On the opposite side of the street the kiosk of the co-operative Przodownik ('Stakhanovite') was burning, and the Cobra shop, a dress shop on Hevelius Street, and a delicatessen were broken up.[4]

It is significant that all those events that suggest the total breakdown of social order took place close to the railway station, and can be blamed upon the mobile element that made fires and then escaped. This is traditionally the gathering-place for people out to cause trouble, as quick access to trains acts as an incentive for irresponsibility. The fire was serious, but the objects were empty buses (one doesn't know what was written on the buses) and little wooden kiosks. We learn from the *Calendar* that at 21.00 on the same day the crowd was destroying the station, trying to erect barricades on the rails that would effectively cut off the centre from the rest of the agglomeration, and that this was prevented by the forces of the railway police and general police, who emptied the station area at around 22.00. The army was not used in this area of vandalism but 160 soldiers from the local unit of the Interior Ministry armed forces were introduced into the offices of the PUWP.

---

[4] Bucholc, 8.

The attacks on the party headquarters and the general turmoil in the area brought to Gdansk, at 22.25, some top political figures from Warsaw, who came with the knowledge of First Secretary Gomułka: Politburo members Zenon Kliszko, Gomułka's closest collaborator and secretary of the Central Committee, Ignacy Loga-Sowinski, chairman of the Central Council of the Trade Unions, and General Grzegorz Korczyński, Deputy Minister for National Defence. Throughout the area police and security forces had made arrests, and a telecommunication and transportation blockade of the area was prepared for next day. The official account of injuries and damage on the first day of rebellion claims 99 policemen wounded, 16 persons (no further information available) hospitalized, 7 cars, including 3 police cars burnt, 2 vans and 1 bus destroyed (we are not told what happened to the second of the two buses set on fire close to the station), 1 'battle vehicle' (probably an armoured car) damaged, and 16 shops demolished, of which 10 were looted.

The night also was not quiet in the Gdansk port area. In some sectors of the port there was no work, but the urgent unloading of coal and ore continued. Port workers assembled in the premises called for a strike at 7.00 in the morning. It seems that at 4.20 the strike in the port was in full swing, and dock workers were motivated in their work-stoppage by solidarity with the earlier strikers. At 6.00 the new shift in the Gdansk Shipyard, the Northern Shipyard, and the Gdansk Repair Shipyard had not begun work. In Gdynia some of the workers in the Commune of Paris Shipyard went on strike as well. Strikes started also in the metalworks, the furniture factory, and in the railway repair works. It looks as if the arrests that were made during the previous day and night had failed to quell the unrest.

Already at 6.45 around 15,000 people had gathered in front of the Gdansk Shipyard management office and whistled out the party secretary who tried to appease the employees. Demands for the freeing of those arrested the day before were shouted, and threats made that they would be liberated by force if necessary. Gatherings took place in other workplaces too, and groups of employees left the premises to join others. Visits were made to other work-places aimed at gathering support. After 7.00 the procession of about 3,000 employees, joined on their way by passersby, left the Gdansk Shipyard for the city. Processions were also leaving smaller work-places and heading for the regional PUWP headquarters. When the front of the Gdansk Shipyard procession arrived at the party building at about 7.15 in Gdynia, a procession was formed in the shipyard as well and set out on its way. While the Gdansk procession was passing the party building it encountered a surprise attack by police and city officers. In the meantime the party building was almost totally evacuated, with only seven political activists, two workers, and 'a group of soldiers' left inside.

Workers armed with iron poles, shields, paving-stones, and Molotov cocktails attacked police headquarters, aiming to liberate colleagues arrested on the previous day. The first shots were fired 'from the crowd', as the party research group claims, and three policemen were wounded. The police answered with teargas, and batons. Police headquarters were attacked through the windows, and a policeman was 'massacred by the crowd with the wooden staves'. Around 8.45 police removed the attackers from police headquarters before they could approach the jail. Another office, that of the regional trade union, was then ransacked and set on fire. Cars were driven hard against the walls of armed police, which led to the suicidal death of a youth. The regional party office was besieged by a crowd of between ten and twenty thousand people who prepared themselves for attack, while the incoming railways brought more and more fresh people who entered the battle.

At the same time Władysław Gomułka, the man who had returned to power in 1956 after the repudiation of the bloody pacification of riots in Poznań, opened a meeting of the inner political decision-making élite. As the meeting was more formal and at the same time more crucial than earlier ones, not the names but the functions of those convened by the First Secretary are important: the formal ruling nucleus included, apart from the Number One, the chairman of the Council of State (the collective constitutional head of state), the chairman of the Council of Ministers, three secretaries of the Central Committee of the party, the chief of the Administrative (that is, interior) Department of the Central Committee of the party, the Minister for National Defence (General Jaruzelski), the Minister of the Interior, and the Commander-in-Chief of the Civic Militia (police). The three policemen wounded by shots fired from the crowd and the murdered policeman were brought to the attention of those gathered, as well as the avalanche of difficulties spreading out of the strikes. 'In this situation Gomułka [were the others of a different opinion?] decided on the use of firearms by the forces of order and the army.' Firearms were to be used only in case of direct assault on soldiers and militiamen, of setting fire to or destroying premises, or of danger to human life. The rules for the use of firearms were defined by Władysław Gomułka as follows: after a spoken warning the first shots were to be made in the air, then after 5 to 10 seconds, in the case of a crowd approaching soldiers and militiamen—*concentrated fire (salvo)* to the legs. This decision was kept secret (as was the meeting itself, about which nothing was said at the time), and the decision was passed by Premier Cyrankiewicz over the phone to General Korczyński at 9.50 in the morning. At exactly this moment the crowd succeeded in setting the party headquarters in Gdansk on fire.

### Demands

Rebellion and revolution always find some means of expression, perhaps through speeches given in clubs, or through pamphlets, newspapers, and bulletins. Some write on walls, others prepare a list of demands. Polish social unrest after 1956 took the form of lists of demands. These were related to the work-place, as the environment in which the upheaval and social movement began. Social action is performed by colleagues at work in the midst of collaborators, both superior and subordinate. The power against which one rebels is also the power of the functionaries in the work-place, whom one does not simply reject. Labour rebellion thus develops in some way through the forms of the discipline of work. 'Present your demands, in written form and through your delegates!'—this is the first and most obvious reaction of anybody who directs a work-place, to separate the rebellion from the work that needs to be done. From this point of view the rebellious work-place is the one where the work goes on as usual while the demands are discussed by those entitled to do so. In Communist society the state is a large work-place, and thus the same categories apply when those employed withdraw their subservience to the state. Withdrawal does not equal rejection of discipline. In

time of need the employed themselves will organize the protection of the work-place and its property, production, and even
management. When in rebellion they will appear as disciplined,
not wishing to seem an anonymous crowd of rebels whom journalists, politicians, and the social scientists of the regime will call
'hooligans'; instead, wanting to appear as a recognized free
agents, their choice being limited to whether one is employed or
not, in the world of labour and the working masses.

The normative language of the authorities is that of propaganda and planning. Propagandist and planner use this language
through creating the appearance of description. Instead of
'Poland should be a country of social justice', both will say
'Poland is a country of social justice'. The rebellious worker
rejects appearances and instead says that 'Poland should be a
country of social justice', and puts such a demand on the list.

In this way a set of texts is created, mostly short resolutions,
demands, and declarations, as documents written in the of the
conflict are called, which often finish with remarkably explicit
statements such as: '. . . the presented demands we treat as an
ultimatum, and if they are fulfilled the staff will resume work.' A
group of thirty-eight documents from the days of direct confrontation in 1970, edited by Elżbieta Kaczyńska and Beata
Chmiel, are of great value, as they demonstrate the hierarchy of
the things for which people were ready to pay the price of blood.
All the documents come from Szczecin and were formulated during the events of December. For analysis they need to be divided
into more basic elements, a procedure which is always arbitrary
and therefore needs to be corroborated by the independent findings of other authors. Fortunately this is the case, as I can compare my results with analysis of the same set of documents made
by Beata Chmiel and Maria Woydt, and with the study of a partly
different set of documents from the same period by Roman
Laba.[5] In all the Szczecin documents under study I was able to
distinguish at least seventy elementary kinds of demands, such as
'better provisions' or 'removal of the Party-State leadership'. If
those demands that were made only once are removed from the
set, then thirty-nine thematic units remain that may be subject to
further analysis. By removing those that appeared only once we

[5] Roman Laba, 'Worker Roots of Solidarity', *Problems of Communism*
(July–Aug. 1986).

make it more certain that the demands formulated in the particular companies or units of the work-places represent the common
way of acting. The frequency of particular demands, the ranking
on the lists, and the content of the demands can then be studied
further.

When the mere frequency of the demands is considered, three
are clearly to the fore: (1) the demand to lower the prices of food
items, which in practice meant a demand to revoke the food-price
increases declared by the authorities in December 1970; (2) the
demand for pay rises, most often of 30 per cent, though twice by
as much as 50 per cent; and (3) the demand to establish the independence of trade unions from PUWP in particular and from the
authorities in general. This is the group of demands made most
frequently, that is, twenty-eight or twenty-nine times. The next
group in order of frequency are as follows: (4) to inform the public about the demands made by the strikers; (5) to guarantee the
personal safety of participants in strikes and demonstrations,
especially members of strike committees; (6) withdrawal of the
decree that allows opening fire on the civilian population in the
streets; (7) guaranteeing communicating by the mass media of
information on events in Poland; (8) punishing those responsible
for giving orders to shoot the civilian population; (9) removal of
the armed forces from the vicinity of work-places; (10) punishing
those responsible for the economic crisis (yes, this demand was
already being made); and (11) securing compensation and assistance for victims of repression and their families.

The question is whether this order reflects the different importance of the particular demands? One might think that demands
put on most lists are exactly those that are placed at the bottom
of those lists, and are therefore relatively less relevant. One can
ask if the order on the lists is of any importance at all? We have
been able to see ourselves that in such circumstances the order is
not accidental. It does not mean that the most important
demands will be put first, as tactical considerations might prevent
this, and for tactical reasons the most important demands might
not appear on the lists at all, or might be hidden amongst the
others. All this is true, but at the same time experience shows that
the authors of such lists try to create them in such a way that the
order reflects the way the demands one thought about it in private discussion, before they are made public. Ordering reflects

thus the objective hierarchy, even if this objectivity is given life by the common will of the collective authors of the list.

If a second list is made, therefore, that takes into account the average ranking of a demand, and takes into account even those demands that have been put forth only once, the order is different from the one shown in the first list. It is clear that the demands put in first place most often are not necessarily the demands that are put forward most often. Under these circumstances one comes to the conclusion that the best method would be to take into account both criteria, so that the place of the demand on the list reflects both the frequency and the average ranking. This, then, is the list that best reflects the hierarchy of issues. The first three demands are those that define the goal of the strikes— withdrawal of food-price increases, increased earnings (and thus an increase in the welfare of the people instead of its worsening), and the independence of the trade unions from PUWP and the authorities. Only later do we realize that the last demand, which was totally neglected by intellectual independent opinion-creating circles, was of an almost constitutional character. It was through the independence of trade unions that the breakthrough in the totalitarian structure of the Party State was attempted, with the subsequent democratization of public life, creation of a legal instrument for mass influence and participation in politics, and pressure on the apparatus of power secluded behind *nomenklatura*, promotion and arbitrary selection. The strikers' vision of influencing the shape of the work-place through the trade unions was related to this, as well as to control of wages and conditions of work.

Perhaps a fourth demand should be added to this group, namely that of punishing those responsible for the country's situation. This was an essential item and it should be emphasized that nobody from the other side of the barricade had then made the slightest remark about the crisis. On the contrary, progress and development were widely stressed and the food-price increases were to serve as only a minor correction, as Gomułka often said of excessive consumption that needed to be subsidized by the state. In fact, consumption was already exceeding the real economic possibilities, but contrary to Gomułka's view the fault lay not with the consumers but with himself and his economic managers and planners, and the stagnation that marked the

Gomułka period, after the initial boost due to a short-lived rise in individual entrepreneurship and Western aid. It is important to remember that after the change in power and the initial improvements of Gierek's regime, that the same situation began to emerge, but this time on much higher level of investments, debts (which Gomułka was not involved with), and social aspirations. Official social science, represented then by people such as professors Jerzy J. Wiatr, Włodzimierz Wesołowski, Stanisław Widerszpil, and Zbigniew Sufin, developed a theory of developed socialism, a stage which Poland was supposed to have already entered, similar to Soviet and Central European Communist societies. Official acknowledgement of the crisis, amounting to a failure in what was treated as the basis for the legitimation of the system since Khrushchev and the post-Stalin era, was the most difficult thing for the Communist ruling class to do, whereas the truth had already been seen by society from the beginning. Strikers were speaking about the economic crisis as early as 1970, whereas the Communist rulers did not agree to the diagnosis until as late as summer 1980. This means that, due to censorship, not a word about the crisis (and above all, not even the word 'crisis' as such) could be published anywhere in Poland, nor used on television or radio in this period. The responsibility of the leaders was less threatening—Communists were always quarrelling and intriguing about who would be held responsible for past problems, rather than confronting the reason for the problem for which the responsibility was to be established.

After these top four, the remaining demands from the first dozen deal with the consequences of protest against the crisis, that is, against the terror applied by the authorities. Here one can discern a large group of demands that focus on the resumption of the need for individual and public security. We find demands for the withdrawal of the army, above all from work-places and their vicinity, and then from the city streets; withdrawal of the police (MO) and security forces (SB) from work-places and their vicinity; withdrawal of the decree that allowed forces to open fire on the civilian population; and prohibition of the use of army uniforms by the police. The latter demand is understandable with reference to the fact that, until 13 December, society preferred to uphold the myth that the army as such was not used for internal terror and repression—a myth that was recognized by those directly involved in applying security measures, since, while the Poznań riots of 1956 had been pacified with the help of the army, the army as such was never attacked in contrast to police, security forces, and party officials. The demands go on to seek the punishment of those responsible for ordering the shooting, as well as of those who fired; an end to the use of the concept of 'hooligans' when referring to demonstrators and strikers; personal protection for those involved in freeing arrested demonstrators; assistance for the families of those killed and wounded; legalization of strikes and strike pay; the restraining of armed formation and the reconstitution of the feeling of security amongst the civilian population; the creating of a workers' militia that would protect workplaces against the forces of order; the removal of the telecommunications blockade; abolition of the curfew and state of emergency; the punishing of the commanders of the police; and the abolition of the security forces.

The next set of demands consists of those aimed at general changes in the political situation of the country. Here we find the demand for the abolition of the Central Council of Trade Unions (CRZZ), which served as the main tool for controlling trade-union activity from above; for compromised politicians to step down from office, and for reducing and making public the incomes of those in the apparatus of power; abolition of privileges such as cheap canteens and internal office shopping systems for the authorities; reduction of the number of staff in the administration of party and state; making promotion and earnings independent of membership in the PUWP; putting the administration under the control of the trade unions; providing employees with the right to strike, demonstrate, and hold general meetings; introduction of proportional ethnic representation clauses in the apparatus of power; providing the public with reliable information on events in the country; the abolition of censorship; consultation with the public over increases in food prices and other equally important decisions; ceasing to aid Vietnam and the Middle East countries; and for calling an extraordinary congress of the PUWP and changing the leadership of the party.

Finally, a separate set of demands focused on work relations and differentiation of living conditions. The majority relate to the situation in the work-place but some go beyond. Employees demanded equalization of the extra earnings paid in various departments of the same work-place; improvement of the housing situation through setting up targets for the next three to five years; a five-day working week; ethnic proportional representation clauses for selecting students for higher education (though ethnicities are unmentioned). (The previously mentioned demand for stopping material aid to Vietnam and Arab countries gives ground for suspecting that this latter demand was directed against foreign students from those countries visible in Polish academic institutions at a time when competitive entrance examinations were held for Poles, while the ethnic *numerus clausus* in the case of the power élite was most probably addressed against Communists of Jewish origin.) The list goes on to include demands for stopping the export of food; equalization of the status of those working with their hands, and those working with their heads (as the Polish jobs classification put it); extending paid maternity leave to one year; giving a right to three years unpaid nursing leave; increasing pay for night-shifts, work in conditions detrimental to health, and work on days declared non-working days by law; increase of the lowest pensions and lowering of the pension age to 55 for women and 60 for men; abolition of the criteria for establishing the duration-of-employment allowance; giving the so-called coal allowance in kind and not in money; equalization of increments; and improvement of work conditions and shortening the working day.

However detailed this might seem, some details still remain to be discussed in discussion in connection with demands made by the Gdansk Shipyard workers later on. One sees in these demands dissatisfaction with various aspects of work and life, and the resulting frustration is directed not only against the ruling class but also against ethnically defined surrogates. It is interesting to note that in this respect Szczecin differed from the Gdansk region, where xenophobia was never manifested either in 1970 or in 1980/1. Ten years after the events and demands we are describing now (in 1990) it was again in Szczecin that the Solidarity leader Marian Jurczyk made a public anti-Semitic attack on Rakowski's ruling group.

The demands of the Gdansk shipyard workers were collected in January 1971, when the heat of the events was over and the direct threat to life had passed. This may explain the variety of topics that are raised there, from order in the state, to demand

No. 47/60: 'The Workplace Council (of the trade union) should justly distribute free tickets for all entertainments.' Such detail is nevertheless of great value, as it allows us to reconstruct relations in the great socialist work-place by finding what the sources of dissatisfaction were. How *should* work relations look? Can the conflict be reduced to money? Certainly not, as the greater part of the demands may be expressed in summary form by demand No. 47/128: 'To treat the employees according to democratic principles.' But what are those principles? This can be reconstructed only through looking at the protests provoked by the most extreme cases of dissatisfaction.

First, there were inequalities which needed to be abolished. White-collar workers ('mental employees' in the Polish classification) according to the Decree of 1928 had a right to full salary to be paid by the employer for the first three months of illness, and were only afterwards put on the sickness allowance from social assurance amounting to part of the lost earnings. Workers were put on the sickness allowance immediately. The demand was made for equalization of the rights of both categories of labour. One would be disappointed, however, if one was looking here for 'class' hatred against white-collar workers, as in another demand, No. 47/53, we read: 'Equalize the earnings tax with workers—the white-collars earn much less, so why should they pay higher taxes?' Another anachronism of that kind was the difference in obituary allowances, which were lower for workers. The demand for equalization seems to be an indicator of the widespread feeling of the absurdity of the very division into workers and white-collars, a division blurred by the fact that 'workers' were paid in the work-place more on average than the 'white-collars', and were often assigned more important tasks.

Equalization of status for 'workers' and 'white-collars' was not the only objective of the rebellious work-force. Management should not offer privileges that were not directly justified in terms of actual duties performed, supervision, and responsibility. Differences in earnings were tolerated, but not differences that transgressed the direct relations of supervision and subordination in the work-place. This is indicated by demand No. 47/56:

Equalize for employees the class of train compartment on duty travel—until now in the same business and for the same journey, where an employee and a boss were sent, the employee travelled by the lower class while the boss was always sent first class by express train, which is improper and abusive.

One can understand that this is both abusing the employee financially and humiliating his sense of dignity.

We do not know what the other hidden privileges of management were, but the work-force demanded 'to inform all employees in the work-place about the premium earnings awarded to workers and the management (No. 47/29). It was thought less important to abolish premiums and bonuses, although one may find this demand in the set of those formulated in various departments of the shipyard which are not fully comparable, but above all the cry was 'to establish the just division of all premiums and awards and abolish the great disproportions in distribution between rank-and-file employees and the management' (No. 47/3). This was accompanied by the demand to flatten the differences from the bottom, best expressed in demand NO. 47/14: 'To compensate for the losses of the worst-paid white-collars', or in another one: 'To decrease the outrageous differences in premiums and awards between the worst- and the best-paid employees of the Gdansk Shipyard' (No. 47/792).

Another dimension of differentiation results from the existence in the work-place of a local oligarchy of party and trade-union activists which provided a focal point for the resentment of the staff. This led to the demands that 'employees doing public duty during work hours should not be privileged when premiums are distributed' (No. 47/13), and that employees delegated to trade-union activities should be paid out of union fees and not the work-place budget (No. 47/24). Furthermore, 'the Chairman of the Shop Council should not work in isolation separated from the remaining staff, as has happened until now, so that his eager and sole interest was given to the matter of distribution premiums and awards first to himself and then to those closest to him, his satellites' (No. 47/51). This demand describes how from the official trade-union posts the work-place clique worked out the distribution of awards, premiums, non-refundable loans at personal discretion (No. 47/52), and free tickets (No. 47/60).

Deprivation of the party activists' privileges was also demanded (No. 47/76: 'PUWP secretaries should work too', as they are on the work-place payroll). 'The bond between party members and non-party members among employees should be reinforced', and 'sincere trust in everyday life' was demanded (No. 47/69). This suggests that neither the bond nor the trust existed. One should remember that 'trade unions should be non-partisan' (No. 47/146), and the trade-union officialdom should be reduced in numbers (No. 47/302 and others). In order to break the cliques, a limit of two terms for the maximum length of office-holding was also advocated.

There were other irritating differences between staff within the work-place. Thus there was a demand for equalization of the situation of bachelors, childless people, and women. Technical staff should be treated equally with the group that is paid according to work done. Again, the demand that appears in the list of demands made in the various departments of the shipyard, and which led to the participation in the rebellion of the Industrial Guard as well as the administrative-social management, focuses on equality of chances of getting premiums.

In general, '(i) in order to secure the bond with the staff general meetings need to be organized in order to pass information directly and to receive the demands of the staff' (No. 47/388), while the PUWP should act publicly, and be open to the work-place staff (No. 47/420).

In the Gdansk Shipyard, among the demands that go beyond the workplace one may, as in the Szczecin case, distinguish three sets that deal respectively with personal and public security endangered by the repression by the authorities, material issues, and various aspects of political life in the country.

Within the first set one encounters the demand for the release of those arrested during the riots, except persons against whom a criminal offence was proven; for stopping repression, especially beating and using other illegitimate methods of investigation; for making certain that in future the use of arms against the civilian population could not be repeated; for punishing those responsible for the massacre; for making public the full list of victims; for releasing workers who, as a means of repression, had been drafted into the army; for releasing those imprisoned since 1968; for the abolition of tear gas and police batons; for limitations on the numbers of police and security forces; for taxation of those services and of the army and cutting down their budget. One meets also the demand for withdrawal of insults addressed by the government media against participants in the events on the sea-coast in December 1970. It is important to note that all this was demanded in January 1971, after the riots had ended, order had been restored, and the government changed. On the one hand, there was appeasement in the relations between society and the ruling class; on the other, the apparatus of control and repression continued its work as if nothing had changed. The list of victims was to be published several times in the local press but never in the national media. The arrested were not released. The methods of intimidating the population through punitive drafting into the army, indiscriminant police checking and arrests, beatings at police stations, and continuous surveillance by the security forces and its informers did not cease for a single day. The pact between the new PUWP secretary and Edward Gierek, sealed when, to his request 'Will you help me?' the chorus of labour answered in January 1971, 'We shall help!', was made within the context of the unbroken machinery of terrorizing society, a fact which is readily forgotten.

Within the demands that deal with the political life of the nation one finds clearly developed the issue of reform of the trade-union movement. Apart from general demands that trade unions should fulfil the role provided by national and international standards, the Gdansk Shipyard workers demanded independence of the trade unions from the PUWP so that the unions would be directed by non-party members, or at least that party members would not be over-represented amongst the general membership in trade unions. It had been pointed out that the president of the trade-union movement should not, as had always been the case, be a member of the Politburo of the PUWP, a position of intra-organizational loyalty and subservience. A two-term limit for office-holding was demanded, as well as a new election and a change of structure (lack of detail prevents us from knowing whether this new structure was to be of territorial character, like the one designed a decade later for Solidarity)—and publication of an independent trade-union journal. Those demands that dealt with the desire to establish personal responsibility for the crisis have been mentioned earlier and seem self-evident, but let me add here that in the Gdansk region the PUWP secretary Stanisław Kociołek (in Szczecin his twin was Antoni Walaszek) was often held responsible for the massacre of the shipyard's employees because of his message asking them to come to work where they were met by force of arms. To tell the truth, the shipyard employees demanded a change in the whole leadership of the PUWP throughout the country (No. 47/3150), although only one particular sanction—confiscation of accumulated personal property—against those responsible for the crisis was mentioned. The demand was also made to change the system of elections to state authorities (removing opportunities for the PUWP to influence parliamentary decisions), enforcement of the constitutional freedom of speech and of beliefs, and the introduction of the right to strike into the Constitution.

The freedom of belief mentioned above is related to religious freedom, and this issue was absent from the demands made in Szczecin. The demand was made a few times for a permit to be issued to build a church in Przymorze which the authorities had been postponing for years. A more general demand was also made for granting the right to build churches in the country as a whole. The demand was also made for full freedom of action for church authorities, exemption of the Church from taxation, and the reintroduction of some religious holidays previously abolished.

Further demands from this set include the request for reliable (this word is always used in this context to express what is thought about official information on what is happening in the country) and detailed information about the demands made by the shipyard workers. Construction of a memorial monument to fallen colleagues, protection and care of their graves, and the erection of commemorative plaques and obituaries were also demanded. As one sees, all this was impossible without explicit permission from the authorities. As to the monument, was finally approved by the authorities after the demand was repeated during the strikes of summer 1980, a decade later. Lesser demands were granted in 1971. The truth is, however, that the Communist authorities succeeded in 1971, as well as during the riots in December 1970, in keeping the whole matter localized. People living outside the Gdansk and Szczecin areas would never discover that anything had happened at all, if not for the one or two days of brief news-items on the riots and looting of shops, and information about the change of guards in the Politburo, and later the visit of Gierek to the coast. The full description of events, as the government allows it to be published, was for the local press only. The censorship ban was reintroduced soon afterwards in the local press as well, so that not a word could be printed of what had happened. Obituaries could be published, but the memorial could not be erected as it would threaten the control of information. Knowledge of the events was deemed to be private, not public, and the suppression was successful to such a degree that opposition-minded intelligentsia in Warsaw or in Cracow have had very little information about what really happened in Gdansk and in Szczecin. The living memory of the events surprised the intelligentsia when it came to the fore again the demands of summer 1980.

To end this group of demands, limitation of the size of the administrative apparatus was required as well as limitation of economic aid to the developing countries. Finally, there was a willingness 'to make all party and trade-union activists elected by the nation [*sic*] aware that they ought to serve the nation, and not rule and manage it' (No. 47/276).

In the social and material sphere, the demands already known from Szczecin for five-day and forty-five- or forty-hour working weeks appeared, as well as equalization of the situation of manual and white-collar workers, lowering retirement age by five years, abolition of bachelors tax and childlessness tax, cutting the earnings tax by half, removal of the food-price increase, and shortening the waiting period for housing. New demands were made for the right to a free choice of physician (since, in order to maintain work discipline, each person was linked to a particular physician either at his local health-service unit or at the work-place); for a quota of 50 per cent of entrants to higher-education institutions to be for young people of working-class origin (this time the 'workers' were mentioned explicitly); for the introduction of free competition in commerce; and, related to regional inequalities, a demand for free import and export of fruits and vegetables between the sea-coast and the rest of the country, as restrictions had led to higher prices on the coast. The lowering or at least freezing of housing costs in the housing co-operatives controlled by the state was also demanded.

This summary may now be considered in the light of the conclusions of other authors who have dealt with the same or similar sets of demands. Roman Laba[6] presented demands collected by

---

[6] See Table 5.1.

himself. His collection embraces fifty-nine lists of demands from December 1970, thirty-nine from the beginning of 1971, and 305 from summer 1980. Though this is a much more extensive set, it may be that by not taking into account those collected by the team directed by Elżbieta Kaczyńska, Laba did not encounter any trace of chauvinism, whereas in the demands I have analysed there were at least two clear cases of this. Laba certainly operated with different thematic units in his content-analysis of the material, as he discerned ninety-four demands in his paper. The ten demands analysed in detail, probably the most frequent, led Laba to conclude that first (and here we are in agreement), the demand for independent trade unions was no invention of the political opposition formed in the 1970s, and even less of the strikers in summer 1980; and secondly (and on this we are in disagreement), that Polish workers represented radical egalitarian beliefs in their concept of political justice. Laba is certainly right in saying that the demands of 1970/1 are as political and systemic as the demands from 1980, and that long before the emergence of the KOR (Committee for Defence of Workers) and the social activization of the Catholic Church, the programme formulated could easily be that of Solidarity: for free trade unions independent from the party, government, and management. Laba is also right when he stresses that the demands from 1970/1 went far beyond wages and conditions of life, and criticized the very essence of the Leninist state, and that the demands as formulated then were full of constructive and positive proposals, not destructive and negative. His historical comparison is best summarized in Table 5.1.

Analysis of the 1970/1 demands made by Beata Chmiel and Maria Woydt independently of Roman Laba led to a classification into six basic types: (1) political-social demands; (2) economic; (3) organization of work in the work-place; (4) conditions of work; (5) social services; and (6) living conditions. In such a classification the problems of personal and public security that I separate are put together with other demands of a political character. The authors ascertained from the Szczecin lists of 1970/1 that 47.5 per cent of demands dealt with the actual political situation, compared with 13.8 per cent of such demands made in Gdansk. When the Szczecin and Gdansk documents are compared further, respectively 24.7 per cent and 18.3 per cent of demands were classified as aimed at the system in general; 0.5

TABLE 5.1. *Labour demands on the Baltic Coast in 1970, 1971, and 1980*

| 1970 (n = 59) | | % | 1971 (n = 47) | | % | 1980 (n = 308) | | % |
|---|---|---|---|---|---|---|---|---|
| 1. | Wage increases | 68 | 1. | Reform of wages system | 59 | 1. | Wage increases | 65 |
| 2. | Free trade unions | 61 | 2. | Free trade unions | 59 | 2. | Equalizing family allowances with those in the power apparatus | 63 |
| 3. | Safety of strikers | 58 | 3. | Wage increases | 56 | 3. | Free Saturdays | 53 |
| 4. | Release of arrested | 44 | 4. | Earlier pensions | 54 | 4. | Free trade unions | 52 |
| 5. | Pay for strike time | 44 | 5. | Punishment of those responsible for shooting civilians | 51 | 5. | Reform of wages system | 51 |
| 6. | Punishment of those responsible for shooting civilians | 39 | 6. | New trade-union elections | 46 | 6. | Better housing | |
| 7. | Full public information about the strikes | 32 | 7. | Release of arrested strikers | 44 | 7. | Support for the Inter-Factory Strike Committee | 42 |
| 8. | Publication of strikers' demands | 31 | 8. | Protective work dress | 36 | 8. | Improvement of working conditions | |
| 9. | Punishment of those responsible for economic crisis | 31 | 9. | Abolition of privileges of the power apparatus | 36 | 9. | Abolition of privileges of the power apparatus | 39 |
| 10. | Abolition of privileges of the power apparatus | 24 | 10. | Reform of work organization | | 10. | Earlier pensions | 37 |

*Source:* Roman Laba, 'Worker Roots of Solidarity', *Problems of Communism* (July–Aug. 1986), 53.

per cent and 3.2 per cent were related to taxation; 0.2 per cent and 10.0 per cent related to the organization of work; 15.5 per cent and 41.5 per cent to working conditions; 2.9 per cent and 9.6 per cent to social services; and 8.7 per cent and 3.65 per cent to living conditions.

In connection with this comparison one needs to bear in mind the fact that the Szczecin documents were made during the events while the Gdansk list is later, and this fact alone suffices, in my opinion, to explain why in the later document one finds more reference to work, and relatively less reference to problems of the system in general. The fact that under less stress the organization of work was also raised supports the general impression of a constructive approach to problems. The employees wanted to work in a meaningful way, and meaning is given above all in the work-place as well as in the way the whole national economy is run; that is, the demands are following, and not opposing, the basic economic rationality that one acquires by managing one's own household economy.

Beata Chmiel and Maria Woydt, when comparing these data with documents from 1980, stress the presence of certain unresolved problems (excluding a few settled after 1970), such as equalization of sickness-leaves, allowances, and the abolition of earnings taxation (the taxation was removed in what amounted to simply a change in the state economy's central bookkeeping system). They stress also that the demand for independent trade unions was made by strike committees in Szczecin in 1970 more often than in the departmental demands of Szczecin Shipyard in August 1980. The greatest difference they see, in fact, is that in 1980 personal issues were not raised at all, due to the realization that changes to the system and not personal ones were necessary in order to improve the situation.

The first conclusion to be drawn from these three independent surveys of documents accumulated in 1970 and 1971 is that one should approach all figures in this area with caution, no less than in other areas of study; not because the calculations could be unreliable, but because individual differences in classification might lead to great differences of interpretation, the addition of new documents can greatly change the results, and the same source may give rise to different ways of grouping the data. The analysis of demands from 1970/1 illustrates this point well, and freedom of choice as to classification of the demands would be desirable for the reader.

Whatever the results of this methodological choice, some issues become clear in the light of the above comparisons. The sharpness with which the demand for free trade unions was made by strikers in 1970 is very marked, particularly if one remembers the disbelief with which the opposition intelligentsia in Warsaw received the information about the stubbornness of the strikers concerning this demand in summer 1980. The demand expresses a certain stable tendency or component in the hidden normative structure of the political culture of Polish society: trade-union freedom as part of this specific constitution. In the strike-demands under analysis other cardinal freedoms are also present, such as freedom of association, of assembly, of speech, of belief, individual freedom and personal integrity, national sovereignty, elective authority and responsibility before the electorate, power as service to people, and justice in social differentiation if merited by different input of work and burden of responsibility. In a situation where censorship and administrative coercion made the everyday expression of aspirations, feelings, and convictions impossible, documents such as these become the only possible vehicles of expression.

It is not useful to discuss the role of such documents as sources of information. It is more important to discuss the layers of normativity to which they refer. I have already pointed out several times that normative expression made under direct threat to life is of the highest reliability. It does not mean, however, that the normative structure is fully manifested, since, first, it remains unknown to those who sustain it, and secondly, even the text created in such way is limited by convention. Creators of demands do not create the language anew. They use the language they have encountered. Moreover, it is neither the language of their everyday exchange with friends nor the language of everyday exchange in the midst of the élites that rule a work-place or the country. In order to set forth demands publicly one needs to use public language. The difference is that, while the representative of power like to use what is good as a description of the reality under their control, those in rebellion take what is good as the normative ideal that allows them to reject the surrounding reality. Albeit this use of public language is made half-consciously, it nevertheless is not under the control of the user. This is why the category of rebellion applies here better than that of fully fledged revolution. New language is not yet created. But one may ask whether the raising of abnormal items in normal language accepted for dialogue between those in official relations is not, *par excellence*, of a revolutionary character? To speak concretely in the language of demands (which serves as the inversion of the language of plans and commands) about the need for controlling disorderly security forces, about the right to build a church, about the need for responsibility in party officials . . . Perhaps this grey language in which the hidden normative constitution of society is expressed is much more revolutionary than it seems to be at first glance. Demands are the normative expression of this hidden constitution, but by no means the sole or full expression. Independent of what was said in the demands, what was done is important. Independent of what was done, what was a possible threat and what was felt to be possible was important. This is why a knowledge of demands should be taken as a very important, but still partial, source of knowledge about the normative structure. The lawgiver who thought it a simple task to translate the core of demands into a constitution, and in this way to satisfy the political aspirations of the nation, would be doomed to failure. Basic rights and obligations are much more fundamental and wider than can be read from the expression of demands.

# 6

# *Daily Conflicts*

'We still suffer but we suffer in a different way'
(a Carpathian small-town resident, re-interviewed in 1981)

A well-established tradition of social science tells us to look for a key to understand the character of social life, if not to grasp the essence of it, in conflicts between people. Modern social sciences, on the other hand, point to the theoretical tension between the sphere of direct human experience that is conventionally described as the microsociological and the sphere of social events at the upper level of modern society in the form of political, economic, or cultural institutions within which the life of millions takes place. One often hears that focusing reflective and investigative attention on the first set of events prevents realization of the way they are determined by the events that take place on the larger scale, while on the other hand complaints are made that a perspective on society from above makes it impossible to observe successes and failures actually experienced by human beings in their common everyday existence.

All this is a well-researched area, and if we start this chapter with such a reminder of one of the fundamental sociological dilemmas the sole purpose is to make our own interests more clear. The question is simple, even though the answer is not so simple; that is whether, in conflicts with others, Poles in the 1970s were involved in conduct which might be interpreted in terms of some wider structure that framed everyday life in those years. Here, we shall not focus on those collective conflicts that manifested themselves in summer 1980, but on the most mundane and trivial—a conflict with a neighbour. The question is thus: are there any patterns in those conflicts, and do those patterns fit the schemes that one develops for society as a whole when taking a more detached point of view, and looking at events that, due to their political impact, attained historical importance?

When an electrician passed through the closed gate of the Lenin Shipyard in Gdansk, the act could have been as trivial as any other person entering under any other circumstances. When for the first time in my life I approached a socialist factory for military aircraft in the 1970s south of Lublin, the worker I met simply guided me through a hole in the fence, so that it took a while before I convinced him that I needed to register at the entrance in order to get a permit to visit the director whom I was going to interview. Thousands had been crossing the fences and gates daily, but only once did it make a historical difference. In some sense the macrosociological is what has not made a direct impact on others' lives, while the same act microscopically may gain in significance. So, the dilemma is that of equality and inequality of significance. My problems are unimportant for almost everybody on earth, somebody else's problems are of much greater importance because he or she is in the position of making consequences of a larger scale. Drop a light stone in the water and the waves might be almost invisible; a heavy one will make more noise and disturbance. Equality lies in the fact that both are acts, though the assessment of the consequences might differ.

In the second half of the 1970s we were involved in a series of studies on dispute-resolution involving the private interests of an individual. We collected information on the frequency and degree of strength of various types of disputes in contrasting social environments, the metropolitan as represented by Warsaw, and the small town as represented by two former county seats[1] of under ten thousand inhabitants, one in the Carpathian Mountains and the second in Upper Silesia. Though the reader might be more interested in the interviews from the metropolitan capital area, quite deliberately what follows will focus mostly on the small towns. Warsaw, as we all learned suddenly in 1980, does not reflect the social life of the country. There were practically no strikes there, except the city bus transportation strike in 1980 and a symbolic strike in the local steel plant. The government is there,

---

[1] Edward Gierek, perhaps under the influence of his personal experience with France, in 1975 had authorized administrative reform of the country that diminished the power and importance of the traditional seventeen provinces (voivodships) through multiplying their number to forty-nine, and abolishing traditional lower-level *powiat* counties or districts.

and government workers are over represented in the social structure; police and military are over-present in the social space; the capital is privileged in material and other ways, and its inhabitants, who until the 1980s (typically for all Communist countries) could live here only if they had an individual residence permit, were not willing to surrender their better life-chances. Last but not least, what is more microsociological than the small town where everybody thinks she or he knows everybody and where, thus, institutional relations are at the same time personal relations, even between strangers? It is here, therefore, that our attempt to cross the bridge between two apparently different levels of sociological interpretation should be made.

In all three locations interviews were conducted with several hundred people randomly selected from the lists of residents. The material gathered was then subjected to quantitative analysis aimed at establishing differences between the environments and social subcategories as to the frequency with which participation in various types of disputes as well as the procedures and outcomes was reported. Of special interest, then, was how often and under what circumstances—according to those interviewed—the official, especially judicial, way of dispute settlement was used. It was also clear from the very beginning that quantitative analysis can only be very approximate in view of the complex socio-psychological nature of conflicts in general as well as the way in which they are defined and interpreted by participants.[2] The codification and quantification left most of the detailed descriptions unused, a waste that I intend to repair in this chapter by combining previously established conclusions with new interpretation of the old material. The reader is advised that this chapter is indirectly linked to Chapter 3 on 'Organized Injustice'. There I attempted to show how, with the passage of time, Draconian Stalinism took on a more benevolent appearance and became domesticated under the guise of 'socialist legalism'. The all-persuasive principle of institutionalized dualism that culminated in the Party State political organization of society was an adaptive mechanism used by the party to gain passive acceptance at the lowest cost. In terms of the Barrington Moore Jr. equation, this

[2] Jacek Kurczewski, 'A Sequential Model of Disputes', *The Polish Sociological Bulletin* (1979) 83–96, and *Spór i sądy* (Dispute and the Courts), *IPSIRUW* (Warsaw, 1982).

was the net attempted optimum of relations with the ruled. In a sense, the present chapter deals with the same set of institutions and mechanisms but from the perspective of those ruled. Most post-war history describes stability at the surface level. This stability is due to the fact that the ruled have also devised their own ways of adjusting the existing institutional structure to their needs. How this was effected is again best seen in the golden age of Polish Communism, that is, in the mid-1970s.

From the institutional point of view the paramount instrument of conflict-settlement and the public forum in which a dispute should ultimately appear is the state court. If one looks into the statistical data on the number of cases coded as conflictual which brought citizens before the courts of first instance, the striking fact is that from the mid-1950s until the mid-1970s, a period for which comparable statistics are available, the ratio of conflicts measured per capita was roughly the same. It should be remembered that some of the conflicts could have been taken into court as private criminal accusations, and that systemic changes have resulted in taking the whole area of state administration out from judicial dispute resolution. Most of the economic transactions between companies and so on also lost their private character.

The making public of interpersonal conflicts in the form of a civil suit or private accusation is very rare in comparison with the frequency of such conflicts, even when assessed according to capricious declarations on the last occurrence of such a conflict made during an interview. Even with our best efforts one cannot establish the 'dark figure' because, in fact, there is no such thing as the opportunities that have not been exploited by those interviewed or remembered by them. One needs to read the court statistics with this in mind.

In one of the small towns under study, where a district court is located, in the years 1973–7, 1245 civil and private accusation cases were filed in which both parties were local residents. This means that in a town of roughly seven thousand inhabitants about twenty-five conflicts find their way annually to the public judicial forum. One should remember that in this and the following analysis the marital conflicts that find their manifestation in divorce proceedings are outside our consideration, because these were within the jurisdiction of the court of the upper, regional level. The largest group—49 per cent—of conflicts that went before the local court were between actual or former spouses. Divorce does not end mutual conflicts; in fact some disputes arise out of matters unresolved in a divorce settlement. Alternatively, spouses may dispute some property arrangements without appealing to the ultimate sanction of divorce; in a Catholic country like Poland divorce will not be sought by some who are otherwise in a quite intolerable position, being maltreated by a spouse, battered, or not maintained. All this gives rise to conflicts in this category. If the unknown number of divorce proceeding were to be included it must be said that the marital bond seems to link most opponents in a dispute before the court. This fact will be discussed later, but let us note in passing that the family seems to be not only the most valued social unit (in which Polish society does not differ from others), but also under Communism the only private unit of an economic character that is recognized by the authorities as not only legal but also ideologically legitimate. Not surprisingly, the majority of the legitimate and illegitimate economic actions undertaken by individuals who are acting on behalf of their family group and who are supported by the group are concentrated here.

The second most frequent type of conflict was that of a private-property and financial character, where neither actual nor present spouses were involved (31). Defence of one's dignity and personal integrity against strangers through a civil or private accusation procedure emerged in 11 per cent of cases, and bodily integrity in 7 per cent. Any more detailed classification would make the analysis too fragmented in terms of the legal as well as sociological characteristics. This is the most general classification that makes sense. Together, all four categories take in 98 per cent of the disputes between residents in the small town under study in the period, and we may take it to be fairly representative for the country as the whole.

The statistical distribution of the various types of dispute has been reported for representative samples in both small towns and in Warsaw. One should bear in mind also, however, that the categories used in the interviews do not correspond to the classification used in court. Why is this? Above all, it is because the working of the court and the lawyers is in itself a collective process of classification of disputes under legal categories, and also because technical legal discourse would not be easily comprehensible in conversation with lay citizens when speaking about their everyday experience. The interview schedule pre-cluded family conflicts and included various conflicts with public commercial and service establishments, the public employer and public administration that had been excluded from the statistics of private disputes because of the complex issue of the inaccessi-bility of common judicial procedure in some of these cases. Expe-rience of disputes of the various types occurring at least once during three years preceding the interview is reported in Table 6.1.

TABLE 6.1. *Incidence of disputes of a given type amongst the citizens in three communi-ties studied in 1977/8* (in % of the respective samples)

|  | Small town in Silesia (n = 229) | Small town in Carpathians (n = 211) | Warsaw (n = 334) |
|---|---|---|---|
| Personal reputation | 16 | 15 | 14 |
| Physical integrity | 7 | 9 | 5 |
| Neighbourly relations | 13 | 10 | 14 |
| Property borderlines | 8 | 7 | 4 |
| Tenancy rights | 6 | 4 | 2 |
| Debt | 10 | 14 | 11 |
| Quality of goods | 10 | 10 | 12 |
| Conflict with administration | 10 | 9 | 12 |
| Labour relations | 16 | 11 | 14 |

One should remember that all judgements about frequency reported during the interviews should be set against the back-ground of the arbitrary typology of disputes. The figure does not give the incidence of disputes reported, because one person might have reported three disputes with the administration and another only one of that type, but both would be coded in the same cate-gory of those who reported experience of at least one dispute of a given type. The whole enterprise taught me a lot about the vol-ume of assumptions that are necessary in order to achieve a set of data of this kind. This belongs to sociological methodology rather than to the subject of this book, so let it suffice to say here that I now subscribe to the view that the research product as above should be accepted if it allows an insight into similarities and dif-ferences between particular subsets of data within the set pro-duced under the same conditions and assumptions.

Material goods are, then, the main cause of conflicts experienced as disputes, followed by threats to personal reputation and bodily integrity. If we look at the potential numbers it is evident that particular conflicts appear extremely rarely before the court. Taking into account the random character of the sample (tables of random numbers were used to select the respondents from the residence registers), one may estimate that between one-third and a half of the citizens took part at least once during the three years before the study in a dispute that could have been brought before the court. The last qualification is important as, in fact, the paradigmatic disputes as sketched in the interview schedule were means to develop in the respondent the image of a dispute that could well have been brought to court with the help of a skilled lawyer. The rank-order fits that of the court statistics, if the disputes between spouses or ex-spouses are kept, evidently quite arbitrarily, out of the picture.

How artificial this exclusion is in fact becomes clear from the following extract from an interview carried out in one of the small towns under investigation in 1977. A 41-year-old artisan complained:

So I have been fighting with my wife and mother-in-law. They have beaten me, I have fought back. She married me because she thought I was rich, she is very greedy. After five years of marriage we built a house. That was still not enough for her, all the time she wanted more and more money. She was shouting at me, sir, she was beating me. We called the police, they used to come two or three times a day, later they were unwilling to come. I like her but I am afraid, she used to beat me and afterwards pretended it was me who beat her up.

Divorce had not been granted by the court and the respondent had lived outside the home for a year and half. 'I would like at least to recover my workshop', he said. 'Everything was left there.' This case, which is outweighed by much more frequent cases of women complaining about being battered by their male partners, could of course be classified under several headings. This is an explicitly recorded marital dispute that could have ended in divorce, involving physical abuse accompanied by noisy accusations that threatened not only the personal dignity of the parties but also the peace of the neighbourhood. Finally, tangible property rights were involved in the dispute. On the other hand,

one sees that however complex the case and overripe for adjudication, the court had been approached over only one aspect of the
conflict, and the urgent feelings continued to leave room for a
wide variety of future developments. Sociologically the case is
instructive too, as it points to the private material preoccupations
that remain outside official economic life. Private artisanry, not
falling within the official criteria of capitalism, that is, private
employment of more than a few workers or pupils, was tolerated
under Communist rule, though this tolerance was very limited as
the administration was able to put a firm out of business at any
moment with the help of arbitrary taxation, legally at its sole discretion. The number of private, small, though sometimes lucra-
tive, businesses was deliberately kept low with the help of licences
and taxes. An artisan of this kind would also normally be at the
mercy of the local police and administration, not only when trying to win the struggle with his wife but in any other circumstances too, as he would inevitably be dependent upon illegal (or
at least illegitimate) means of securing the resources, (spare parts
and so on) needed in the business.

It is commonly assumed of small towns that everybody knows
everybody else. One would expect, therefore, that the various
ways of official conflict-resolution would be contingent upon the
knowledge of some specific persons that might secure the chances
of satisfying one's own interests. To ask whether one knows somebody who is influential would be rather meaningless in this context, as under conditions of lowered anonymity it is either too
general or too private a question. On the other hand, there is
always in sociology the vague idea of community leaders who, as
heroes of the community, assist others for altruistic reasons. The
truth is usually less edifying, as books testify that they are concerned with local-level politics, bribery, patronage, and influences
through which careers and power are built. One would need, however, a study of a different kind to approach this issue directly,
rather than a study of the political careers of individuals. The sad
truth is that, according to my knowledge, no study was ever made
of Communist political careers along ethno- and biographical
lines. In both small towns under study, however, I put the question whether people knew individuals who served others by helping to arrange various matters and settling problems. The results
tell us something about social life in a Communist country.

In one of the small towns twenty-six names, and in the second five names, were given. The list included a retired judge, the president of the town, the secretary of the PUWP, ex-secretaries of the PUWP and ex-officials, policemen, activists of the Women's League, teachers, and finally an accountant who 'helps various victims of injustice', as one of the interviewed put it. The fact is that the list, in which I was quite naïvely expecting to find politically independent moral authorities, includes those of influence because of their position in the system of power, or those who know how and with whom things can be arranged. The list might say nothing to a reader who does not know the Communist political system at the local level. In the case of Poland in the late 1970s, it should be recalled that the organization had just changed. Previously, there had been the district-level national council 'elected' from the single, no-choice list distributed among the voters. The council, in theory, controlled the administrative body presided over by the chairperson of the council. The small town under study was one of several hundred of the sort that were seats of such bodies. Gierek's reform abolished the districts and strengthened the executive element by making a difference between the president of the town (*naczelnik*) and the chair of the local council. The strengthening was a theoretical operation, as in fact under the previous system the council had had little say about matters, even if some concern over local issues might be raised by members of the council carefully selected by the Communist party politicians. This resulted from the fact that the council's administration was legally subordinate to the upper level of the national administration, and therefore there was in fact no local self-government, even if there was a locally 'elected' representation. In the new system, the town president was also directly subordinate to his regional authorities, in turn dependent upon the central government, while the chair of the council was what the name says. This local government was again embraced by the political power of the local Communist officials, the secretary of the Municipal Party Committee being under the orders of the regional secretary and monitoring the life of the small town and its public government. The former district's capital would still have the district court and that would mean a parallel district procurator who would control the general territorial structure independently of the party, but as a party member remaining under the authority of his regional procuracy also composed solely of Communists. In this way the local political authority was not allowed to have a feeling of unchallenged total power. The procurator's power, on the other hand, is indirect in that he or she might open an investigation but rarely give direct orders. Moreover, procuracy power is legalistic and specific: if a procurator decides that a factory is to be closed it is because of imminent danger as defined by law; while the secretary's power is political and general: the factory may be closed on his or her order, but public, that is, legal reasons need to be found and this decision might always be overturned at a higher level of the internal party political structure.

It is interesting that the procurator is not mentioned in either small town. It is even more interesting if we are reminded that one of the official functions of the procuracy was to safeguard the rights of the citizens against their fellow-citizens as well as against the administration. The explanation is simple. One does not arrange things with a procurator. All matters may, however, find their ultimate solution in being presented before the procurator. It is not so much in the public open forum of the court, as we have already pointed out in Chapter 3 on 'Organized Injustice', but behind the closed doors of the procuracy that the private issue becomes subject to the public interest. This simply precludes the procurator from our lists.

We interviewed all thirty-one persons found on those lists and from the interviews it became clear that, apart from persons of actual decision-making power, it included only those who were related to the decision-making process through membership or office held in political or administrative authorities. Council members are not listed, except those who belong to the very small circle of the presiding board or have some functions that put them in a personal decision-making capacity in relation to such areas as control of local schools, employment agencies, and so on. This explains the presence of the Women's League activists on the list. Traditionally, some areas, such as provision of extra goods for households or careers for girls, were felt to be within the female area of influence. In their meticulous attempt to leave no area of life uncontrolled, the Communists abolished all independent women's organizations and set up the monolithic, quasi-feminist structure called the Women's League, the paid officials of which represented women in all appropriate bodies, except in the 'internal' government of the party as such. In normal cases a Women's League official was expected to serve as a representative of the personal interests of a woman if requested to do so, especially in conflict with her spouse or in the traditionally female area of household economy and child-care.

From all this one should not deduce that the map of influence reflects the bureaucratic division of competence of the functions performed officially by those listed. They will be approached in their area of competence directly, or they will be asked privately to assist in a matter outside their area. Party officials such as the secretary do not have any specific area of competence at all; they can deal with everything. This is the basic principle. It is interesting, though, that it becomes clear from the list that in a local community it was quite easy in the 1970s to get access to those who play a crucial role in local decision-making. This easy access (and this is most important in order to understand the inefficiency of the system as such) does not mean that an issue may be equally easily settled. In a larger community, though, even the accessibility would be limited while living conditions remained generally bad and, since 1976, were visibly deteriorating.

The political aspect of everyday life will inevitably reappear if one looks into another set of data collected in one of the small towns under study. This was a study aiming deliberately at an assessment of the awareness of rights among the public. Fifteen hypothetical conflict situations were presented in another part of the interview, and the subjects were then asked how they evaluated the legitimacy and justice of the claims made by the wronged in the story as well as the best method of executing the claim advocated. The situations were (as one may see in Appendix 1 at the end of this chapter) related to various types of social relationship. Marital relations this time were included on a par with relations between neighbours, friends, commercial establishments, and public administrative agencies. In each of the fifteen situations the responses were coded into four basic types—withdrawal from pursuing the claim; conciliatory settlement in private; fierce action in order to fulfil the claim with no referral to the public agencies; and finally, making use of all possible official agencies such as PUWP, municipal authorities, formalized conciliatory commissions, trade unions, police, or finally the court.

The main findings accord with what might be expected. In general, with the decrease in perceived legitimacy of claims the frequency of those advising withdrawal from pursuing the claim increases. Advocacy of compromise, on the contrary, increases with legitimacy of claims. Compromise is not advocated as a way to achieve those interests that are perceived as illegitimate, but is felt instead to be the best method to achieve what is fairly and legitimately claimed. One would need comparative data from a democratic country in order to check whether this should be interpreted in termed of the political context. Those who are of the opinion that one should enjoy his or her rights to the full, will understandably suspect that in the Communist political context one would prefer to negotiate his or her due with others in order to avoid being put under scrutiny by an irresponsible government. This is an interpretation to which we shall return later on, but first let us look more closely into the patterns of answers given. The institutional way was advocated most often in relation to institutionalized actors, which is hardly surprising if one does not consider that it might quite well be the opposite, that is, that a compromise and negotiations through personal contacts might be sought in order to achieve at least partial fulfilment of one's rightful expectations. This apparently trivial finding may gain in substance, thus, as opposed to the previous one. Compromise is advocated when one has a right, but no contact with institutions. Personal private conflicts are to be kept out of the official, public, and political world. Patterns of conducting the conflict are thus determined by at least two factors: the legitimacy of the claims put forward and the private or public relationship with the opponent.[3]

As to the particular situations that were presented during the interview, there are twelve items to which at least three-quarters of the sample pointed as legitimate grounds for claims made by those who, in the interview schedule, defined themselves as the wronged parties. It might also be of interest why the remaining three have not been defined equally often as legitimate. Less than

---

[3] This is reflected in the particular positions because Spearman's *rho* coefficients of rank-order correlation between the legitimacy of claims and each of the patterns of conflict reactions are equal to $-.55$ in cases of withdrawal, $.71$ in case of compromise and direct negotiations, and $-.16$ in case of the institutionalized reaction.

half of the sample (46 per cent) thought a patient had a right to protest against waiving the confidentiality of medical information by a hospital when requested by the place of employment. Those who rejected the claim to privacy and confidentiality most often explained that, according to their knowledge, some types of illness are exempt from the rules of medical confidentiality. Only 26 per cent supported someone whose house and building plot were expropriated by mandate for a public purpose. In view of the debate that developed in Poland after Communism and the mood of re-privatization prevalent among Solidarity-related legislators, it is worth noting that, apart from the evidently arbitrary procedure and equally arbitrarily lowered compensation, the principle was accepted by the majority of those questioned. The next situation is similar, that of when, in face of a shortage of a given good in a shop, the staff decide to sell only a limited and equal volume of that good to each of the buyers. We will come to this soon, but let us first mention the fifth situation of a spouse who has retained for her own use the inheritance from her parents. Less than one-third of the sample support the claims of the husband. The rest stress the fact that the possibility of legal dissolution of the marital union through divorce favours the right of a spouse to hold separate property within the marriage. This interesting detail sheds some light on the normative beliefs of Poles who, independently of the stress put on family solidarity, extend individualism into this sphere, as well as showing that family solidarity is based upon the equality of gender and individual rights.

Coming back to the restricted sale of goods in shops, it is necessary to point out that the oft-repeated descriptions of Poland in the mid-1970s as a society before crisis have no foundation in reality. On the contrary, economic crisis as experienced through the shortages in supplies and price-increases led at least three times, in 1970, 1976, and 1980, to public unrest. Even if Communism in the 1970s emerges more and more clearly in the course of this book as the most domesticated form of the system, the truth is that this was effected (probably only as the result of huge foreign loans) under conditions of permanent structural crisis. The political and non-political behaviour and attitudes of this society cannot be isolated from the chronic crisis in which various ways of adjustment developed, such as the mercantilization of public relations accompanied by dishonesty, combined with the networks of personal loyalties and support extending far beyond the family bonds.[4] The hypothetical antagonism between somebody willing to buy in a shop as many goods as he needs and the other consumers was not hypothetical, as it reflected the everyday experience of each Pole. This is why 'situational rationing' developed, in which the sales staff served as the agents of supply and demand, deciding how many loaves of bread or how many ounces of ham each consumer was to be allowed to buy. Those were the problems that the common people were forced to decide, without the help of any theory of justice, as an everyday matter.

The majority (64 per cent) of those asked found this rationing to be legitimate and morally justified. The justification was made mostly in terms of egalitarian social justice. Some division must be made; if not, one would have everything, another nothing. Society is like a family that needs to share. People should understand each other if there is such a situation, as a man with university education said: 'there must be equality', elaborating on what the less-educated had expressed by saying: 'everybody needs to eat.' On the fringe, however, one may note the more egocentric statement that pointed to another type of social conflict which could have developed from the critical market shortage of supplies: 'Retired people queue from five in the morning, while somebody else works from seven and gets nothing for it.' The small (7 per cent) category of those who did not grant the sales staff the relevant right, while at the same time finding their conduct proper, made use of the same arguments. On the other hand, many of the 12 per cent who disagreed with the right of the sales staff to allocate goods, justify their dissent through criticism of the Communist economy in general—'because this is the fault of the People's Republic economy'; 'this is the fault of the whole economy'; 'the goods should have been there'. All three categories of responses I have listed above are united by awareness of the discrepancy between the ideal pattern of reality ('it should have been enough for everybody') and the actual one ('it needs to be enough for everybody'). Such a majority (83 per cent) is rarely opposed by those in whose view the sale should follow the general

---

[4] Janine Wedel, *Private Poland* (New York, 1988).

rules of the market, independently of the circumstances: 12 per cent of the sample thought that sales staff had no right to introduce restrictions, and they referred to the principle of the freedom of sale ('everybody has a right to buy as much as wanted'), or to the fact that the needs of buyers are different ('people have varying needs'), that they had made different investments of energy in shopping ('the one who gets there first and wakes up early should buy as much as he wanted, while sleeping beauty should get nothing'), and to the equalization of chances in the long run ('today I will buy more and tomorrow it will be your turn'). Among the opponents to situational rationing one finds not only adherents to the idea of an unrestricted free market but also those who favoured the ideal of a universal system of rationing, like that introduced in relation to sugar in the late 1970s, but soon to become the demand of the strikers in the summer of 1980. This development will be discussed in Chapter 11.

Of equal interest is another situation in the interview schedule, the example of a policeman beating innocent bystanders. I should, perhaps, have dared to deal more directly with political abuse of power, but then the situation would certainly be remote from the everyday experience of the people interviewed. The regular abuse of power arrogant policemen would usually indulge in was, however, like that depicted in the interview. Police in Poland arriving at a drunken brawl would first 'pacify' those in the area and then investigate who was responsible. Of our sample, only 10 per cent were willing to accept such a general right to use physical coercion for the sake of a higher necessity. Of these, 3 per cent mentioned public order as a good of supreme value, and 2 per cent pointed to technical difficulties in distinguishing between the innocent and the guilty; and here too order is implicitly held to be a higher good. Some, however, mentioned different reasons for their approval of police beating. One said that lack of help from bystanders indicated their co-responsibility and participation, another that curiosity should be prevented, and so on. Three people granted the relevant right to the police patrol, but from the context it became clear that this was in fact observation of a widespread practice rather than acceptance of such conduct. Amongst the majority that reject use of force by the police against innocent bystanders, justifications emerge that do not allow a clear division into different themes. It was pointed out that one should not beat the innocent, by which it could be understood implicitly that the guilty could be beaten; others said that nobody should be beaten in public, while the guilty could possibly have been beaten at the police station; finally, there were those who were against beating in general. While in the case of situational rationing the legitimization of the practice was so overwhelming that no pattern could be detected concerning the reaction to one who had been prevented from buying as much as he wanted, here it was different as the majority supported the legitimacy of the claims made by the wronged party. Most often it was said that the claims should be pursued in an institutionalized way, that is, through grievances laid against the police and, if that did not work, the judicial route. Nevertheless, the most characteristic remark made was that 'one could make a grievance but that would not lead to anything'. A social pattern emerges here, for the first time, as the institutional way was advocated less often by those under 30 years of age, which might be explained by their experience of conflict with the police.

The two situations compared here demonstrate that contrast between two apparently identical structures of action. To subordinate oneself to restrictions on sale could suggest subordination in general, but such an interpretation is clearly disavowed when the attitudes towards police behaviour are taken into consideration. The contrast is easily explained. People opt for limitation of subjective rights, even if they are of great importance. We should consider here approval of the disappropriation of property for public purposes, on condition that it is related to the provision of some good for the greater number of individuals who are in a 'worse' situation or to whom the wronged party himself belongs. One should underline here the concreteness and the universality of the case which is necessary in order to be recognized as such. An acceptable public good seems to be a good which is of value for a large number of people as individuals—this would include the natural community such as individual families—though also any individuals or families. A right to an indeterminate amount of bread is to be surrendered before the right of anybody within the community to buy bread. The street which is to be built will be public, that is, it will be used by anybody, including the former owner of the land in particular. Whenever a calculation ending in favour of anonymous individuals cannot be made, individual rights and claims will be supported even if there is no chance of fulfilment.

Speaking about the claims as a way to obtain fulfilment of rights, one needs to immerse oneself again in the various ways of action that may serve this purpose. The 'institutional' way mentioned up to now has not been analysed. All cases where the interviewee named an institution to which he or she applied or which she or he advocated, were classified as meaning a direction of the conflict into the public forum. This is an evident over-simplification.

Let us start with the lists of those to whom people in a small town would go in case of an irreconcilable dispute or a difficult problem. These included past and present public figures such as secretaries of the party, town presidents, municipal officials, activists of officially recognized social organizations, teachers, and policemen, to whom one would go in order to arrange the matter, or to learn with whom and where the matter could be arranged. In case of dispute the authority of the organization or institution represented by those persons should have suffered to overcome the resistance of the opponent, irrespective of whether it was a private person or institution. The important principle was that the opponent should not be beyond the potential influence of the person approached. Thus, do not ask the town president to help in a quarrel with the party procurator. Travel to the regional town centre or to the capital is, therefore, needed from time to time. Letters of grievance were also a publicly recognized form of appeal, which was formalized and served as a useful instrument of pressure applied against the local authorities, efficient only under the assumption that the central authorities are willing to support the case and were not directly involved in support for this or that particular local official.

Such a procedure had very human features, but its informality, most valuable from the point of view of those who gained, was also its major weakness. Actions of all those influential persons were made according to decisional discretion, and were exempted from the control of interested parties. Such a control could have been maintained only through direct personal influence on continuation in office or indirectly through referral to rules defining procedural and substantial borders of discretion. Although from the formal point of view making one's claims through influential persons meant use of official channels and institutions, in practice it meant something opposite, that is, private action developing on the basis of public institutions.

This may be supported by an *a contrario* argument provided by the lack of widespread support for the Social Conciliatory Commissions.[5] This institution seemed best suited for the settlement of disputes in a collaborative and conciliatory spirit. In contrast to the *Tovarishcheskiye sudy* (workshop committees) censoring Communist subjects at the workplace and in their place of residence without any concern for formalities, the SCCs were based upon the voluntary principle, and even when they were extended to cover out-of-court pre-trial mediation attempts, the agreement was fully dependent upon the will of both parties. The commission did not have any means of forcing parties to accept the agreement. Commissions established by the local administration at the lowest possible level were also not empowered to impose penalties of any sort. I think that my sympathy for this institution might be forgiven. I could not, however, understand why so agreeable an institution, the principles of which were widely supported, was not well supported in practice. From careful analysis of some actual cases it emerged that clients preferred not to repeat their experience with the SCCs, even if their assessment of the commissions was favourable. Some simply pointed to the fact that commissions were offered the least-significant type of disputes—neighbourhood quarrels over the joint use of land, borders, private debts, and so on, but this seemed to me a typical reaction of the intelligentsia, showing disdain for the lower classes and common people's interests. In fact, what could be more important than a fair and efficient way of rendering justice to a poor and uneducated old lady from a village? If this works, other things are likely work as well, while the opposite is not true. It seems to me now that the failure of the SCCs to gain real ground among the people to whom they were addressed is clearly related to the problem being discussed now. The problem with the SCCs was that they were devoid of authority which supported even informal action by any of the influential incumbents of some of

[5] Jacek Kurczewski and Kazimierz Frieske, 'Social Conciliatory Commissions in Poland', in Mauro Cappelletti and John Weisner (eds.), *Access to Justice*, vol. ii, pt. 1, *Promising Institutions* (Milan and Aalphen aan den Rija, 1978).

the roles in the local power structure. Apparently the sharp division of the world into public and private, meaning the opposition of the official to the informal, was in practice dismantled through the development of access to influential people interested in opening some access, as this gave them a base on which to build their influence in the developing 'second life' of the community, not to speak of the accompanying development of favours and personal loyalties, and sometimes pure corruption. It also explains why in the subjectively significant social relationships, Social Conciliatory Commissions were numerically as insignificant as the regular court with its fully institutionalized procedure of adjudication of rights.

Privatization of the public institution seems to be the ruled's counterpart to the domestication of the terror described in Chapter 3. The important thing to note here is, however, that those adjustments are of a secondary character. Here as well as in the economy, the public reacted to the oppressive structure by developing various ways to pursue their own rights and interests, but whatever the rate of individual success it was evident that the structure itself was hostile to private rights and the interests of the public. In fact, as we see here, individual success was proving this general principle. One could develop individual ways of adjusting the official structure to one's needs, but the structure as such was not changed. In this way institutional 'second life' developed on a massive scale.

For a sociologist law seems to have two basic and strictly related tasks: dispute-resolution and securing general acceptance of legal norms. This is not so evident for the common people, who recognize the functioning of official law usually through contact with the rank-and-file agents of public order, and the detailed regulations that, with growing specificity, regulate social life. Studies conducted in 1977/8 in Warsaw provided an occasion for deciding how important dispute resolution seemed to be to public opinion as a function of the legal system. The majority (57 per cent) when asked what, according to them, were 'the goals the law should serve above all', selected from our four possible answers the reply: 'law secures order and discipline in the state'; while 'the law is the instrument of dispute- and conflict-settlement among the people' was placed second (21 per cent), before the answers: 'law makes possible change and development

in our society' (11 per cent), and 'law makes possible the fulfilment of the personal needs and interests of the people' (8 per
cent).

One can never formulate survey questions to achieve full and
precise expression of human thoughts in a satisfactory way, but as
earlier answers to an open question on what the law is and what
purposes it serves were monotonous, and stereotypically linked
law with regulation and social order, one may suppose that,
although law is perceived by the minority as primarily the instrument of dispute-resolution, this is still for the majority only its
secondary function. On the other hand, much of what is included
in the most popular function of law, conflict resolution and
upholding social order, requires direct reference to individuals,
groups, and social organizations. We know also that the major
part of institutionalized legal material accumulated over centuries
is directly related to conflict: the best example of this is the
importance of civil law in the life of state societies and the
development of the various institutions of dispute-management.
This topic, under-represented in sociological literature, takes on
increasing importance all over the world today as one sees growing dissatisfaction with the institutions of dispute-management.
We observe this process in Poland also—though it has been slow
to develop. In the 1950s several institutions for resolving neighbourhood conflicts were tested. Then changes to the procedures
of labour-law disputes followed, and finally procedures for disputes between the citizen and the administration evolved, leading
to the establishment of administrative adjudication which was still
too limited but which raised the hopes of the citizens.

There were negligible differences between the three samples
surveyed concerning the dominant types of behaviour in the dispute situation. Taking into account the fact that some of the disputes people talked about were, according to those interviewed,
already over, while others were still continuing, one could, however, assume that at least on this aspect there were no differences
between the milieux under comparison, nor serious differences in
the relative frequency of the institutions in which the dispute
develops most often, that is, the agencies for grievances, applications, commissions, and more rarely the courts.

Withdrawal, bilateral negotiations, and the introduction of
extra-judicial institutions into the dispute are the three basic pat-

terns of reaction, and are found frequently in the milieux under study. The degree of 'urbanization' of a milieu—in other words, the degree to which local bonds exist—was unrelated to the frequency of these patterns. Vengeance, passing information to the authorities, or brutal self help appear only sporadically in the interviews, but one cannot doubt that these occur often in private conflicts. Our data may, therefore, say more about the desired hierarchy of acceptable patterns of dispute-settlement and the ranking of the patterns followed in practice. It is evident that in the latter the importance of official procedures increases.

These results offer the following definition of the role of the court in Polish society. Conflicts rarely pass to the official plane, and for the disputes that found their way to the official forum this is taken to be the tip of the iceberg. Of all the various conflicts that affect an individual, the disputes that found their way to the official forum form another iceberg of which the disputes in the court are only the tip.

Petrażycki once observed that, apart from procedural issues and the internal arrangement of the organs of authority, the real foundation of the proper social 'legal order' and the real engine of socio-legal life is not the positive but the intuitive law. '*Only in exceptional, pathological cases of conflicts, transgressions, etc., does the issue need a positive law to be applied*' (emphasis added). This is supported by our findings. Petrażycki, however, did not pay attention to the factors that, as it were, secondarily pathologize the pathology of conflict. Our data show how often claims are given up and that lack of perceived legitimacy for those claims is only one among the many reasons given here. Moreover, settlements made by the court that are automatically assumed to be the most fair and just, in legal ideologies are the last resort, invoked in a minimal percentage of cases, even though the judicial channel may remain open after the filters of resignation, attempted compromise, and finally after several attempts at settling the case through other 'official channels' have been exhausted, such as pressure on the administrative hierarchy, political and trade-union organizations, press, television, radio in the case of conflicts with (official) institutions, and pressure through the inhabitants' committees, local council, police, or political and social organizations in the case of conflict with private individuals.

It is perhaps a detail, though probably an interesting one, that when we asked in Warsaw about preferred ways of settling various kinds of disputes, with one exception only the principle of a-priori resignation from one's own claims emerged independently from traits such as class membership, age, education, gender, and income. In the case of action to be taken against somebody who does not repay a private loan, the level of income per capita within the family had a weak but clear influence. When we move to the lowest income quartile we find increasing percentages—12 per cent, 16 per cent, 19 per cent, and 25 per cent of those interviewed in each of the respective categories. Ceasing to press a claim may result not so much from the lower value of the loans made between the poor—the relative value is the same as the larger loans between the rich—as from an understanding of the debtor's situation, as he will certainly be in financial difficulty.

On the other hand, the choice of the court as the authoritative technique of dispute-settlement is related to a social characteristic of the people surveyed only in the case of decisions concerning disputes over a possession. Only 15 per cent of workers as compared with 25 per cent of white-collar workers would use the court for such a dispute. Looking at education, one sees how the frequency of using the court increases from 20 per cent of those with elementary education and 19 per cent of those educated between the elementary and secondary levels to 27 per cent of those with secondary education and 33 per cent of people with higher education. One may suspect here the greater attachment to 'privacy' in general and to private property in particular amongst those higher on the social ladder, though the unclear picture of relationship with the level of income should prevent too hasty conclusions.

At this moment we recall an important result of the earlier national survey.[6] When asked 'How would you advise participants in a dispute in order to achieve the most just settlement?' 68 per cent of respondents pointed to bilateral agreement, while the court (17 per cent) ranked third after the Social Conciliatory Commissions. The state courts had a better standing when the question was asked about which way of settling a dispute best secures a lasting settlement (24 per cent). Official conciliatory

---

[6] Kurczewski and Frieske, 'Social Conciliatory Commissions in Poland'.

agencies were cited by 21 per cent and bilateral private agreement by 50 per cent. In the majority's opinion the court does not emerge as an instrument of either the most just or the most efficient dispute-settlement. On the other hand, there is a subgroup of people who think that courts are the most just and the most efficient forums for the settlement of interpersonal disputes in general as well as of such petty cases as a hypothetical insult. Although this subgroup is relatively small (on average 20 per cent of respondents) and decreases when moving from the issue of efficiency to applicability in an insult case, nevertheless it varies little when education and socio-economic categories were taken into consideration.

Apart from the significant though still-unexplained minority, the court remains the ultimate resort, understood as a necessary evil. One may conclude that more people give up their claims because they do not want to use the courts than use the court in order to enjoy their rights. The question asked in Warsaw as well as in the small towns on whether one agrees with the statement that to go to court is always unpleasant, even if one has the right, and then what this unpleasantness consists of, provided answers that support the prevailing stereotype. These answers are difficult to quantify, and in order to avoid misrepresenting them one can only point to some major concerns. Those interviewed referred above all to the shame of appearing in public, the time it would take, fear of vengeance, ignorance of the procedures, lack of trust in the administration of justice, and fear that aspects of one's private life might be revealed in a public forum. The survey made by the research team of Borucka-Arctowa[7] complements this picture with quite visible mistrust by the majority as to the impartiality of the courts and the equality of parties before the court.

It is interesting that some people persevere in the action they have started irrespective of their success or failure. This may be illustrated with data from Warsaw. Those who described a dispute in which they took part in the three years before the interview were asked about what they would do if a similar dispute were to occur in the future. With difficulties and inescapable

---

[7] Maria Borucka-Arctowa (ed.), *Poglądy społeczeństwa polskiego na stosowanie prawa* (Attitudes of Polish Society Towards Application of Law) (Wrocław, 1978).

arbitrariness the answers have been coded into three main categories: 1) resignation from following one's claim; 2) striving for a conciliatory settlement through direct negotiations and agreement with the opponent; 3) pursuing the claims in the official way including the court. This analysis was meaningful only in the Warsaw sample in which 310 were cases described, sometimes more than one for each person interviewed, though for approximately half the cases the information was incomplete.

Even this incomplete data, however, made it possible to realize that resignation of a claim as a future strategy is most often discussed by those who have recently withdrawn their own claims. Similar congruence between previous and future action emerged for the remaining categories. Of the cases where full information was available, 44 per cent of respondents planned to repeat their most recent kind of behaviour. Among those planning to change in future, a significant change of preferences could be seen. Bilateral negotiations and agreement which had been the most popular choices for actual behaviour became the least popular strategies for the future, and official action came to the fore. It is possible, therefore, to sketch the following scheme of development as a hypothesis taking into account the more frequent changes of direction:

> bilateral agreement
>> resignation
>>> official action.

This scheme points to the specific dominance of official action as the most popular choice not so much for the present as for the future. Success and failure in disputes slowly lead to the emergence of people who will pursue their course of action. Those who are losing today in bilateral negotiations, when withdrawing begin to think of seeking official action in future. (Note that the simplified codification of the data records total withdrawal before any attempt was made to pursue a claim as well as withdrawal after failure of attempted negotiation as resigning a claim.) Those who achieved a compromise present the widest range of possible future options. Those who used the official way will follow it in the future. If use of the courts is considered as official action, one will find that the above scheme describes quite well the generation of the 'querulants', that is, the people who repeat their contact with courts or at least with the offices repeatedly fulfilling their claims.

This hypothesis is supported by work on criminal procedure with private accusation, that is the *sui generis* remnant of the old private penal procedure, functioning as a peculiar way of settling conflict related to abuse of one's good name, personal integrity, and so forth. In interviews with accusers and accused in 1978 in the judicial districts of Warsaw-Praga, Lesko, and Kepno it appeared that if the interviewed were to be engaged in a neighbourhood dispute resulting in insults, beating by a stranger or by a neighbour, or a libel dispute, in most cases they would follow the official route. The court was mentioned most often (39–49 per cent of those interviewed), followed by the police (33–42 per cent). Those who played the role of private accuser were more likely to take the official route. It appeared, however, that a more or less favourable verdict of the court in criminal cases with private accusation is *unrelated* to preference for courts or other official ways of dispute-resolution in the future. This supports our suspicion that 'failure' or 'victory' are not to been seen as the explanatory mechanism. I think that all this results in a large measure from specific habituation. People are full of antipathy towards court proceedings, and in daily life treat these as absolutely the last resort, the threat of which serves as a special sanction against others in case of transgression of their various rights and duties. Unpleasant thoughts about the court act as a threat, helping the non-conflictual interpersonal or informal and conciliatory settlement of potential conflicts. Once the barrier that divides everyday life from the courtroom is passed, people are able to learn quickly that this world is ruled by quite simple rules which can be exploited in their own interest. This is made even easier as the courtroom is frequented by those more stubborn and energetic in defending their own position. The deterring stereotype of the court seems to facilitate the peculiar selection of its clients, although the clients once in the courtroom quite quickly find their way back there.

# APPENDIX 1.

## Catalogue of disputes used in interviews in three communities investigated in 1977/8

We told you earlier that we are interested in various ways in which people settle disputes between themselves. We would like to learn about your personal experience. During the last year (and if not, in the course of the last three years) have you had a dispute of the kind listed, or a similar one? [Instruction to the interviewer]: What is a dispute? If a respondent does not know how to use the word we assume it is a 'difference; or quarrel; you want something, another wants something different'; in general, it is a conflict that leads to incompatible claims. One will not be able to apply sharp criteria during the interview and therefore we need to use an extended definition of the word 'dispute'. It is important to learn about all possible dispute situations experienced, and simultaneously to know if disputes as described in the catalogue happen. Each of the types is to be described first in general terms and illustrated later with an example.

*Catalogue of dispute situations*

1.  Conflict and dispute about an individual's reputation. For instance, someone retails malicious gossip about you, people you know are told of this, or, a person you know abuses you verbally on the street.

2.  Conflict and dispute related to the abuse of personal integrity, for instance, beating or slapping in face by someone at a dance or at a festival.

3.  So-called typical conflict with neighbours, for instance, regularly make a noise at night and you cannot sleep.

4.  Dispute over the borders of property or possession, for instance, two farmers dispute over the border between their land or two neighbours in an apartment house quarrel over who has a right to use the basement.

5.  Dispute between owner and a tenant, for instance, the owner of a house wants a tenant to leave and the tenant resists.

6.  Dispute over borrowed money from a private persons, for instance, the respondent lent 1,000 zlotys a year ago to a colleague and has not got the money back despite repeated requests.

7.  Dispute between a respondent and a firm that sells something or supplies some services for instance, you gave back your television-set to the state's Tele-Repair Shop after the guaranteed repair period, and money is paid but they fail to repair the set.

8.  A dispute with the administration, or an office, for instance, over the level of taxes you must pay.

9.  (To all employees): A work-related dispute with a superior or subordinate, for instance, a superior refuses you a job reclassification and promotion, though according to you you have the right to it.

10.  Any other dispute? For example, an intra-family dispute not listed in the interview, or a dispute with colleagues at work.

# APPENDIX 2.

## Fifteen hypothetical disputes over rights presented in interviews made in the Carpathian small town in 1978.

1.   A woman coming into a shop in the morning meets her neighbour who tells her about the quarrel that took place at night in the house of the former.

2.   Mr Kowalski's children were beaten by a neighbour because they were misbehaving noisily under his windows so he could not rest after work.

3.   Two neighbours share access to a piece of land convenient for gardening purposes. Each thinks he has a right to plant vegetables, so there is no room left for the other.

4.   Mr Kowalski's friend gossips about him among friends, so the former slapped the latter's face in the presence of others.

5.   A friend borrowed 1,000 zlotys and did not pay it back despite requests to do so. The latter therefore went to the debtor's house and took an item worth 1,000 zlotys.

6.   Two people who know each other well were working together. One became a manager. When the promotions were discussed at a meeting the manager objected to the promotion of his acquaintance, referring to something he knew about him privately.

7.   An employer sent to a hospital a request for information about the illness for which an employee was being treated. The hospital gave an answer to the request which was used against the employee.

8.   In the evening a quarrel started near a restaurant. During the disturbance the police patrol called in used batons against other persons not taking part in the quarrel in order to restore peace quickly.

9.   Mr Kowalski has recently put up a small house for himself but the [space-use] plans have been now changed, and the authorities order him to dismantle the house.

10.     In a shop the management ordered checks on every hundredth client in order to deter potential thieves.

11.     In a shop they do not want to sell some goods in a quantity needed by a client, saying that there should be enough for others as well.

12.     Mr Kowalski was taking pictures in a photography shop. Passing by, he sees his picture exposed in the window. He does not like the picture and wants it to be removed but the manager refuses.

13.     There is a dispute within a family as the wife has inherited 20,000 zlotys, has put it in her saving account and does not want to put it into the common household budget.

14.     A husband has beaten his wife up because he suspected that she made a secret appointment with a man.

15.     A wife teases her husband by telling her female friends some details from their intimate life, exposing him to their ridicule.


*Questions asked:*

(i)   Did X have a right—according to you—to behave in such way? Why?
(ii)  How should Y have behaved towards X?
(iii) Independent of whether X has a right to behave in such a way or not, do you think his/her behaviour to be proper or improper?

# APPENDIX 3.

Patterns of reaction advocated in 15 hypothetical
situations presented to the interviewed sample of
inhabitants of the small Carpathian town in 1978
(100% = n = 211)

| Hypothetical situation | Reaction advocated: | | | | |
|---|---|---|---|---|---|
| | Subject's rights | Withdrawal | Private com-promise | Private pursuit | Official pursuit |
| 1. Neighbour telling gossip | 93 | 39 | 37 | 12 | 7 |
| 2. Beating children by neighbour | 98 | 11 | 53 | 12 | 15 |
| 3. Taking garden by neighbour | 84 | 13 | 29 | 6 | 43 |
| 4. Face slapping by friend | 84 | 31 | 17 | 19 | 27 |
| 5. Taking item by friend | 89 | 17 | 41 | 3 | 35 |
| 6. Refusing to promote friend | 79 | 19 | 10 | 12 | 48 |
| 7. Waiving confidentiality by hospital | 46 | 25 | 7 | 6 | 49 |
| 8. Beating by police | 85 | 26 | 2 | 2 | 66 |
| 9. Expropriation by town | 26 | 28 | 4 | 7 | 51 |
| 10. Random check-up in shop | 78 | 27 | 5 | 32 | 31 |
| 11. Restrictions on sale | 18 | 72 | 4 | 3 | 11 |
| 12. Putting picture on show | 82 | 15 | 8 | 9 | 52 |

| Hypothetical situation | Reaction advocated: | | | | |
|---|---|---|---|---|---|
| | Subject's rights | Withdrawal | Private com-promise | Private pursuit | Official pursuit |
| 13. Inheritance kept by wife for herself | 32 | 53 | 25 | 7 | 9 |
| 14. Wife beaten by jealous husband | 82 | 18 | 17 | 10 | 36 |
| 15. Wife gossiping about husband | 98 | 9 | 47 | 21 | 15 |

# 7

# *Union Democracy in 'Solidarity'*

## INTRODUCTION

For those who are familiar with the debate initiated by Robert Michels and his Iron Law of Oligarchy[1] it is surprising that in the literature on Solidarity, both in Polish and in other languages, so little attention has been paid to the internal democracy that is one of the most conspicuous features of the movement. This may result from the fact that, as the movement was strongly oriented towards democracy in the political life of the society, it might have been obvious that the corollary of this was bound to be the stress on internal democratic organization. One may point in vain to the fact that even sympathizers with organized labour accept as an unwelcome weakness, perhaps attributable to some innate trait of working-class character, a lack of respect for proper procedures. It may suffice to recall that what was from the beginning an obvious assumption of the Polish unionists—secret ballots and elected officers—was imposed practically by force on the British trade unions by a government otherwise accused by the same people of abusing democracy. But this peculiarity of Solidarity ceases to be remarkable for this reason, that in fact it was not a trade union but a political rebellion disguised in trade-union form. There are several arguments to this effect, but still it cannot be doubted that, apart from its other functions, Solidarity as it developed tried to fulfil all the functions of a trade union. It negotiated salaries and wages, discussed health and safety conditions at work, was concerned about old-age pensions and sick pay. At the same time Solidarity was also interested in a hundred other matters ranging from abortion to the rights of minorities but, nevertheless, there is no trade-union function that it could be accused of ignoring. It seems better, therefore, to assume that

---

[1]  See the seminal volume by Seymour Martin Lipset, Martin Trow, and James Coleman, *Union Democracy* (Glencoe, Ill., 1956).

official trade-union structure under Communist rule differed from the traditional one, although the traditional functions were performed, so that the counter trade-union movement in the context of the Party State was also peculiar.

Solidarity's particular nature could not be reduced simply to better performance of the traditional functions. Those who have tried to put the accent on 'trade' functions soon discovered that when confronting the political resistance of the ruling Party State they were unable to do anything without questioning the very basis of the system, as if the accusations by radical critics of reformist movements were to be applied more literally in a socialist society than in a capitalist one. The paradox is apparent only because socialist society has been shaped by the Communist party, and is political to a much greater degree. Here everything, even the grocery shop, its location, and its functioning depends upon the will of authority, so that nothing can be changed without coming into the scope of the power of the authorities. Discussion of the price of cigarettes, pollution of the environment, or the terms of labour contracts, are all political from the start.

## UNION DEMOCRACY

The beginning of Solidarity can be traced back to the evening of 16 August 1980, when, in the Lenin Shipyard in Gdansk, in opposition to the prevailing mood in favour of ending a strike (one of the many in that hot summer of 1980), the decision was taken to form the Inter-Factory Strike Committee including at first representatives of twenty-one firms and companies, and soon more. The word 'factory' in English does not render the full meaning of the Polish *zakład*, which describes any work-place except the administration. The design bureau would be included under this name, as well as the shipyard. The demand for free unions had existed ever since the Committee was set up by self-conscious opposition activists from the coast—Wałęsa, Gwiazda, Walentynowicz, Borusewicz, Kaczyński, and others—the first being the most important on the list. Since this demand was defined in such terms, the strikes of 1980 changed from a diffuse, spontaneously arising and withering away activity into an organized social movement, and the rationale of strikes changed from largely economic into outwardly political. The monopoly of the official organization for representing this group in society was questioned on one of the weakest and at the same time politically most sensitive grounds, that of the representation of workers in general by the official trade unions, something even the Communists were ready to admit in private was failing as a convincing achievement in terms of socialist ideology and Marxist theory. Whatever their private views, especially those who took part in the vivid and turbulent social battles fought by the independent trade-union organizations in pre-war Poland, the political theory sometimes supported by the official party sociologists, such as J. J. Wiatr and K. Ostrowski, as well as by the legal doctrine, was that the existing central organization of trade unions perfectly suited the purpose of expressing the interests of those employed. The Communist trade organization assumed that everybody belongs to a trade union within a given trade or branch. Membership was not obligatory, as my personal experience of being unaffiliated shows, but in practice 99 per cent of the employed belonged to the trade union as it was given the right to express concern over individual and group conditions of work at the individual work-place and in the industry as a whole. Unions were also subsidized from work-place and state budgets, and were given the monopoly of decision-making concerning subsidized holidays for all those employed in the socialized economy. At the work-place the role of the union activists was different from place to place, as some were eager collaborators with the management, helping to discipline the labour force and to encourage its productivity, while others were genuinely concerned about conditions of work and safety, as well as with fighting against corruption and cliques at the top. The undemocratic milieu of the socialized work-place gave rise to the opportunity for a politically well-established manager to organize a group of willing collaborators around himself or herself. This group, in order to be effective, would include the deputies, the bookkeeper, the secretary of the Communist party cell in the work-place, and chief of the trade-union shop. Such a group could then control the illegally acquired surplus in money and goods, and decide on the allocation of access to better-paid positions in the work-place, thus controlling the whole staff, and would then qualify as an organized economic crime gang. In order to survive the clique had to develop an efficient system of surveillance in the work-place to prevent the rise of opposition to its rule, as well as to corrupt or support the otherwise corrupted political authorities at local or supervisory level. The fact that honest trade-union shop activists were soon fired while compromised managers and corrupted trade-union officials were offered a position in another socialized work-place cannot be documented but was felt to be the rule.

So the unions were seen not as an efficient instrument for opposing management (not to speak of the management of the industry or economy as the whole—that is, the ruling party administration), but as the efficient way to organize one's own and one's children free time, holidays, and vacations. This was felt to be a good area of activity, and several thousand union activists were engaged with goodwill in this type of activity. Some of them even tried to improve the level of health-and-safety regulations and practice, as well as to influence management decisions on the extra payments which, in the socialist economy, were often of equal value to basic wages and salaries. In exchange, the unions were supposed to organize the employed, the organization meant the ability to raise a show of support throughout the country should such a need arise, as was the case in the Stockholm Peace Appeal in the early 1950s, support for Vietnamese Communists fighting the Americans, or support for the government in case of increased food prices and the pacification of the related riots. Such support was organized through meetings of employees in the work-place, where absence was treated as illegitimate leave even after working hours, as in the May Day parades where presence was obligatory. The number of trade unions was strictly controlled, and the establishment of the new union of sea workers after October 1956 was an exception to this rule, and fiercely debated. It is interesting to note the role of the sea-coast economy as early as 1956 in the context of future development. (The sea-related economy did not fit easily within the pattern of socialist organization of the economy as commanded from central offices in Warsaw; the bonds between employees were quite strong, and knowledge of the conditions of life and work in foreign countries was often directly acquired.) Trade unions were united with the help of the Central Council of Trade Unions within the nomenclature of the Central Committee of the Communist party, and the chairman of this council was chosen by the

Politburo itself. The Council was controlled from above by the personal policy of the leading élite, whose less-gifted members were given positions in the top offices of the trade-union movement. It was then given the power of legislative initiative. Nothing is known about how this was used, except that sometimes changes in labour relations were declared by the party leaders as initiated by or in consultation with the trade-union movement. And as the already-cited party sociological production shows, the sheer numbers of union members were to serve as proof that socialist society was behind the system, and party to it.

The demand for independent trade unions formulated by the small group of sea-coast dissidents, who did not find in this the interested support of the dissident intelligentsia from Warsaw or Cracow, was first meant to express the needs of workers on the Baltic Coast. The demand had been raised in 1970, then rejected and channelled into the new elections to shop positions in the existing union organizations. The same strategy was suggested this time but it did not work, as the illegal independent trade-union movement was already in full swing. The proponents were thinking in terms of the local trade-union movement when signing the local Gdansk and Szczecin agreements. Such was the meaning of the agreement as signed. But it soon became apparent that the movement was overstepping the framework of the original agreements. First, the movement mushroomed throughout the country. The Strike Committees of summer 1980 were to change themselves, according to the agreement, into the organizing committees of the new trade unions in the work-places, according to the model that where there was a strike, there should be a new union. The representatives of the staff of workplaces throughout the country were coming to the Inter-Factory Founding Committees in Gdansk, Szczecin, or Wrocaw and signing their participation declarations. Within a few days at the beginning of September 1980 the new Inter-Factory Founding Committees were established in various local centres, as well as the only Independent Self-Governing Trade Union of Scientific, Technical, and Education Workers, of a traditional character that recruited several thousand members, and after a month (10 September to 13 October 1980) disbanded itself and joined the new union of Solidarity collectively.

The official history of Solidarity, though traced earlier, starts therefore on 17 September 1980 when representatives of thirty-four work-place, inter-factory, and trade (Sciences, Technics, and Education) unions claiming membership approaching 3 millions met in Gdansk. The National Co-ordinating Commission was formed, and its board and its president, Lech Wałęsa, were elected. In a few days the charter was agreed. This temporary charter included, however, an element which was a surprise to the initiators of the movement. While people from Gdansk were thinking about a loose confederacy of regional unions, the charter finally accepted the unified (though as we shall see federal) union names Solidarity' as proposed by Karol Modzelewski, academic historian and former Communist revisionist imprisoned under Gomulka for political activity with Jacek Kuroń.

To understand Solidarity one needs to take into account a fact often not understood by outside observers, that this trade union was not organized according to trade but according to the principle of territoriality. The Communist trade unions emphasized the functional unity of society by putting the manager of the factory on the same footing in membership as the cleaning lady. There was no distinction into trades or positions within the factory, or within the office and the whole socialized economy. Almost the whole economy outside of agriculture was unionized. The work-place was the functional unit in practice and the work-place was the unit of the rebellion against the system. People from different departments and people from different positions—workers, clerks, engineers—took part equally in strikes. Though the language used was that of 'workers', in fact indifferentiated labour, that is, employees of all kinds from particular work-places were the groups taking part in conflict and in reaching the agreements eventually signed. The confrontation with the Party state was firmly localized in the sense that it was in a particular region of the country that strikes occurred in one or another work-place. In summer 1980 strikes were held in many work-places all over the country. A new stage was reached in Gdansk and in Szczecin when several work-places from the same area went on strike, and the strike took on a regional character. This is why it was successful. In a private economy, labour confronts the management of a particular trade or industrial sector: the same happens in a given branch of public services if the state is confronted by its employees. In Communist society the economy-holders are the state, and they rule on the territorial principle. The party secretary in Gdansk has control over the shipyards as well as the schools and kindergartens there. To succeed in opposition you need to confront not the particular trade ministries, but to use the territorial principle, and this was done by the activists of the new movement even though the need for the new structures to express specific interests was stressed by the minority, and remained the basis for the internal 'trade' dissent within Solidarity throughout its legal existence. The charter gave precedence to territoriality. Regional authorities were to be formed by the representatives of the shops, and trade interests were to be expressed in the form of the trade or branch sections. The tension which we mention here continued though in the form of disputes over the powers of those branch sections, as some of them (the miners for instance) wished to stress their autonomy. The competition of the old trade unions that remained organized according to branch lines (remember, however, that the affiliation of an individual in this system is determined not according to his or her individual occupation but according to the character of the work-place that employs them) undermined the strength of the trade dissent, as those committed to particular interests had much more room for expression in the old 'branch' unions as they soon started to be called once the compromising Central Council was decapitated. A second reason for the territoriality, the need for solidarity within Solidarity, was underlined. It was assumed that even if differences between various groups, sectors, and trades were genuine, that the conflict with the Party State took precedence, and therefore only strict adherence to the path of unity and solidarity could prevent the peaceful revolution from falling apart. Trade interests were to be postponed or relegated to a minor position. It was also felt to be good for the common interest that the stronger industries, like mining or steelworking, should not be given further opportunity to pursue their particular interests above the interests of health services or education.

At the end of the first stage of its history, during the first Congress held in the Olivia sports hall in Gdansk in autumn 1981, Solidarity remained a federation with regional organization as opposed to a unity structure or a confederacy of regional unions. There was one union with various regions, and that remained the important political fact throughout the next stage of short-lived, post-Congress, official legality, and the long period of illegal underground Solidarity. The characteristic features of Solidarity's internal democracy of interest for us here by no means disappeared in this second period, but due to the unusual circumstances of repression and secrecy these were less clearly manifested. This is why discussion of Solidarity in its first stage, that is, until the First Congress, remains the major concern for this chapter.

The natural history of Solidarity involves the process of regionalization. The local Inter-Factory Organizing Committees could have developed in any locality; the scope of regional co-operation was not limited by any rule. On the other hand, the factors described earlier worked towards the gradual adjustment of the internal structure of Solidarity to that of the state. Sometimes it was at the initiative of the regional party secretary who, in order to control the situation, would prefer to have one representative of the insurrection to deal with; in another case it could have been exactly the opposite, that is, the initiative of local Solidarity activists willing to overcome the division that weakened the new organization in relation to the political local party 'landlord'. The KKK (Polish acronym for National Co-ordinating Commission of Solidarity, its supreme body until the First Congress) soon passed the motion of 'regionalization' of the structure. This involved three important elements under one general heading: first, that the adjacent shops together form a base for union structure in a region; secondly, that once the regional structure is formed, the union shop belongs to it and not vice versa; thirdly, that the regional structure is to be equivalent at least to the voivodship, that is, the highest-level territorial unit of national administration. It might be difficult to understand why this motion had to be repeated, if it were not taken into consideration that originally some of the shops of the emerging union had registered themselves in the 'historic' first organizing committees, above all in Gdansk, even if they were located at the opposite end of the country. Local ambitions would not allow them to achieve reunification at the level of administrative borders. Those borders were also challenged as not responding to 'natural' frontiers. This was true in the sense that the division of the country into forty-nine voivodships instead of the previous twenty-one had been made in middle of Gierek's rule, with the openly expressed aim of

following the French example of departmentalization and the
hidden objective of strengthening central power over the smaller
units at the expense of the provincial party secretaries' power.

On the eve of the First Congress of Solidarity, in its twelfth
month of existence, the union was composed of thirty-eight
regions if by region we mean an area of at least one full voivodship, but in two voivodships the regional structure of authority
had still not evolved. Solidarity regional structure therefore
remained different from the state's structure in that the union's
regions were of three types: (1) the potential regions where,
within borders of the same province, a voivodship, two mutually
independent local union authorities continued (Płock and Kutno
in Płock voivodship and Przemyśl and Jarosław in Przemyśl voivodship); (2) thirty-one regions which in their jurisdiction corresponded to one of the voivodships; (3) four regions which
encompassed more than one voivodship—such was the case of
the Mazovian region encompassing seven voivodships, including
the city of Warsaw; Lower Silesia and Little Poland with three
voivodships in each; and the Central-Eastern region encompassing two voivodships. In this connection it is noteworthy that the
territorially largest Mazovian region, including Warsaw, had by
no means the largest membership, this being found in the single-
voivodship region of Katowice. The organizational debate at the
First Congress was in part devoted to this issue as there was a
strong urge to rationalize the structure of the union, and on the
other hand there was the willingness of some quasi-regions (illegal from the point of view of the rules voted by KKK) to fight for
the preservation of their highly valued local independence.
Though one may point to some other manifestations of the
mutual antipathy between inhabitants of the two voivodships
under discussion, there are no data to say whether this was due to
the ambition of the local Solidarity leaders or rather that they
were in this simply following the will of the membership. However (and this needs to be stressed), the resistance against being
accommodated into the larger voivodship was expressed at local
meetings of representatives from the particular shops. And,
finally, it should be added that on the eve of the First Congress
throughout the country there were some shops which, in open
disregard of the decision of the KKK, belonged to regional structures different from the one in the voivodship where they were

located. According to my information the membership in such 'exterior' shops did not exceed 10 per cent at that time, but it could still invalidate the bargaining power of the particular regional structure of the union from which the secession had been. One should remember in this connection that regions, as well as voivodships, differed very much in their industrial power as well as in other characteristics.

The question of regional structure is related quite closely to that of the ladder of authority within the union. The practical push in the direction of large-scale regionalization was achieved with the help of the elections that were arranged deliberately by the KKK in such a way as to enforce the rules described on regionalization. In order to elect representatives to the First Congress—and it was assumed that everybody was interested in taking part in those elections—regional representation was given to particular local units but put to the ballot by the general regional electorate body or (and this was less often practised), the electing regional body approved the voting in the elections made by the composite units of the region. Looking at the second solution one sees that even the KKK's motion to have those delegates validated who were elected by the regional body (regional election of meetings of delegates elected proportionally in each of the shops) had not sufficed to prevent localism as expressed in both the solutions adopted in the regions, the first and most frequent being partial lists of candidates, and the second, less frequent, partial elections that were formally held as pre-elections but were voted in total by the regional electing body.

The original idea of local shops federated in regions that met in the KKK did not provide space for another level of authority structure between regions and shops. The need for this was evident in the proliferation of various non-statutory bodies at this intermediate level. The pattern and the labels were different in different regions, but the principle was the same, in that the regional authorities were proclaiming the establishment of, say, a local chapter, and giving it a charter. But here two opposing options were followed. In one case, it was accepted that the chapter was to be managed by those members of regional authorities who came from the area covered by the chapter; in the second, the new elections were arranged and the new body, unauthorized by union charter authority, emerged above the shops and under the regional authority. Basically, however, this level was not afforded the right to proclaim a strike, and was therefore limited in its power, though cases were not unknown of conflict developed or, more often settled at this local level. It was also evident that regional boards felt willing and obliged to allocate funds and positions to be filled at this level from the pool of resources in the possession of the region, with specific rates, for instance, of one position for every five thousand members of the union.

### SOLIDARITY AND THE MIDDLE CLASS: ONE OR TWO CLASSES?

'Solidarity' was a union joined by people with various characteristics, different in age, gender, life condition, income, and education. The common thread was dependency upon the state employer, more exactly upon the Party-State administration of economy, culture, sciences, health, education, and public life. The dependency was so essential that making further differences in interests, beliefs, and habits is of lesser importance. Still, the question was often asked about the class character of the Solidarity movement and Solidarity membership.

Which classes? One can talk about class in two ways. First, when by a class a social collectivity is understood, as defined by some common features, independent of whether people belonging to this collectivity are aware of the commonality, such as small-farm holders or shareholders. Secondly, class can be understood also as a feeling of some commonality to which one belongs. Those two criteria may coincide but this is not necessarily the case. Solidarity members in principle did not have doubts about their class self-determination, and used two conventional categories in answer to our question 'To what social class do you feel you belong?' Answering this question, 62 per cent in the Mazovian region and 74 per cent in Katowice region answered that they belonged to the 'working class', while 26 per cent in the Mazovian Region and 13 per cent in the Katowice region said that they belonged to the 'intelligentsia'. In social consciousness, then, those two classes were the basic constituents of Solidarity. But what were the differences between the members of those two classes? Let us examine further the Mazovian region data, where the proportion of 'intelligentsia' was much large than in the heavily industrialized Upper Silesian region of Katowice, thus making comparison between two 'classes' more reliable.

Among the 'intelligentsia' belonging to the union the majority were women (63 per cent), and among the 'working class' members, men (61 per cent). Union intelligentsia were, on average, older than union workers. The intelligentsia as a whole had completed secondary education, while of workers only 17 per cent had completed secondary education and 37 per cent had completed elementary education only. The data concerning the relationship between class affiliation and the job performed is also of interest. Of workers, 84 per cent identified themselves with the 'working class' and none with the 'intelligentsia', while of white-collar workers 16 per cent identified with the working class, and 77 per cent with the intelligentsia. The rest either did not identify themselves with these classes or in a few cases listed other ones, though not numerous, such as 'peasant-worker class'. We can see that among Solidarity members the 'working class' is the most attractive denomination, but while people with higher education may declare themselves to be workers the opposite does not happen. In effect, therefore, the 'working class', is composed of 81 per cent workers, 8 per cent service workers such as mailmen or sales-girls, and 9 per cent white-collar workers, while the 'intelligentsia' is made up of 3 per cent service workers and 96 per cent white-collar workers. The self-defined intelligentsia more often filled managerial (7 per cent) or intermediary (20 per cent) positions than the working class (respectively 2 per cent and 12 per cent). Average income per family member was also higher among the 'intelligentsia' than among 'working class'.

The two subjectively defined classes do not differ in their political behaviour, as 13 per cent of the 'working class' and 13 per cent of the 'intelligentsia' in Mazovian Solidarity belonged to the PUWP, though when we asked about their religious affiliation 66 per cent of the 'working class' as opposed to 46 per cent of the 'intelligentsia' declared themselves as regularly practising Catholics. Within the union the intelligentsia were involved more often in various functions which could be explained not only by increased promotion opportunities within a work-place as a result of education and specialist knowledge, but also because they were coming from more numerous shops with smaller membership, such as research institutes, offices, schools, bureaux and the like. In effect, among the 'working class' 91 per cent of rank-and-file union members were not involved in any union function, while among the 'intelligentsia' the respective figure was as low as 65 per cent, with 33 per cent performing some official duties within the Solidarity structure.

These findings also need to be discussed with reference to the division into workers and white-collar workers, which only partially coincides with the division into 'working class' and 'intelligentsia'. The results were nevertheless similar: there were more men than women among the workers, and conversely in the white-collar sector women dominated. White-collar workers unionized in Solidarity were older than workers. And of the workers, 42 per cent had no more than elementary education, while the respective figure for white-collar workers was 2 per cent. Among workers 25 per cent, as opposed to 9 per cent of white-collar workers, were in the lowest income bracket of less than 2,000 zlotys of monthly income; 91 per cent of workers and 70 per cent of white-collar workers did not perform any union function; 14 per cent of workers and 15 per cent of white-collars belonged to the PUWP, and 68 per cent of workers and 51 per cent of white-collars were regularly practising Catholics.

From two nation-wide surveys, one made by the Polish Television and Broadcasting Public Opinion Research Centre with a general population sample, and the second by the Mazovian Solidarity Social Research Centre, one could conclude that membership in Solidarity was basically the same for both genders, and that the preponderance of men resulted from their greater share in the labour force employed in the socialized economy. Solidarity was most popular among those in their twenties, while few pensioners belonged. Solidarity was best represented in the larger towns (above 20,000 inhabitants), but the proportion of Solidarity members in the countryside was also quite high (20 per cent), and this included people with two jobs, employed both in industry offices and self-employed on their own private farm.

The two surveys differed concerning the education and occupational background of Solidarity members. As to the first characteristic it might be said that, despite all these differences, the better-educated part of the labour force found its place in the union, as the average level of education of Solidarity members

TABLE 7.1.    *Education of Solidarity members and the labour force in general* (%)

| Categories of education | Employed in socialized economy according to Central Statistical Office | Solidarity membership | |
|---|---|---|---|
| | | (a) according to OBOPiSP 1981 survey | (b) according to OBS Mazovia 1981 survey |
| Elementary | 42 | 33 | 24 |
| Occupational and secondary incomplete | 24 | 36 | 27 |
| Secondary | 27 | 26 | 28 |
| Higher | 7 | 5 | 11 |

was higher than in Polish society in general, as well as for those employed in the socialized economy (see Table 7.1).

The higher average did not mean, however, higher education. Certainly, Solidarity had not attracted people with secondary or higher education in a higher proportion than were in the work-force, while on the other hand, those with elementary education were under-represented. The divergence of the data concerning the occupational background of Solidarity members was much larger (a fact that may be explained by reference to the growing and changing nature of the membership of the union). Two things were certain nevertheless: first, that skilled workers were the most numerous category of union members (between 42 per cent and 58 per cent), and secondly, that white-collar workers without higher education were next in numbers (23 per cent to 29 per cent). Those rankings correspond to the general occupational structure of the work-force in the socialized economy and state.

Some additional information on the social composition of Solidarity is provided by figures on membership in the Communist 'branch' trade unions. Though the data, as given by the management of those unions in the spring of 1981, has no guarantee of reliability, still the differentials in the outflow of membership from particular 'branches' as noted in comparison with pre-summer 1980 statistics can be taken as informative.

In the first group of branch unions where the loss of members, presumably in favour of Solidarity was highest, and amounted to at least three-quarters of membership as recorded in 1980, one finds the unions of energy resources; of the media (publishing, the press, broadcasting and television); forestry and the timber industry; the steel industry; sailors and dockers; textiles; and leather and clothing industries. In the second category, where the losses were lowest and amounted to 50 per cent or less, we find the state and social (that is, PUWP and other licensed organization employees unions); agriculture (mostly state-farm labourers), and teachers. The third group included all the other trades that took an intermediate position in this ranking.

Of course, there were sometimes very concrete and particular reasons for differential outflow figures for particular trades and unions. Sometimes tradition could have been of importance, as the Polish Teachers Union, for many teachers, was a symbol of social significance of their otherwise neglected profession, and so they remained members. But basically even this case supports our main hypothesis that Solidarity attracted fewer of those who had either been linked personally with the authority and power of the Party State (state and social organization employees), or the lowest paid (sales-people or farm labourers), who were socially passive and had developed other, illegal ways of compensating for their low wages by controlling the supply of products sought on the market or by simple appropriation. Solidarity was most attractive to those who had been relatively better educated, and not linked materially with the *ancient régime* either by a share in power or by participation in the black economy.

## Solidarity Values

Attempts to point out the basic values to which Polish society was historically oriented have also been made by the independent movements, sometimes with the help of the same sociologists who otherwise attempted purely descriptive formulation. A good example here is the debate on the basic ideological premises of Solidarity occasioned in 1981, when the forthcoming First National Congress of the union was expected to present to society the programme that would finally set forth a clear distinction between Communist rhetoric and the new one developed by society itself. But there is no such thing as 'society' itself. It was, therefore, first the Centre for Socio-Occupational Research and its programmative-consultative council which served as the formal advisory body of experts to the National Co-ordinating Commission of Solidarity that was asked to present the document that would start the debate, and then, secondly, society expressed itself in the form of a series of counter-drafts, individual proposals, and articles, and collectively in the form of the ballots taken on the various versions of the ideological document of the union, until finally the programme was decided through voting at the First National Congress in Olivia Hall, Gdansk. 'Society' did not, therefore, mean society in general, but the specific milieux and their very formalized procedures; it was not, however, individual or clandestine manipulation either. The authorship really was collective, and the debate really was open, even though the decisive motions were made by a few thousand of the formally legitimated representatives.

The first draft of the programme, of which little remained in the final document, was prepared by a small circle of collaborators from the Solidarity research centre, and then modified in the course of the informal discussion as well as the four full meetings of the said Programmative-Consultative Council. The document, entitled *Directions for Action of the Union in the Present Situation of the Country*, included a chapter on 'Basic Values' in which four such values were listed:

The best tradition of the nation, the ethical principles of Christianity, the political message of democracy, and socialist social thought—these are the four basic sources of our inspiration. We are deeply affiliated with the heritage of Polish culture, immersed in European culture, strongly related to Catholicism although linking various religious and world-view traditions.[2]

The draft programme then stressed in two places the place given within the union to all members independent of their religious beliefs, world-view, nationality, and political beliefs. Solidarity, comradeship, and brotherhood of labour in the common cause of struggle against exploitation were mentioned as values related to the associational character of the union. A large paragraph was devoted to social justice, and this value was put forth as the 'foundation for the functioning of the State, its offices and institutions, and to lie at the foundation of all decisions concerning social policy

---

[2] After *Dyskusja nad programem i taktyką związku* (Discussion on programme and tactics of the union) (Gdansk, 1981), 3–4.

and the organization of the collective life'. Social justice was based in the draft programme on the principle 'of the innate dignity of the human being, the dignity of the labouring man and his efforts' (it should be mentioned that in the original Polish the formulation is much more gender-neutral than in the almost literal English translation). There were two corollaries of social justice derived from the aforementioned dignity of the human being. First, 'from the principle of social justice, from the dignity of the human being comes the result that in deepest essence all people are equal. We shall therefore strive for social egalitarianism' as manifested in the priority given to a social minimum wage before pay according to effort. Secondly, 'from the principle of equality it follows that in public life full democracy needs to be fulfilled'. Democracy is linked, then, with the promise to support the widening of public participation as well as all political freedoms, such as the right to free expression of one's beliefs, freedom of speech and print, the right to reliable information, the right of assembly, and the right of free association. The link with the workers' movement was then mentioned, and cautiously limited to 'those elements of this tradition which will reinforce us in the ideals of social justice, democracy, freedom and independence'. The draft took as obvious that national values were of great importance. National values were held to be 'the fundamental bonds of our society, the modern world, and the ultimate foundation of our independence and sovereign statehood'. It was remembered then that the strikes of summer 1980 were, amongst other things, directed against the suppression of national values in the social consciousness. Finally, the chapter on values emphasized that, though the union is a meeting place for people with different attitude towards religion, 'the great majority of our members as well as our nation were educated in the Christian religion' and thus religious inspiration served as one of the main sources of the programme and will continue independently of the lay character of the union.

Such was the draft, and this may be read as the first attempt by Solidarity-related Polish opposition intellectuals to read what was in the minds of the several millions who united in defiance of the Communist regime. In the draft there was both reading and teaching, two sides of the interpretative work that cannot be separated in any such enterprise. Drafters aspired to offer this verbalized intellectual justification of the mass movement and so to direct normatively the actions of the movement in the near future. Such documents are never satisfactory from an intellectual point of view, as well as being subject to partisan debates. So what, in fact, was the purpose of draft itself? The debate quickly started, and in this the draft achieved its expected goal.

The intellectual arguments, as soon became apparent, were not necessarily devoid of partisan spirit, as one does not state simply that a draft programme is incoherent without saying in what the supposed incoherence lies. Thus Marcin Król in *Solidarity Weekly* soon observed that, instead of a programme for the functioning of democracy, the draft served values which although noble, could not be reconciled with each other and were ambiguous. Król asked what were the 'best national traditions' and the 'political message of democracy' in the context of the bicentennial fight for independence that put aside the problems of the functioning of democracy? What 'socialism' and which 'Christian ethics' were referred to by the authors of the draft? The counter-argument, that the principles invoked in a document of similar character cannot and need not be specified, was rejected by Król when he wrote that:

The naive presumption that such incoherent values or inspiration may co-operate in the practice of social life without tension is based upon a dangerous moralistic illusion. This part of the chapter on 'Basic Values' can be intellectually justified only if we accept that the members of Solidarity will take inspiration only from what is good and mutually consistent. I am asking therefore why members of Solidarity are likely to be better than people anywhere else and at any other time have been? This has not been explained to us. In the whole chapter there is not one word about the difficulties, conflicts, and struggle of interests to achieve compromise and concessions. Once again in Polish history in this way a programme emerges that appeals to moral unity and neglects the democratic unity that is the unity evolving out of conflicts.[3]

Król observed that as early as 1926–39 it had been attempted in Poland to base social and political life upon the moral principles that finally led to the limitation of democracy and the creation of the moral regime under Solidarity. According to him, not moral values and the virtues of the individual but an efficient

---

[3] After *Dyskusja nad programem i taktyką związku* 47.

and democratic social system should be attempted. The Church should be concerned with improving the individual, and Solidarity with improving society. Moreover, the principle of individual freedom and not individual dignity is fundamental when speaking about values, and the draft should take into account the abuse of the principle of equality that emerged in history when individual freedom was not respected.

Leszek Kołakowski has described why he was a conservative-socialist-liberal-and-whatever-else, and why it was impossible not to be so at that time. Król attacked the draft programme precisely for attempting to be a patriotic-christian-democratic-socialist-egalitarian cocktail, and not helping the people to become aware of what were the causes and aims of their public engagement. Professor Stefan Kurowski, while not accepting the left ingredients of this cocktail, was unconditionally in favour of the normative axiology as an indispensable part of the programme. His own proposals, some of which found their way into the cited draft, went much further in that direction, and Kurowski, who was especially keen on the liberal economic element in the programme, travelled around the country and mobilized support for his version. According to Kurowski, setting out the values in the Solidarity programme was necessary in order to legitimize the union in society.[4] As a movement of protest and social reconstruction, Solidarity was above all the creation of a democratic environment for developing various values (but which ones he preferred not to pronounce himself), while for Kurowski and others like him in this respect Solidarity had a much more detailed task to perform. A more general difference of standpoints is manifest here: for some, the union was an instrument for the promotion of democracy in Poland, while for others, even with democracy, some additional values were to be pursued by the union. One could imagine some who might have preferred values other than political democracy as those to be realized with the help of union action. In Kurowski's case the structure of axiology was clear. At the top was the set of universal ideas most brutally abused under Communist rule: honesty, solidarity, comradeship, brotherhood, the innate dignity of man and labour, public participation and social control, democracy, social justice, the rule of

---

[4]   After *Dyskusja nad programem i taktyką związku* 33 ff.

law, civil liberties, national values, and religious Christian inspiration. By publishing his version Kurowski made it possible to see that the elements of the collective draft programme which refer to some of those values from his list had been prepared by himself. It is interesting, however, that while the role of dignity in the hierarchy of values was accepted into the collective draft, the notion of human dignity being the distinctive mark of John Paul II's social teaching and theological anthropology, the good old notion of honesty, that served in Kurowski's conception as the first principle, had been eliminated through ballots in the council because of fear of over-moralizing. In Kurowski's version honesty was of great significance. He stressed that 'contrary to appearances it is by no means a trivial principle leading to shallow moralism but a directive for social action with wide consequences and great reconstructive force'. The union as a whole and its members as individuals were to be honest. Honesty in social life meant the acknowledgment of equilibrium, in that 'the gains we achieve from society or other people cannot exceed our services'. This social ethic of reciprocity allowed Kurowski to condemn all undeserved privileges, corruption, and theft of public property. Honesty as the best policy meant that 'Solidarity' would be against the exploitation of labour, but also against the corrupt and bad performance of one's duties in labour. Honesty meant truth in public life, that is, good faith in negotiations and agreements. It meant also the fight against social pathologies, above all against alcoholism as present in the life of members of Solidarity and in society in general. This vast moral programme was formulated in individual categories so that it could not be accepted through the democratic procedures of approval and amendment. In a sense this worked against Król's argument. The vagueness of the programme in this part resulted from the application of true democracy as the procedure for the creation of the programme. If you vote on ideology, it cannot be detailed, consistent, and unambiguous. Perhaps the answer is simply not to vote on values and ideologies. But Król himself—and the dispute between Król and Kurowski in my opinion well illustrates the dilemmas of those days—was for a programme, but with a different structure, that is, with a different axiology. Król wrote: 'In my opinion, in the forefront of values there is now and always the freedom of the individual. And therefore at the top of the hierarchy of tasks there should be the construction of a democratic regime and education for democracy.' The draft was ambiguous in rejecting Kurowski's detailed axiology of honesty, and by neglecting Król's axiology of individual freedom. Both would perhaps agree that the patriotic-democratic-christian-socialist-egalitarian cocktail is too strong. But the cocktail was created by people who came together from divergent traditions, and the very fact of their presence and co-operation could serve as the argument for the mixture, as at least reflecting the reality of the ideological landscape.

The final document emerged in the last days of the First National Congress after weeks of debate and bargaining, in which the so-called fundamentalists opposed the so-called pragmatists on several issues, of which one, then the most important, was the attitude towards open rejection of the Communist Party State with its corollaries.

## Solidarity: Functions

Towards the end of 1981 Solidarity had over 9 million members and—if the Roman Catholic Church is left temporarily outside the picture—was the largest social organization taking part in public life in Poland. It was a voluntary association of people with various background and other social characteristics, as described earlier. Solidarity's main function was to fill the void between the private world of the individual, family, and friends, and the official world of the Party State. We refrain here from discussion of the political function of Solidarity, which has been a major concern for those who have written on the subject in the past. One cannot refrain, however, from mentioning the various social functions of the new organization as a politically engaged social movement organized as a trade union in its original structure. What is even more pressing is the feeling that the closed triangle of discussion about whether Solidarity is a party, trade union, or social movement also had a specific social function. Those who held that Solidarity was a trade union were stressing this in order to legitimize it within the frame of the Communist political system; those who underlined the party character of Solidarity, if doing it in the open, were criticizing the movement and weakening its position by reference to this political frame; and finally, those who spoke of Solidarity as a social movement attempted, with the help of sociologists, to legitimize its demands and aspiration without transgressing the limits set forth by the Gdansk Agreements and later political practice.

As all these attempts were related to tactical necessities and opportunities, it emerged that in order to better understand the social role of Solidarity in Polish society in the 1980/1 period, one should forget about this magic triangle and look for some other functions as manifest in social practice. At the Sixth Polish Sociological Congress in Łódź on 9 September 1991 I suggested the following functions of Solidarity, referring to the dialectical functionalism and the tensions involved in each of the particular functions that emerged from interviews, observation, actions, and declarations of the actors.

The first of five functions to which I draw attention was the mobilization of the wide mass of members who, though acting in various directions, were nevertheless within the confines of the one organization, and who in this way were achieving their aims ten years after the abortive strikes of 1971. Apart from groups which had taken part in those events, the offices of Solidarity were filled with meetings of Home Army veterans from 1939–45, victims of Stalinist persecutions, Trotskyites, and patriots, and people of many other persuasions. The stronger the movement became, the more strength was attached to it from the various nuclei of social action that would otherwise have developed their own structures. In this way Solidarity was held responsible for the activities of various movements such as, for instance, the KPN (Confederacy of Independent Poland) which was the standard object of attack of Communist propaganda. The process of construction of social self-government was also slowed down in this way, as instead of the proliferation of free voluntary associations and other forms of organization the activities of Solidarity were becoming more and more diversified. Solidarity was also undergoing a process of totalization, as with the growing variety of interests among its membership—political, ecological, cultural, and so on—the union was encompassing a wider and wider part of the members' lives. Consequently, within the union one could observe a process which was called by Marxists the transformation of a *Klasse en sich* into a *Klasse für sich*, a process resulting from the fact that the resistance exerted by the Party-State bureaucracy into second place while the unity of interests achieved priority. The more society was forced to be united through this process, the more the process of polarization developed as people were more and more often forced to declare themselves on one side or the other in the major political conflict. This polarization weakened the position of those elements in Solidarity and in the ruling class who were favourable to compromise, and therefore the conflict became more and more severe, and positions moved wider apart.

The dialectical functionalism might be best illustrated by an apparent paradox, the fact that the tension in the country increased the more the ruling camp was surrendered its previous patterns and accepted the rules of conduct typical for a democratic society. This process and the relevant functions might be termed the civilization and barbarization of the enemy. Significant relaxation of censorship and the opening of the secrets of power after August 1980 led to a progressive demystification of the ruling power. Various mechanisms for the abuse of this power which had worked for decades were finally made known to the public. One should remember that, although everybody was repeating that there was corruption, almost nobody was aware of the fact that corruption was of a more and more complex character. Solidarity, with more than 9 million members, was the most numerous organization in the country. As pointed out above, it was for those people most often the only accessible public forum in which they could manifest their beliefs and exercise their right to expression. Forms of participation differed, but most of them were similar and ranged from the union shop meeting to the mass meeting held in the work-place or a public place under the sign of the cross and union flags. The popularity of strikes will not be fully understood unless it is considered that in fact the strike was a manifestation of beliefs and the exercise of newly resurrected rights as well. So the fact that about three-quarters of the members of two union regions took part in at least one strike cannot be interpreted without taking into consideration the expressive functions of a strike. Strikes and mass meetings were the legal form of public participation as opposed to the more passive one which consisted in affiliation with the new trade union. But even in the latter case it should be kept in mind that membership in Solidarity was an act of conscious political decision involving risk and felt to be so by almost everybody, though not evidenced by standard sociological methods. Some strikes were certainly greeted with joy by local activists, who saw in it the occasion for the involvement of the masses in the union, and this experience of testing abilities and loyalties was, as was well known to Solidarity members, considered crucial for the proper and healthy development of the union in a given area.

After activization and the corresponding totalization of the experience of the membership that resulted from taking part in one overwhelming organization, Solidarity's next function was both the unification and the polarization of society. In fighting against the steady resistance on the part of the Party State's bureaucracy, Solidarity became stronger, though this strength was at the same time a burden. Whether willingly or not, Solidarity was forced to serve as an umbrella under which shelter was found by various social movements, tendencies, and orientations. In the middle of 1981 the sharp division into two political camps was already evident, with the opponents labelled respectively the *korniki* (from KOR—the Polish acronym for the Committee for Defence of Workers) and 'true Poles', a division that can be traced back much earlier and which will reappear on the national political scene. One should mention here also the events which, under normal conditions of public life, might also have taken place, such as brutal intervention by police forces or a politically biased trial of the leaders, but which in the conditions of heightened expectations and motivation for change in 1980/1 would have been seen as overstepping the threshold of tolerance. All this had the result that during the process of 'civilization' of the opposition, that is, during the time when the Communist authority assumed more democratic rules of conduct, rejection of it was also increasing together with the negative attitude resulting from various current and past abuses. The demystification of authority proceeded in this way. So long as the economic system was unchanged and the Party-State apparatus remained in control of the enterprise, the strike, an event both legal and normal after August 1980, made it clearer that this affected the employer in relation to labour both within Solidarity and outside. 'One need not explain why this process is so dangerous to further developments in Poland. If it continues I will need to withdraw from my previously expressed optimism about the possibility of a stable, peaceful, and glorious development of change in Poland within the bipolar model.[5]

Egalitarianization without egalitarianism seems to be another on the list of the internally contradictory functions of Solidarity. In contrast to what the majority of sociologists and journalists expected, Solidarity was not a movement aiming at the fulfillment of egalitarian programs, although the role of the egalitarian element in the motives, actions, and declarations of the union had not yet been fully exposed. From all the axes of social differentiation as perceived by pre-August 1980 society, Solidarity focused on the most important, albeit not the only one, that is, on the division into rulers and ruled, 'government' and 'society'. Nothing pointed to other areas of interest. The people who took part in the movement and who led it came from various social milieux, and the better educated and better paid were strongly represented. In my survey I was able to discover that the majority (80 per cent) of union members were against radical egalitarianism and supported differentiation of income and, more generally, of living conditions according to input of work, skills, and quality of performance at work. One should remember in this context that in summer 1980 the strikers in Szczecin rejected the advice given by their expert Andrzej Tymowski to introduce a maximum income into their list of demands.

Egalitarianism was formulated, therefore, only in relation to the authorities who, after losing their legitimacy in the eyes of the ruled, lost also the legitimacy of the privileges linked with posts held. At the same time, within the movement itself privileges related to top offices were accepted when it came to the union's own élite. If Merton's terminology of manifest functions is followed, then the struggle for freedom of enrichment, based upon one's own work and initiative as well as the universality of access to everyday as well as luxury goods, should be mentioned. The right to enrichment through one's own efforts is common to all those manifestations mentioned above.

On the other hand, Solidarity is an immense force for equalization in society as a whole, not only of the relationships between the apparatus of power and the remaining mass of citizenry. This egalitarian function manifests itself in many different ways. As an

---

[5] J. Kurczewski, 'Funkcje społeczne NSZZ "Solidarność," *Sprawy Związkowe* (Sept. 1981), 28.

illustration one may cite actions aiming to level inter-regional differences in living conditions. Those differences had not been well enough exposed by sociologists before August 1980. Summer 1980 meant the rebirth of social activity outside the capital of the country in Lower and Upper Silesia, Little Poland, the Lublin and Łódź areas, Gdansk, and the Western sea-coast. Great Poland provided Solidarity both with militants and with ideas. It is symbolic that nobody questioned the role of Gdansk as the capital of the union. Gdansk, as opposed to Warsaw, represents the capital of Solidarity as opposed to the capital of the Party State. Solidarity helped to equalize conditions in various sectors of the economy by preventing the development of trade and branch sections within its structure. If one accepts the concept of the 'new middle class' as the active force for change, and the resulting drive for opening up various channels of well-being and advancement, one expects also that those processes will hamper the fulfilment of aspirations held by the social base of the union, at least during the economic crisis that also produced the egalitarian effects for the part of society that belonged to the union.

Finally one should list the institutionalization of revolution as the last function of Solidarity, though in fact it has been most often mentioned by others, especially by Jadwiga Staniszkis.[6] In fact so much has been written on this that there is little to add. The dilemmas of 'self-limiting revolution' are at the same time dilemmas of institutionalized revolution. It is exactly the institutionalization of social protest in the form of the independent and self-governing trade union 'Solidarity' which led to the multi-functionality of the union, and to the fact that it needed to act at the same time as the defender of the interests of employees in the work-place, as a partner in negotiating the new socio-economic system, as an extra-parliamentary opposition pressing for changes in the political system, and as organizer of strikes which in a sense went against the economic interests of the strikers and at the same time (inevitably in this political regime) had a political character. Certainly, free elections would have been better for the health of the national economy at that time than the revolution effected through strikes. This is related to the work-place and region being the structural units of Solidarity. The work-place

[6] Jadwiga Staniszkis, *Poland's Self-Limiting Revolution* (Princeton, NJ, 1986).

shop corresponded to the traditional objectives of trade-union activity in Poland, while the regional structure corresponded to the needs to develop activity above the work-place level and to play the part of independent labour organization. At the same time, the regional structure helped to politicize Solidarity, which had to oppose the political power so long as this was married to the economic power. This had been accompanied by a process that turned out to be of capital importance for the future, that is, the emergence of the new post-August 1980 political élite of Solidarity activists who acted beyond the work-place, epitomized by Lech Wałęsa. This alternative élite was political, as it was engaged in conflict and negotiation with the Party-State apparatus. Solidarity at this stage was an organization aiming to win the support of the majority of society without physical elimination of the opposite side. With the PUWP being the apparent force, Solidarity was the real 'leading' force of society. But as the PUWP was not a political party in the customary meaning of the term, neither was Solidarity. Nevertheless, it was both a trade union which, in these political circumstances, needed to play the part of a political force, and a political force which, under these circumstances, was forced to take the shape of a trade union. If asked what these circumstances were, the answer for 1981 was that in Poland a system of confrontation democracy had developed built upon the tension between two polar forces. The system could survive so long as the two camps were basically equal in power, that is, when Solidarity was supported by, say, 90 per cent of society and the apparatus of power by something like 10 per cent, but with its own means of support. The imposition of martial law on 13 December 1981 was sociologically possible because first, state power had been strengthened by foreign support at the moment when General Jaruzelski decided to execute the operation that had been planned earlier by the Soviet and Warsaw Treaty international Communist ruling class, and secondly, when support for Solidarity corroded due to the impossibility of achieving further progress without recourse to armed struggle.

But Solidarity was a social movement not directed only from outside the existing social environment, but also creating a new, independent, and autonomous one for its members. Within this environment new patterns of thinking and of acting were formed. Union members determined their identity through manifesting their membership in Solidarity and through taking part in various collective activities such as field mass, strikes, or election meetings. The majority also had close friends within the ranks of the union, especially in the case of workers.

The survey I conducted under the auspices of the Mazovian Regional Centre for Social Research (OBS) in May 1981 in the Mazovian region, and in July–August 1981 in the Katowice Inter-Factory Organizing Committee area of highly industrialized Upper Silesia, made it possible to assess the scope and forms of the public activity of Solidarity members. As many as three-quarters of the membership took part in a strike at least once after summer 1980. But strikes were not the only form of public activity, and the widespread involvement in other forms as well is noteworthy, such as petitioning the authorities or presenting one's own views in the government-controlled media or in public meetings outside the work-place. The public activity of Solidarity members developed, thus, mostly within the work-place, within the community of work colleagues, and through the work-place union shop. This is self evident, as the Communist Party State had not removed its control from the media. The restrictive laws on associations, assemblies, press, and publishing had not yet been amended and the new law on censorship was passed as late as in May 1981. In this context the role of Solidarity in creating a liberated zone of free speech and action within the work-place is more visible. The freedom was there at work, as it was achieved by the employees of the Party State fighting as the trade union.

The high level of public activity of Solidarity members is also evidenced by the fact that only from 12 to 13 per cent of them had not used any of these forms, while from 38 to 50 per cent had used at least two. Again, activity outside the work-place was limited as, while from 25 to 31 per cent of union members took part in the last month before the survey in the union meeting at the shop, the figures fall dramatically from 4 to 7 per cent of union members who took part at least once in such a meeting outside their respective work-place shop. These data are particularly striking as in the Mazovian region, for instance, between 69 and 73 per cent of union members did not belong to any other political, social, or cultural organization. In a country devoid for decades of free voluntary association, Solidarity in 1980/1 remained the only organized public activity and participation offered to most people.

The uniqueness of Solidarity is also manifested by the extremely favourable assessment of its activities by its members. When people were asked to evaluate and choose between four scores ranging from 'unsatisfactory' to 'very good' (this is the system of scored used in Polish schools), most of the evaluation was made using 'good's and 'very good's. In both samples the three levels of union authorities— the shop organization, the regional organizing committee, and the National Co-ordinating Commission were evaluated on three aspects of their activities: (1) Do union authorities take care of the membership? (2) Do they inform the membership about their actions? (3) Do they take into consideration in their action the union members' interests? In total, the average score in both regions was lower when assessing the regional authorities than in the case of shop or national union authority. Concerning informing the membership and taking their opinion into consideration, the best assessment was given to the shop authority, but when assessing promoting the members interests the first choice was given most often to the national union authority. One needs to point out that, contrary to the busy activity of the regional activists, the difference in evaluation between regional on the one hand, and national and work-place activity on the other could have been due to the lack of a clear distinction between the roles of the bottom and top union structures, and the intermediary regional ones. If one takes into account the above-mentioned tendency to develop a fourth, sub-regional level of hierarchical structure, doubts concerning the relationship of this elongated pyramid of authority and the real perceived interests of the membership could be raised. The vague role of those intermediary structures was also implicit in the answers given to the question about the functions which the various structures could fulfil. In an open question about the tasks of the shop union organization, problems such as social security, organization and efficiency of work, health and safety at work, wages, control over the size of work-place administration, and problems peculiar to particular firms were listed. As the most important and urgent tasks of the National Co-ordinating Commission, actions aiming at fulfilling agreements with state authorities, economic reform, and improvement of food provision were listed, and for the regional authorities, food provision and defence against unemployment.

# 8

# *Union Democracy in Action:*
# *A Meeting*

The Union meeting is only one way in which a legitimate
opposition can get a hearing from the rank and file.

Lipset, Trow, and Coleman, Union Democracy

The purpose of this chapter is to look more closely into the procedural democracy practised by Solidarity as it emerged in 1980.
Though such organizational rules are defined at the macro-level,
the debate about democracy within the organization resulted
from the experience of individuals in the concrete situations of
elections, ballots, meetings, debates, and the like. It seems obvious, therefore, that however carefully we study the various rules,
and practices, at the institutionalized level, this cannot be
divorced from observation of the organization as it evolves day by
day. Classic work on union democracy touches on this question,
but only briefly. The vivid atmosphere at local meetings in the
context of the two-party politics of the American ITU (Independent Typesetters Union) is compared with the less-appealing
atmosphere within the other unions.[1] In the case of Solidarity,
the role of meetings in a democracy was widely acknowledge
from the beginning, and sociologists were busy preparing helpful
hints.[2] But apart from the thousands of union meetings held at
the local or regional level, the union meeting in 1980 was an
exercise in democracy at the national level also. There was no
freely elected parliament at that time. The Seym continued in its
previous form though the debates were more heated. In fact, only
three or four of the hundreds of representatives were in any way
close to the opposition, and to the mood of the nation. The

[1] Seymour Martin Lipset, Martin Trow, and James Coleman, *Union Democracy*
(Glencoe, Ill., 1956), sub-chapter 'Union Meetings' in chap. 13.
[2] Jolanta Babiuch *et al.*, *Jak prowadzić zebranie* (Warsaw, 1981).

debate over national policies was, therefore, going on in two
opposed and separate political camps. The meetings of the
National Co-ordinating Commission were a counterpart to the
plenary meetings of the Central Committee of the Communist
Polish United Workers Party. The performance of the one was
judged in comparison with the second. This is why the study of
how those meetings were held is an important part of the study of
democracy in action as practised by Poles at that time.[3] From the
volumes of documents on Solidarity that were edited underground by a team headed by Professor Andrzej Paczkowski, let us
take for this purpose unauthorized transcripts of the sometimes
inaudible tapes of the meeting of the National Co-ordinating
Commission on 23 and 24 March 1981,[4] debating one of the
most important events of that year, namely the beating-up of Jan
Rulewski, the regional leader of Bydgoszcz Solidarity, and
activists of the agrarian movement by police who entered the
premises of the regional council where a delegation from Solidarity invited by Council members was engaged in public discussion. The upheaval that resulted from this incident—three
unionists were beaten—was exacerbated by the overtly menda-
cious reporting of the event in the state-controlled media, and by
Warsaw Treaty military manœuvres held on Polish soil with the
participation of the Treaty Commander-in-Chief, Soviet Marshall Kulikov. This brutal action, held by many to be a provocation, was condemned by the Solidarity leadership on 20 March as
an attack on the union itself, and a strike alert was announced
along with an appeal to postpone actual strikes throughout the
country until the decision by the NCC had been issued. The
country was on the verge of civil strife, and rumours of Soviet
intervention were spreading by word of mouth. Mieczysław
Rakowski, the deputy prime minister, kept referring ominously to
the Warsaw Treaty manœuvres during his meeting with leaders of

[3] The documents of the Solidarity Congress that took place later on 5–10 Sept.
and 26 Sept.–7 Oct. 1981) in Gdansk-Oliwa are less useful sources for our purpose, as being better edited and thus devoid of the details that help to reconstruct
the micro-sociology of the meeting; cf. *The Solidarity Congress, 1981, The Great
Debate*, ed., trans. and introduced by George Sanford (Houndmills, 1990).

[4] *Posiedzenie Krajowej Komisji Porozumiewawczej NSZZ Solidarność 23–24 marca
1081 r.*, Archiwum 'Solidarność', Seria: Dokumenty (Warsaw, 1986). Henceforth
referred to as 'Transcript'. The translations are as literal as possible, preserving
important shades of meaning in Polish, even at the cost of some awkwardness in
the English expressions.

the union. This was the atmosphere in which the two-day meeting of the NCC was held, ending with what was generally described as a compromise. The Bydgoszcz affair, as it was called, was the first confrontation of such a size between the Communist power structure and the independent social movement, and has been recalled many times since then for various purposes, one of which, the debate on the state of democracy within the union itself, is our concern here.

At the meeting itself the majority was in favour of a general strike of indeterminate length, starting on 27 March. The idea of a general strike was permanently present throughout the early 1980s, and several teams were busy preparing the technical details. It was widely assumed that such a strike (excepting food stores, health services, railroads, gas and electric works, and oil- and gas-pipelines) would put an end to effective Communist rule in the country and would thus amount to a declaration of civil war, or rather, as it was felt, of national independence. Lech Wałęsa, following his inconclusive tête-à-tête with General Jaruzelski (then prime minister) and his political advisors Tadeusz Mazowiecki, Bronisław Geremek, Jan Olszewski, Władysław Siła-Nowicki, and Jacek Kuroń defended the compromise solution, throwing all their authority into the balance.[5] Finally, the Commission, by a majority vote, adopted the Walesa proposal to conduct a four-hour warning strike on 27 March, then to recommend negotiations with the government and, if they failed to produce results, to start the general strike on 1 April.

However fascinating for contemporaries and for historians the political substance of this meeting may be, we need to leave it aside for this discussion. Our concern here is with the collective activity which can be interpreted in terms of procedural democracy or the lack of it. There is, of course, a problem of boundaries. A meeting does not start whenever people meet; it has an arbitrarily set beginning, if not an end. There is usually some agreed definition of those limits. In our case this was not problematic, as the meeting had already been advertised in a

---

[5] This aspect of the meeting has been described in J. Kurczewski, 'Between Power and Wisdom: The Role of the Expert in Contemporary Polish History', in A. Montefiore and I. Maclean, *Political Responsibility of Intellectuals* (Cambridge, 1990).

memorandum issued by the acting board (Prezydium in Polish) of the NCC on 22 March and agreed by national and Bydgoszcz union leaders at their meeting on 20 March. The meeting was due to begin at 4 p.m. in the regional union headquarters but started one hour late due to overcrowding, as more than one representative from each region came. Forty-two mandated delegates took part, and several advisors, as well as members of the boards from the Gdansk region, the Gdansk Lenin Shipyard chapter, the Bydgoszcz region, and the Bydgoszcz railways chapter that had hosted the National Co-ordinating Commission. Altogether a hundred people took part in the meeting, while up to four thousand people listened to the proceedings through the local amplification system outside the building. On the first day dozens of journalists were allowed in the meeting room or in the next room where permanent transmission was given, while on the second day only the union press was allowed in. The whole thing started at 5 p.m. and ended at 8 p.m. the next day, with breaks between 9.30 and 10 p.m. on the first day and 3 a.m. to noon, on the second day, altogether about seventeen-and-a-half hours. Detailed transcripts, though with some unreadable and inaudible parts,[6] are available for the first part of the proceedings. The meeting was run as usual by the secretary Mr Andrzej Celiński, who later rotated this task with Ryszard Kalinowski and Bogdan Lis. It opened with a short discussion on the order of proceedings as proposed by the Board of the NCC and accepted by the majority: (1) the demands of Bydgoszcz Solidarity region and the state of talks in Bydgoszcz; (2) the situation of the farmers who were occupying a part of the Bydgoszcz Agrarian Movement headquarters and who were supported by Solidarity in Bydgoszcz; (3) a briefing on talks held in Warsaw to prepare for talks here in Bydgoszcz; and (4) decisions that, under given circumstances, should be taken by the Union. Then a series of questions posed by the representative of other regions was answered by those who themselves took part in the events. This ended in agreement, to quote from the transcripts:

ANDRZEJ SOBIERAJ (*Radom*): Just a moment, but at this moment I'd like to ask [ . . .]?

---

[6] All citations from the transcript are translated as literally as possible. The author's notes and comments are always within square brackets.

ANDRZEJ CELIŃSKI (*chairman*): I'm sorry, Adam Niezgoda is willing to introduce the procedural motion, so I need to . . .

A. SOBIERAJ: Just a moment, but this is related.

A. CELIŃSKI: I'm sorry, if there is a procedural motion on the order of proceedings I must give the floor to the procedural motion on the order of proceedings.

ADAM NIEZGODA (*Zielona Gora*): Ladies and Gentlemen,[7] what are we discussing today? Our representatives from an organization of nine or ten million have been invited to a session of the provincial People's Council in a manner [*noise*]. Just a moment please. From the discussion, from the documents and from what we have heard it looks like open provocation, and while we investigate the details we'll get lost in them, and we'll never know, let us finish the discussion!

A. CELIŃSKI: I understand that if . . . I understand the procedural motion is for ending questions about the matter, yes? Questions or discussion?

A. NIEZGODA: Questions, questions.

A. CELIŃSKI: So, the procedural motion to end questions. I need to put this motion to the vote of members of the National Commission. Who is in favour of the motion, please raise your hand. We vote with mandates. One, two, twelve, eighteen. Eighteen for. Who is against finishing the questions on the matter? One, two [*counting*] fifteen. Eighteen persons were for stopping the questioning, fifteen for completing it. Therefore,

---

[7] The Polish form *Państwo* that was used at the Union meetings is a ceremonial plural for both female and male, and in this it is equal to another form, *Panie i Panowie*, also used, though more ceremonial and thus more rare. I render both forms as 'Ladies and Gentlemen', though this is the literal equivalent only of the latter form. It makes sense, as at least one participant in the meeting was female, Ms Elżbieta Petrykus, representing the Koszalin region in the NCC. I also render *Pan* as 'Sir' when used as a form of direct address, and as 'Mr So-and-So' when used as a referential. The female equivalent would be *Pani*, rendered by 'Lady' and 'Ms' respectively. All these minutiae are important if only because they were important for the people involved. These forms belong to the traditional Polish manner of address, and were not in use in the official language, that is, on television, in the press, within the Communist party (where one used *Towarzyszu* or *Towarzyszko*—'Comrade' plus a second-person plural form), official unions (*Kolego* and *Koleżanko*—'colleague'), or on public occasions for non-party members where *Obywatelu* and *Obywatelko* ('Citizen') were the only forms accepted. Readers of the Transcript will soon realize that in practice two styles of formal address were used (but Party members, even if in Solidarity, would not address each other as 'comrades'), along with an informal one, amounting to calling people by their first (if acquainted) or last names.

well, this is not important we will end questions. There is time for discussion only on this matter and possibly comments. Members of the National Commission who want to take the floor are asked to raise their hands. Just this once the other side of the (room) will be given the floor. Please raise hands. Please, Mister in the white shirt on that side, you first.[8]

The debate followed, but the task of the chairman was not always so easy. The next speaker raised a point of fact, and immediately became *primus inter pares* in this body. Lech Wałęsa put in his contribution although it was not his turn, nor was he addressed directly. The chairman reminded everybody about taking turns for the floor but after a while another delegate, Professor Karol Modzelewski, made use of the procedure to make a direct political appeal:

A. CELIŃSKI (*chairman*): Karol Modzelewski wishes to speak on a procedural matter, I emphasized on a procedural matter.
KAROL MODZELEWSKI: I propose that such things should not be done because the time for fighting with paper is over [*applause*].
VOICE FROM THE ROOM: Exactly that![9]

One cannot refrain from reflecting on such an abuse of the declared procedural motion, that through it Professor Modzelewski cut through the debate to the heart of the matter. His statement was obviously meant to set out the radical point of view to help the toughest policy to be adopted. As any participant in formalized debate (such as the one that was taking place on that anxious day in March 1981 in Bydgoszcz) would know, procedural motions are given priority and, in this way, even if postponed may influence the further course of proceedings. At the same time, Ryszard Ornoch from another region put forward the motion that would condemn the Bydgoszcz incident, though, as if meant as a contrast, it was not introduced as a procedural motion. One should add, in this context, that in Polish culture the whole concept of seconding a motion, so obvious to an Anglo-Saxon reader, is missing, and the introduction of it through a declaration: 'To suggest we put the motion to the vote if someone else supports it!' would cause a rebellion amongst

[8] 'Transcript', 14.        [9] 'Transcript', 15.

those assembled. I did not introduce it myself into a brochure on how to run meetings[10] which I helped to prepare for Solidarity members in 1981 simply because, though knowing it, I had not paid attention to it. When I tried half-heartedly to introduce it later, in the academic context, it was never taken seriously. Upon reflection I think that this derives from a different concept of procedural democracy. The devil is in the details. Polish understanding of democracy was as procedural as the Anglo-Saxon, but more individualistic. It would be thought contrary to individual rights of expression to impose such a limit. Despite some historical discontinuity, this can be traced far back into Polish political history, with its stress on the principle of consensus and its corollary, the *liberum veto*, which gave the single individual a right to veto parliamentary decisions of major substance.

Another typical issue for any meeting is that of keeping to the purpose of the meeting. This divides into two issues: keeping to the substantive agenda of the meeting; and even more important, maintaining the power structure of the meeting. These decisions may seem purely procedural but are in fact substantial, as the boundaries of the 'matter at issue' are to be decided arbitrarily, the only remaining problem being who makes those decisions and how. Let us follow the meeting into the next exchange. All this so far relates to the first of four points on the agenda—discussion of the demands of the Bydgozcz regional Solidarity chapter—which arose when Edward Strzyżewski from the neighbouring Toruń chapter described in detail aggressive police and security monitoring of the union there, supposedly because of the initiative for co-operation with Bydgoszcz and other adjacent regional chapters. Celiński broke in:

A. CELIŃSKI (*chairman*): I'd like to ask you to take a stand on the Bydgoszcz affair.

E. STRZYŻEWSKI: This is the Bydgoszcz affair, I have put it clearly.

A. CELIŃSKI: [inaudible].

E. STRZYŻEWSKI: I have spoken clearly and so please do not interfere, Mr Chairman.

A. CELIŃSKI: I am entitled to interfere, I'm afraid. Please [ . . . ], I don't interfere [ . . . ], please address the Bydgoszcz affair.

---

[10] Babiuch *et al.*, *Jak prowadzić zebranie.*

E. STRZYŻEWSKI: I am already addressing it [He then argues for a short while that there is a direct link between what happened in both regions.][11]

It is obvious when read afterwards that the intervention by Mr Strzyżewski was linked directly with the Bydgoszcz affair, but it is also obvious that it could have developed in another direction, judging from the content, until the chairman's intervention. Moreover, if we look into the wording of the agenda, it is problematic whether the whole discussion, and not only the Toruń detour, is related to the demands of the Bydgoszcz chapter. This is one of those cases where the arbitrary nature of the decisions made is clear. This is also one of those nice cases where cause-and-effect appear heavily dependent upon interpretation, and also upon the time and individual perspective of the interpreter. From one point of view the chairman interrupted the line of argument; from another, he caused the speaker to change one line for another, i.e. the Toruń story gave place to the Bydgoszcz story. In fact, nobody can establish which of those two interpretations is more valid. If we were able to ask the actors, they would also have to answer after the event. No fresh and innocent interpretations would be available. Another point is, however, indisputable, that is, that the chairman reaffirmed his authority over the debate, as the grounds for his intervention but not his power to intervene were contested. It may be noted, by the way, that this exchange was soon followed by closing of the discussion on the first point of the agenda, a discussion which had taken up 19 per cent of the first day. A causal link between the two events may impress itself upon a reader, but remains open to interpretation.

The second point of the agenda, presentation of the demands of the independent private farmers Solidarity organization, began with an incident that once again highlights the negotiable character of the structure of the proceedings. Antoni Tokarczuk was invited to present those demands. His speech was, however, interrupted several times by noise in the room so that the chairman felt obliged to invoke his authority and to subdue the level of noise and free movement. At the end of a long summary of the issue the following conversation was recorded:

---

[11] 'Transcript', 17.

A. TOKARCZUK: [. . .] And that would be that, from the developments.

UNRECOGNIZED VOICE: [information is given that the farmers themselves are present and may answer additional questions]

A. TOKARCZUK (?): Please.

A. CELIŃSKI *chairman*): I'm sorry, but is that the end of your presentation?

A. TOKARCZUK: In fact [. . .] I'd like to recommend, that it would be best, because there was a motion for supplementary interventions. [He himself furnishes additional information].

KRZYSZTOF GOTOWSKI: [Gives additional information too.]

A. CELIŃSKI: Have you finished the presentation of the matter at this moment or not? Because it is not clear.

UNRECOGNIZED VOICE: So much, that is . . . but I'd recommend that the colleague president [of the farmers' union] should add something.

A. CELIŃSKI: [. . .] information?

UNRECOGNIZED VOICE: Of course.

A. CELIŃSKI: Please.

Roman Bartoszcze from the farmers union starts the next lengthy presentation at the end of which the chairman asks again: 'Thank you very much. Now I . . . that presentation is completed, yes? On that matter. Questions, therefore, if there are any.'[12] The discussion of this point of the agenda took about 16 per cent of the transcript.

As the third point, the current state of talks with the government was reviewed, with a detailed introduction from a second-rank leader from Szczecin, Marian Jurczyk. This is a very important moment: the leaders of Solidarity give a public account of their negotiations with enemy. The opening sentence clearly indicates how tense the atmosphere was and how relations between the two structures were regarded with suspicion: one being the links between all parts of Solidarity as represented in the National Co-ordinating Commission, and the second, the link between the leading team of union representatives and the Communist government. One should consider the fact that it was Jurczyk, and not Wałęsa himself, who gave an account of the talks as meaningful too. A presentation by Jurczyk might have been

---

[12] 'Transcript', 22 and 25.

interpreted as 'objective'. Such a meaning can be construed only if there is a serious possibility of bias on behalf of the leader, or if there is serious suspicion that such a possibility is considered by the audience.

M. JURCZYK: Colleagues, I'll begin perhaps by saying that I have nothing to hide. I will convey to you, ladies and gentlemen, the content of the talks according to my conscience; that means whatever was talked about. At the same time I'm asking Colleague Tokarczuk from Bydgoszcz, as a colleague who was with us, to pay attention now to my words. If I forget something, and this is certainly possible, I'd like to ask my colleague to supplement my contribution afterwards.[13]

Jurczyk's reference to his conscience sounds to an outsider like a mechanism to avoid possible suspicion. But if someone stresses his or her conscience, the hidden meaning is also that someone else's conscience may be not so clean. Jurczyk calls Tokarczuk as a witness and thus a moral guardian for himself only. Wałęsa is not mentioned at all, so whatever is said by Jurczyk will not cleanse Wałęsa's conscience, if it is unclean. In this way Jurczyk, though speaking on behalf of the whole delegation in talks with government, in fact speaks only for himself. It is stressed that he is not there, in another structure, but that he remains with those assembled here. No wonder that after his presentation, supplemented by some recollections from Tokarczuk, the basic question troubling by the audience is posed first:

A. CELIŃSKI (Chairman): Thank you. Any questions concerning the talks?

VOICE FROM THE ROOM: What did Wałęsa say?[14]

[Wałęsa enters and tells the story from his side. This is understandable, as Jurczyk has explicitly left space for it.]

M. JURCZYK: [. . .] Leszek Wałęsa[15] took the floor first. I will not talk about what Leszek said under the circumstances [it was] very tough, Leszek's intervention was very resolute. After

---

[13] 'Transcript', 36.        [14] 'Transcript', 40.

[15] In Polish you use a diminutive in order to express, among other things, affection. When applied to first names, a form like 'Leszek', the diminutive of 'Lech', indicates close friendship. Its use by Jurczyk is notable in the present context.

Leszek's intervention I took the floor next [*he continues with the presentation of his speech*].[16]

From this reference, it seems that Jurczyk, while dissociating himself from the union–government talk-structure, is not willing to attack Wałęsa. Not a word of criticism is passed. On the contrary, there is open praise of the leader that, of course, can also be interpreted as a sign of objectivism and therefore an instrument for distancing oneself from the critical object. Such distancing also allows Jurczyk to present the official view of both leaders—in fact, we know that these two were to compete for the post of president of Solidarity at the Union Congress in Autumn of 1981.

M. JURCZYK: [. . .] As Andrzej Celiński already said at the beginning, this meeting [with the government] ended with a fiasco. Nothing was agreed, nothing was arranged. We thought as Leszek already said today, that four people from the Board[17] . . . we did not have any right to take any decision, this would not be in accordance with the Charter. These are very serious matters, Ladies and Gentlemen, you know yourselves that the tremendous responsibility for the whole of Poland cannot be put upon those four persons alone. We have decided to follow emergency procedures and call an extraordinary meeting of the NCC today and I hold that you should take the appropriate stand today.[18]

But for the singular 'I', this could be read as a joint communiqué by all four members of the delegation, presented by Jurczyk to make it safer from the suspicions of the remaining members of the National Co-ordinating Commission. In fact both ways of reading the text are equally plausible and not only do not exclude, but, as these small inconsistencies such as inserting an egocentric 'I' in the collective message suggest, rather complement each other.

After the initial discussion of the Bydgoszcz events this

---

[17] Those four being Lech Wałęsa, Marian Jurczyk, Andrzej Celiński, and Zbigniew Bujak, accompanied by two advisors Tadeusz Mazowiecki and Władysław Siła-Nowicki and three union representatives from Bydgoszcz, among whom was Antoni Tokarczuk.
[18] 'Transcript', 39.

communiqué comes to define the matter. It is understood that subsequent debate should revolve around this statement. For our purpose it may define the meeting as a model exercise in democracy: it is up to the people to decide. Moreover, it demonstrates democracy under the rule of law. Jurczyk cites the Solidarity Charter that forbade the Board to make decisions of the kind.[19] Once Wałęsa enters, however, the centre of gravity moves for the third time. In his speech he moves from reporting what he has said during talks with the government, to an account of the talks, to the political stand he favours. In his typical elliptical style,[20] with jumps, elaborations, and ambiguities, Wałęsa ends up with the suggestion that even if the reliability of the Communists is dubious, one needs to assume reliability in political action or, if not, the power must be taken directly. In the context of what happened nine months after this speech this sounds impressive once the meaning is attached to the text:

L. WAŁĘSA: [. . .] And now, considering things reasonably I don't say withdrawal! I don't say: no pressure. But at the same time I say, in a tight corner, that some rules of the game are to be kept. And therefore, if we look at it this way, General Jaruzelski in my opinion is unable to do anything unless we as Solidarity say this or that. He is unable to do any thing reasonable. So I come to that . . .

VOICE FROM THE ROOM: [inaudible].

L. WAŁĘSA: Right. No, I am in agreement with you, of course, they have abused, abused . . . But to someone we will declare

---

[19] Art. 19: '(1) Within a scope of the National Commission is (i) representation of the whole union before authorities and agencies of the state and economic administration and other organizations and institutions; (ii) co-ordination of the regional union organizations; (iii) budgetary decisions; (iv) setting forth principles of creation of branch and trade sections; (v) entering collective contracts; (vi) election of the president of the National Commission and members of the Board. (2) The Board monitors execution of the decisions of the National Commission, directs the office, and performs legal actions.' (Charter as before the 1981 Congress according to 'Transcript', pp. xviii–xix.)

[20] On that subject see the elaborate though partisan analysis by Marek Czyzewski and Sergiusz Kowalski made during the presidential campaign of 1990, 'On the Rhetoric of Wałęsa', where they conclude that: 'According to pragmatic criteria of political discourse the way in which Wałęsa communicates with society turns out to be consistent, efficient, and effective. At this level the logical contradictions lose their relevance: opinions, mutually exclusive otherwise, operate at different levels, serve other purposes, are stated in different contexts' (personal communication).

selves, to someone from out there, or from here. To someone
or to ourselves. Or to me as a president. Of course, I don't
accept, no, I have enough. Thank you.[21]

Speakers who use blank space so that anybody can insert any
meaning he wishes are successful in politics, though this is not a
technique to use without restraint and reason. In fact, the reader
should take into account here the high probability that the participants in the meeting easily understood what was not explicitly
said in this passage. The Warsaw Treaty armies under Soviet
command were on manœuvres on Polish soil. The mysterious
'out there' could (I repeat, *could*) refer to the Soviets and the possibility of indirect negotiation with the Kremlin itself, while 'here'
refers to Jaruzelski as the local, Polish Communist, dealing with
whom is an alternative. Either Solidarity was to take full political
responsibility for the nation, or choose between deals with either
Polish or Soviet politicians. Wałęsa envisages all options at once,
but the first, with himself as President of Poland (no such constitutional office had then been re-established), is rejected. So, however dubious the reliability of the other side, the negotiations are
to be continued. Some minutes later he will speak for the four-
hour warning strike, a pressure, but by no means a withdrawal by
Solidarity. The deputy prime minister, by his rejection of Solidarity complaints about the Bydgoszcz events, had blackmailed
Solidarity into the choice of either seizing power or withdrawal.
The brutal police attack which the government was not willing to
condemn was the instrument of this blackmail. By this action the
government seems to imply clearly that it is unreliable, that Solidarity cannot be negotiated with, but must simply fight or surrender. Wałęsa sketches a way out of this dilemma by not accepting
a definition of the enemy as unreliable. This is the third interpretation of the problem that this meeting is presented with, but this
definition is superimposed upon the one given by Jurczyk, as it
includes the same starting-point, that is, the demand resulting
from the Bydgoszcz events and the peasants' demands around
which those events started. The meeting until now seemed to
consist of the natural meandering by which the consecutive
speakers generalized the issue, up to the point made by Wałęsa.
But then, suddenly, another line opens up, a line that is germane

[21] 'Transcript', 43.

to our topic here, as the meeting is now not only an exercise in democracy but is also about democracy as Jurczyk had already suggested. His statement of the problem was as ambiguous as his way of speaking. The meeting cannot be understood if the Bydgoszcz affair is used as the only interpretative key. The final 'thank you' by Wałęsa as the ritual ending of the speech provides a very instructive display of his art of polysemiosis and may be taken to show both his unwillingness to take on the burden of presidency, while at the same time, indicating that such a possibility is under consideration. The last reading is suggested by the representative of a Silesian Bytom region when he exclaims (and because of the polysemiosis, we even don't know whether it is invocation or interruption): 'Wait a moment, please [. . .]', and asks for information on the talks held between Wałęsa and General Jaruzelski on 10 March 1981.[22] From the heat of the moment that can be felt even now on reading the transcripts of the meeting after Wałęsa enters the debate, it is evident that something is being hidden. Cierniewski brings back the expectations that were linked with those close talks. In the light of what was to happen on 13 December 1981, the introduction of martial law and non-violent resistance, it is all the more important to note those expectations.

A. CIERNIEWSKI: Wait a moment, please. There is a certain problem here linked with your intervention. The talks that the National Commission in a certain sense charged you with, and in so far as I remember [charged you], were to be held with Mr Jaruzelski in person. There were great, immense hopes, hidden or, shall we say, unexpressed, both in the nation and amongst our membership. First, because he is a general, second, because this is a historical moment and third, because it is said that he is a strong man. All this when things are so murky [around] and counted only on that . . . Lech, do you hear me? In a word, you were to have had talks with Jaruzelski. Can you tell us . . . whether Jaruzelski had talked with his deputy [Rakowski, who had met the official Solidarity delegation after the Bydgoszcz incident] and why those talks were held with Rakowski and not with Jaruzelski. It is vital that you explain to us those two issues, those two questions.[23]

---

[22] 'Transcript', 43–4.     [23] 'Transcript', 44.

At this stage the point on the agenda is no longer being redefined but a new item has emerged and the dispute has been redefined. It no longer matters what happened in Bydgoszcz, or how the government reacted to Solidarity complaints. Now what matters is the content of the private talks between Wałęsa and Jaruzelski. Wałęsa's power lies not only in the elected leadership, but also in his monopoly over important information. In fact, the information might not be so important if it was to be revealed, but it will never be known whether it has been fully revealed, and the privacy of the talks and the resulting monopoly is an important political fact. As a comment, we may note that it is a monopoly even if two men were involved, and perhaps also some clerks or servants with coffee, even though translators were not necessary as often happens in important international meetings of statesmen. Even if one of those involved pretends that the full content was revealed, there is always the possibility of challenge by the second; even if they make a statement together, there is the possibility that in future one will present it differently. Those private meetings, therefore, give each of the participants a monopoly over the contents, but it is a relative monopoly, as it is established not only towards those not having access to information but also towards another participant. Joint ownership of the information would fit the situation better, and this why such intimacy is both profitable and dangerous for politicians to share. Wałęsa entered the intimacy of ultimate power on 10 March, and now nothing can enable him to leave it behind. Whatever he will tell, there will always remain the suspicion that something could have been hidden. In this context one often sees repeated, even at the most sophisticated level of the professoriat of which the Advisory Council of the CCN was mostly composed, demands for full openness of negotiations and no secret diplomacy (as in Russia in 1918).

It is interesting how Wałęsa deals with the problem. At first he answers Cierniewski by telling why Jaruzelski himself could not see him and why the talks as such, even with the deputy prime minister Rakowski were important:

L. WAŁĘSA: First, the general-prime minister was on [Warsaw Treaty military] exercises. Second, in Bydgoszcz the temperature was so high, as the Board was sitting, and we have achieved nothing and only the main issue was that Bydgoszcz people should start for these. Third, I did say often: I will do everything, even without asking, in order to serve this union. And therefore, I will not, of course, undertake any decision that will not be agreed upon but I shall attempt a meeting in which something will be achieved. Here the moment of the talks was important.

One may note another dilemma. On this occasion Wałęsa expresses himself by making seemingly contradictory statements about decision-making. But this is exactly the problem that each democratic leader faces: what is assumed to be his duty, to actively pursue organizational goals, and what is to be agreed upon directly with the constituency. Whether to ask before acting, or to act when there is a chance to act. In choosing the first, the leader risks being ineffective, or at least seen as ineffective; to choose the second risks the accusation, more and more well-grounded, of authoritarian proclivities. There is no way out of this dilemma, unless we go back to ancient procedures of electing short-term dictators who are forced to go into exile after serving their term. But let us return to the real question that remained unanswered, even if it seems that Wałęsa has given an answer to the explicit questions posed. He is reminded, and this becomes a democratic ordeal for the leader:

A. CIERNIEWSKI: Lech, you do not understand. I am not attacking you. [First, this is typical polemics; secondly, it should read: 'I am attacking you on another point.'] Simply, we are still concerned about the question whether you have talked with General Jaruzelski and if so, what have you agreed upon. So, this is a detailed question.

L. WAŁĘSA: Everybody know that I had talks earlier, and therefore . . . [*noise*] What is it? The briefing was given [by Wałęsa on NCC meeting on 12 March]. Today I don't remember, so many things happened, so many nights without sleep. Did I sleep yesterday? And . . . I didn't sleep.

PATRYCJUSZ KOSMOWSKI (*Bielsko-Biała*): Leszek, there was a communiqué to appear. It has not appeared. Let us say, my MKZ [*regional body*] doesn't know anything about your talks with Jaruzelski. We would like to know.

A. CIERNIEWSKI: Lech, this is really not an attack upon you.

P. KOSMOWSKI: Enough secrets?[24]

If it might be thought that my interpretation of Mr Cierniewski's question is unfair, the last intervention by Mr Kosmowski makes clear what the message was. I do not suggest that Cierniewski was not sincerely interested in the content of the talks, or even that he might have been of the opinion that the secrecy of such talks should be accepted. The interpretation one gives in such a study should not be mistaken for the reconstruction of the real motives, as such a reconstruction of subjectivity is always hypothetical, and independent of what was really felt. If I am told by a confessor or analyst that an act of mine resulted from hostility I have not felt, I may still be convinced that this is a plausible interpretation of what happened. A good subjective interpretation is the one that Mr Cierniewski or Mr Wałęsa would agree on as convincing, but we are in no position now to carry out interpretative co-analysis, nor confession. The validity of interpretation must remain open to the doubts of a reader. Let me add here that I understand the analytical task here as concerned with the interaction. The interpretation aims to make the statements meaningful in the context of the meeting, the collective interaction game played by those who met in the crowded room of the Bydgoszcz railway workers Solidarity shop on 23 March 1981.

Wałęsa says that he has decided to reveal everything, to disclose the secret of the talks:

L. WAŁĘSA: No, there are no secrets. Don't play the fool, man, be serious. At first, even if you were a gentleman, what is said should not be made public, if you would understand. But I will say more because I don't risk anything now. So I may say more. Of course, we have considered all the possibilities with friends, with enemies and other matters [. . .][25]

And he goes on to say that apart from the possibility of Soviet intervention, which is suggested by the last words, they have also discussed the fact that none of them has enough power fully to control their constituencies; that is, Jaruzelski has no more hold over the Communist Party ruling apparatus than Wałęsa, or the

---

[24] 'Transcript', 44–5.      [25] 'Transcript', 45.

whole NCC has over the union. It must be said at this point that the tension might have resulted from some misunderstanding, though it would be stupid not to observe that misunderstandings result from the tension. Cierniewski might very well not know about the talks, or rather, as he corrected himself, his region did not know. This is a very important point on which we need to dwell. Participants in the meeting are not private individuals, they represent their regions and they need to report before their respective regional constituencies. The remark made earlier by Cierniewski, that he is sorry that his region does not know the content of the talks, is to be read then as a reminder to Wałęsa that even if, in his capacity as a private individual or even as a member of the National Co-ordinating Commission present at the Meeting on 12 March, Cierniewski knows about the talks, he does not know about the talks 'as region', as his region does not know. Therefore he asks here for information as a representative of the region and not as Mr Cierniewski or as a member of the NCC. Then another discussant makes the following lapse.

RYSZARD SAWICKI (*Lubin*): Leszek, I've got a question. In the context of yesterday, talks with Jaruzelski, yesterdays talks . . .

L. WAŁĘSA: There were no talks with Jaruzelski yesterday!

R. SAWICKI: Yesterday's talks with Rakowski [. . .] [This may be attributed either to a genuine slip of the tongue or be taken as a manifestation of the general disorientation prevailing in the room.]

L. WAŁĘSA: [. . .] Other matters. Please? [NB This 'Please' means that Wałęsa has appropriated the role of the chairman for himself, and Celiński has been temporarily ousted, an event in line with previous interventions by Walesa jumping the queue for turns. A Voice from the room then proposes a break, and confidentiality of proceedings after the break.][26]

But Wałęsa is against confidentiality, arguing that the press is important to disseminate the balanced and pragmatic opinion of the Commission. This is very wise, and shows that Wałęsa is able to see the whole meeting as an element in the political struggle, not only the final outcome of the meeting in the form of the decisions. On the other hand, this rejection of confidentiality serves

[26] 'Transcript', 46.

another function as well: it strengthens Wałęsa's message that nothing has been hidden, a message already dramatically reinforced by the rejection of rules of gentlemanly conduct. It is also important to note that a motion to close the meeting to the press would move the secrecy from the Wałęsa–Jaruzelski talks to the NCC meeting itself, something that happened on some occasions and gave the regional representatives a feeling of power over their constituency, while at the same time it was not themselves but their colleagues, the Commission as such, that could be blamed. We can see how the issue of 'closed' versus 'open' is played. In the first part of the meeting, it was government–Solidarity talks that were to be opened. Then suddenly the problem of closedness lies somewhere else, in the earlier talks between Wałęsa and Jaruzelski. This could, however, be overcome if a new border was to be delineated which would include Wałęsa, representatives of the NCC, and of the Commission altogether. The motion to close the meeting to the press is a peace-offering to Wałęsa and an initiative to recreate the original equality within the body. Is not this why Wałęsa rejects the motion? By telling everything he thinks he has already cleansed himself, since acting at that moment in a collective conspiracy would dissolve his political uniqueness. He surrendered his monopoly of information in order not to surrender his individual power.

After a meandering discussion on the political situation in the country, the break comes. When the meeting resumes, and it is well understood that the meeting is both surrounded by 'unofficial' talks whispered in the room or developed freely outside, and divided by such 'free talk' that continues during the break, the technical reality of the confidentiality issue comes to the fore:

E. STRZYŻEWSKI: [Inaudible, but in the footnote by the editors we read: 'He puts forward a motion to allow in all the press, including the official and the foreign.']

A. CELIŃSKI (chairman): Is any journalist not allowed in?

A. NIEZGODA: Let him say himself [*sic*].

A. CELIŃSKI: If it comes out that there is a journalist who has not been allowed in, if you know that a journalist has not been allowed in, then a motion could be put to the ballot.

K. MODZELEWSKI: My proposal is: if there are already journalists in the room do not throw them out as that would be a waste of time. The door was closed because [if] tapes from our meeting are passed over to the Security Service[27] [tapes] of the Security Service cannot be used legally in the press for propaganda. If, however, the press is present in the room, anything, any 'words and music' could be made up.[28] Perhaps it is not so important. If the press is already in the room I propose not to throw them out now. What do you think, ladies and gentlemen, may we vote on that?

A. CELIŃSKI: Do you want to vote on allowing the press to stay in the room?

A. NIEZGODA: All right, let us vote.[29]

The press was allowed in. I wanted to cite this part of the transcript in full to make a further point about secrecy and confidentiality. If the Commission declares its proceedings closed to the press it would not mean that no press at all is allowed in. In fact, it seems that secrecy here means cutting contact with Communist power. A secret meeting of the Commission is the one about which the Communists, the enemy, is not informed. It does not follow from that that the membership of the union is uninformed. This is of course the theory, as it would not be possible to follow this rule to the letter: first, because some members of Solidarity, even of the Commission, were themselves members of the Communist party, though not the 'Communist power'; secondly, because nobody would assume (and this was clear in Professor Modzelewski's statement), that the Communist powers would not know through bugging what was said at the meeting. The real secrets were handed over, as I witnessed, in private between two or three people in the rest-room, and certainly not said aloud in public. The meeting of the Commission is public even if closed; it is not hidden from the union membership. Paradoxically, how-

[27] The Security Service, known also under its Polish acronym SB, was the name of secret political police with a commander in the rank of general of the Ministry of Interior (MSW), that included also the special army units and ordinary police called the Civic Militia (MO), supplemented by mobile strike anti-riot forces (ZOMO) and voluntary national police reserve (ORMO) plus firemen.

[28] Wrong. Fictional recordings like those he envisages were made and distributed over official radio and television just before the introduction of martial law in December 1981, even though the meeting of the Commission was closed. One should observe that at closed meetings the 'Solidarity' press, not subject to the Union censorship, was present.

[29] 'Transcript', 52–3.

ever, such a decision was leading to the situation in which the Commission's proceedings were known to the Communist authorities but not to the Solidarity membership, that is just the opposite to the reason given as justification. This may illuminate Professor Modzelewski's sudden inconsistency and flexibility on the issue. It may also help us to understand better the reasons for Wałęsa's reaction to the demand for confidentiality.

In the meantime, after the break the representatives started to present the standpoints of their particular regions. This marks the official beginning of collective decision-making.

This presentation, occupying roughly 11 per cent of the recorded text, unfolds in three stages. First, a regional representative makes a statement, then the debate on secrecy emerges immediately after the first voice from the floor unabashedly asks for speed,[30] after which the second, third, fourth, and fifth representatives speak on behalf of their regions. The statements are long; arguments for postponement of the general strike or for its immediate calling are presented. The badly constructed and unclear moderate stand by one of the delegates provokes a violent reaction from the floor.

M. JURCZYK: Ladies and gentlemen, a procedural motion. There are about sixty persons represented [in] NCC. If each of us reads the decisions of the region we will sit here for four hours. Everybody knows what the situation is in Poland, please stand up and say if a given region is for or against. If yes, then which: strike warning, general or general without warning and vice versa. This should be a decision. Don't be children, like the colleague from Stalowa Wola. I am asking: don't they have there a person who would come up here and put up a problem in a manly way or only like kids. I am sorry for tough words, but there must be order. Thank you [*applause*].[31]

This motion is translated by the chairman into an official one and accepted with a visible majority for, and one vote against. After this decision in the third stage thirty-seven participants briefly present for their regions, though not without some varia-

---

[30] J. Szulc (*Wałbrzych*) asked for short presentations, 'as I don't have time', but the chairman was irresolute: 'I think, as a suggestion. I cannot make a motion . . .' ('Transcript', 52).
[31] 'Transcript', 56.

tions. Some are very fast, while some take longer. We can make a quantitative assessment with help of a word-count for each of the speakers. This should help us in assessing the validity of the common-sense hypothesis about the relationship between the length of a statement and the political significance of the speaker. However, the fact is that there is no way to assess the importance of the speaker independent of the size of the region, and only some approximative information can be given for the majority but not for all of the regions, as presented in Table 8.1.

Looking at the word-count, the uneven distribution of the appetite for rhetoric is observed as expected, but more interestingly, a pattern of pulsation is manifested with several ups and downs alternating. The motion that put an end to unlimited intervention was passed, and the new procedure reduced the average word-count from 302.4 in the first two stages to 53.9, a dramatic result. It is more interesting that Jurczyk's motion limited the substance but not the length, though the length was mentioned as the rationale for the rule. Nevertheless, all this amounts to a good case of how an unquantified rule has resulted in a numerical effect as explicitly expected. How does this work? The ups and downs seem to explain the process. The shortest possible statement is exemplified by the four words of Mr Prajzner: (Białystok): General strike on Friday.'[32] This would in fact have sufficed for everybody, but this was one of the shortest statements. Basically it looks as if those who were speaking after this statement felt obliged to develop the argument, to add weight to it (the weight being shown by the number of words spoken), while those who spoke after the peak of length was attained felt obliged to cut their pronouncements. Here it would be useful to know the amount of unruly behaviour in the meeting, but this was not recorded in the transcripts except for an extraordinary amount recorded in the statements themselves. The relative importance of the speakers being related to the length of intervention is hard to establish, as this seems to be more influenced by the ups and downs that determined the length of speech tolerated. Jurczyk, who initiated the motion, himself uttered 102 words, more than twice the average but certainly not the longest, as he was fifth on that score in the third stage. One should also

---

[32] 'Transcript', 61.

TABLE 8.1. *Length of presentation of regional standpoints*

| Speaker | Region | Word-count | Membership in thousands* |
|---|---|---|---|
| (*Stage 1*) | | | |
| Ornoch | Gorzów | 245 | 120 |
| (*Stage 2*) | | | |
| Strzyżewski | Toruń | 232 | 150 |
| Gotowski | Bydgoszcz | 44 | 280 |
| Krupka | Stalowa Wola | 648 | n.d. |
| Wieczorek | Częstochowa | 343 | 150 |
| (*Stage 3*) | | | |
| Sawicki | Lubin and Głogów | 45 | n.d. |
| Słowik | Łódź | 111 | 460 |
| Sobieraj | Radom | 37 | 110 |
| Kurnatowski | Słupsk | 84 | 80 |
| Cyran | Little Poland | 51 | 640 |
| Jurczyk | Szczecin | 102 | 360 |
| Wach | Tychy | 84 | n.d. |
| Dymarski | Poznań | 49 | 380 |
| Anonymous | Sieradz | 24 | 30 |
| Kopaczewski | Rzeszów | 24 | 200 |
| Lechowski | Olsztyn | 45 | 150 |
| Nowicki | Włocławek | 12 | 70 |
| Wiścicki | Płock | 17 | 100 |
| Kijanka | Przemyśl | 12 | 70 |
| Zawojski | Krosno | 28 | 70 |
| Cierniewski | Bytom | 107 | n.d. |
| Niezgoda | Zielona Góra | 217 | 160 |
| Przydział | Wrocław | 55 | n.d. |
| Chojecki | Leszno | 34 | 40 |
| Prajzner (?) | Białystok | 4 | 110 |
| Śliwa | Kalisz | 15 | 160 |
| Lis | Gdansk | 77 | 530 |
| Petrykus | Koszalin | 45 | 120 |
| Piesiak | Jelenia Góra | 82 | n.d. |
| Rozpłochowski | Katowice | 79 | n.d. |
| Domińczyk | Holy Cross | 32 | 260 |
| Kosmowski | Bielsko-Biała | 17 | 240 |
| Skoczylas | Konin | 4 | 60 |
| Bartczak | Middle East | 32 | 300 |
| Prędki | Opoczno | 10 | 100 |
| Szulc | Wałbrzych | 92 | n.d. |
| Jedynak | Jastrzębie | 24 | n.d. |
| Bujak | Mazovia | 125 | 920 |
| Kalinowski | Elbląg | 69 | 100 |
| Przybylski | Grudziądz | 90 | n.d. |
| Biegalski | Lakes | 45 | 60 |
| Kirsztejn | Opole | 15 | 240 |

*Note*: * As figures are taken from the Summer 1981 pre-Congress campaign only approximate membership could be established, and in several cases due to the mergers no data at all are available.

consider that the order of presentation was not determined, at least according to our knowledge, by the size of region or political influence of the speaker, except for interventions by Wałęsa (others needed to use a procedural motion to jump the queue) and the aggrieved region of Bydgoszcz that served as both host and the party whose wounds were to be healed (as can be seen by the chairman's response to a representative of the Bydgoszcz region: 'I'm sorry, I have been impolite, I should give the floor first to the Bydgoszcz region. Fatigue has its effect. Please, go on.').[33]

The question of order emerged, however, in the most heated exchange of this part of the NCC meeting, when the political advisors of the Union rose to speak. The experts were not members of the NCC, their formal position within the Union was secured through establishing a Consultative-Programme Council of the studies centre affiliated at the National Co-ordinating Commission. In fact only some of the members of the Council were treated as political advisors of the NCC, and expected to appear at its meeting and invited to the delicate talks with the Communist government.

Theoretically, they were seen as continuing the role of the intellectuals who supported and advised the workers on the Baltic Coast in Summer 1980. In practice, neither then nor now was the division so clear. In the room, Professor Karol Modzelewski was a full member of the NCC from Wrocław, while his old friend and political colleague from the revisionist Communist opposition, Jacek Kuroń, was present as an expert. Kuroń (MA, education), could not however take the floor on his own, while Andrzej Celiński (MA, sociology), expelled from the University in 1977 and re-established after 1980, chaired the meeting. Experts were always a scapegoat for the internal politics of the union leaders. They were blamed for a wrong course of action if Walesa himself could not be attacked directly by his competitors for reasons of political expedience. The group as a whole could also delegate moral responsibility for unpopular decisions to the experts. In political games, the unpopular decisions advocated by union leaders were to be supported by the voice of knowledgeable people of the highest moral standing. This was the expected role

[33] 'Transcript', 54.

of the advisors. Not accidently, Zbigniew Bujak from Warsaw, one place where the influence of the intelligentsia was at its greatest, invited the experts to speak:

A. CELIŃSKI (*chairman*): Zbyszek Bujak wants to put the procedural motion [. . .]

Z. BUJAK (*Mazovia*): I'm asking for statements by experts on the proposed deadlines for the strikes. Short. Thank you.

A. CELIŃSKI: I think this is going back as this is not subject to the vote. Unless the National Commission doesn't wish to listen to experts. Therefore I'd like to ask the experts of the National Commission to take the floor. Let the experts themselves decide about who is willing to speak and in what order, only about the deadlines. Bujak's motion was limited to the commentary by experts, or the opinion of experts about the deadlines for the strike.

P. KOSMOWSKI (*M. Engin., Bielsko-Biała*) Procedural motion.

A. CELIŃSKI: [. . .] contrary motion is.

P. KOSMOWSKI: Yes, contrary motion that on the deadlines of the strike and generally, the methods of its execution should be pronounced by those who have led the strikes. Those who have led the strikes can tell most about it, not the experts. There are no experts on strikes.[34]

The dramatic exchange that follows is in fact part of the general turmoil in the discussion. We may point in a more detailed way to what this turmoil consisted of. Several lines of discussion developed simultaneously, that is, they cut across each other. Celiński attempted to put Kosmowski's motion to a show of hands, while one of the experts, Professor Bronisław Geremek, declined the invitation to speak only about the deadline and proposed that experts should take part in the general discussion to follow; and this reminder of the need for general discussion came at the moment when the advocates of the general strike promised to limit the remaining debate to the specification of deadlines; Celiński proposed the break in order to rethink the order of proceedings, but as chairman he felt obliged to postpone voting on this motion and accept a motion from another participant, Jerzy Szulc, who suggested that a small editing group should be set up

[34] 'Transcript', 64–5.

immediately to prepare the document to speed up the proceedings. The way out of this turmoil was found by focusing on the words 'no break'.

A. CELIŃSKI (*chairman*): I understand that this was a motion to open discussion now. Yes?! Do we open discussion or, do we make a break and . . . Good, please. Please take the floor.[35]

The 'discussion' starts, the pros and cons of various decisions to be taken by the NCC are debated by anybody who wishes. In fact, Jerzy Szulc repeats his call for speed and by rejecting the notion of discussion he stresses that he did not want the decision to be debated, as almost all of the speakers were for the general strike. At this moment the issue of experts arose again. Both Wałęsa and Jurczyk stressed the seriousness of the decisions to be taken and requested the opinion of experts.[36] The first expert, Władysław Siła-Nowicki, took the floor:

W. SIŁA-NOWICKI: Ladies and gentlemen, I take the floor on a procedural issue as one of the experts. We know each other from way back. I can take various posts and assume various functions, from the meanest to the higher ones. But I will never be a just a puppet. If all decisions were taken by the union after listening to the opinions of experts, and the most important is to be taken without our voice, I am very sorry but I will bow to the Commission and leave! To be a court-jester—never! Therefore, ladies and gentlemen, if we are to be taken seriously, please listen to colleagues Mazowiecki, Geremek, Olszewski, and me [*applause*].[37]

This was a short but well-constructed intervention. Siła-Nowicki had been an excellent defence lawyer in political trials for years. Several of those in the room were his clients, including Professor Modzelewski, who finally introduced the formal motion

---

[35] 'Transcript', 65.
[36] Wałęsa: 'What do we have experts, various people for? In order to tell us even what a general strike is. I don't know if even a half of you, ladies and gentlemen, know what a general strike is [. . .] Therefore, again I request the discussion and experts, with experts invited in order to explain to us this problem.' And M. Jurczyk: 'I'm very emphatically asking for experts to speak on the subject. Let us do everything reasonably and deliberately. It will not at all harm you, ladies and gentlemen, if experts, one or two, take the floor' ('Transcripts', 65–6).
[37] 'Transcript', 66.

to cut down interventions to five minutes and to allow experts to take the floor on a par with the members of the NCC. Significantly, this motion was simply put into practice, not voted on; a spirit of consensus might have been sensed among the congested audience. However, several minutes later the whole issue was raised again:

Z. BUJAK (*Mazovia*): [. . .] I ask again to hear the experts on this point—what are the arguments for the strike deadlines?

R. KALINOWSKI (*chairman*): I understand that, Zbyszek, as a motion to hear the experts [. . .]

A. CIERNIEWSKI (*Katowice*): But we have already agreed that experts have the right to speak, so let them speak, what is this motion for?![38]

S. M. Lipset, M. Trow, and J. Coleman, in their study of local meetings, found a marked difference between the climate of the oligarchy-controlled union where: 'local meetings are characterized by the steam-roller tactics of an entrenched an arrogant administration, punctuated from time to time by the hysteria and violence of bitter factional struggle', and the meetings within the two-party union democracy system where:

[p]arliamentary rules largely prevail . . . the chair recognizes opponents as well as political supporters; debate is usually thorough; votes, both hand and secret, are promptly and accurately counted, with representatives of the opposing sides doing the counting. The chair often leans over backward to avoid the impression of railroading resolutions or suppressing opposition motions, and any leading opposition spokesman who wants the floor gets it almost automatically. Though the local president, who ordinarily chairs the local meetings, often use the power of the chair to gain political advantage through all kinds of parliamentary tactics, his manœuvres are almost always within the bounds of parliamentary law, and though they sometimes engender opposition resentment, they almost never earn the bitterness that would be associated with actions felt to be violations of the basic norms governing legitimate political conflict. It is in such an atmosphere of heated partisan debate and manœuvre within the bounds of mutually accepted rules of procedure that issues are raised and discussed.[39]

---

[38] 'Transcript', 75. And see my 'Between Power and Wisdom . . . (n. 5 above) for some other aspects of this exchange.
[39] Lipset, Trow, and Coleman, *Union Democracy*, 300–1.

This quotation is given in full not only to offer a comparative picture, but also because, with all its adequacy if applied to the Solidarity experience as illustrated by the NCC meeting described above, we should note the basic difference in the political context. Lipset, Trow, and Coleman explain the peculiarly democratic atmosphere of the ITU meetings by reference to its internal two-party political cleavage. Solidarity, though torn by several internal conflicts, institutionalized slightly in the second half of 1981, never developed as an internal party structure, though knowledge about the ITU solution was to hand.[40] The democratic atmosphere of the union meetings, both at local, regional, and national level, resulted from another set of circumstances, that is, from the fact that the union was and wished to be seen as the paramount force for democracy in Poland, and therefore it distanced itself from any practices that belonged to the anti-democratic tradition of Communism.

The remaining discussion was very dramatic and full of spirit, especially in statements made by experts who compared the decision to be taken with that made by the Home Army command in Summer 1944 when the unsuccessful Warsaw Insurrection against Germans was proclaimed. It was also more chaotic and tired, due to the length of time participants had been concerned about the situation. Wałęsa was repeatedly advocating a warning strike first, while most of the representatives from the regions were stressing the need for a decisive show of strength by the union. Independently of how often Wałęsa entered into the discussion, his motion was not voted on until night, when it was passed by 23 votes to 19. In the morning the voting had be repeated. Wałęsa had left the room that night saying that he had a sick wife and children and did not want to be in a union with those who sought political suicide.[41] This vote went 25 votes in favour of Walesa's original motion, 2 votes against with 4 abstaining. The ultimative stand taken by Wałęsa was criticized. But, whatever the stands and critiques, the fact is that all those hours can in effect be summarized as full and open discussion of the motion introduced by the president of the union. The meeting

---

[40] J. Kurczewski, 'Demokracja związkowa', a paper reproduced in several Solidarity journals in 1981.
[41] 'Transcript', 105.

was thus devoted more to debate on Wałęsa, than to the Bydgoszcz affair.

The discussion was not concerned with Wałęsa as a person, but the leadership was at stake, and the powers of the leadership were discussed. Let me take from the transcripts of the first day another interesting element that was not so overtly contentious as the issue of the experts, but was of greater importance in terms of the constitution of Solidarity. This was the question of who was going to run the strike and who was going to talk with the government. Let us remember that some speakers were quite simply against any further talks with the government, but a direct takeover of power was not mentioned, except when rejected by Wałęsa. One may wonder what was behind the radical speeches when one reads the objections of such an extreme proponent of refusal as Kosmowski:

P. KOSMOWSKI (*Bielsko-Biała*): [. . .] I think that absolutely no talks with governments should be undertaken. There have already been enough attempted talks with the government and now we should remain on strike, of course on strike, until the government asks us for talks. It doesn't matter what government it will be, of prime minister Jaruzelski or of Mr X. The government has to come to us and negotiate with us. Not with any group, as I think that we cannot trust any small negotiating group. Now, there is an end to all trust. We know how we trusted some people and how we've become disenchanted [. . .] And, of course, those talks should, . . . talks should take place live, in the presence of TV, so the whole society would know how these talks go [. . .].[42]

This is the idea of a final settlement that will amount to a new agreement, or possibly an act of surrender, that will be made with the Communist rulers; their settlement will be made in public, by the public—a speaker of course felt himself to be the public—and for the public.

On the other hand, there is understanding that if the NCC is to run the strike the leaders must disperse and go back to their regions. In fact, time was a crucial factor here, as representatives were in a hurry to go home and organize their followers for the

[42] 'Transcript', 99.

decisive struggle. There was, therefore, an organizational need for
somebody to be burdened with the task of co-ordination. The
Co-ordinating Commission is, therefore, trapped in its own organizational logic: being composed of leaders, it cannot both co-
ordinate and direct the strike on the ground. The leader who is
not back with his followers will lose his following. This is why
there was the idea that no responsibility for running a strike
should be left with Wałęsa or a Board. In this context we can
understand the proposal made by one of the experts:

JACEK KUROŃ: I'd like to point out to you, ladies and gentlemen,
that in principle everybody is in agreement. There is the problem of a deadline, and of the order [of the warning and general
strike]. but this is a problem that would disappear in only one
way and I think that this is the way. A situation has developed
in which any group that is having talks with the authorities
now, even composed of radicals, was held by the remaining
members of the NCC to be too weak and prone to compromise. This is why I'd like to propose, in any case, I have no
right to put a motion, but I advise somebody to make it, to
accept the principle that: subordination to the leading team in
all matters, except the cancellation, that only the National
Commission [*in corpore*] may cancel the strike. This is realistic,
as if there is a problem of cancellation, there is an agreement
with the authorities and the Commission should be convened.[43]

The reader is entitled to know the substantive outcome of this
discussion. The Commission finally decided to proclaim (on the
coming Friday) a nation-wide four-hour warning strike, demand-
ing punishment of those responsible for brutal police action in
Bydgoszcz, safeguards for Solidarity functioning in future, for
political opponents active in 1976–80, legalization of the farmers'
trade union, and full strike pay. If those demands were not met,
the general strike would begin after the morning shift.[44] The successful warning strike paved the way to the compromise achieved
in the further negotiations, though the Bydgoszcz affair as such
was never fully investigated.[45]

---

[43] 'Transcript', 97–8.
[44] Resolution of NCC, 24 Mar. 1981 on strike action ('Transcript', 110).
[45] However, it seems appropriate to cite here Andrzej Słowik (Łódź): 'Słowik

Writing about the Solidarity Congress which took place toward the end of 1981, George Sanford comments on the procedural debates that '[t]he delegates had traditional Polish attitudes and resented any limitation on their rights to speak, to vote and to submit formal motions . . . Solidarity activists understandably had an almost pathological fear and hatred of being manipulated because of their experiences with the communist bureaucracy, but this emotional feeling extended to what are the normal mechanisms producing the majorities which make democratic politics work.'[46] However critical Sanford is, he observes that the procedures curbing individualism evolved slowly, and that something more substantial was at stake, that is, the relationship between the role of leaders and experts and their relationship with the Solidarity membership, 'in other words whether Solidarity's internal functioning could reconcile democracy with effective leadership'.[47]

There is another important aspect evident in the proceedings of the Solidarity Congress as well as in the Bydgoszcz meeting of Solidarity's NCC, and which escapes our attention if only suspicion and tradition are stressed as underlying the unionists' behaviour. Concern with procedure was too well-marked a characteristic of Solidarity to be relegated to an external factor. More direct issues of the central experience of living in Solidarity were at stake. In fact we are dealing here with a more traditional and more suspicious concept of democracy that remains as an element of the Polish political ethos even today, after Communism has vanished. This is best termed the aggregative and individualistic concept of democracy, as opposed to the organic, and modernization of political life with the development of representative institutions and its corollary in the form of representative private voluntary associations.

But we need to go a long way from general statements to the details of the Bydgoszcz meeting to make the interpretation consistent. Keeping in mind that consistency should not be imposed upon the event under analysis, let me move to the bridging appeals to the representatives from Bydgoszcz not to allow ambitions to prevail as there are more cases of the kind. For instance, yesterday in Łódź a man was thrown out of a window from the second floor of police headquarters. The struggle goes on for the most important affairs: the country and the union' ('Transcript', 108).

[46] Sanford, *The Solidarity Congress*, 11.     [47] Ibid. 12.

remarks. The Bydgoszcz meeting is an event with different planes of meaning which have already been alluded to. The first is the affair that gave the impetus to the actions. Bydgoszcz unionists raised the alarm throughout Poland and the rest of the world about the beating, and now they want this to become the motive for the tough stand of the union. The situation at this point is, however, inconsistent. The unionists are not interested in the cause that lay behind the aborted participation in the regional council session. The cause of the agrarian unionists was referred to but was of lesser importance, in fact it takes a very small share of the time. The conflict is between the Union and the Government, or rather the System, as the Prime Minister himself and his Cabinet are seen as indirectly involved in what was done and what is going on. The attack on the unionists is to be answered by a general strike that symbolizes defiance of the Communist system as such. Though we are not in the room we may feel that the unspoken expectation of final victory over the hated regime is in the air. This is a politically consistent plane of the debate. But this by no means exhausts the talk that continues hour after hour. In fact, the talk and the meeting is more exhaustively explained if one assumes that its central meaning is the exercise of union democracy. The test is in those sentences and interventions that do not make sense if the previous, rational and political interpretation is assumed. Could they not simply cast ballots and leave their regions to prepare for the struggle? But one after another, the representatives of all the regions present their stand as the stand of the regions. Equality is the common theme. Everybody is equal on behalf of the membership that is represented. The crucial issue is not how to combine efficiency with democracy but how to combine leadership with equality. This is why Wałęsa's conduct of Union policy is the subject of debate. On the direct procedural level the chair is at the centre, the discussion is mediated through him, so there is permanent dialogue between the chair and each of the speakers. But this is the surface of the debate. If we listen to it we discover that Wałęsa is the real focus. From time to time this comes to the surface, as when Wałęsa takes the order in his own hands and enters directly into dialogue with his opponents without the procedural mediation of Celiński. The whole meeting took place after Wałęsa had talked with the government and it leads towards the establishment of control by fellow unionists over their leader; the dialogue is between him and the regional union politicians. This is expressed in the ambiguous statements by Jurczyk, number two in terms of the inter-regional hierarchy of prestige. Jurczyk speaks about the talks with the government as an observer of what Wałęsa was doing. Though he was a member of the negotiating team, he dissociates himself in such a way as if he both was and was not present at the talks. Formally, the line is drawn between the negotiating team and the remaining majority of the members of the NCC; Jurczyk makes it clear that at the level of the 'intended' or 'subsumed' meaning, the division separates Wałęsa and the rest. The four different readings of the text may be presented as below:

(1)  Solidarity attempts to abolish Communism through a general strike;
(2)  The beating of Bydgoszcz unionists cannot go unpunished;
(3)  The government has to agree to register agrarian Solidarity;
(4)  Wałęsa is to be made responsible before his constituency.

The four readings, of which the top (1) and the bottom (4) are both implicit and unstated, obviously interpenetrate each other and cannot be simply dismissed as irrelevant. But the deepest one is the reading (4), that is activated through the events (3) giving rise to (2) and (1), and that could be activated under any other circumstances. The government in those days suspected Bydgoszcz activists of provocation, legitimating the (1) interpretation; Solidarity activists suspect government provocation that might be interpreted at the same (1) level. Parallel, however, is the interpretation (4) that describes the meeting. In fact we could have erased all the substantial references made at (3), (2), and (1), and the whole debate would remain meaningful.

One may doubt, however, whether at the internal level of meaning (4) the debate is rightly reduced to the role of Wałęsa. Obviously, it is unimportant what decision will be made. What is important is that the leader will be forced to listen to the arguments presented by his fellows and that he will explain his past or future policies. Once the debate is going on, the basic principle of union democracy and the responsibility of the leaders before their constituency is satisfied, even if finally his policy will be approved against all odds made by those who take levels (3), (2), and (1) into consideration. The game is played also between Wałęsa's colleagues. The procedural rules are meant to allow equal expression for all, independent of the size of the region they represent. This is reinforced by the assumed federal structure. Everybody speaks for his own region. The caustic remarks by Jurczyk about a colleague are possible exactly because Jurczyk himself is an anomaly in the union government composed of equals and the leader. If there is a second-rank leader, as the history of Szczecin represented by Jurczyk would legitimate, there is also room for the development of a complex pecking-order that would run against the egalitarian political democracy of Solidarity. The participants can maintain this stance only by a legal principle that each of them speaks on behalf of their respective region. The principle of representation is not used here in order to set up a central representative government but in order to dismember the government into its confederated constituents. In this way individualistic and aggregative democracy is effected. This is manifested in another paradox: although decisions are made by majority vote, every speaker presents the stand of his individual region. The apparent waste of time in reality is necessary to overcome the contradiction between the equality of the participants and the need for joint decision. They vote, but first they present their opinions; sometimes, not surprisingly, the stands are made even after the voting had taken place. In this strange way the history of union democracy is rendered possible: everybody is equal but there is a leader, everybody is independent but a joint decision is made. The solution needs extemporality that is embodied in those apparently absurd procedural motions and controversies that are independent of the outwardly expressed political aims. A leader is put on equal terms after being empowered to act as leader; presentation of the news is made after the votes have been cast. The only way to resolve the contradictions involved in such union democracy is not to give priority to any of the contradictory principles. The result is that the power to act on behalf of the collectivity and the decisions made collectively through voting are always open to discussion. Problematic leadership and problematic decisions will accompany Solidarity throughout its history.

# 9

# Self-Limited Freedom of Expression: Censorship

Thus problems, even practical problems, are always theoretical. Theories, on the other hand, can only be understood as tentative solutions of problems, and in relation to problem situations.

Karl Popper, *Unended Quest*

The debate within Solidarity exposed us to the reality of the rights as enjoyed by the members of the democratic society created by the movement in 1980/1. In a democratic society it is often assumed that basic freedoms are safeguarded on the macro-level of society, so that one should be less concerned with these when dealing with the internal life of private organizations such as the Church, trade unions, or political parties. A concept of 'one degree minus' seems to operate by which it is understood that once a number of freedoms exists in the society at large, one degree less of freedom within an association might be tolerated unless the association is really voluntary, and it is of one's own free will that one surrenders one of the freedoms while entering it. If there are free, universal, and secret ballots held in the polity for all major offices, this theory would suggest that it is not a problem that in the trade union or church which I have decided to be a member of the senior posts are not elected but occupied by appointment or by revelation. To a degree this seems true, though one can hardly envisage the democratic society in which the major voluntary associations would be run on non-democratic principles. A degree of adjustment on both sides is inevitable, a fact that makes the theory of organizational democracy so important for society as the whole.

In the Polish circumstances of 1980/1 the situation was paradoxically opposite. Here we had the major force of society trying to institute democracy within the hostile environment of the Communist political organization, that existed both at state level and beyond it. Communism in Poland, as in Czechoslovakia or Hungary, was part of the wider international political system of ambiguous and unregulated internal constitution of power. The hostility of this wider environment was to be taken literally after the experience of the armed invasions treated as internal pacifications in East Germany in 1953, Hungary in 1956, and Czechoslovakia in 1968. The example was sufficient to make the local Communist leadership as well as the population aware of the threat in case the lid of liberalization was taken off too quickly. For those who were living in the satellite states of Central-Eastern Europe it is less easy to understand the complacency with which the so-called national Communist regimes in Yugoslavia, Albania, or Cuba were treated, although one could never exclude the willingness of the international Communist political leadership to enter those countries also in case of a threat to the system. The lesson may be that the everyday order is less to be explained by reference to external power than it seems, and more by personal conformism. It would mean that one needs to look more closely at the mechanism of social order under Communism, and this is to be attempted in the final chapter. The Solidarity experience seems to be crucial in breaking away the old order in that it had proved that here and now a different social life can be established, and that contrary to the Communist suggestion free ballot, free speech, and free association are not Utopian ideals but can be realized just here and now at the Solidarity meeting or in the Solidarity press. This is the opposite case to those normally acknowledged: Solidarity was more democratic than the polity inside which it acted, and this shows not only that weakness of internal democracy of voluntary associations may hamper the development of democracy in society at large, but also that the democracy recreated within the scope of the mass voluntary association Solidarity may prove decisive in changing the undemocratic context. Decisive? Yes, because it seems that the example gave the final blow to the support which Communism enjoyed in intellectual circles in the West, that it helped to separate the socialist cause of the workers and underprivileged from the 'real socialism' practised in the East, that it changed Polish society so much that even under General Jaruzelski the life was more brutal but more sincere than in the 'domesticated Communism' period of the 1960s and 1950s, and that it warned the Communist ruling élite of the possibility of mass dissent beyond calculation and control.

We know now how the idea of democracy and democratic rights functioned within Solidarity.[1] But how were the rights implemented in the public sphere as such? Solidarity not only practised some rights at its meetings, in its organization, and in its own media but also radiated its political philosophy. The union, as we know, had definite political goals, and these were explicitly formulated in its Programme and implicit already in the Gdansk Agreements of summer 1980. The question is relevant, as the voluntary association Solidarity cannot cut itself out of the environment. There was in 1980/1 the feeling that it was possible to do so, and that an alternative social life would be developed within the realm of Solidarity, but its members in some aspects of their daily lives were also subject to the Communist rule, however strong the union seemed and however weak the party. Even Wałęsa had to ask for a passport to be able to leave the country. Electricity bills were to be paid to the state company. The union was meeting in premises of state enterprises, and these were subject to the political power and this would remain unchanged even if the move to expel Communist party cells from the factories that started in Autumn of 1981 would be successful. The border between Solidarity and the Communist state was strict but it could not be made strict in the life of the people. It was inevitable that Solidarity would have to be involved in public rights, even though some thought it better to be involved only with internal matters and disputes with management. Management, however, was just the lowest level of the Party State administration. So there was no escape from political involvement and this is the mechanism that explains the positive, corrosive role democratic associations play in an undemocratic environment. This involvement took the form of various detailed initiatives through which the vague notion of democracy and freedom was undergoing actualization. When one speaks about democracy one soon discovers that speech itself is one of its main components. Not surprisingly, the struggle for free speech was one of the major avenues for implementing democracy in Polish public life.

[1] On the ideology of 'Solidarity' see also Sergiusz Kowalski, *Solidarność Polska* (Polish Solidarity) (Warsaw, 1988).

Acknowledgement of the right to freedom of speech seems to be one of those basic, even definitional, components of a democratic legal system and of democracy as such. It is by no means accidental that this right was at the forefront of the political struggle in 1980/1. Free speech seems, therefore, a perfect example to be studied in order to understand the way it was interpreted and construed. Before we go into details, however, we need to understand the particular way in which the Communist legal system used the word 'right' and its peculiar concept of 'rights', which encompassed also the constitutional right to freedom of speech.

## Rights à la Bourgeois and Socialist Rights

Inga Markovits already in a 1978 paper provided us with a comprehensive analysis of the difference between the Communist and democratic, or bourgeois and socialist, concept of rights.[2] The fact that there were two German states neighbouring each other with totally opposing political and legal philosophies helped to make this comparison more clear than in the case of Poland or Hungary, where comparison would have to have been made either with the local past or with the contemporary alien culture: the first leaving doubts as to the influence of passing of time and modernization on the issues, the second on the incomparability of the distinctively different cultures. Markovits's approach is also methodologically close to ours when she writes that her interest is not so much in the theories of rights as proclaimed by politicians and scholars under both legal systems: 'but in that theoretical understanding of rights that can be extracted from the numerous ways in which individual rights are actually interpreted and handled in the legal process. How are rights viewed by those who deal with them; what is their purpose and justification? . . . I will try to distil, from practical differences, the theoretical essence of bourgeois and socialist rights.'[3]

I will simply cite the basic characteristics which, according to Markovits, distinguish two concepts of rights. We shall check

---

[2] Inga Markovits, 'Socialist vs. Bourgeois Rights—An East–West German Comparison, *University of Chicago Law Review*, 45: 3 (1978), 612–36.
[3] Ibid. 612.

afterwards how well this applies to the previously described area of freedom of speech. Markovits thinks that:

1. Bourgeois rights are individual entitlements conferring autonomy in a limited area to be exercised at the discretion of the right-holder, while socialist rights are policy declarations that set public standards for desirable goals and behaviour. Markovits compares socialist rights to railroad tickets that entitle the holder only to travel in the indicated direction.

Socialist constitutional rights are thus as weighty as the policy they are designed to express. In the case of traditional civil rights like free speech, which rank low in their socialist hierarchy of values and actually run counter to important organizational principles such as democratic centralism, the constitutional pronouncement of a 'right' will be unsupported by any political corroboration and will thus be worthless. In the case of rights like the right to education or to work, which always have figured in Marxist ideological history and are in line with present-day political requirements, the constitutional right will be sustained by actual policy and will thus have meaning. As political guidelines, however, constitutional rights will not only legitimate benefits but also justify interference: while 'the right to work' protects employment, its alter ego, the 'duty to work', help to enforce it. Socialist constitutional rights thus not only ward off state intrusion, but, on the contrary, facilitate it by serving as a funnel through which official standards can be infused into individual lives.[4]

2. As an entitlement, the bourgeois right is oriented towards enforcement, if necessary throughout litigation, that will provide the right-holder with a result, while socialist law focuses on a right as a means by which a useful social process of disclosure of the inefficiencies in functioning of the state administration and the elevation of the general level of the socialist civic awareness will be initiated.

3. Bourgeois law that focuses on rights as entitlements to be enforced in court aims at exact definition of rights, while socialist law, putting greater emphasis on the realization of the policy as behind the right than on the right itself, often intentionally blurs the definition of the right in question.

4. Bourgeois law leaves the enforcement of rights to the personal concern of the individual right-holders, even if it assists

---

[4] Ibid. 616–17.

them in asserting their interests and makes proceedings public in order to check the exercise of state power.

Socialist law, which views rights as policy pronouncements, sees the violation of a right as a threat to the policy in question and therefore as a social affair, in need of a social solution. Socialist procedure knows many forms of public participation: social representatives, who comment on the parties' personal character or circumstances; social defenders or accusers, who represent the view of the work collective in criminal proceedings, visiting sessions held at the locale—a factory or school, for instance—of a particular dispute or offense; court invitations to an 'organized public' that is especially affected by the issue before the court.[5]

Though Poland has never achieved as high a level of the development of a socialist concept of law and rights as East Germany did (for instance, techniques such as those cited here of, say, factory visits or running a *Rechtspropaganda* course have been experimented with only occasionally), still the basic description by Markovits holds valid in this case as well. She is certainly right, too, when she links the different concepts of rights to the different concepts of the relationship between law and rights as well.

We expect from law the protection of what is our due. Hence the bourgeois fascination with procedure: since we understand a legal conflict as a match of right pitted against right, with both potentially of equal weight, we have to see to it that the rules of the match are impartial. Bourgeois law is basically a horizontal affair: it co-ordinates purposes, balances interests. Our figure of justice is blindfolded and holds a scale— a neutral arbiter of rights [while] rather than balancing right against right, a socialist will look for the policies embedded in particular rights, then rank them accordingly to their importance and urgency. We try, or pretend to be, neutral; socialists try, or pretend to be, partial—not to the parties to a dispute, but to the Party as the authoritative guide towards social progress. We want to be fair; socialists want to be correct. Law under socialism is a vertical affair: order, direction, discipline, command. A socialist figure of justice would not be blindfolded, but seeing, and she would show the way with outstretched arm and pointing finger.[6]

Another author recently commented on human rights in a totalitarian society supplementing the legal characteristics with the political one.[7] Podgorecki lists five basic features of the way

---

[5] Socialist vs. Bourgeois Rights—An East–West German Comparison. 621.
[6] Ibid. 626.

totalitarian society treats human rights: (1) presentation of human rights in the most abstract terms possible in order to divorce the rights from the concrete experience of the people; (2) elimination of all organized attempts to act independently on behalf of the rights; (3) attack on non-totalitarian societies by pointing to actual cases of human-rights violation and, more importantly, by pointing to the mass categories of invisible victims of social-rights violations, such as the victims of economic exploitation; (4) attempt at extinction of all independent associative behaviour ruled by the intuition of human rights; (5) overt denial of mass crimes committed against human rights. This policy makes it possible for the countries of 'real socialism' both to reject human rights in practice and to present themselves as champions of human rights as socially understood.

## CENSORSHIP LAWS

Not without direct involvement of the intellectuals, the Gdansk Agreements of 31 August 1980 included the following clause:

Concerning point three of the list of demands: 'To uphold freedom of speech, press, and publication as guaranteed in the Constitution of the Polish People's Republic, not to repress independent publications, and to make access to the mass media available to representatives of all religious denominations', it was established that, firstly, the government would introduce into the Seym within three month a draft law on control of the press, publications, and performances based upon the following principle: censorship ought to secure the interests of the state. This means that protection of the state and economic secrets should be closely determined by legal rules, covering both state security and important international interests, the protection of religious sentiments as well as the sentiments of non-believers, and the prevention of dissemination of messages harmful to accepted customs and beliefs. The draft would include also the right to appeal against the decisions of the authorities concerning control of the press, publications, and performances, before the Supreme Administrative Court.[8]

[7] Adam Podgórecki, 'Toward a Sociology of Human Rights', Department of Sociology and Anthropology, Carleton University, Ottawa, Ontario, Canada, 88–5 (October 1988).
[8] Dokumenty. Protokoły porozumień. Gdańsk. Szczecin. Jastrzębie. Statut NSZZ Solidarność, KAW (Warsaw, 1980), 3.

There is no need to tell the full story of censorship in Communist Poland. Let it suffice to say that it had developed into a complex bureaucracy based upon vaguely formulated legislation which controlled all publicly uttered words or images, from printed wedding invitations to cabaret performances, not to mention newspapers, television, and broadcasting. The special agency was called the Office for the Control of Press, Publications, and Performances, its chief ranked as a minister, and there were regional offices throughout the country. The censorship was preventive. This meant that no printed or mimeographed piece could be published, no word spoken on radio, no play be performed in a theatre without obtaining authorization in advance from the office. For radio and TV it meant that a censor was always listening to each item and could decide to stop the broadcast even when it was on the air. Scripts had to be approved, and rehearsed, sometimes before an audience whose reaction was carefully checked before authorization was given for a public performance. Some authors were forbidden to publish at all; some topics were forbidden to be mentioned. The special index of forbidden names and topics as well as the exemplary censorship's failures and achievements were published for the censors on a regular basis.

It is difficult to say how widespread knowledge was, and how far sentiment was directed against censorship in Poland. People were listening to foreign broadcasts which pointed to censorship as the institution through which the party was attempting to control minds. But when I presented the issue to my students in Autumn 1980, I realized that the majority of them did not know what I was talking about. This attitude is likely to be even more pronounced in the case of the less-educated majority of the population. The issue was never forgotten amongst the intellectuals, however, who raised it regularly since at least 1956. Censorship was not only the concern of writers and artists. As an official of the Polish Sociological Association in the late 1970s I remember repeated grievances being addressed to us by the authorities, who finally, through the intervention of the special body that the party has created from its member sociologists, agreed to arrange a meeting between us and the censors. The main censor of the People's Republic, Mr Koziński, arrived equipped, as we were, with various examples. Heated exchanges developed, during

which we showed how innocent the texts or fragments of sociological prose were over which the censors had intervened, while
the other side pointed out how important for national security
censorship was in general, and the disputed interventions in particular. The representative of the Sciences' Division (*sic*) of the
Central Committee of the Polish United Workers Party, a sociologist by education herself, was present at the meeting trying to
point out to us the merits of the institution, which could be mitigated if it seemed to go to unnecessary extremes of intervention.
For a few issues the English-language publication of our association, the *Polish Sociological Bulletin* was quite well treated, and a
chapter by myself and Mr Frieske on the Polish economy was
finally allowed to be published.[9] But soon new interventions
occurred, and the struggle resumed as usual, with grievances
being further aired before the Sciences' Division which was the
only institutional mediatory body between the scientific associations and the censorship itself. It is, though, important to know
that apart from this type of unconstitutional mediation there was
no procedure that could be used by a frustrated editor, author, or
performer, against the arbitrary and discretionary power of the
said office.

In view of this and similar experiences, the paradox lies in the
fact that the previously cited clause of the Gdansk Agreements
reads as agreeing to censorship. The first question that comes to
mind is why censorship is needed at all? If it was so oppressive,
why did the strikers agree to its continued existence, and why
were intellectuals soon found to be eager to introduce it in its
new legal form? Professor Jerzy Stembrowicz, who negotiated the
clause on behalf of the strikers, explained later that:

I need to stress that the negotiations on this subject were basically going
very smoothly. Both sides finally agreed that censorship ought to be preventive. In particular, events in Czechoslovakia were referred to, as the
abolition of censorship there led to widely known effects. When the matter was decided within the Strike Committee itself no further difficulties
in talks with the government subcommission were encountered.

---

[9] J. Kurczewski and K. Frieske, 'Niektóre problemy prawnej regulacji
działalności gospodarczej przedsiębiorstw' (Some Problems of the Legal Regulation of the Activities of Economic Institutions), in A. Podgórecki (ed.), *Socjotech-
nika* (Warsaw, 1974).

The allusive character of Stembrowicz's remarks result from the self-accepted censorship. At that time, under the accepted rules, no direct mention could be made of the Warsaw Treaty invasion of Czechoslovakia in 1968, though the whole event was freely discussed in this context between the government's and the strikers' experts. The danger of a Soviet-led invasion was imminent throughout the hot summer of 1980, and the memory of Czechoslovakia in 1968 was enough to make those feeling responsible for the fate of the country accept self-limitation on various freedoms, beginning with freedom of speech. In this context I recall a scene from the mid-1970s when, on a winter holiday close to the Tatra Mountains, I asked two friends who were soon to become quite active dissidents what their first move would be if the liberation of Poland were to happen suddenly. To introduce censorship they answered, without hesitation! I had this scene vividly in mind in September 1980 when joining the group of lawyers who began drafting the law on censorship as a contribution to freedom.

The Gdansk Agreements clause on censorship was a real achievement if we take into consideration the fact that, until then, the power of censorship was arbitrary, secret, and discretionary. In vain one would look for laws describing the jurisdiction of the censorship, in vain one would look for appeal against the verdict as well as the grounds of any decision. In this context, the most revolutionary aspect of the clause consisted of reference to the Supreme Administrative Court as the apellate body. Now, as soon became clear, the crux of the matter was to change the role of the court in question from one which was supposed to judge only the procedural propriety of an administrative decision, into that of judging the merits of the case. The Supreme Administrative Court that existed in pre-war Poland was duly eliminated by the Communists as not fitting the unitary model of centralized power, and only in the 1970s was it allowed to be reconstructed after heated debates within the political and legal establishment. It came back into existence at the beginning of 1980, a fact that proves that in August 1980 strikes were possibly the unpredicted element in the chain of events, some of which were initiated by the ruling group itself. The court, however, was given limited powers in that it was empowered to deal only with cases, within a limited scope. Moreover, it was to inspect the formal quality of the decision, its legality in accordance with the general rules, and not the substance of the case. The powers of this court were debated until the end of the negotiations, which continued throughout the first half of 1981. We, the authors of the independent draft of the law on censorship, wished to develop a judicial review of the merits of the case, and the Communists, as represented by Professor Jerzy Bafia, then Minister of Justice, were willing to retain or review the legality of a censorship decision. The latter solution would mean that, if a censor's decision was made in proper form, in proper time, and with due reference to the proper rules, then no protection could be achieved for the censored citizen. Our goal was to have the judges of this court— separate from the common courts of the country—decide whether a publication or performance in question had really abused the law, and therefore had to be prevented.

As the Gdansk Agreements set forth the deadline for the governmental draft, it was decided in our small group of colleagues of Professor Stembrowicz, that in order to prevent the authorities from introducing limited review by the Supreme Administrative Court, we needed, to prepare our draft before the authorities could complete their work. On 27 October 1980 the so-called 'social draft of the law on control of publications and performances' was prepared and signed by Jan Górski, Stefan Bratkowski, Jerzy Ciemniewski, Jacek Kurczewski, Stanisław Podemski, Andrzej Wielowieyski, Jan Wojtyński, and Janina Zakrzewska.[10] In the negotiations that followed the composition of the group changed a little, but we will return to this later.

The draft was based on three main principles and these were listed in the introduction to the draft as printed in a relatively liberal newspaper *Życie Warszawy* due to links with the editor-in-chief, Henryk Korotyński, published on 27 November 1980 beside the official draft prepared by the government. The authors of the 'social version', as this type of the legislative proposal came to be called, were of the opinion that:

First, the principle of freedom of speech and print is a basic norm (art. 83 of the Constitution), respect for which is a general duty. All limita-

---

[10] Those and following details have been systematically collected and recorded by Mr Waldemar Kumor in his unpublished thesis on censorship in Communist Poland (University of Warsaw, 1990).

tions of this principle are exceptional and therefore need to be strictly regulated by law and cannot be interpreted by extension.

Secondly, the role of the agency of control over publications and performances is limited only to prevention of disseminating the contents mentioned in this law. The said agency is the sole institution in the state that is entitled to this function.

Thirdly, the agency of control of publications and performances must act in accordance with the basic requirements of the rule of law, that is legality, publicity, and appealability of the decisions. Therefore the draft determines the grounds for the intervention of a censor, makes it necessary to inform the author about the decisions of the censorship, and introduces appellation including appeal to the Supreme Administrative Court.[11]

In order to shape those principles in letters of law we introduced in our draft a list of exemptions—as wide as possible—and a list of grounds for censoring as precise and limited as possible. In the letter we felt, as I recollect it, limited by three factors. First some decisions had already been made in Gdansk, that is, 'interests of state', 'protection of the state's and the economy's interests', 'the state's security and its important international interests', 'the protection of religious sentiments as well as the sentiments of non-believers', and finally 'prevention of messages harmful to [good] customs' listed in the respective clause. Very soon we discovered that these formulations were much too vague to serve as a safeguard against arbitrary administrative practices. We could not, however, embark on an open rejection of the Gdansk formula as this was the only normative ground for the whole enterprise. The Gdansk Agreements never became a part of the legal order and have not been ratified by the Seym or acknowledged as part of the law of the country by the Supreme Court, as could have happened. Their legal status was ambiguous while at the same time they served as the normative frame of reference for thousands of claims, negotiations, and finally, the legislative initiatives of which the law on censorship was just the first one.

One should, however, mention at this point that the Gdansk Agreements were the basis for the Council of State decree that paved the way for the creation of the free trade unions, with Solidarity at the head, and was still referred to deep in the martial-

---

[11] *Życie Warszawy*, 27 Nov. 1980.

law period by the Communist Government when showing that it had fulfilled most of its obligations. In this sense it might be rightly said that the Gdansk (and related Szczecin and Jastrzebie) Agreements served as the written, though implicit, Constitution of Poland after August 1980. The importance of this constitutional role of the agreements can be proved in one aspect. The Constitution of the Polish People's Republic since the contested amendments of 1976 acknowledged the 'leading role of the Polish United Workers Party'. The amendment was in fact a Soviet one. The Soviets had introduced such a clause in their Brezhnev Constitution and the Polish Communists felt (were?) forced to repeat it, together with some corrupted lawyers like Professor Wojciech Sokolewicz and intellectuals such as Edmund Osmańczyk (then non-Communist, allowed to sit in the Seym, and in 1989 elected as a senator on the Solidarity ticket) supporting the motion against protests by dozens of Polish intellectuals. I feel particularly angry whenever I contemplate the incident, as after signing the protest I was forced to resign from my elected office in the Polish Sociological Association (as my running for the next turn of the presidency of the Warsaw Chapter would harm the Association) and then was expelled from the university only to be accepted back in its out-of-town outpost on condition of a written promise of political non-alignment in future (a condition which I considered was imposed against my free will, so I did not feel bound by it afterwards). Before this time the Communist party was ruling the country *via facti*, and then by tradition. Since 1976 its rule became acknowledged in writing. The Gdansk Agreements of 1980 made a change, in that in exchange for recognition of the 'leading role' of the party, society was granted some specific safeguards of rights such as freedom of association and freedom of speech. This exchange was the essence of the agreements and everybody behind the agreements was aware of that. This constitutional assumption was broken with the dissolution of Solidarity in 1985 by an act of the Seym, and not unnaturally the decomposition of the 'leading role' of the party soon followed.

This is why the new draft aimed at implementation of the basic constitutional achievement and could not undermine its foundation. In our case Professor Stembrowicz was an eyewitness to the agreements, and this inhibited our attempts even more. These were not the only considerations, however. Secondly, one must mention that within the group we developed a keen sense of the 'public good' which the law on censorship needs to serve. The philosophy was as follows. Once censorship is accepted at all (and this was already done in Gdansk), the role of the experts on 'society's side was felt to be that of the guardians of the deep truth of the agreements themselves, even against the will of the participants. We felt that our duty was to make an independent interpretation in terms of basic freedom of speech and the public good that was involved in an act of deliberate and voluntary agreement to the existence of censorship. Let us assume that free citizens from their free will decided to limit their freedom of speech. The question we were involved in answering was, what are the goods that could justify such self-imposed limitation? Thirdly, one of those goods was clearly the peace and sovereignty of the nation, then endangered by possible Soviet intervention if Soviet interests, as we thought them to be defined, were to be threatened. (Note that nobody even dared to consult Soviets on that.) All this may explain, I hope, why we were seriously engaged in drafting a law on censorship that would limit the freedom so dear for us.

As a result, the list of grounds for the censor's intervention was changed a little from the original Gdansk formulation as these were now to include:

1. Incitement to abolish the constitutional regime of the Polish People's Republic;
2. violation of freedom of conscience and religion;
3. disclosure of state and economic secrets, with the definition of state secrets to be determined by law;
4. incitement to commitment or approval of crime;
5. disclosure of information from pre-trial proceedings and dissemination of information from a trial behind closed doors;
6. propagation of ethnic and racial discrimination;
7. incitement to violate alliances made by the Polish state;
8. profanation of foreign countries and their diplomatic representatives in Poland.

To this we added a list of publications exempted from preventive censorship. The list included: (1) normative acts (*sic!*), speeches, and interpellations made by the deputies to the Seym and transcripts of sessions of the Seym, local councils, and their commissions; (2) publications controlled by other institutions such as statistical data controlled by the Central Statistical Office; (3) 'publications of political and social organizations, trade unions, denominations and associations designed for their members and labelled as such'; (4) coverage of religious services in the mass media; and (5) publications of a strictly scientific character. Of those exemptions the third one was to become politically the most important. In relation to this one needs to say that it had been a long-standing practice that some information, including publications, were distributed only to members of the Communist party, 'for intra-party use'. The internal truth was more detailed the more closed the circle, so some of the public-opinion poll results were published only in one copy—as I was told by the director of the Centre for Public Opinion Research at Polish Radio and Television—and addressed to the Director of Radio and Television and through him to the First Secretary. All research reports from this centre were designated 'for internal use only'. There were also many publications for varying degrees of limited publication, and the graduality of truth was never before better manifested than with those various 'for internal use only' messages. The introduction of such an exemption into our draft was preceded by long debates. Basically our attitude towards it was negative. Citizens were to be equal before the law, and we saw no reason why an organization or association should be put on a better standing than individual citizens. Moreover, with organizations like Solidarity recruiting millions of members the whole idea of reasonable censorship as focusing on a common good was becoming compromised. With a label 'for intra-trade union use only' one could (and as the future has shown, one did) disseminate any type of message that was otherwise understood as being harmful to the common good as defined in the Gdansk Agreements, of which we suddenly felt ourselves to be the authoritative interpreters.

Our draft was approved by the Committee of Arts and Science Associations which we asked for support in order to institutionalize the draft which was, in the light of law, an innocent hobby of a few private citizens. The Committee was also a body without legal powers, even more so as—in contrast to the component associations—it was not registered under Polish law, but at least it gave us an aura of organizational support. After all, the Polish United Workers Party also was not registered. The legislative process was developing into a dispute between organizations like the party, trade union, and associations. Ministries and parliamentarians were to play a role subservient to the 'leading force' of the Communist state. The Gdansk Agreements gave us, however, *de facto* constitutional entitlement to promote the draft as the self-appointed representatives of the will of the now-defunct strike committee that signed the agreement in August 1980.

The government, through the Minister of Justice, presented its draft first on 21 November 1980. The draft was a much less liberal interpretation of the Gdansk Agreements. The grounds for censor's intervention were defined vaguely—to tell the truth, as vaguely as in the Gdansk Agreements—as follows:

1. Enjoyment of freedom of speech in press, in publications and in performances cannot violate the interests of the People's Republic of Poland, that is:

(i)   principles of regime as guaranteed by the Constitution of the Polish People's Republic and by other laws;

(ii)  state secrets, including military and economic secrets;

(iii) state security and its important international interests;

(iv)  good customs.

2. Enjoyment of freedom of speech cannot be abused in order to violate the reputation and dignity of man, for incitement to discord based upon ethnic or racial differences, or for approval of crime as well as undertaking other actions that are criminal.

The official draft included some exemptions from censorship as well. These were to be normative acts, official forms, reports from the open meetings of the Seym and its commissions, textbooks used in schools, universities, and institutes, 'texts and images communicating message of faith, liturgical texts, cathetical and prayer texts published by the denominations', 'records containing music only' (yes, Schubert not exempted), printing-material for commercial or personal uses', and original works of art. The governmental draft also included the right of appeal to the Supreme Administrative Court, though the merits of the case were not to be judged in the review, contrary to the provision in our draft. The critique of the official draft was well orchestrated and came from the press and journalists, who in the meantime shook down the shock of the August strikes and agreements and started to develop an autonomous editorial and informational policy in various journals that had been until then under direct party control.

The Law On the Control Of Publications and Performances was passed by the Seym on 2 August 1981 after months of negotiations between the representatives of the government, headed by the Minister of Justice, and the representatives of the committee of Arts and Sciences Associations, including the authors of the 'social draft'. This ended the dispute in favour of 'society'. Practically all the principles upon which we had based our draft were accepted, as well as the new role of the Supreme Administrative Court. The list of exemptions was extended to include also any publication as a manuscript in up to a hundred copies, a clause I was personally proud of as it survived the amendments made under martial law and later on made possible the legal publication of some books in sociology as well as in history.[12] The most debatable clause on intra-organizational publications was also accepted, though even the independent deputy Mr Karol Malcuzynski acting on behalf of the Committee was formerly against it. But the authority of Solidarity, represented on this issue by Jan Józef Lipski, co-founder of KOR, was so great that without our support and without independent representation in the parliament appointed by the Communists the law was passed in its most liberal version. In fact, it was the power of the strikers that allowed the issue to be brought to the fore, and it was the power of Solidarity that allowed it to legislate the freedom of speech, even if in the form of a law on censorship. Hundreds of bulletins published by local chapters of Solidarity with the inscription 'for intra trade union use only' were inundating the country, in hundreds of thousands of copies, freely criticizing Communist rule as such, its 'leading role', and the Soviet leaders. Drafters felt it to be in contravention of the Gdansk Agreements;

---

[12] This supports the argument for freedom of pornography. During the negotiations Minister Bafia asked why I wanted to have this clause included, as the country was full of free publications. 'But what about pornography?' I asked. 'Would not fifty copies be enough?' replied Professor Bafia. 'But what about pornography of such quality as those by the well-known Polish 19th-cent. playwright Count Fredro?' We agreed on one hundred copies, even if the clause was used later to publish, for instance, the collection on *Food Rationing Under the Gdansk Agreement* (Umowa o kartki) which I edited in 1985.

the Agreements, however, were static, while the political process was developing in the direction that everybody recognized but few on both sides dared to pronounce in public until 13 December 1981.

### RIGHTS IN GENERAL

There is no better place to stop and discuss the concept which is essential to this book. Though I have not aimed at a philosophy of rights in the traditional style, my hope was that through telling the story about a society desperately trying to secure the good life for itself, I would be able to convey some more general considerations on rights as well. Philosophers like to commence their investigation by imagining the *tabula rasa*, an empty screen on which no rights or order are represented. Hobbes did this with the political order, some others followed him; de Sade forced maidens on the brink of losing their virginity to imagine a society in which no prudish feeling of shame, modesty, and love would be felt. In the area of rights this philosophical method is also used. Mark Tushnet, in his 'Essay on Rights',[13] opposes the world-of-rights to the world of solidarity and compassion.

The reason behind my lifelong opposition to this way of thinking is that, together with hundreds of millions of people, I have participated in the tragic experiment of Communism that will mark the twentieth century. Instead of the speculative 'zero-state' we have experienced the Paramount State, with power elevated to its supreme level. The experience of other civilizations is still beyond our comprehension, but the fight for freedom of speech by the Chinese students that culminated in the Tiananmen Square massacre is too familiar not to raise doubts as to assumed cultural differences. But let me speak for the part of the experiment I witnessed myself: there was the concept of rights which was involved in the action of the individuals and there was the concept of action involved in the action of the rulers as well. The liberating force of the concept of rights could not have been proved better than by the revolution of Solidarity in the 1980s.

Human rights were, often seen in a negative way in the democracies because of the 'human-rights policy' seen as a manipula-

---

[13] M. Tushnet, 'An Essay on Rights', *Texas Law Review*, 62: 8 (1989).

tion by politicians and the ruling Western establishment. The sad truth is that judgements of policy need to be divorced from our ability to discover the hidden national, class, or personal interests behind what seems the impulse of conscience. This is exactly what all the demystifying ideologies miss—be it Marxism, Freudianism, or Hypercriticism—good acts are in no way worse in effect for the recipients if the motivation behind them is base. Nobody will deny that a politician who supports human rights against the Communist polity might use double standards and prefer to be blind to the abuses of human rights in countries oppressed by friendly governments. No one will deny also that the stress on human rights might have been seen by some as an instrument used in pursuing international policy and not as the goal in itself. Will such considerations make any difference for those who, soon after the signing of the Helsinki Agreements, discovered that consideration for Western pressure and credits make it much more easy now to raise the issue of political freedom against the Communist administration? In the Soviet Union and Romania the right to emigrate was the one around which externally supported resistance based upon the philosophy of rights developed in the 1970s. In Poland it was not freedom of movement as such, which since 1956 was basically much less restricted than in other Communist countries, but the administrative *discretion* in granting the right which was the point raised by the little groups of the right-conscious opposition which were active since the mid-1970s. Western support for human rights was seen as of absolute value independent of hidden motivation. Here I think one should follow the simple difference between what is the meaning of an act to the recipient and what is the meaning to its author. The author may be judged—or perhaps will judge herself or himself—according to ulterior motives. Kant was not eager to accept the moral value of an act unless morally motivated; the pleasure felt by an altruist would relinquish the value of an act that needed to be done out of pure duty, that is, because of adherence to a principle. True, no one should be prevented from contemplating the base hidden motives behind her or his apparently noble deeds. At least, I see no reason why a totalitarian thinker should have been given the right to clean our consciences and to perform moral surgery on everybody in pursuit of easy happiness. But it is a different thing to say that consequences of an action are good for those who make use of it. There is a widespread tendency to speak of the recipients of an act, but this is too subjective a perspective. The recipient is a projection of an author who does something envisaging somebody—Peter, Margaret, or mankind as beneficiary. Parents quickly discover that their children do not easily accept such theories and a benefactor may rarely be so happy as to be accepted as such. The reason is prosaic: we live in a world and not in a chain of exchanges. The reality we experience is not composed of separate effects of actions by someone else, reality is all the actions and results taken together, and to be able to tell who did what for whom is practically impossible. 'Practically impossible' does not mean totally impossible. Whenever a claim is made we may be able to isolate the partial configuration of the actions and blame the results on Adam, Eve, or the government. In doing this we confront some actions with the remaining reality. The normative responsibility or lack of it does not amount, however, to full acknowledgement of what was done. One could enjoy love even if it was always offered for money or prestige; human rights are enjoyable even if supported for secondary political reasons.

The 'original state' of the police society under Communism was that there was a discourse of rights held by the rulers. As needs always to be stressed, socialist jurisprudence and *Rechtspropaganda* is full of 'rights'. The subject of the Communist Party State is raised in the knowledge that there are some rights that are due to the human being, that the state has certain rights towards the subject, and that sometimes rights are to be refused to individuals because of the impropriety of their moral standing. The 'class enemy' has no rights because he or she is not a fully fledged participants in the socialist society. Rights are not universal. This element needs to be stressed as it is not so clear from the preceding analysis. Marxist ethical doctrine, elaborated by the official theoreticians, holds that values are changeable and always relative to the given historical context. It took the post-Stalinist 'thaw' to make some of the most liberal and revisionist Marxists consider the possibility that there are some general 'human values' such as truthfulness or maternal love. Quite rightly, no universality of this kind was acknowledged earlier. The ideal Communism, as best approximated under Stalin's rule, does not have room for universal values. This is difficult to understand for those raised in another civilization, but Communists literally rejected the universality of some ethical concepts. The area of micro-social bonds, expectations, and duties such as family was not left exempt from the principle of political expediency. Sons were expected to denounce fathers and spouses were really expected to denounce each other, in fact tortured to make them do so. This experience makes one suspicious of the charms of academic relativism, however convincing the arguments might seem.

The specificity of the Communist concept of right is that it is conditional upon the discretion of the political authority. The right to move around might be acknowledged but circumstances might force one to acknowledge the necessity that the rural population would not be allowed the right to travel freely from county to county. Vertical obsession, of which Markovits wrote, means that there are no rights at all. The concept of rights assumes, in our opinion, that there are no rights at all. The concept of rights assumes, in our opinion, that right-holders are mutually autonomous of each other.

The critiques of capitalism used to stress that rights enjoyed by an employee against the employer are illusory because the former is dependent upon the latter. Communists concluded from this that rights are illusory in general and created the system in which ideally nobody could choose their employment as everyone was allotted a given job and put under a centralized system of supervision and management. On the other hand, defenders of capitalism used to reply that this dependency is an illusory one because nobody is forced to work for a given employer. It would be too easy for a sociologist to deny the role of factual dependency in those matters. There is, however, some difference between the situation of the starving peasantry, thrown out of the countryside into the town where they beg for employment, and the situation of the citizen of a modern capitalist economy who chooses in fact between better or worse welfare benefits, wages, and salaries. What is called capitalism may be called with justice the free society: the individual is given a free choice as to his or her destiny. Free society does not necessarily mean free citizens. It is possible to undertake the task of improving the social situation in order to allow as many individuals as possible to enjoy freedom of choice; but to abolish freedom of choice, as the Communists did, is certainly not the solution.

This short polemic of an ideological character allows me to present my personal view on rights. Contrary to what average sociology tells us, it seems to me simply impossible to speak of the social world without taking into consideration the normative. To dispose of the 'ought' is beyond our mental capacity. The world we live in, even when filled with Marxist or racist nihilists, is the world of the normative, though some prefer to manifest it through commands and orders. Certainly cultures differ as to the way the normative is expressed. Masaji Chiba long ago introduced the distinction between the European culture of individual rights, the traditional culture of kinship-status, and the Oriental culture of duties. Other typologies may be in place as well. Those cultures should not be seen, however, as the full realization of the individual potential of mankind, but rather as various ways in which the common faculty of normative judgement is structured.

Adam Podgórecki stresses in his 1988 essay that human rights are neither divinely created nor derived from 'human nature'. In his view human rights are the particularly influential components of the intuitive law, that is, the 'mutually related set of rights and claims that have obligatory force for the involved parties in a given social situation, irrespective of written norms and of any state control that might apply, support, or sanction these norms'. Moreover, human rights develop as the intuitive law develops through specific social conflicts, processes, and situations, which he lists in this exceptionally clear paper.

The only trouble I have with this approach is that it does not pay tribute to the ontological foundation of human rights. I will return to this topic at the end of the book. Let me here state simply that there seems to be a way out of the apparently irreconcilable opposition between the doctrines of the absolute law of nature, including human rights, on the one hand and the mutable and relative positive or intuitive law on the other. In the constitution of man as social being one is able to detect basic rights, or rather the basic ability to be a right-holder. This means, as I have just observed, the ability to be on an equal footing with other human beings. Equality is a necessary condition of autonomy; autonomy means that one has certain rights against the other,

[14] A. Podgórecki, 'Towards a Sociology of Human Rights'.

and vice versa. Women have no rights in a male-dominated society; acknowledgment of their rights against men needs to be preceded by acknowledgment of their equality. But what does equality mean in this context if not reciprocity of rights? Two beings are equal, not if they are the same in height, intelligence, wealth, or other substantive aspects, but if and only if the rights of one towards the other are the same as the rights of the latter towards the former. The reciprocity of rights constitutes equality. It does not follow from this that all rights need to be reciprocal, but only that it makes sense to speak about rights only with reference to human beings who have been acknowledged as equal. It is enough to assume that the situation of ontological equality is the primordial state within the human species in order to assume that rights are at the foundation of mankind and are, in this sense, a constitutive part of human nature.

Why, then, are there systems that are not rights conscious? Why are there systems that make use of rights in a way that is contrary to the essence of rights? Why is there so much talk of rights towards superiors and of inequality of rights?

There is a dangerous use of the term 'right' that makes it almost indistinguishable from 'duties'. Leon Petrażycki, the great legal philosopher who coined the term 'intuitive law' indiscriminately calls any 'mutually related set of duties and claims that have obligatory force for the involved parties in a given social situation; a law.[15] There is, perhaps, a slight difference between a right consisting in having a right to get a receipt for goods confiscated by the authorities, and my right not to have the goods confiscated without the due process of law. There is, however, a great difference between my right to be shot once my treason towards the state has been proved, and my right to choose my country of residence and citizenship. The fact is that the language of rights and duties, if applied without due care, may construct any interaction and corresponding relationship in terms of the respective rights, duties, and claims.

Zygmunt Ziembiński, who has made one of the most thorough analyses of elementary legal concepts, observes that the term

---

[15] Leon Petrażycki, tr. H. W. Babb, *Law and Morality* (Cambridge, Mass., 1955).

'claim' has in recent years led to several misunderstandings of a similar character:

Following common intuition, when one says that one's action towards B—touching B's personal or tangible goods—is subject to a right of B, the person's behaviour which is beneficial for B is stressed. One speaks then of somebody's right to get remuneration for work, as receiving remuneration for work done is commonly taken as something beneficial. One does not speak, however, usually about the right of a subject to be imprisoned by the prison administration or to be hanged by a hangman, as services to a citizen of this kind are commonly taken to be not beneficial, unless one contemplates hanging as somewhat more beneficial for a subject than impaling, tearing apart by horses, burning on a pyre, or breaking on a wheel.[16]

Ziembiński points out other ambiguities involved in the common use of the term 'rights'. He thus introduces a distinction between the oppositions 'right/obligation' and 'competence/subordination to competence'. The right has as its object an action undertaken by someone who was obliged to act or to refrain from an act *on behalf* of the right-holder. The competence has as its object the performance of a given conventional action with legal relevance. A citizen is competent to introduce a civil suit before the tribunal and a prosecutor has a competence to introduce a public accusation. The court in both cases is subordinate to the competences of outside agents, but this does not mean subordination in terms of power.

As the third of the main sources of ambiguity concerning the meaning of the term 'right' Ziembiński quotes the practice of speaking about a right when a certain act is allowed, that is, not forbidden. If, generally, driving on the wrong side of the road is forbidden except in some specifically designated areas, it is customary to say that a driver has a 'right' to drive on the other side, especially in circumstances when the scope of our duties towards some other person have been limited or when a competence of a person to whom one is subordinated in some way was limited.

In effect—as Ziembiński observes wryly—if Paul has taken upon himself an obligation to deliver a bottle of milk to Peter daily except for Sundays, it is said both that Peter has a right to receive from Paul a bottle of milk every day except Sunday, and

---

[16] Zygmunt Ziembiński, *Analiza pojęcia czynu* (An Analysis of the Concept of Action) (Warsaw, 1972), 178–9.

that Paul has a right not to deliver milk on Sunday. Simultaneous reference to 'rights' in the proper sense and to competences leads to a similar confusion. Not surprisingly, Ziembiński is sceptical as to the scientific value of the term 'right':

Not neglecting the usefulness of the term 'subjective right' in order to designate a set of rights, competences, and freedoms of a subject, and acknowledging the richness of the ideological content traditionally linked with the concept of 'subjective rights', one should, however, take into consideration that the decision as to what ultimately the given 'subjective right' consists of reduces to establishing what are the correlative duties of other subjects. One can, of course, pompously declare that someone has this or another 'right', but if this is not followed by the establishment or acknowledgment of duties that are adequate to given rights, competences, or freedoms imposed upon other subjects, then thus understood 'right' is, from the legal point of view, only something superficial, a mere appearance, void of any essential social significance. The further important issue is whether the duties to behave in this or another way which are related to a subjective right of a given person are secured with the respective sanction proposed for their transgression, and whether the initiative of the efficient production of such a sanction is within the competence of someone interested in the fulfilment of the mentioned obligations.[17]

This is, though, just the beginning of the difficulties. Where one sees irreconcilable diversity on one side of rights, another will see the variety on the side of duties. And even the apparently obvious linkage of rights and claims will soon be abolished under closer scrutiny, as when Feinberg, quite convincingly, ended up his tour of the realm of rights and duties, opposed to the other original Utopia of no-rights no-duties, Nowhereville, by saying that:

To have a right is to have a claim against someone whose recognition as valid is called for by some set of governing rules or moral principles. to have a *claim*, in turn, is to have a case meriting consideration, that is, to have reasons or grounds that put one in a position to engage in performative and propositional claiming. The activity of claiming, finally, as much as any other thing, makes for self-respect and respect for others, gives a sense to the notion of personal dignity, and distinguishes this otherwise morally flawed world from the even worse world of Nowhereville.[18]

[17] Ibid. 195.
[18] Joel Feinberg, 'The Nature and Value of Rights', in Philip Pettit (ed.) *Contemporary Political Theory* (New York, 1991) [originally published in *Journal of Value Inquiry*, 4 (1969), 243–57], 34.

## CLAIMING AS SOCIAL PROCESS

This brings us back to the classical area of disputes. My assumption has always been that legal sociology is just a specific way of looking at the same social facts that are dealt with differently by other approaches. Far from tending to avoid conceptual and disciplinary disputes, I wish to make it clear that legal sociology starts not with the law as understood in an official way, but with legal facts, that is, social facts which are interpreted in terms of rights and duties and the derivative categories. Only after the domain of social facts interpreted in this way is created, is the proper sociological study of law, or more adequately legal sociology, possible. Whether such a reconstruction of social reality seems to be a distortion of the latter or not, it is a step that is a necessary condition for any scientific inquiry, be it in physics or psychology.

The second point is that, if we agree that rights and duties are materially rooted in the events of mental life, then the proper way of building up scientific theories of legal life is to assume the mental reference of our basic concepts and not to seek the primordial elements in codes, written texts, official utterances, institutional behaviour, or metaphysical facts, as happens in the common assumptions of the sociology of law or the theory of law in general.[19]

Thirdly, the lessons that are taught by the continuous debate between the interpretative and objectivistic currents in sociology include the contention that social events cannot be fully understood without taking some peculiarities of the human mind into consideration, and that even if our existence is limited by the environment and by our organic apparatus and its needs, still we do create and keep alive the specific cultural realities that on their side are influencing our conduct, even if this reality is totally dependent upon our and others' intellectual and other activities, that is to say, that it exists conditionally. All the recent new sociologies and meta-sociologies seem to play precisely that tune, although in different keys.

---

[19] This point is the shortest summary of the basic premises of the theory of law and morality as it has been formulated by Leon Petrażycki at the turn of the 19th and in the first decades of the 20th cents. See e.g.: the chapter on Petrażycki in Adam Podgórecki, *Law and Society* (London, 1974).

With these three basic premises: that legal sociology is a study of social facts through the concepts of rights and duties; that these latter are to be interpreted as psycho-cultural facts; and that this interpretation needs to take into account both what exists in the common, psycho-cultural reality and in the individual mind—though the list of the basic premises of any legal sociology still seems far from being exhausted—we must attempt a reconciliation of this humanistic approach with the already too-familiar systematic theoretical thinking and investigation that is called the scientific approach.

The phenomenon of dispute seems to be one of the best battle-grounds to select for this purpose, and it would deserve our attention even if this purpose were not considered. First we must, however, agree as to what is the meaning of the term. As understood here, it refers to any set of interactions that are intended, by at least one of the actors, to fulfil a claim that is not acknowledged by at least one of the remaining actors. Such a definition allows for a study of conflicts in a way that is specific for legal sociology, as it both cuts out the events and problems that are peculiar to it, and yet still refers to the social action. And this, by no means original, definition is humanistic as well, as it takes into account human intentions, the neglect of which would make the study of disputes impossible.

The first thing that comes in mind here is that a dispute may be put under scrutiny whenever we are able to represent it in a matrix of pay-offs which result from the investments made by the actors according to their subjective utilities. Vilhelm Aubert has remarked, however, that the disputes we are interested in are mostly not the zero-sum games which have been studied most thoroughly by game analysts.[20] The classical game approach has also little in common with the practical games people play when disputing, as the dispute in reality is not a closed process that may be easily reduced to a static matrix. More adequately it would be represented by a series of different matrices that are changed by the participants in time. Moreover, a dispute normally does not involve one and only one hierarchy of preferences on the part of the actors. Rather, they play a simultaneous game on several chessboards. Making things even more complicated, and still far

[20] V. Aubert, 'Courts and Conflict Resolution', *Journal of Conflict Resolution*, 11 (1967).

from the reality, we may say as a metaphor that both opponents in a dispute play different games with each other at the same time, and that developments in each of these games influence the decisions taken by the players in other games too.

Such a complex array of processes and influences makes it preferable to think of a dispute not as a game but rather as the game of games. In this meta-game the choices are between the various particular games of dispute. This is why a rational model may be quite easily produced for the particular game, for instance, a civil trial involving a definite financial value, and still it will neither predict the real conduct of the parties nor satisfy them when instructed. The same reason lies, probably, at the root of the frequent dissatisfaction of the parties with the rational solution of their dispute which, after painstaking efforts, has been worked out and offered them by the court or a mediatory body.

Valuable as it might be, for instance, in helping the parties to understand their own and their opponent's position in a dispute, the game approach will lead us inevitably into the obvious traps of *ex post facto* explanations which are linked with the social exchanges and the more-than-problematic attempts at measurement of the subjective utilities involved.

Disputes may obviously, be approached from many possible directions. Here, however, we follow the steps made, more or less consciously, by all the interested scholars who deal with disputes, that is, the division of these into some stages of development. This diachronic, sequential analysis is involved even in the simple opposition made between a conflict and a dispute, which presupposes a precedence of conflict in order of time. Any such division made in humanistic terms involves, however, an assumption of the 'normal' or, better, the 'natural' course of human actions that together constitute a dispute. Thus, we are not allowed to make simplistic behaviouristic intrusions, such as that made, for instance, by Richard L. Abel in his otherwise valuable survey of the hypotheses concerning dispute-management institutions, when he declares that any state of a dispute is its outcome.[21] It is a different thing to say that a dispute may be stopped at any time (at least, because the global holocaust has taken place), and to say that the states of affairs that are intended by the parties to a dispute can be

---

[21] R. L. Abel, 'A Comparative Theory of Dispute Institutions in Society', *Law and Society Review* (1973), 228.

neglected by a theoretician. Of course, these teleological elements may be discarded by an ethnologist who compares various zoological species, but then the whole notion of dispute becomes useless and inapplicable. We cannot consistently use both anthropological concepts, such as rights, duties, claims, and disputes, and zoological ones, such as that of the outcome (instead, for instance, of dispute settlement) at the same level of analysis of a total social fact. The whole concept of dispute thus involves the intended 'natural' development of interaction, and these intentions need to be taken into consideration also when dealing with the typical processes that emerge during the disputes. We need not assume that in every dispute these processes occur, as the 'natural' course of action may be broken. We may, however, assume that in the standard structure of disputes, the following basic processes occur, or rather begin to occur in the following order.

*1. The Jural Definition of the Dispute*    The terms 'jural definition' and 'jural interpretation' as used throughout this paragraph are intended to cover all intellectual apprehensions of reality made by the actors in the specific categories of rights and duties and their derivatives. This definition and interpretation may be made by the professionally trained and acknowledged legal authorities as well as by any average citizen, even by a child if already socialized enough to be able to do so. For a legal sociologist a dispute starts if a conflict—an objective conflict of interests as subjectively felt—has been translated by an actor into the specific legal language he or she thinks in and talks with others. At this stage, the basic problem is whether there will be any dispute at all and, if so, then what is its content and in what jural discourse has it been formulated. The mutual relation of these definitions as made by all the sides to a dispute add the inter-actional component to this problem, which, however, is not peculiar at this stage, as the multiple perspective provides for the sociological dimensions of the dispute at any stage of development.

We shall wander now through these stages trying to point out some detailed issues which the parties confront. These issues may be both interpreted at the more theoretical level and, at the same time, at the level of empirical observation. The theoretical problems to be formulated will also be rooted in the practical problems which the participants in a dispute must deal with.

One of these problems is related to the very content and justification of the claims made, and, in general, to the processes of jural definition and interpretation which, from the first stage onwards, permeate any dispute. The degree of precision with which we use terms like rights, duties, and so on is far from the desired one. There is nothing strange in that, as these are some of those words which being thoroughly linked with conflicts of human wishes, interests, and aspirations, are richly endowed with value-judgements and ideologies that make them full of affective significance. And if such a state of affairs exists in theoretical speculation, it is by no means strange that in the everyday legal intuitive thinking of people the same ambiguities, discrepancies, and vagueness may be found too.

It would be superficial to hold that everybody has strictly delimited and unambiguously understood concepts of various jural relationships that link himself or herself and others—fictitious beings included—into the subjective legal systems. The gaps and vagueness to be encountered in average legal thinking may also be held responsible for the apparent order that governs standard interactions, whether of a private or public character. The *ad hoc* interpretation allows in a majority of cases for the inter-subjective order to function without crises. Indeed, attempts at precision may both engender and stem from some clashes of interests and of concepts. This makes disputes one of the focal points in the development of the legal order, as it both follows from and causes changes in the subjective legal systems in existence.

The development of the legal system through disputes need not be a continuous progression towards an ideally precise system. New situations will always reveal some new gaps and new ambiguities in the law. In general, it seems appropriate to look at legal systems as being in a process of continuous development in which the attainment of a relatively precise and well-defined body of rules appears to be rather a symptom of stagnation of the very social system in question, a stagnation that may be followed either by the resolution of the social system itself (for instance, a dispute-free period that often precedes the divorce), or by a series of radical changes (the elaborated Code of Napoleon is surrounded by major changes and innovations in law challenged by the speeding-up of industrial growth). So, in individual, local, or national legal systems the legal fictions are necessary to keep an image of the stability of law independent of continuous change and reinterpretation.

One of the basic issues that must be settled in one way or another by a potential participant in a dispute concerns the justification of his or her claims. They may remain self-evident, as it would be the case with intuitive legal emotions. The wider the social distance separating an actor and opponent or third party, the greater the risk that such a legal intuition will not correspond to the views held by the other participants. The more experience one has with disputes in general and with particular procedures, the more one is open to the possibility of a fault in interpretation of the dispute, that is, to define one's claims in a way which will not be found justified by the others. We may reasonably expect that such experience increases a chance that the rights and duties, claims and obligations will be justified on a positive basis, as by the invocation of a common practice or a written legal rule, and the experience with official procedures such as the court will increase the use of official positive justification. Possibly, social distance increases a tendency for positivization and officialization of legal interpretation too. Another thing is one's ability to make the jural definition of one's own and other people's problems. The resignation from a dispute may result as well from the fear of the consequent developments or asserted lack of interest as from legal imbecility in this respect. As the psychology of claims remains sadly undeveloped there is little to be said here on this subject, except for some apparent trivialities. Disputes are cyclic processes, the last stages influence the first ones, and thus, the dispute experience will make someone more trained in the appropriate reasoning. In developed societies some people get professional training in this, and they are later paid for this ability and receive the exclusive privilege of recognized competence as 'lawyers'. This ability they claim to possess may, however, be irrelevant for some types of dispute that people have. That official jurisprudence will be of no use, or almost none, in the disputes emerging among the parties to an officially illegal transaction seems possible. Finally, it has often been observed that the development of the ability for legal reasoning may be controlled by more powerful persons, groups, and organizations through various means.

*2. Entering into a Dispute*     After the jural definition of the matter at dispute and the related claims have been formulated one may enter into the dispute or leave it.[22] The first actor who, instead of avoidance, enters a dispute opens it. This is why it is important to observe the order in which the entrances are made, as some decisive effects for the whole further development of the dispute are thus possible. Next, actors must join the dispute (some of them cannot avoid it), and some others must even intervene. At this point the real character of the developmental stages makes itself clear as the first definition must precede the first entrance, that is, the opening of the dispute, while for some next participants the jural interpretation of the dispute may happen after they have been involved in the matter.

A dispute seems to be a painful experience for those involved. It creates a stress in mutual relations. In this sense it is a pathology. People will try to forget about this experience as soon as possible. They will try to invent a better justification for their participation in the dispute. The disputes will, therefore, be justified on ethical grounds even if there is no apparent ethical motive felt by the participants. Moreover, there is a strong tendency to avoid disputes and to end them as soon as possible. The responsibility for the dispute and the blame for it is put on the other parties. Any dispute triggers the tendency to settle it.

When I reviewed the observations I made in the late 1970s I felt pressed to insert the words 'under normal circumstances'. The dispute I participated in during 1980/1 does not fit this characterization. Moreover, once the collective action took place it became obvious that it is the lack of some kinds of dispute that was pathological for society in the sense of the prolonged suffering, frustration, and dissatisfaction that was hidden behind the surface of a tightly controlled public life. Then I hesitated: what are 'normal circumstances' after all? The life under the terror or civil strife? Let us, therefore, assume temporarily the truth of the above statements without further comments. The obvious 'Why' may be answered in terms of social motives. We are taught and we teach others that a dispute is something abnormal, to be

---

[22] Cf. W. L. F. Felstiner, 'Avoidance as Dispute Processing: An Elaboration', *Law and Society Review*, 9 (1975), and related article by R. Danzig and M. Lowy, 'Everyday Disputes and Mediation in the United States: A Reply to Professor Felstiner', id.

avoided as long as possible. All this belongs to our set of assumptions on normal social interaction which gives us a feeling of security among other human beings. Furthermore, this is related to some more general premises of social order. We are taught and we teach others to follow certain rules of social intercourse so that this order will not be endangered by mutual hostility, and at the same time we forgive and we are forgiven for a fairly large amount of 'mistakes' and other faults in following these rules. In this way the psychological rooting of a human being in the social situation is brought about. Some positive reinforcements for compliance with the social order are supplied, and negative sanctions are visible in some cases of failure. And all this is linked to the sediments of previous experiences that work out in our personality a disposition to act in a certain way.

Still, disputes are common events in social interaction. They are practical problems both to the social order and to an individual who is rooted in it. If irenic motives were so important for people, how would it be possible to dispute at all? The instigation by persons of positive reference is probably a great influence here, as is the need to defend one's own image. Vitality of endangered interests is another type of factor that tends to influence the decision to enter a dispute. There are also pro-social motives which may be involved, as when someone starts a dispute in order to make a precedent either of the action itself or of the settlement he or she hoped to achieve. Various positive and negative, egocentric and pro-social motives may render the entrance into a dispute psychologically possible. Thus, we cannot expect to find some of these motives as predominant for disputes in general, although some peculiar combination of motives may be related to the specific types of disputes or the specific types of participants. Still, it seems worthwhile to make a distinction between two types of motivational orientation that may play a role here: first, when the effects of settlement are considered, for instance, the value of a land tract to be adjudicated by a court together with the subjective probability of winning the case; and second, when preponderance is given to the immediate effects, such as a display of one's determination or respect payed to the local customs. There is nothing in the first type that makes it more rational. The longer it takes to obtain the effects of one's action, the more the possibility increases that the estimated probabilities of success will change, as the utilities seems important, however, in another aspect. The orientation to immediate rewards is a stronger motivation for entering into a dispute than is the full realization of one's initial claims. In such a case a compromise is more likely than in the second type of case in which claims-orientation prevails.

Another important distinction is whether the person of the opponent is important or just the issue at stake. In the first case, even the full satisfaction of one's claims may be not enough for one to withdraw from a dispute, as the wish may be for the other party to be humiliated, while in the second such motives may not play any significant role, when only a settlement of some sort is desired. This is also of importance for the next decisions, as some procedures which will lead eventually to the fulfilment of the formulated claims (a civil suit, for instance) may be of less appeal to someone who is interested more in, say, the final humiliation of an opponent (then, for instance, a criminal trial would serve this motive better). Intervention into a dispute made by the third parties, the various official agencies included, may also be studied in relation to these distinctions, as when we observe that a police action may be primarily personality oriented, aimed at the immediate effects of pacification, while a court aims at the settlement of a dispute in terms of final allocation of assets according to some official standards. Inadequacy of these motives and orientations assumed by the whole set of participants in a dispute produces one of the most acute adjustment problems that will affect all the subsequent stages.

The decision to enter a dispute is to be contrasted to the decision for avoidance. An actor avoids if she or he thinks that there is an incompatibility of claims, and second, if he or she decides not to undertake any action that would make the fulfilment of claims he or she supports possible. As an example of hypotheses related to the avoidance—entrance opposition, one may be formulated that is linked to the previous comments on dispute as pathology of the social order. As a state of ordered social interactions need not be—and some would even say, never is—equally rewarding for the participants, dispute avoidance may be expected on the part of those more interested. These 'interests' are, however, to be understood widely as human wishes of a material, as well as of an ideological, character, and the 'social order' in a more specific way than often happens in sociological literature. An old, poor widow has as much interest vested in the quiet maintenance of her relations with neighbours, shop assistants, and clerks as a manager has in his relations with supervisors and subordinates in a factory he manages. Thus, for instance, disputes in 'in-groups' will be opened relatively less often, even if conflicts happen more often, while disputes with 'strangers', with whom one interacts sporadically, will result from conflicts more frequently.[23]

*3. Choice of an Action* Here the choice involved is between the various procedures that may lead—according to the knowledge and experience of the participants—to the fulfilment of the respective claims. Contrary to some views, we will thus not treat avoidance as a procedure, although avoidance of some particular types of action may be seen as a choice of procedure. Procedures understood as types of actions leading to the fulfilment of one's own claims are a familiar subject both for the sociology and the anthropology of law, which deal with it in terms of the variety of procedures that are at the disposal of the potential participants in a dispute and in terms of the variety of motives that underlie the practical choice made. Procedural interactions which usually constitute the main object of study are, however, incomprehensible if the earlier problems and solutions were not taken into consideration.

There is one more thing that should be raised at this point. An analytical distinction may be made between agonistic and irenic actions and procedures. While the former may be described as attempting to bring about a fulfilment of a claim that is incompatible with someone else's claims, the latter are intended to reduce exactly this incompatibility of claims. The areas of agonistic and irenic procedures cross-cut each other, and it is my contention that each of them has its own theoretical as well as practical problems. For some purposes it might even be wise to divide the whole domain into the theory of disputes and theory if dispute settlement, and it is at this stage that being intermingled they start their separate lives.

A third important issue that thus arises during the participation

---

[23] People, if asked, themselves express this point directly.

in a dispute is the choice of procedure for action and, for the next participants, of procedure for counter-action. The classical now, for both the sociology and the anthropology of law, is the question whether the institutionalized or uninstitutionalized (or informal, as it is more often called) way of action will be chosen. Two basic approaches may be illustrated by a typology of those actions into mediation, adjudication, and administration as developed by T. Eckhoff,[24] or the more quantitative approach as advocated by R. L. Abel[25] when he makes use of the concept of the 'degree of institutionalization'. Less theoretical are the numerous studies in which the concrete forms of institutionalized dispute settlement and management are discussed, as for instance courts, conciliatory bodies, arbitration tribunals, and so on. For years I have been using a taxonomy based upon a cross-section of two dimensions: (a) whether the entrance of a third party depends on the will of the disputant(s) or not; (b) whether the settlement made by the third party is binding dependent on the will of the disputant(s) or not.[26] In this way four basic procedures, mediation, arbitration, mandatory conciliation, and authoritative settlement may be distinguished. This approach, as well as Eckhoff's and Abel's, are more abstract and enable us to describe the various concrete institutional choices in general terms. This means neither that those studies which take into account the distinctions elaborated by the local (official) legal systems can be enriched with theoretical interpretation, nor that the abstract definitions of the procedural alternatives must of necessity lead to some deeper theorizing, as when a theoretical definition of adjudication will be used only for the purpose of identification of civil procedures on which the statistical data will be collected in the sociographic way.

I think that the main risk involved in the choice of procedure is not that of efficiency in dealing with claims. In an earlier paragraph I have tried to point out that only some disputes do really focus on the ultimate fulfilment of the claims worked out by the participants. For all disputes, however, independent of the motives and orientations behind them, an important question

---

[24] T. Eckhoff, 'The Mediator, the Judge and the Administrator in Conflict-Resolution', *Acta Sociologica*, 10 (1966).

[25] R. L. Abel, op. cit.

[26] J. Kurczewski, *Prawo prymitywne. Zjawiska prawne w społeczeństwach przedpaństwowych* (Primitive Law. Jural Events in Pre-State Societies) (Warsaw, 1973).

remains as to the degree of control the participants may enjoy over further developments. If a neighbour sues someone in court, it may well happen that he will be cross-questioned, and eventually he may even be punished for perjury. In the socialist system the risk of this kind is even greater as courts are obliged actively to seek the objective truth for themselves, but even in adversary procedures all these things could happen. Courts or the police may take the dispute into their own hands, and even with voluntary conciliation some loss of control occurs. The various procedures differ, amongst other ways, in the degree of power and control the various types of participants have over the further development of dispute processes. From the viewpoint of a private 'opener' the various interventions *ex officio*, as, for instance, a police patrol which tries to pacify a quarrelling couple, are at the same pole of this dimension, and the bilateral fights, bargains, and negotiations, as the quarrel in itself, are at the opposite pole.

Were it safe to assume that on average people prefer situations which, at least apparently, are under their own control—and I see no reason to reject such an assumption—then it may be predicted that as the first procedural move, the choice of bilateral action will occur. The less control, the less probability of choice until the more controllable procedures have been used. Thus, after the opportunities of bilateral action have been used, the next choice will involve above all mediation, and later on, an arbitration or mandatory conciliation, with the authoritative settlement as the last choice.

Some further qualifications seem in place, however. In claims-oriented disputes the subjective probability of winning the case through each of the available procedures will be important. If one feels this probability almost equals 0 in the case of authoritative settlement, and equals 1 in the case of direct negotiations, then everything will agree with our previous predictions, but it would be contrary to it if the subjective probabilities are inverted, at least, because the further developments are controlled as to the predictability of those. So why are these conflicting predictions introduced at all? My answer is that, first, we may expect the over-all tendency to be to choose those procedures that give more control, while at the same time different procedures will be selected as appropriate in a given case. This is not without practical effects as the same people may advocate informal conciliation to others, and

at the same time choose authoritative adjudication for themselves. Secondly, the whole issue may now be formulated theoretically as the question why people choose ways of action over
which they have less power and control, and thus the practical
problems of choosing the court assumes a rather more general
interpretation. Let us observe that for opponent-oriented disputes
our answer would be different. The procedure will be selected
that allows for more power and control over the opponent. So, if
I have more power over him than he has over me, then I will
select bilateral contacts or mediation, while if in a worse position
I will allow other persons to enter the case as, since I already have
little control I am losing relatively little in contrast to my opponent. In a family quarrel it may pay for a wife to call the police;
and in this way the power relations are restructured even if the
most efficient way of settling the matter at dispute might be the
mediation of the relatives.

Thus, a hypothesis seems justified that in disputes involving
opponents with unequal power, the underdogs will choose a loss
of control in favour of third parties, either in order to put the
opponent under alien control in opponent-oriented disputes or in
order to increase the chances of winning his own case in claims-
oriented disputes. We may expect, therefore, that in labour disputes for instance, individual workers will prefer courts and a
manager direct negotiation or mediation; on the other hand, organized labour will prefer bilateral action or mediation and the individual manager will then prefer a court. In these processes the
subjective status congruency seems to play its role also. A well-
known idea in social psychology is that incongruency of components in one's social status results in insecurity of status because
others tend to react to the individual as if he had a lower status
than the real one,[27] real according to the individual in question.
The perceived status incongruency will make an actor afraid of
bilateral procedures, above all because of the fear that underesti-
mation of status will lead to the expectation of a too far-reaching
compromise. The procedures that involve authoritative settlement, and especially the procedures in which settlement depends
upon the external standards and not on the wishes of participants,
will be, therefore, more appealing for such individuals or groups.

[27] After Andrzej Malewski, *O zastosowaniach ogólnej teorii zachowania* (On the
Applications of the General Theory of Behaviour) (Warsaw, 1964), 161.

*4. Choice of a Solution*   If we accept the use of the word 'settlement' as in the expression 'they settled their dispute by a fight', then there is nothing to prevent us from including the various types of forced (negative) settlements here. A settlement may be enforced by a third party even to the open dissatisfaction of the original opponents or it may be, also, imposed by one of the opponents upon the second who must subdue himself or herself, for instance, for political or financial reasons. Practically, the indicators of final settlement offer the culturally and inter-personally understandable signs of acceptance of what may be termed an exit from the dispute. Solutions are planned already when the legal interpretation and definition of the issue at dispute is worked out, but achieving the solution needs the previous stages to be completed. Even in the case of the resignation of one of the opponents, the choice of solution is a social event involving the decision of all the participants.

As in the preceding paragraphs some points have been raised that refer, more or less directly, to the last two remaining stages in the standard structure of dispute development, we feel free to mention here only one issue specific to each of these two stages as an illustration. As disputes focus upon the incompatibility of claims, any outcome of the dispute process that eliminates this incompatibility is a solution or settlement. It seems safer to deal here with the settlement as an agreement as to the elimination of the incompatibility of claims and to putting an end to actions aiming at the fulfilment of mutually incompatible claims, even if this agreement is imposed on the participant(s) with the help of coercion and one or all interested opponents are left unsatisfied. The individual choices of solution can be made from the very beginning, but the social settlement, as defined above, is not effected in every dispute that has been opened.

As the previous deliberations may seem over-psychologized for the reader's taste, it would help to locate the dispute processes in a wider social perspective. These processes may be dealt with in terms of social regulation, and of the latter the three following most general types may be discerned (see Table 9.1.).[28]

The four cells in Table 9.1 can be reduced to me three basic cases that will be called respectively authoritative (B and C),

[28] Cf. J. Kurczewski, 'Legal Motivations and Economic Order', in Kalman Kulcsar (ed.), *Sociology of Law and Legal Sciences* (Budapest, 1977).

TABLE 9.1. *Three types of social regulation*

|  | Outside influences: | |
| --- | --- | --- |
| Autonomy of individual: | others influence ego's decisions | others do not influence ego's decisions |
| Ego makes decision | A. CONTRACT | B. EGO'S POWER |
| Decision not made by ego | C. EGO'S SUBMISSION | D. CONVENTION |

conventional (D), and consensual (A)—as this type of contract is considered here—regulation. For our two quarrelling neighbours, a settlement negotiated directly or through mediators will evidently belong to the consensual dispute regulation, while a settlement imposed on them by the police or a court is an example of the authoritative one. It could happen, however, that another neighbour will remind the two at dispute that there is an old rule (local 'custom' or national 'law') that says exactly what their respective duties and rights as to the matter are. If this suffices, we will tend to call it a conventional regulation.

Now, an interesting question may be posed as to whether there is a homology between the regulative processes that operate at the level of disputes and the type of regulation that is prevalent at the scale of the wider social system in which the dispute takes place. Some evidence may be quoted in favour of the hypothesis of homology. The authoritatively regulated societies will tend to maintain the same approach in the official agencies that deal with disputes. The development of *cognitio extraordinaria* in the Roman Empire with the growing absolutization of power, the administrative character of the court's action throughout Chinese history, or the active role of the judiciary and public procuracy and the doctrinal rejection of adversary civil procedure in the socialist legal doctrine may serve as the corroboration. A series of examples could be cited also in order to prove this point as to conventional and consensual regulation. *Legis actiones* clearly represent the conventional type of procedure that is historically related to the most traditional stage of Roman society until they gave way to the more consensual procedures that allowed for more autonomy on the part of the participants. Economic liberalism during the capitalist industrialization of Europe is correlated with relaxation as to the various aspects of contracts and civil procedure. The conventionality of the basic procedures of dispute settlement in the traditional pre-state societies (covered with the label of 'customs') is also easy to document, even if it need not be linked with restrictive formalism. On the other hand, all these societies leave room for unofficial procedures and settlements, either *de facto* or *de iure*. Thus, the hypothetical homology is limited to the levels of the official structure of society and its wider occurrence may be doubted, although it still should be subject to an investigation, this time on the relation between the basic mechanisms and premises of the official legal systems in force and legal psychology and culture.

*5. Redefinition of the dispute* This or another solution being, at least involuntarily accepted, the final stage in our model standard and 'natural' structure of disputes involves the processes of redefinition and reinterpretation of the whole experience. The result of these processes is decisive for the further conduct of the participants. They may come back to the mutual interactions as before the dispute had started, or they may decide to continue it further by repeating or by changing the claims and procedures. The enforcement of the solution depends heavily on the effects of this stage. The whole experience will add to the already accumulated legal psychology of the participants as well as of the observers, and it may be included in the institutionalized law as when, for instance, a precedent is made or a change in written legal texts is made as a result.

The issue we have chosen to deal with briefly in relation to the last stage we have distinguished, that is, the redefinition and reinterpretation of disputes, is the one that, at least once, may appear only at this stage. This is the problem of how to memorize the dispute experience, one of the most important problems for someone who studies the disputes, historian or sociologist, while, at the same time an acute problem for a participant, for whom such an experience may be traumatic. Simple self-observations suggests that people should be able to remember all the disputes in which they have participated. As some types are the common and obvious parts of everyday life, the categorization of them as disputes involves not only a decision as to subjective rights and duties but also as to the rank of importance. It is quite probable that in a given society people differ not so much as to the content of their subjective legal systems but as to the importance they attach to the various abuses of their own and of other people's (and human in general) rights. To label a dispute as a 'dispute' to interpret past experience in terms of the rightful claims endangered and fulfilled, even if these claims have been formulated in a full and sincere feeling of rightness, and followed by the respective actions, may be a result of complex intellectual and emotional processes influenced by situational and cultural factors.

All this may be stated as the following problem: will this be remembered as a dispute, and on what conditions? Some purely psychological questions may be involved here as, for example, the disputes in which I lost my case or did not fulfil my expectations in their totality will be better remembered. More reasonable, on the grounds of common observation, is the suspicion that we all remember better the more difficult cases (where 'difficult' can cover many aspects), whether with satisfactory solution or with negative or no solution at all. But apart from this, one thing is certain: that these reinterpretations will differ among the participants.

We have already mentioned that there is a need to justify entrance in a dispute on moral grounds. One of the effects of these justifications is that usually one's opponent is defined as responsible for the dispute, even if not defined as 'guilty' or 'responsible' for the specific action or inactivity that led to the dispute. Even if the parties are reconciled it is most often observed that at least one of them still needs the opponent to be defined as 'guilty' and 'responsible' and to perform some symbolic act of humiliation. The meaning of such an act and such a conciliatory agreement is differently recorded by different parties. What for one is just a sign of approval of conciliation, can be for the other the right punishment for conduct which led to a dispute. In this way, not only the dispute as such but also its content and the structure of the roles played in it by the participants will undergo a selective reinterpretation which helps them to keep their image, and to fulfil those claims which have been practically left unfulfilled after a settlement ended the whole affair. These different interpretations may very soon give impetus to a renewed dispute if an opportunity arises for each side to learn how the other had reinterpreted the past.

# 10

# *Self-Limited Freedom of Market: Food Rationing*

> This queue is after what?
> After greyness, greyness, greyness.
> Ernest Bryll, *Psalm of Queuers*

Calls for political freedoms and democracy were stressed in foreign media coverage of Polish events because the conflict within Polish society was translated into the terms of international politics as a conflict between democracy and Communism. For Poles themselves it was seen rather as a conflict between society and the Communist, whether Polish or Soviet. Poles thus also internationalized (or rather externalized) the conflict. In both cases the Soviet Union was commonly held to be the main protagonist in the political drama of Polish society. All this was with good reason, though on reflection it was not necessarily the Soviet state as a whole which should be held responsible but rather the 'inner circle' of the Soviet Communist party which acted as the ruling élite for the whole Eastern bloc and the Communist movement, except when split into rival factions as was the case when Trotskyites opposed the Stalinists in power or during the Sino-Soviet dispute which allowed the non-ruling parties to achieve some independence. The dependency was sometimes direct, and on another occasions much subtler, as in the dispute which still continues today over whether or not general Jaruzelski, by assuming dictatorial power through the introduction of martial law on 13 December 1981, in fact prevented a Soviet-organized Warsaw Pact intervention.

Communism is a collectivist doctrine and practice, though the collectivism is of a peculiar flavour in this case, organized on hierarchical principles into a total state, ruled authoritatively by an individual or an élite group. The conflict between Communism and democracy is then seen in terms of an opposition between the individual and the collectivity, the citizen and the Party State, the rights of an individual to express himself and the arbitrary power of the administration. The debate on censorship illustrates this point. But the conflict that is inherent in this type of social organization (and after all the Polish example is intended here as a case study of such a form of social organization) may be posed in different terms as well. The seeds of it are seen already in the way the participants see developments. The rulers are afraid of what 'society' will do and 'society' is fighting against 'them', those who rule. This is a very collective point of reference, though the society in question might be construed in individual terms as well. I hold that it acts both as if composed of individual rights-holders, and of participants in some collectively enjoyed rights as well.

National independence might have been an easier illustration, but the social distribution of economic rights will be taken in this chapter because it is possible to document point by point how the collective right was enforced by collective action against the Communist government, and how it was interpreted by the individuals who form public opinion, and how it was put into practice through social networks and transactions between individuals. In the end, though, it is the central authority that is supposed to organize the distribution of individual rights, and mutual co-operation which puts this into practice. Food, and specifically meat rationing in Poland in the 1980s illustrates such a collective right to just distribution as enacted by the people against the Party State, based upon collectivist doctrine.

In sociology and in journalism Polish society in the second half of the 1970s is often referred to as 'society before the crisis'. This is, of course, misleading if the food-shortages appearing then which coloured everyday life are forgotten. It is also important to note that it was the crisis in market supply, prices, and shopping that led to subsequent outbreaks of social discontent in 1970, 1975, and 1980. After a short period of developmental impetus in satisfying the basic needs of everyday life such as food, housing, and clothes, the 1970s were marked by continuous shortages of goods sought. As the official party sociologist wrote later on, the

regression in consumption manifested in the significant decrease in sales of consumer goods was delayed in relation to the symptoms of the economic crisis which, as present analysis shows, began to appear in the middle of the 1970s (falling exports, lower increase in gross national product), ruining the market equilibrium.[1]

Official statistics on the average consumption of meat and meat products for the period were as follows:[2]

35.5 kilos annually per person in 1950
42.5 kilos in 1960 (116 per cent in comparison with 1950)
53.0 kilos in 1970 (145 per cent)
56.1 kilos in 1971 (154 per cent)
59.3 kilos in 1972 (162 per cent)
62.1 kilos in 1973 (170 per cent)
65.6 kilos in 1974 (180 per cent)
70.3 kilos in 1975 (193 per cent)
70.0 kilos in 1976 (192 per cent)
69.1 kilos in 1977 (189 per cent)
70.6 kilos in 1978 (193 per cent)
73.0 kilos in 1979 (200 per cent)

Within thirty years, therefore, the consumption of meat had doubled, but this increase was irregular over time. In fact, if we did not know that the differences were accompanied by the related social events, we would perhaps never have thought that such relatively minor changes might be of such great social significance. The increase was very small within the period of accelerated industrialization in the years 1950–60, when it amounted to 16 per cent. In the years of Gomułka's rule, otherwise characterized as a time of stagnation, the increase was 25 per cent for the period 1960–70, while for the dynamic period of Gierek's rule it was as much as 40 per cent in 1970–80. In the 1970s, however, apart from the impressive figure for the decade as such, one should note the irregularity. Until 1975 there was a 5 to 7 per cent annual increase, then a decrease of 2 per cent in the years 1975–7, after which an increase was achieved again, though at a slower pace than in the first years of the decade and ranging between one and two percentage points per year. The achievement of the peak level of meat consumption in 1980 was preceded by the acceleration of consumption to which the supply of

[1] Zbigniew Sufin, 'Społeczne uwarunkowania i skutki reglamentacji' (Social Determinants and Effects of Rationing), in *Społeczne i ekonomiczne skutki reglamentacji oraz warunki i sposoby odchodzenia od niej* (Warsaw, 1983), 2–3.
[2] *Statistical Yearbooks* from 1975, 1978, and 1981 (Warsaw).

goods—if we assume, for instance, a model in which the consumption level is extrapolated as expectations for the next year—corresponded less and less. This model would then agree with James Davies's well-known theory of the increase in revolutionary activity with the widening of the gap between expectations and opportunities, and not with simple deterioration of material well-being. If, for instance, a point of reference for an average Pole was to be the increase in consumption, as in the first half of the 1970s, then the expected figure for 1980 would be at least 88.3 kilos per capita and not the 74 kilos achieved in reality. Even the great leap forward made in the 1970s was in total only 84 per cent of the expected level if we simply assume a continuation of the trend started in 1971.

When a nation-wide sample was interviewed by the respected Polish Television and Radio Public Opinion Research Centre in 1974,[3] 34 per cent of those asked evaluated the supply of food in the vicinity of their home as very good or good, 32 per cent found it so-so, while 30 per cent found it weak or bad. Evaluation was more positive the higher the material standard of living, 'as the greater pool of material resources permitted greater freedom of manœuvre, substituting cheaper items for more expensive ones, and financially gave the buyers a better basket'. Signs of the crisis were kept hidden then by the introduction of more expensive substitute goods that could satisfy the needs of the better-placed sector of society. This inequality can be assessed with the help of data on household consumption. Consumption of meat and meat products in 1973 in the highest income bracket equaled 221 per cent of consumption in the lowest income bracket; in 1974 the figure was 189 per cent; in 1975, 206 per cent; and in 1976, 209 per cent.

It is no accident that the political history of Communist Poland contains such frequent references to meat and meat prices. In the mid-1970s the crisis was most acute and closely related to this ingredient in the Polish diet. For forty-eight food items listed in the already-mentioned survey, four were very often unavailable for more than half of the sample. These were boned beef (65 per cent), ham (62 per cent), beef with bones (60 per cent), and Cra-

---

[3] Stefan Szostkiewicz, *Zapatrzenie w żywność w opinii społecznej* (Food Provision According to Social Opinion) (Warsaw, 1974).

cow sausage (51 per cent). On the list of food always available for less than half of sample, apart from the better kinds of meat listed before, were chicken, fish, eggs, liver sausage, lemons, honey, canned meat, ordinary sausage, oranges, and pork. The survey pointed to the more privileged situation in great cities, especially concerning provision of meat. Regional differences were also important, with industrialized Upper Silesia as the most privileged.

Of the 17 food articles mentioned, 14 are described as always available most often by better off people. Those include all the meat items on the list (. . .) and butter, freshwater fish and natural honey. Interpretation of those differences seems simple. Those are the expensive articles that are not sought daily by those worse off, and were not part of their thinking. This is also indicated by the higher percentage of those uninterested in buying those articles in this category of respondents.[4]

I should stress again that this characteristic applies to all the meat items on the list presented to those interviewed in the 1974 survey.

The 1975 survey by the Institute of Philosophy and Sociology of the Polish Academy of Sciences showed that, while market problems such as poor supplies and lengthy queues resulted in the greatest dissatisfaction to 13 per cent of farmers, 15 per cent of unskilled and skilled workers, and 20 per cent of white-collar workers, one social category, namely that of unskilled workers, clearly described more often than others lack of proper food (20 per cent, as compared with 8 per cent of farmers, 11 per cent of skilled workers, 9 per cent of white collars without higher education, and 1 per cent of those with higher education).[5] Some were dissatisfied because they didn't have enough money to buy the food, others because they could not get what they could afford. And still, according to studies made by the Marxism-Leninism Institute at the Central Committee of the PUWP, in the second half of the 1970s

the need for food was characterized by the lowest degree of tension in Polish society. The market situation in the years 1975–9 resulted in making this need more acute in all social groups, but still this was the need

---

[4] Szostkiewicz, 42–3.
[5] Wacław Makarczyk, *Struktura społeczna a warunki życiowe* (Social Structure and Living Conditions) (Warsaw, 1978).

relatively best satisfied in comparison with family income, both in declared and realized consumption.[6]

One may say, therefore, that conflict about meat is, in this society, a conflict about the almost symbolic satisfaction of minimum social needs. If those expectations are not fulfilled, nothing remains for a citizen permanently deprived of consumption and possession.

The situation was becoming even worse with time. In a 1975 survey by the Marxism-Leninism Institute, approximately 61 per cent of respondents assessed the provision of meat and meat products as bad or very bad.[7] While in 1974 a survey by the Polish Television and Radio Centre of the provision of food shops was assessed as bad by 'only' 36 per cent of the public, in 1975 such an assessment was given by 48 per cent, and exceeded 50 per cent in the years 1976–9, oscillating between 53 per cent and 57 per cent. In the 1977 survey of the Marxism-Leninism Institute, 72 per cent of the sample had observed 'difficulties in national development' pointing to bad supplies, shortage of food, and its low quality. In the 1979 survey again, over 70 per cent 'had complained about difficulties in supply. Demands for the introduction of coupons for the sale of meat appeared.[8]

The readiness of consumers to accept rationing may be illustrated by my own survey of a random sample of 211 inhabitants of the small town of Lesko in South-East Poland. I asked respondents if they thought that sales personnel had the right to introduce emergency rationing in the face of a limited supply, and to decide that only  certain amount of goods could be bought by individual clients. This situational mechanism with norms established *ad hoc*—one loaf of bread, one chicken, half a kilo of meat—was in those days a permanent mechanism applied by sales personnel in order to balance needs and the means of satisfaction. A clear majority (72 per cent) was in agreement with such a procedure, and it was legitimized above all by reference to egalitarianism and social justice: 'Everybody needs something';

[6] Lidia Beskid, 'Przemiany spożycia, w gospodarstwach domowych w Polsce w lalach siedemdziesiątych' (Changes in Consumption in Polish Households in the 1970s), in Z. Sufin (ed.), *Diagnozy społeczne w okresie narastającego kryzysu* (Warsaw, 1981), 43.

[7] Zbigniew Sufin (ed.), *Społeczństwo polskie w drugiej połowie lat siedemdziesiątych* (Polish Society in the Late 1970s) (Warsaw, 1981), 33.

[8] Ibid. 3.

'Some distribution needs to be secured. Otherwise one would have everything, and another nothing. Society is a family that needs to share between its members. People need to understand each other if there is such a situation', as a university-educated man answered, expressing in the most elaborated form the majority position. This was related to acknowledgement of the difficult economic situation: 'as it is now', 'one needs to understand the difficult situation', 'such is the social situation'. Many of those who agreed to situational rationing at the same time criticized the situation that lay behind it—that is, the shortcomings of the economy of the Polish People's Republic—'this is the fault of the whole economy'. Others, opposing situational rationing by sales personnel in the shops, demanded direct rationing and the reintroduction of coupons that had been in force during the war and immediately afterwards. In 1977 the government had introduced coupons for the sale of sugar, and in 1976 there was an attempt to control market problems through price increases, an attempt that ended in riots in Ursus and Radom, and bloodless but brutal pacification. The increase was rejected, and as a new instrument the market for met was stratified with the introduction of special 'commercial' shops—one of the strangest linguistic innovations of Communism—in which prices were higher and where soon the whole supply of more interesting meat items was directed. 'There are only a few commercial shops, while the butchers are empty, and thus there are queues to commercial shops that run for kilometres', as one of the leaders of the Gdansk strikes, Bogdan Lis, observed during the negotiations of August 1980.

The situation that summer may be summarized by quoting Sir William Beveridge on the British administration in 1917:

In this matter the government . . . seems to be improbably slow and hesitant, clearly lagging far behind public opinion, pushed by events and not controlling them, fearful of what should not be feared. Rationing was in fact expected by society long before the government was ready to decide that it is necessary and that society will withstand it.[9]

The similarity of the government's attitude is striking, but is it due to accidental factors such as the fragility of the political situation, or are there some more essential common features in the

---

[9] After R. J. Hammond, *Food*, vol. I, *The Growth of Policy* (London, 1951), 120, n. 3.

politics of rationing? To answer this we need to dwell a little upon rationing as such, and its place within various economies. This is important in order to understand why, in the light of the prevalent feeling that the government had tried to postpone the introduction of food-rationing in Poland for too long, the strikers and later Solidarity forced the authorities to surrender on this issue and to introduce coupons in 1981.

Direct administrative rationing of goods, in which we are interested here, is a set of politically determined conditions of entry for an individual consumer into possession of a specific amount of the good in question. If we look into the legal literature on the procedure, the negative definition seems to be the only one at our disposal. Thus we read that: 'Sometimes rationing of scarce social goods is introduced that amounts to total or partial exemption of the distribution of those goods from general circulation regulated by civil law.[10] Socialist legal literature on the issue is shamefully lacking, and those few authors who diverted their attention to this otherwise basic social fact are divided. I agree with the already quoted Stanisław Biernat who thinks that: 'acts of allocation of scarce goods have all the features of administrative decision and should be classified as such even if perhaps this doesn't fit fully the general picture of transformations in administrative law and in the forms of administrative functioning.'[11] No doubt the decision on allotting coupons to a particular subject is an individual administrative decision, and should thus be related to responsibility for realization of the decision granting the right to make the specific purchase, although this does not lead to the duty to fulfil the resulting claim when there is no supply of goods of the given kind even if there is a duty to secure the fulfilment in future or to compensate for the failure at the given moment.

Such a point of view differs from the one most often encountered when dealing with rationing:

Introduction of rationing should be treated as administrative intervention of the state in the system of market relations, taken when a sufficiently fast and efficient solution of economic problems through economic actions is impossible. Such intervention was necessary in view

---

[10] Stanisław Biernat, 'Charakter prawny aktów przydzielających obywatelom deficytowe dobra społeczne' (The Legal Character of Acts Allocating Social Goods in Short Supply to Citizens), *Państwo i Prawo*, 9–12 (1981), 85.

[11] Ibid. 82.

of the market situation, social pressure, and circumstances, making it impossible to increase the supply, or economic limitation of demand. In its effect a quasi-equilibrium was achieved that enabled consumers to satisfy their most imminent consumption needs. It should, however, be taken into consideration also that in this way, the consumers and the commercial and productive establishments are at least partially disenfranchised.[12]

This general characterization of the causes and immediate results of rationing points to the limitation of freedom of choice that results from rationing. This limitation should therefore be counterbalanced by reinforcement of the rights that, on the basis of rationing, are to be enjoyed by subjects, that is, the rights to obtain a good in the quality and quantity allotted. This is not the only expectation that is put forward by participants of the economy under rationing. Normative expectations are not limited to the relationship between the rationing administration that rules the economy, and the individual consumer, but also between consumers in general. Surveys of public opinion discussed below point clearly to comparative justice as being the foundation for the acceptance of rationing by the population. Just rationing in this context secures just treatment for each consumer with reference to others. Rationing through safeguarding the chances of each of those entitled to buy goods up to the prescribed limit automatically equalizes individual positions as against the possible competition which, under conditions of shortage, would lead to an otherwise unmanageable catastrophe. The universality of rationing makes it just for each participant, at least in that it secures the minimal equalization of buying chances and consumption chances. In other words, the introduction of rationing is related in the mind of the public to a *sui generis* contract, under the terms of which each of the consumers surrenders the right to buy a good of an indiscriminate value and transfers the right of establishing the relevant limits of value to the administration, in exchange for the obligation on the part of the administration to secure the supply of the allotted rations, and to safeguard the enjoyment of the allotted right against possible transgression by others.

[12] A. Kantecki, 'Uwarunkowania i skutki reglamentacji w sferze funkcjonowania gospodarki narodowej' (Determinants and Effects of Rationing in Economic Functioning), in *Społeczne i ekonomiczne skutki reglamentacji* . . . ,11.

Social contracts of this type are usually theoretical constructs of an abstract character, to be presented to students or to clarify a point to the general reader. In the case of food-rationing in Poland which started in 1981 one may, however, point to the reality of such a contract taking place. The introduction of meat-rationing led to the mushrooming of rationing for other items forced upon the administration by participants in the long strike on the Baltic Sea coast in summer 1980 that ended in the signing of an agreement between the government and the Inter-Factory Strike Committee. One should remember again that the strikes in 1980 were started in reaction to the increased meat prices at the beginning of July 1980, in a situation where, due to the developing crisis in the food market, the state had introduced the new system of so-called commercial shops where supposedly better-quality meat was sold for much higher prices, while people were queuing for hours for food.

In the official records of the agreement signed in the Gdansk Shipyard on 31 August 1980 we read the following:

As regards Points: Ten, which reads, 'Supplies of food to the home market should fully satisfy needs, and exports should be concerned with surplus only'; Eleven, which reads, 'Specially raised prices and sale for foreign currency (the so-called home exports) should be abolished'. Thirteen, which reads, 'Rationing of meat and meat products should be introduced (and should remain in force until the market situation can be controlled)', the following has been agreed:

The supply of meat for the population shall be increased before 31 December 1980, as a result of the increased profitability of agricultural production, reduction of meat exports to the necessary minimum, and additional imports of meat. Also before the above date, a programme should be put forward of extension of meat supplies for the population including if necessary the introduction of rationing. Scarce articles of daily use produced in Poland shall not be sold for foreign currency in 'Pewex' stores. Society shall be informed about the decision, and steps concerning market supplies, before the end of this year.

The Inter-Factory Strike Committee moves for the abolishment of special shops where meat is sold at raised prices, and for regulation and unification of meat prices at a medium level.[13]

This is the contract itself, a rare case illustrating social theories. The transcript of the Gdansk negotiations summer 1980 includes

---

[13] Gdansk Agreements as signed on 31 Aug. 1980.

further arguments concerning the contractual base of the rationing in question. Deputy Prime Minister Jagielski, who was leading the governmental delegation, reacted on 23 August to the demand for rationing with a lack of enthusiasm.

The thing is exceptionally difficult, it is difficult for technical reasons. Well, yes . . . meat is different from sugar, with the latter the introduction of coupons was much more easy, without troubles. The very system of division of meat for coupons could be very expensive in itself. Will all regions and all groupings or milieux accept such a system? We do not know. We may, however, take this into consideration. It might be considered. When I am thinking about this matter the following questions come to mind, how to approach the question of distribution of meat among the private farmers? How technically would they have to buy it? Should therefore the employees in heavy industry get more? If yes, then how much more? I think that on this matter detailed proposals should be presented with variations quickly, so that society could present their view. We have had coupons once. I should say that this led to transgressions. This is why I'd like to say again that personally I believe the way to improve the situation in the supply of basic items—here I mean meat— lies in increase of production.[14]

However tragicomical this last piece of wisdom may sound in the mouth of the representative of the Party State that took upon itself the responsibility for all the minutiae of the national economy since the late 1940s (and certainly it provoked laughter, if not amongst the representatives of the Inter-Factory Strike Committee then at least amongst the strikers listening to the negotiations transmitted through the loudspeakers), it evidences the resistance of the authorities up to the last moment, trying to postpone the relevant decisions. Throughout winter 1980/1, in negotiations with the new Solidarity as well as with the other trade unions, the government came step-by-step closer to a detailed programme of rationing as the food market was deteriorating under the influence of frozen prices and increased wages. No miracle occurred, so finally on 20 February 1981 the Council of Ministers issued Decree No. 38 on rationing meat and its products. This was still meant to be a very temporary procedure, as the decree introduced the rationing from 1 April for a period of three months only. The next decree was also made in terms of three months, and only after the introduction of martial law on

[14] *Gdańsk-Sierpień 1980* (Warsaw, 1981) 45.

13 December 1981 did the whole procedure become more routinized. In fact, it would be difficult until then to find the constitutional base for the introduction of rationing that limits the freedom of the market—rather self-evident in a socialist economy—but also a freedom for the individual consumer. Paradoxically, legitimization of rationing was forced upon the administration by the strikers with the support of the majority of society in a normative act, the legality of which is very dubious, in the Decree of the Council of State of 12 December 1981 on martial law as printed in the *Journal of Law*, No. 29 of 1981 (item 154): 'Art. 31.3. The Council of Ministers may pass a decree introducing a full or partial rationing of the basic articles of food and of certain other [*sic*] articles.'

The Council of Ministers, then, issued decrees on rationing meat and other articles, but this time it was realistically assumed that the provisions would be valid for the whole of 1982. Food rationing was to be in force until 1989. The martial-law rationing included not only meat and its products but other basic items that came to be rationed through 1981 such as butter, edible oil, soap, sugar, alcohol, flour, cigarettes, chocolates, washing powder, and baby food and hygiene products as well as powdered milk, unskimmed milk, and rice, eighteen items altogether, plus temporary rationing of other articles such as shoes, cocoa, coffee, citrus fruits, carpets, and paper and paper products such as notebooks, and so on, not to mention petrol. Małgorzata Fuszara, who studied the relevant administrative regulation in detail, stresses that though the basic philosophy of rationing underlying the demand for rationing was equality of chances, once the process started the administration developed wider and wider use of the system of direct redistribution, where more and more differentiation of rations according to age, gender, type of job, and so on were introduced, and in effect the whole system became impenetrable and subject to both manipulation and exploitation.[15]

It seems worthwhile, however, to stop at the first government decree of February 1981 in order to examine how the details of rationing looked in practice. Each of those entitled received a coupon on which was printed that a certain quantity of a good

---

[15] M. Fuszara, 'Patologia systemu reglamentacji' (Pathology of Rationing), in J. Kurczewski (ed.), *Umowa o kartki* (Warsaw, 1985).

was to be exchanged for it, if the price had been paid. One needs to remember that rationing, practised in states of emergency independent of the political system, gives the right (or more specifically, entitlement) to buy, not to get, an item. It means that, unless price control is introduced as well, equality of entitlements to buy need not be related to equality of the market situation of prospective consumers. In the Polish case price control was executed with full vigour simply because of the state's economy, within which no item could have bene priced without the approval of the respective administrative agency which, throughout most of the history of this system, had simply set the prices for all items except goods sold on the private market. One needs to remember that this was an economy in which most people get their wages or salary from the state, and everybody buys bread, meat, or television sets from the state shop. The state sets both the price for labour and for other goods and services. The value of all goods and services determined by the specifically designated administrative agency according to administrative discretion. Those decisions are then almost (except when limited and controlled by state commercial relations with the external economy) totally subjective. The planned and commanded national economy is thus totally subject to the free will of the economic administration of the country. This free will, however, is limited by some external factors, including the behaviour of the consumers. The food market in Poland was determined by the administration's policy, but consumer reaction, when it could not be expressed in the decision to buy or not to buy for a given price, was manifested through strikes. If the economy is political, then consumer behaviour must take political forms as well.

The February 1981 decree on rationing meat for the period 1 April to 30 June introduced no less than nine different types of rations (A, B, C, D, E, F R, RD, and P). The basic ration offered to the widest circle of people gave the right to buy 3.5 kilos of meat and its products in the month for those employed outside agriculture, pensioners, the handicapped, members of households of those listed previously, youths aged above 18 if still at school, members of artists' and other creative associations (this point explains the importance of being a member of the writers' association and not just a poet who lives from day to day), religious associations (the same for priests and preachers), free professions (if registered), owners of private enterprises, foreigners if entitled (it meant that a foreigner should apply in person), professional soldiers, police and security forces, and employees of the administration. Lower rations were offered to children aged 1 to 9 years, children and young people aged from 10 to 18 years if living in the countryside (this illustrates well the necessity of introducing superficial precision in such regulations that either leads to bureaucratic paradoxes in practice or to arbitrary adjustment by the rulers to the exigencies of the case), farmers and members of their households, as well as 'those who live in the city, are not excluded from the system of rationing, and do not have a right to other provision coupons of any kind'. All these persons were then allotted 2 kilos of meat per month, while children between 10 and 12 were given 2.7 kilos per month. In three instances higher rations were given: 4 kilos of meat per month was offered to those who perform menial jobs (the full, lengthy list of jobs was attached to the decree); 4.5 kilos of meat per month were offered to young people aged 13 to 18 years; and the highest ration C (5 kilos per month) was offered to nursing mothers, pregnant women, and miners. To this it should be added that 'miners' included also supervisory staff and workers, police on patrol duties, and professional military personal if on battle duties, while subsequent supplements gave the Commerce Minister discretion to establish the list of job positions entitled to an extra kilo of meat. Fuszara observed that in time the discrepancy between the lowest and highest ration increased to 6.5 kilos, while the basic ration went down, and farmers—except the smallest farm-holders—were excluded, so in effect: 'rationing in practice has led to large differentiation [in rights] between various groups of clients and inequality in access to the goods.'[16]

In the post-war history of Poland, as well as in the history of mankind as a whole, rationing of necessities is not a novelty. In Karl Polanyi's outline of the basic types of economic systems, it serves as an example of the mechanism of redistribution which has been practiced from time immemorial by centralized 'Asiatic' systems. The mechanism replaced principles of reciprocity, only to give way to market mechanisms in Western conditions. According to Zsùzsa Ferge, redistribution is the basic economic

---

[16] M. Fuszara, 'Patologia', 132.

and social mechanism in socialist systems. This is consistent with the opinion about the collective social system which has prevailed since the first socialist and Communist utopias. Leon Petrażycki, who was the first to outline the model of a centralized economy—before Stammler and the doctrinal disputes of 1950s—treated redistribution in the social system as the basic mechanism to satisfy living needs. The supposed distinguishing mark of socialist redistribution is the principle of egalitarianism as the substantial rule for just distribution of goods and services.

Zsüzsa Ferge points to the fact that in real socialism, redistribution failed to fully supersede market mechanisms and the principle of reciprocity which still governs 'borderline' and family conomies, despite expectations to that effect cherished during the revolution. Nevertheless, such market elements are surrounded and dominated by redistribution, just as elements of redistribution found in the economy and social policy of modern capitalism are surrounded by the dominating market mechanism. Whenever the supply of a certain type of goods exceeds perceptible demand, direct redistribution through various allocations, allowances, coupons, and ration cards is replaced by free sale. This trend is not the subject of sociological thought and is treated as obvious. Redistribution is assumed to be abnormal from the natural point of view of a member of a socialist society; what is normal is the possibility to buy and sell goods and services freely on the market. The redistribution mechanism is also assumed to be abnormal from the economic point of view, and the market mechanism to be normal. The latter assumption is historically wrong; the former, on the other hand, has never been submitted to reliable empirical study. Treating rationing and redistribution in general as abnormal and transient phenomena, we have never given to them the attention they actually deserve. In socialist society, redistribution is the basis of social life (planning being just a means), and its imperfect functioning is the everyday problem for the mass of citizens.

The contractual character of prices, treated as a weak point of the centralized system, is a logical component of a system based on redistribution. In the socialist system social conflicts concentrate on a struggle for a share in redistribution which would be the most profitable for a given social group or category.

The rationing of meat and other basic food products introduced following the events of August 1980 is a good example of the above-mentioned theses: in the period August 1980 to December 1981, overt actions of separate groups of interest were noticeable. From society's point of view, coupons were to guarantee a just distribution of goods and help reduce the lines. From the point of view of the authorities and the economic policy, they were to become an efficient instrument of balancing supply and demand. The rationing of meat, forced by the strikers on the coast, expressed both their dissatisfaction with indirect forms of redistribution through a double, if not triple, system of sale, and their belief in the possibility of creating more egalitarian redistribution. The insistent demand for rationing alarmed most economists, who perceived it as a threat to the economic reform that was to introduce a market instead of redistribution. From the government's point of view rationing proved to be an effective step: it helped meet social demands with the overall amount of meat for distribution unchanged, nay reduced. This solution had already been tested in 1974, when sugar rationing was introduced due to the profits then derived from the sale of Polish sugar abroad.

Rationing was introduced during an acute political and economic crisis. As Hagemejer wrote in the summer of 1981,

the market situation gives rise not only to mutual hostility among the population and to hostility towards those in power, but also to conflicts between whole social groups, the regional and professional above all. The central distribution lists that were to secure a 'just' distribution of a limited amount of goods all over the country break down. Tendencies can be found in the separate regions to distribute everything that is manufactured in their respective territories and to prevent any exports of such products to other regions; the introduction of local rationing promotes such tendencies. Barter develops between the separate plants where scarce market goods are manufactured. The system of rationing of meat created conditions in which the separate professional groups rival one another trying to win recognition of their work as particularly hard and thus to obtain a larger ration . . . On the one hand, the universal mistrust in the presented balance resulted in the negotiating of ration norms which allowed for no reserves to cover fluctuations of purchase and irregularities of supplies; on the other hand, the adopted principle of allotting different rations depending on the character of work brought about the frequently successful demands for differentiating rations, voiced by the separate professional groups.[17]

[17] Krzysztof Hagemejer, 'Społeczeństwo w kolejce' (Society in a Queue), *Ruch Związkowy* 1 (1981), 148.

The outcome of the struggle was not obvious. On the one hand, the trend towards equalization of supply norms of the separate regions improved the situation of those living in small towns and agricultural regions to the disadvantage of the hitherto privileged agglomerations of manufacturing industry. On the other hand, the regional structure of the strongest trade union facilitated local corrections through the above-mentioned closed autarchy of provinces and towns. The economic needs soon led back to a privileged position for certain categories of workers such as those performing harder work; the special miners' privileges—the bone of contention in the disputes between Solidarity, departmental trade unions, miners, and the authorities—were left out of account here. Undoubtedly, to redistribution of this type to be introduced the central authorities must be strong in relation to the lower levels. Before December 1981 the Polish government was too weak to realize that task. (Incidentally, the national leaders of Solidarity were also too weak to force the separate plants, professional groups, departments, and regions to observe the adopted principle of egalitarianism.) Just as the local centres of public and economic power tried to avail themselves of the situation and to win over definite circles, the latter also tried to exert pressure on the local authorities to obtain larger shares.

## MARKET OR REDISTRIBUTION?

The demand for rationing of meat and other food products, formulated most clearly in the Gdansk Agreements, may be explained in various ways. One way stresses society's belief that rationing would lead to the disappearance of queues. According to another view, the demand for rationing arose from society's disapproval of the system of many different markets, operative before August 1980, which created privileges for certain categories due to their social position (the party and state machine) and for certain persons with higher incomes (who could buy goods in special stores by paying higher prices). Both of these interpretations can be found in the above-quoted article by Hagemejer. However, the findings of studies carried out after August 1980 make it possible to include still another and more essential motivation.

The Institute of Domestic Trade and Services carried out two studies of an incomplete and yet rather interesting sample of households (n = 2,326 persons).[18] The first of these studies was made in November and December of 1980, this actually preceding the introduction of rationing during a time of great confusion connected with its introduction. To begin with, nearly a half of those questioned (48 per cent) believed that rationing would secure better supplies of meat and meat products for their households, 18 per cent thought it would only make matters worse, and 25 per cent were of the opinion that no changes would result from the introduction of coupons. Five months later, 50 per cent of respondents found rationing to have resulted in better supplies, 25 per cent thought the opposite, and 21 per cent thought coupons had brought about no changes in their households. At the end of 1980 as few as 37.5 per cent of respondents hoped that rationing would help abolish queues; instead, as many as 70 per cent thought that rationed meat would still be scarce enough to make it sometimes impossible to buy the entire amount allocated by their coupons. Five months later, only 33 per cent stated that the introduction of rationing had reduced queues, and 50 per cent quoted instances of shortage of rationed meat. None the less, most respondents (59 per cent) believed rationing to have guaranteed a just distribution of meat, and only 24 per cent thought the opposite. Furthermore, while as few as 25 per cent supported the rationing of other articles besides meat at the end of 1980, the proportion went up to 66 per cent in April and May of 1981.

These data, as well as the answers to our questionnaire, lead to the simple conclusion that support for rationing results not from pragmatic reasons—for example, from a hope for full supplies of rationed goods or for the disappearance of queue lines—but is a matter of principle. Rationing has a moral value. It satisfies the social sense of justice, creating equal chances to buy necessary goods. The approval here concerns egalitarian rationing, though the actual contents of that rationing are not necessarily obvious or uniform for all; this problem will be discussed below.

Our questionnaire survey was carried out in November and

---

[18] Robert Sobiech, 'Reglamentacja w świetle badań opinii publicznej' (Rationing in Public Opinion), in Kurczewski (ed.), *Umowa o kartki*.

early December of 1981.[19] The sample was drawn randomly and included 150 inhabitants of Warsaw; the imposition of martial law on 13 December 1981 made it impossible to examine the entire planned sample of 300 persons. The questionnaire included several questions concerning the above-mentioned problem. The first of them concerned the principles that ought to govern the rationing of necessities and their distribution between individuals and different social categories. As few as 19 per cent of respondents declared themselves against the rationing of necessities. A decided majority (78 per cent) were for rationing. The highest proportion of them (60 per cent) thought that rations should be differentiated according to needs, for example, of the various age groups of persons who perform harder work. The second question concerned the principles of sale of non-rationed articles. Only 10 per cent of respondents were for unlimited sale of such goods. The highest proportion (41 per cent) thought that a uniform principle should be introduced here, with the amount of each commodity sold to one person defined in advance (for example, one bottle of shampoo or one pot, and so on). About one-third of respondents (31 per cent) left the decision about the amount sold to one person with the salesman who knows both the amount delivered to the shop and the demand for a given commodity; 10 per cent were of the opinion that those who stand in a given queue should decide how much they should buy.

Thus, only an explicit minority (from 10 to 19 per cent) insisted on the preservation, or perhaps introduction, of a market mechanism to replace any forms of redistribution. The latter statement is of importance, since we have hitherto discussed rationing as a form of redistribution and treated the distribution of coupons as the only form of rationing. Meanwhile, as follows from a more careful analysis, coupons should be treated as what we have decided to call universal rationing, while various other socio-economic phenomena connected with queues are in fact specific forms of rationing; such rationing will be called 'situational' here.

One should bear in mind in this connection that a 'queue' is

---

[19] In what follows I describe the research carried out with Małgorzata Fuszara and Iwona Jakubowska who are also co-authors of the subsequent section of this chapter.

not necessarily connected with unbalanced supplies of and demand for a certain good: instead, in its pure form, it concerns the problem of satisfaction of needs at one and the same time. Its point of departure is the distribution of time and not of other goods. The basic principle of 'line justice'—*prior temore, potior iure* (first by time, first by right, or first come, first served)—does not necessarily mean that only those first in line can buy at all, and the amount they want. A queue forms whenever it is impossible to serve all the customers at one time. In such a 'pure' queue, which is possible also when supply exceeds demand, what is rationed is not the commodity but the time the salesman has at his disposal. But if demand exceeds supply, which is most often the case in Poland, a queue has a different implication. The position in line determines the very chance of buying a given food. Thus, whenever supply is greater than demand, sale based on the 'first come, first served' principle may indeed be treated as a form of redistribution of commodities and services according to the amount of time passed waiting to buy. This redistribution is situational since it is enough to change the time and situation for the chances of acquiring a commodity or service to be changed also. At the same time, such a situation of purchase is in accordance with the market mechanism, as the customer is allowed to buy what he wants and as much as he wants. No changes of this situation would be necessary had the supply remained greater or at least equal in relation to demand; however, with the actual redistribution done by the salesmen the trade has changed into a normal market situation, which it is *de iure*.

Long before August 1980, however, still another model of the queue situation developed which might be called situational rationing *sensu stricto*. In the face of scarcity, the necessity of rationing commodities was recognized quite soon on a nationwide scale, in the separate localities, and in shops (for example, one loaf of bread, two bottles of vodka, or one tin of preserved meat per person). This principle is situational since the would-be buyer may simply go to another shop and line up for the same commodity there. Moreover, he may even line up again in the same shop, provided the commodity in question is still being sold. What connects this kind of rationing (the principles of which can be determined by trade on administration, by salesman, or by the customers concerned) with the universal rationing which is the mechanism of redistribution of goods among society?

Approval of various forms of rationing was also revealed in answers to other questions. One described a situation where large quantities of clothing materials, vitamin tablets, and baby preparations were bought up by one person. All those commodities together constituted the monthly allowance for the entire town. The articles concerned are not rationed from the legal point of view. Yet in our story the police caused these commodities to be returned to the drugstore despite the fact that their purchase had been legal. It turned out that nearly all of the examined persons (93 per cent) approved of the steps taken by the police. As few as 7 per cent were against a police intervention in such cases. If the possibility of buying a given commodity is to be secured for the greatest number of persons possible, nobody can purchase an unlimited amount of that commodity. Such was the justification given by most respondents. The interest of other consumers and their right to get their share of the redistributed goods is the most frequently quoted motive for accepting police intervention in the discussed case. What is worthy of attention here is the fact that the respondents are seldom motivated by fear of the phenomena frequently quoted by the mass media (for example, as few as 11 per cent were prompted by a belief that the person who bought the commodities was a profiteer). Polish society justifies a limitation of the right to buy commodities by referring to the other person's right to buy at least the minimum amount of goods that are in short supply.

Therefore, the harsh scarcity of goods induced Poles to accept rationing of virtually all commodities and, as was also found in our study, to demand punishment for those who break the rules of rationing. An emphatic majority of respondents declared themselves in favour of punishing persons who buy up commodities in such a situation (9 per cent). Nearly half (47 per cent) believed that both parties to the transaction should be punished, while a quarter thought that a penalty should be applied against the salesman. The most frequently proposed penalties were: a fine (35 per cent) and admonition (21 per cent), but there were also some respondents who mentioned very severe penalties, for example, imprisonment (nine persons, 6 per cent). Those more inclined to declare themselves for punishing persons who buy up commodities are women, persons with elementary education, those who define themselves as workers, and those living in worse conditions, both objectively (who actually have meat less often for meals) and subjectively (who perceive their situation as worse than the average). Among those who were against punishment were a greater proportion of men, persons with secondary and higher education who defined themselves as members of the intelligentsia, those whose living conditions were objectively better (who had meat more often), and those who described their own living conditions as average or better than average.

The above-quoted opinions can be arranged into a consistent system: a prevalence of demand over supply results in a trend towards the rules of rationing which would be known in advance, and towards a limitation of the right to buy goods in some cases so as to make it possible for others to exercise their rights. Transgressions of those rules should be punished and the penalty applied towards both parties to the transaction, the salesman and the customer, or only towards the salesman as the dispenser of commodities. Among the most punitive persons were those for whom the scarcity of goods on the market was particularly painful, poor women. The range of proposed penalties was rather broad and included imprisonment. Although such acts are not penalized, the transgression of the rules of rationing for scarce goods became an offence in the social consciousness: those guilty of such acts should therefore be punished, even imprisoned.

The questionnaire included another example of conduct inconsistent with the norms of times of rationing. A situation was described where a customer helped himself to a chocolate bar, sold only for children's sugar coupons, and left money on the counter—the equivalent of the price. This situation is unclear from the legal point of view: on the one hand, the customer had no coupon and thus was not entitled to buy; yet on the other hand, there were no provisions to prohibit the purchase of the chocolate bar or to impose a penalty on the person who buys it, and the situation can hardly be interpreted as theft. Opinions about the conduct described proved to differ. A little more than a half of respondents (57 per cent) condemned the purchaser, and nearly a half (42 per cent) expressed no disapproval. In this case, as in the one described above, the norms of the times of rationing were also transgressed: the transgression, however, did not result in an explicit reduction of the rights of others, which probably influenced the lack of uniformity of the respondents' opinions. Only one trait proved to have an important connection with the opinion expressed: those with higher education were more inclined to condemn the customer.

In this case, just as before, the respondents were asked about the proposed reaction towards the customer. The most frequently mentioned reactions were admonition (29 per cent) and restitution (of the chocolate bar and of money, 28 per cent). Most respondents (62 per cent) believed that a person who notices such a situation should notify the salesman; 25 per cent would let the customer get away with what he did; and 13 per cent proposed other types of reaction. It appeared that persons with higher education, despite their disapproval of the described act, more frequently proposed reactions other than notifying the salesman or restraint from any reaction. Above all, they mentioned a private intervention: a rebuke, for example.

However, the respondents' opinions were generally consistent: those who condemned the customer declared themselves more often in favour of notifying the salesman, and the imposition of penalties *sensu stricto*, usually a fine, on the perpetrator of the deed (imprisonment was suggested by only one respondent). These correlations made it possible to construct an index of tolerance towards the customer. As also shown by other studies, young people with secondary or higher education and living in objectively better conditions were the most tolerant.

As shown by the findings quoted above, the respondents favoured a limitation of the right to buy commodities to the extent which would make possible the exercise of those rights by as many people as possible, if not by all concerned. It sometimes happens, however, that observance of this principle leads to a reduced utility of the purchased commodity. Our respondents were asked to give their opinion about such a situation, which concerned the sale of hair preparation. Since there were many customers, each of them was allowed to buy one bottle, despite the fact that three bottles are necessary in order for the treatment to bring good results. Most respondents (89 per cent) believed the salesman's decision in this case to be wrong; according to them, it would be better to sell the necessary amount of the preparation to a smaller number of customers. It seems that the trend towards a just redistribution of goods making it possible for the greatest number of customers to buy commodities is limited by common sense concerning the usefulness of a given commodity to the purchaser. Nearly half (48 per cent) the respondents thought that decisions concerning the amount of goods sold to one customer in such situations should be taken by the competent domestic trade organization. The proportion of those willing to leave such situations to the people standing in a given queue was the smallest (19 per cent); according to the respondents, this was due to the fact that the interests of those first and those last in line clash, which makes it difficult to reach a decision that would be acceptable for all. Thus, despite the uniformity of opinions in this case, the respondents did not believe in the possibility of the customers' common sense prevailing in a given 'line situation' of a total economic crisis. With demand greatly exceeding supply, a situation which is keenly felt in society, it was felt that redistribution should be carried out through various forms of rationing. The so-called necessities should be included in universal rationing, with situational rationing applied in the case of other articles where demand exceeded supplies. The latter group includes several forms: first, sale based on principles agreed and known in advance (for example, one loaf of bread or one pot per person). In another form the salesman or, less often, those in the queue decide the amount of commodities per customer according to the relation between demand and supply in a given case. Infringement of those unwritten laws in force in the period of scarcity of goods met with disapproval; whenever the principles of just distribution were glaringly infringed, Polish society supported punishment for the guilty.

To end the present section, we consider how far the legal regulation of rationing agrees with society's opinions in this respect. At the time of investigation, uniform rationing involved the sale of some articles only (for example, meat and sugar). The rationing of other articles varied in different areas (for instance, vegetable fats were sold by coupon in some regions). In those days the provinces enjoyed a large degree of freedom in deciding about rationing and about the introduction of the so-called interchangeable products (for example, coffee instead of alcohol, sweets instead of cigarettes, and so on). Universal rationing on a nation-wide scale resulted from the subsequent resolutions of the Council of Ministers. The lack of uniform regulation, the changing norms, the different interchangeable goods, diverse interpretations of the provisions, and the differences in the rationing policy from one province to another—all of these factors together made the customer's situation unclear, despite the coupons, both for himself and for the salesman whose interpretation frequently determined the kinds and amount of goods sold to the customer. At the time of writing the principles of universal coupon rationing are regulated by the resolution of the Council of Ministers of 12 December 1981, 'on the rationed sale of commodities'. (Resolution No. 264, *Monitor Polski*, No. 32/1981.) The resolution provides for nation-wide uniform norms of sale for separate commodities which agree with our respondents' postulates, as does the differentiation of those norms in the case of particular groups according to their respective needs related to age or the effort put into the work they perform. The relevant findings will be presented in the next section of this chapter. The introduction of a uniform regulation is not, however, tantamount to the disappearance of all doubts and to a just distribution of commodities. The recurring shortages of certain goods bring about a situation where successful purchase of a given article depends not only on coupons and the expenditure of time, but on other factors as well (such as the supplies of definite sorts of meat to a definite shop, the salesman's decision as to the amount of better sorts of meat to be sold to the individual customers, and so on. As shown by this and many other examples, despite the trend towards unification the system of universal rationing is still far from meeting the demand for a just distribution of necessities. Moreover, it is unclear whether or not the government, when issuing coupons, at the same time assumed the duty to secure the supplies which would cover the standards it set. As shown by the creation, through a resolution of the Council of Ministers, of a special Inter-departmental Group for Rationing Commodities, tasks which include supervision of supplies to cover the standards, the government indeed assumed the above-mentioned duty. If this question had been interpreted in a different manner, the whole of the universal rationing system would be nonsensical.

Situational rationing is obviously more difficult to regulate. There are legal grounds for the use of one of its forms, the rationing done by the salesman: the order of the Ministry of Domestic Trade and Services which entitles the shop manager to limit the amounts of commodities sold to the individual customer (1978). It should, however, be added that in some situations the form of rationing was approval, where the amount of the commodity was determined by the order of the superior authority (the trade organization, in our example of the hair preparation). Yet we failed to find legal grounds for this kind of rationing. Moreover (and this seems rather important), although accepting situational rationing by the salesman, the respondents nevertheless had many reservations about this, postulating the checking of the salesman's honesty and supervision of his decisions by a 'line committee' which would check the invoices of the commodities delivered and supervise the fairness of the principles of sale established by the salesman. Today, as the creation of line committees has been banned, the customers are at the salesman's mercy to a much higher degree than before. It is difficult to tell whether this would influence any changes of those customers' opinions about who should establish the principles of situational rationing. There are, however, no legal grounds concerning whether such decisions could be vested with the customers.

EGALITARIANISM, THE PRIVILEGED, AND THE HANDICAPPED

In times of rationing, not only the norms of sale were changed but also certain rules that govern the very order of that sale. There are notices in all shops providing the information that certain categories of persons (the disabled, pregnant women, women with babies) shall be served before others. The interpretation of this principle is unclear in times of rationing. Two lines were formed in shops, the first one composed of those who enjoyed no privileges, and the other of persons entitled to be served before others. Therefore, an additional *metarule* of sale had to be accepted. At the time of investigation, a custom was formed in Warsaw shops according to which five persons from the line of the unprivileged and one person entitled to be served first were served alternately. It should be added here that the related order of the trade authorities gave a much more detailed definition of the privileged categories and of their required certificates compared with the above-mentioned notice-boards, but at the same time was vague about the principles of conduct 'if a longer line of the privileged is formed'. The norm established in practice was both precise and simple: it provided for two classes only, of the privileged and the unprivileged, and one proportion, 1 : 5.

The bulk of the respondents (76 per cent) accepted that social norm. The justness of the 1 : 5 principle was usually motivated by the interest of other customers, that is, by the fact that the unprivileged would otherwise have to stand in line for too long (38 per cent of answers), and by the fear that there would not be a sufficient amount of the commodity for the remaining customers (21 per cent).

As can be seen, the solution already accepted under martial law by the Ministry of Domestic Trade and Services, according to which one privileged and one unprivileged person should be served alternately, is inconsistent with the customers' opinions. One should bear in mind here that the existence of persons entitled to be served first has different consequences for the remaining customers depending upon the relation between demand and supply. The rules by which pregnant women, disabled people, and so on should be served first have a different sense in normal market conditions as compared with the situation of scarcity of goods. 'Normally' we let persons recognized as weaker do their shopping before us in order to lighten their effort connected with shopping. In such a case, the rules granting privilege mean that the privileged persons' expenditure of time spent in line (and the related effort) does not influence their chances of buying the article they line up for. Such rules are sensible if there are enough goods, that is, if all those involved in a given situation of sale can buy—if not on that particular occasion, then at least soon, and in another shop which is reasonably close to the original one. Instead, with the working assumption that demand greatly exceeds supply, those privileged in respect of the expenditure of time and effort related to standing in line become privileged also as regards the chances of buying the necessary article. It is impossible in Polish conditions to draw a line between the two situations described above. However, this can hardly be the only reason for the quantitative relations found here. The smaller the supply in relation to demand, the less chance of buying the necessary article at another reasonably close place in a reasonable time. The greater the extent to which a given position in line determines the very chances of satisfying an important need, the greater also the importance of privileges for the weak, who are perceived as a threat and as rivals by the rest of the queue, and the smaller the part played by the rule that grants privileges in respect of time and effort. It seems that the role of time spent while waiting to be able to buy diminishes, as compared with normal situations. The possibility of joining several queues at the same time, the specific 'turns of duty' in line, reservation of positions, and lists of those in line seem to speak for that assumption. Due to the specific character of a normal situation of sale, it is impossible today to differentiate the customers according to their respective rights resulting from various needs, merits, or faults; what differentiates people instead are the most visible features, such as pregnancy, disability, or special papers which in any case can only be produced with difficulty in a crowded shop. Hence the principle of strict objective egalitarianism (the same portion for everyone) is more easily implemented in line situations than other versions of justice. Of course, buying rationed goods is in reality much more complex, as at least three principles are in force here: (1) all customers are entitled to buy the same amount of goods; (2) the chances of exercising that right depend on the person's position in line according to the principle: first come, first served; and (3) these chances are slightly bigger for certain preferred groups, like the disabled, and so on.

The principle of objective egalitarianism, however, leaves a whole range of separate customers' needs out of account. A single young man may buy the same amount of commodities as a mother of seven. One can hardly demand that appropriately authenticated papers be produced by the customers, thus making the differentiation of needs, otherwise quite obvious to the people, objective. Moreover, the situational character of rationing (what we mean here is not sale by coupons) makes such a strict objective egalitarianism harmless: shopping can be continued in another situation. Thus, as follows from the above, the definite rules of justice accepted in conditions of situational redistribution should be different from those in the situation of universal rationing. Central redistribution through coupons should secure to everybody the right to buy a definite amount of goods; it is assumed here that the person concerned cannot supplement that amount (such supplements are possible through a person's own agriculture, trade, and gifts, for example, from abroad). What is more, differentiation of needs can, nay should, be taken into account in conditions of universal redistribution, as the authority that puts redistribution into effect through the distribution of rights to buy definite shares of the overall amount of commodities is better qualified to define differentiated needs, both on the universal nation-wide scale and for individuals, through the establishment of appropriate parameters of persons entitled to participate in the distribution.

When asked about the principles that should govern the rationing of various necessities and their distribution between individuals and different social categories, most of the respondents (69 per cent) professed the principle of relative egalitarianism, according to which all people should get more or less equal amounts, but with their different needs taken into account, for example, age or the physical strain of work. As few as 10 per cent of the respondents professed the principle of objective and absolute egalitarianism according to which *all persons should get exactly the same amounts*, of soap or sugar, for example. As has already been mentioned above, 10 per cent repudiated the very principle of rationing in general. The acceptance of relative egalitarianism meant that the persons interviewed accepted a certain differentiation in allowances beforehand. As concluded in the study carried out by the Institute of Domestic Trade and Services:

Based on the data obtained, the socially accepted principles of a just distribution of meat may be supposed to result from the existence of two criteria for distribution of goods. The first criterion is that of 'biological' needs, and its application in the case of rationing of meat results in a belief which prevails in society that larger allowances should be granted to groups such as pregnant women, breast-feeding mothers, or those performing hard physical work. The other criterion seem to follow from the existence of negative social attitudes toward those whose behaviour infringes accepted principles of conduct. The reduction of rations for groups such as prisoners or persons who neither work nor learn, postulated by most respondents, may be supposed to be a form of punishment. The fact that smaller amounts of meat are conceded to farmers is another problem.

The groups that proved most rigorous in this respect in the study carried out by the Institute of Domestic Trade and Services were inhabitants of big cities, while-collar workers with the highest

Self-Limited Freedom of Market

income, and those with higher education. It should be added that the negative selection, to determine who should have no right to buy or who should get smaller rations, can be carried into effect more easily in the conditions of universal rather than situational rationing. As shown also by our study, only 39 per cent of respondents were of the opinion that a ration of necessities should be secured for all.

Concerning groups which should be deprived of rations according to the respondents, the most frequently mentioned (49 per cent of answers) were the so-called 'parasites': adult healthy men of productive age who neither work nor study. Instead, as few as 9 per cent supported the exclusion from the rationing system of those whose income greatly exceeded the average, and 10 per cent mentioned other categories of persons deserving discrimination.

With supply problems deepening, the proposed exclusions might be expected to broaden to include other social categories. It is also apparent that the prevailing relative egalitarianism, adapted to individual and group needs and to their external indices, is also related to merit. To all according to their needs, but also according to their work, is the most popular canon of justice according to which the ration should depend on work. A general conclusion may also be drawn here: in conditions of crisis, redistribution and its rules create an opportunity to change the 'privileged' into the 'handicapped' and vice versa. A person who does not work or who has easier access to food is a privileged person—and thus one whom redistribution should handicap. The handicapped, in turn, are those who perform hard work or have particular biological needs—the mechanisms of redistribution should, therefore, privilege them.

At the beginning of this chapter the regional, or the territorial, conflicts connected with access to rationed or non-rationed goods have already been mentioned. Most of the inhabitants of Warsaw who answered our questionnaire (84 per cent) thought that the principles of rationing should be the same in different areas. As regards another, and outwardly similar, problem, that of outsiders' right to buy commodities in a locality they visit, the respondents' opinions were polarized: 49 per cent believed the ban on sale to outsiders, in force in many localities, to be unjust, while 41 per cent accepted that ban as resulting from local differences in living conditions and supplies. The convergency coefficient between the repudiation of limited sale on the one hand and of local differentiation of the principles of rationing on the other hand was, however, high enough (Yule's Q = 0.74) to justify the assumption that in both cases we are dealing with an egalitarian attitude.

The summary index for absolute egalitarianism consisted of four items in the questionnaire. Persons who scored highest in that index were those who declared themselves for equal ration norms throughout the country; equal rights to buy commodities for locals and outsiders; rationed necessities for all without exception; and the general validity of a rule by which the urban population would be provided with household equipment and the like in exchange for meat rations for farmers, if such an agreement were to be negotiated by the competent trade unions. This extreme egalitarianism was shown by 16 per cent of the respondents, while 6 per cent gave no egalitarian answers whatever. Distribution on the egalitarianism index was shaped like a normal distribution, which adds to our trust in its value. One should, however, bear in mind when analysing the index that the highest score fails to reflect the most popular attitude among the respondents: not only 'equality according to needs' but also 'equality according to expenditure on work'. Namely, egalitarianism failed to include the most popular opinion that norms should correspond with needs, and the somewhat less popular one according to which so-called social parasites should be excluded from rationing. Both these opinions could be found in persons with low or medium index values.

Our next step was to compare the divided categories, or respondents characterized by different index values for egalitarian attitudes. In that comparison we used the various possible dichotomies and Yule's convergency coefficient Q:

women = 0.22
younger people = 0.13
the less educated = 0.26
workers = 0.26
incomes below the median = 0.00
medium incomes (quartiles II and III) = 0.00
meat consumed exceptionally = 0.12

material conditions bad in own opinion = 0.00
material conditions average in own opinion = 0.35

As we can see, the relationship between the respondents socio-economic status and their egalitarianism, only one factor, and a weak one at that (significant at the accepted level of 0.05). Those who believed their own and their family's living conditions to approximate to those of an average Polish family were more inclined to show egalitarian attitudes, while inegalitarian attitudes would more frequently be found in categories with extreme (negative or positive) opinions about their own situation. This finding may seem inconsistent with popular sociological knowledge according to which egalitarianism can be found in those least privileged: but the index of egalitarianism concerns not general egalitarianism, but rather its precise and definite forms. In conditions of a serious threat, general principles, such as egalitarianism, are reduced to certain more detailed postulates connected with actual living conditions. One should bear in mind here that the highest score on the egalitarianism scale meant that the person in question accepted a number of opinions: that any agreements on the exchange of manufactured goods for meat rations between those living in rural and urban regions should cover all citizens; that rations of necessities should be provided for all citizens irrespective of their work or income; that rationing standards should be uniform throughout the country since identical conditions must be created for all; and that there should be no differences between locals and outsiders as regards chances for buying goods, again because identical conditions must be created for all. If we take a closer look at the above-mentioned opinions, it becomes apparent that what connects them with one another is not egalitarianism in the broadest sense, in which it functions as a social principle. This form of egalitarianism may be identified with the principle of universal rationing, and equality for all citizens' before the rules of rationing. Here it seems best to characterize the components of the attitude discussed, and of the index used in its measurement.

## THE RULES OF PRIVATE TURNOVER OF NECESSITIES

At the time of writing, most necessities have been rationed for several months. This creates an entirely new social situation and forces people to develop new patterns of interaction and new principles of justice to regulate mutual conduct. In a situation where many people need help in acquiring necessities to satisfy their basic needs, it seems particularly important to investigate the principles that govern the rendering of that help, that is, the transmission to others of the goods they need.

Most respondents (69 per cent) consider it wrong to waste the goods they do not need if those goods might be used by somebody else. Some of them even consider it to be their duty to give such goods to those who need them: not for payment or direct exchange, but as a gift (47 per cent). The principles that govern donations and possibly return services vary according to the strength of ties between the person who has the goods and the one who needs them. The duty to give becomes more bounden with the increasing strength of ties between parties to the interaction. Passing from the family to more distant circles, the duty to help those who expect to be helped weakens. In the present interpretation, that 'expectation of help' possesses the character of a claim: a person's right to expect help is tantamount to his right to demand help. Such a right to a claim is granted to those in need much more frequently if the ties between the parties to the interaction are strong, so that they are more entitled to expect donation. Thus, a person in trouble first asks for help from his next of kin, believing such help to be his due; it is only afterwards, if need arises, that he approaches others, counting on their readiness to oblige. The situation develops differently if the duties and rights concern a return service and not a gift. Both the duty to requite a gift and the right to expect requittal are independent of the strength of ties between the recipient and the donor.

The following data show how strongly the principles concerning gifts and return gifts are connected with the kind of interaction between the partners. If the duty to help a person in trouble is imposed on the disposer of goods, no matter how distant the relationship between him and that person, it is bound also to be imposed if the person who needs help is a member of the disposer's family or his close friend. Those who consider it their duty to help a stranger in need feel even more obliged to help a next of kin. The most frequent opinion here (45 per cent) was that a person who can help is obligated to help irrespective of the nature of his relationship with the person in need of help. The situation is similar in the case of the right to claim help. If that right is granted to a person whose ties with the potential donor are weak, it is automatically also granted to those who are in a close relationship with the donor, but never vice versa. Those who demand help from a stranger who can help them, always demand help from their next of kin as well. Most respondents, however (50 per cent), think they have no right to demand help from anybody: helping is a matter of good-will.

The same trends can be seen in the case of the principles that govern requital. Those who expect requital from a next of kin also, and more so, expect distant acquaintances to reciprocate. Yet the bulk (59 per cent) believe they have no right to claim any form of reciprocation. Those who feel obligated to requite a next of kin for his help, believe that this duty also covers situations when the person who helped them was just a distant acquaintance. According to most, however (83 per cent), requital is not obligatory, irrespective of the closeness of relationship between them and those who helped them.

We shall now discuss the normative regulation of principles that govern private turnover of goods according to the strength of the ties between the parties to the interaction. These principles may be based both on moral norms, that is, on imperative norms or unilateral validity, and on legal, that is, imperative-attributive norms. The former impose the duty to help on one party, but do not entitle the other party to claim help, while the latter—imposing the duty to help on one party—at the same time entitle the other party to claim help. Legal regulation of the principles of rendering help is more frequent if the parties are in close relationship to each other (41 per cent) as compared with the situation of weak ties between them (21 per cent). As we pass from the family to more distant circles, the role of the legal motivation decreases. People feel obligated to help and able to demand help more frequently in interactions with family members than with the members of other groups. Instead, the moral regulation of the principles concerning gifts occurs with the same frequency irrespective of the strength of ties between the parties to the interaction (26–7 per cent). This is shown in Fig. 10.1.

Concerning the principles that govern requital, opinions shape differently, and both the legal and the moral regulation are found with equal frequency irrespective of the strength of ties between

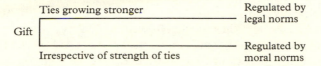

Fig. 10.1. Regulation of the principles concerning gifts.

the parties. Thus the duty of requital and the right to claim requital is not thought to depend on who has helped or who has been helped (see Fig. 10.2).

Private turnover may be regulated by the principles of direct exchange and of gift. We deal with direct exchange if the duty of donation is accompanied by that of requital, and with gift if there is no duty of requital to accompany that of donation.

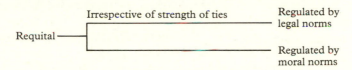

Fig. 10.2. Regulation of the principles concerning requital.

Private turnover is governed by the principles of donation more frequently if there are strong ties between the parties to the inter-action. As we pass from the family to more distant circles, the importance of donation decreases and that of exchange grows.

We shall now compare the rights and duties imposed on one-self and on others in identical situations. The rights granted to oneself and to others are in principle the same. What is signifi-cant, instead, is that people impose a much greater number of duties on themselves than on others (the difference amounting to about 30 per cent irrespective of the strength of ties) in analogous situations, but they do not consider themselves entitled to expect any form of reciprocation. The principle of positive reciprocity—'something for something'—does not apply here; nor does that of negative reciprocity—'nothing for nothing'. It is considered a per-son's moral obligation to help others; this obligation is strength-ened by the belief that other people are not thus obligated, which may also increase the sense of responsibility for others in need. The imposition on oneself of the heavy moral duty of helping others unselfishly if they need help is in accordance with the principle of love of one's neighbour—*caritas*.

In times of economic crisis, struggle and competition for the means to make existence conformable to human needs and habits are said to prevail. Yet despite the endless deterioration of living conditions, charitable attitudes are still widespread irrespective of the chances of reciprocation from the person who is helped. Help is frequently impersonal. For instance, people return the coupons they do not need to the office for further distribution among those in need; coupons can also be given away to a stranger who needs them. As may be supposed, the acceptance of the norm of *caritas* results from the belief in reciprocity in another sense: namely, in a society where the majority are charitable, anybody in need can expect others to help him, too. It should be stressed here that reciprocity in this interpretation is not contradictory to unselfishness in helping, and thus to the principle of *caritas*. In this sense, reciprocity does not involve the element of reckoning which is inherent in the direct positive exchange of 'something for something'. In the former case we count on others to help us in need, basing our hopes on a trust in their kindness and unselfishness only, and not because we expect them to requite us for what we have given them before.

## GENERAL PRESENTATION OF FINDINGS

We shall now present a summary analysis of the structure of attitudes to and opinions about the questions included in this chapter, by means of summary indices which may be treated here as an outline answer to the separate questions. We realize at the same time that an analysis of relations between simple indices— even if those indices include most of the closed questions of the questionnaire, as was the case in our study—cannot replace a deeper and more detailed analysis of relations between the separate questions and the respondents' social and material standing.

Irrespective of the various aspects of the respondents' attitude towards charitable behaviour and the functioning of the principle of reciprocity, a system has been shaped in the social relations of connections between the remaining summary indices we used in the preliminary treatment of the findings. We shall now leave connections that are weak or moderate as measured by the Q convergency coefficient out of account, and discuss those relationships which are significant at the level of at least 0.05. The number of such relations was small. The strongest found was the symptomatic relation between anxiety and *caritas* (Q = 0.81). The respondents' acceptance of *caritas* as an unconditional obligation, and belief in the automatism of charitable actions and inclinations goes hand in hand with their feelings of safety and lack of anxiety in social contacts. One should bear in mind, in this connection, that in our sample of randomly chosen inhabitants of Warsaw anxiety and a sense of threat were relatively rare, and the belief in the unconditional validity of the rule of *caritas* was very strong instead. This statement is rather important in as much as the findings concern the period immediately preceding the imposition of martial law in Poland. The study confirmed our introductory hypothesis, according to which—in a situation of a total economic crisis when it is evidently impossible to work out a system for rationing of goods in short supply which would meet all individual and group needs—the norm of mutual help grows more and more important, and makes further redistribution of some goods possible according to individual needs and powers. Our study justifies the assumption that the decisive role in the process of informal redistribution was played not by the mechanisms of the market but by those of unconditional help (*caritas*) and general reciprocity.

The charitable attitudes are also significantly related to another two summary indices: first, the growth in the index of charitable attitudes, and secondly the rise in pro-consumer attitudes. Despite its weaknesses (Q = 0.37), the relationship between *caritas* and consumerism helps to explain the interdependence between the separate components of the consumerism index. The conviction that we all ought to help one another to the best of our ability is connected with another, namely, that—with scarcity of goods that are not centrally rationed—the will of those directly involved ought to be respected, and the needs of all groups of customers should be taken into account through appropriate settlements by compromise. Thus the pro-consumer attitudes do not result from a denial of the principle that those best informed about overall needs and abilities should carry out a rational distribution of goods. What produces such attitudes is rather the opinion that possible inequalities concerning access to goods in short supply might be mitigated through a further redistribution of commodities, based on the principles of charity, carried out by those who own larger amounts of goods. Another view leading to pro-consumer attitudes is that it should first of all be made possible for the greatest number of those who directly need certain goods to buy them, provided that such persons apply for the goods they need.

The other equally obvious weak relation (0.36) could be found between *caritas* and the index of egalitarianism. Egalitarianism, whose elements concern the rules to be accepted on the macro-social scale in universal rationing, is actually a counterpart of charitable and pro-consumer attitudes at the level of society as a whole. In our sample, however, the relation between consumerism and egalitarianism proved weak and insignificant. This may result from the character of the questions asked. The contents of questions about universal rationing, that is, rationing on the macro-social scale, directly concerned circumstances and problems other than those described in questions about various conflicts taking place in shops and about what we called situational rationing. Another explanation would involve a direct assumption that the accepted rules of situational versus universal rationing differ to some extent, while *caritas* in general adds to the egalitarian character of those rules in both cases. This explanation is likely, as a result of the above-mentioned differences between the questions used for each of the discussed indices.

Finally, the remaining two relationships found in our study should be mentioned. Egalitarianism is very strongly related (0.63) to lack of tolerance of those who infringe the rules of rationing. This relationship becomes quite clear if we realize that a tolerant attitude towards such transgressions is actually tantamount to tolerance of infringements of the rules that provide for a possible equal distribution of goods, which is therefore also equitable or at least as close to equity as possible. Another problem lies in the connection between two indices which were not found to have a relationship with those discussed. With the growing approval of the centralized mechanism of universal rationing introduced by the authorities, went an increased approval of the opinion that some rules have to be adopted in crisis situations—any rules will do as long as we do not let things take their course or leave everything to individual consumers to decide (0.38). Admittedly, centralism and rigorism are highly independent from each other: what connects them, however, is that they both oppose the principle of *laissez-faire* as socially undesirable.

To sum up the problems discussed above, the following can be stated. Rationing of goods, both universal and situational, won a broad acceptance in Polish society. That rationing was to be based on the principles of egalitarianism. What was meant here, however, was not absolute but relative egalitarianism with the rations differentiated to some extent. The differentiation was based on the criterion of biological needs and on another criterion resulting from negative social attitudes towards those whose conduct infringed the accepted rule; the basic canon of justice as regards universal rationing is: to all according to their needs, and to all according to their work.

In society's opinion, the following principles of justice should govern situational rationing: all those standing in line, irrespective of the order in which they have joined that queue, should have equal rights to decide about the rules of situational rationing; it should be made possible for the greatest number of customers to buy the minimum amount of goods, that amount being sufficient, however, to satisfy the customer's needs; a just distribution, which a given person puts into his attempts to acquire a given commodity.

The people believe that the above-mentioned canons of justice will be best carried into effect if decisions concerning rationing of commodities are taken centrally, with the least possible participation of those directly involved in the individual situation. This way the probability of maintaining social order is enhanced. What is indispensable, however, if decisions are to be taken in this manner, is a permanent and efficient system of social supervision exercised by all trade unions, to prevent any deviations from the accepted rules.

Presumably, society's acceptance of the rationing of basic goods according to the principles of egalitarianism was due to the fact that such rationing increased the feeling of safety in conditions of total crisis. Owing to rationing, the right is secured to everybody to buy at least the minimum amount of necessary goods irrespective of that person's dexterity or shrewdness. The sense of threat and dissatisfaction resulting from the scarcity of desired goods was presumably recompensed by the confidence in mutual help in difficulties and in the unselfishness of those who help others whose need is more pressing. The inclusion of individual different needs, impossible in the situation of universal rationing, is made possible owing to the mechanisms of exchange and the prevalence of charitable attitudes among the citizens. Thus the principle of *caritas*, both in the shape of informal and institutionalized activities (for example, of the Church), proves to be an additional support to rationing without which the collective and individual enjoyment of its benefits would be impossible.

# 11

# Daily Bread and Liberation

In 1984–6 at the Warsaw branch of the Polish Sociological Association, I held an open seminar on 'Memoirs of Everyday Life'. It was based on two working assumptions. First, every problem to be discussed had to be a natural phenomenon, something which can be sensed intuitively but requires further explication. Secondly, that the problem should in turn become the subject of independent investigation carried out in various ways in order to overcome the dominance of the standardized questionnaire so typical of Polish sociology since the late 1950s.

The problems were diverse, even though we tried to avoid those which were the most painful after the introduction of martial law on 13 December 1981. We thought that the importance of those events precluded possible profanation in the form of sociological field studies, combined with the desacralization, specific to the sociological profession, of the events and motives studied and their lay interpretation. Such professional cynicism deserves separate treatment and hence will not be discussed here. We shall, therefore, treat the existence of such a professional attitude as given, as part of the sociologist's way of looking at the world.

Let us return to the first working assumption, that is, the naturalness of certain social events. The problem of defining the social fact has fascinated sociologists since Durkheim, who linked the new discipline to the possibility of proving the independent existence of social facts. This school gave rise to definitions of social facts such as that given on one occasion by Stefan Czarnowski, the most eminent Polish Durkheimian and an outstanding sociologist in his own right: 'Any fact whose development, change or outcome is conditioned by the existence of a human community is a social fact. It may be both a general and a particular fact, a fact within a group and between groups, a custom and whatever opposes custom, not only virtue but crime as well.'[1] In this definition which, to be blunt, says little as it leaves little outside the borders of sociology, the most interesting aspect is the stress put on the dynamism of social facts. Czarnowski adds that 'both social facts and their configurations change constantly, each having its own dynamic'.

Such definitions have little meaning today because they express what, in the meantime, has become part of the paradigm of the discourse within the discipline. Durkheim and his disciples emphasized what might be termed the amorality of sociology: 'not only virtue but crime as well' is a social fact. It is common knowledge with what energy Durkheim used to stress the normalness of various phenomena usually treated as pathological. Whether he had to deal with murder or suicide, his first step was to indicate that it was a social fact as well as an individual one. As a social fact it is normal because it is there, and especially because it is always present in a given social type, and because it manifests itself always in a more or less similar way. This is an important issue, as Durkheim thereby imposes on us the attitude of an impartial researcher. What is natural is normal. Whatever is there is natural. It is there, and hence the sociologist finds it, and subjects it to his or her inspection. Every fact found in this way and inspected from the sociological perspective is a social fact. Czarnowski's formula quoted above can be reduced in the same way.

Let us, therefore, follow the beaten track. Imposing a norm on someone's conduct accordingly means making someone responsible for that conduct. It need not necessarily be the person whose conduct is under consideration. If we say that small children should have short fingernails then the responsibility for that hygienic operation falls upon the person who cares for them. In that case we consider the conduct performed upon a person, who is unable to carry out the appropriate operation independently. On another occasion we may say that a certain person's conduct is irresponsible, meaning thereby that whoever acts in a specified way is not responsible, or acts as if he or she were not responsible for his or her conduct. If we feel sure that such conduct is a sign of mental illness, according to standards adopted in psychiatry, then we absolve the doer from responsibility and transfer it to other persons.

---

[1] S. Czarnowski, Preface to the Polish translation of E. Meunier's *Introduction à la sociologie* (Warsaw, 1938).

In the examples given above, and in similar situations, moral responsibility is assumed to correspond to effective responsibility. The person in charge of a child is effectively responsible for its personal hygiene in that he or she may bring it about. Accordingly, to say that a person who is not fully responsible for what he or she does is the doer is, in a sense, a contradiction. When it comes to those who, in view of their mental condition, are exempted from criminal responsibility, we say that they are instruments of an event that is developing outside their will rather than that they are agents endowed with free will, which assumes a definite concept of mental faculties.

Let us, therefore, proceed to 'conscience' as the criterion in that controversy. Attention has often been drawn to the fact that perception of the world in causal terms comes from teleological experience, which at least within the framework of our cognitive abilities must remain exclusively human experience. The nature of the relationship between the human subject who wants something and his or her satisfaction in that respect may remain unknown; nevertheless, from the point of view of that human subject the set of wishes, actions, and emotions is a construction of agency. Anthropomorphization of the world around this would manifest itself in our imposition on the world of similar mechanisms of agency. We may ask why the concept of agency is so important with reference to human beings.

The answer to that question involves the problems of free will and responsibility. Whenever we speak about agency we mean responsibility, and vice versa. In ancient thought these phenomena were identical to such an extent that kings who were quite sane have had the sea flogged, animals have been found guilty of crimes, and human beings have been found guilty regardless of their intentions. The discourse of natural events and causes and moral discourse were still not separated from each other. All this did not imply a lack of ability to make a distinction between the attributes of the various real entities, nor an ability to observe in oneself and to ascribe to others good or bad intentions. The important point was that in the state of natural philosophical innocence mankind treated jointly various things the relationships between which were later forgotten.

People have often thought about whether such cognitive activity can be controlled by rules. This is not a way to deceive either

338     *Daily Bread and Liberation*

oneself or the reader, who is defenceless *vis-à-vis* methodological didactics. How can methodological rules make sense in view of the problematic character of normative regulation, revealed by contemporary reflection? Any experienced researcher is able to list in a quarter of an hour a number of research directives with all the relevant exceptions and reservations. Unfortunately, we also see the constant appearance of studies in the so-called methodology of social sciences written without any grounding in research practice. Current methodology is responsible for the fact that students, young researchers, and journalists resort to the clichéd procedures of questionnaire surveys and in-depth interviews. Under the pressure of these facts the profession as a whole must multiply those quasi-paradigmatic research procedures in order to keep in touch among themselves and with the outside audience.

For instance, the challenge of ethnomethodology to the normative sciences seems at least questionable if it would really mean the total denial of the role of the normative factor in processes which result in any course of conduct. Of course, the very nature of such processes is very debatable today, and the definition of the problem of norms by such traditional terms as determination gives rise to doubts. Few people would hazard a statement today of what underlines such traditional terms as determination, except for certain algorithms of the analysis of co-occurrence and sequence of events, the more so as we know nothing about those algorithms in a casual sense without prior knowledge. But the word 'conscience' in this context is worth remembering, because it may later show us a path along which we may be able to solve our dilemmas.

The advocates of the anti-normative point of view, manifested in ethnomethodology, are inclined to refer to the fact that all allegedly general names and statements are indexical in character. The supposedly revolutionary nature of that observation cannot but evoke a pitiful smile in those versed in normative issues. Take lawyers, for instance, who have had to deal with the indexical nature of norms for millennia, and have developed various practical methodologies accordingly, including a specific legal hermeneutics known as the theory of interpretation. This is so because it is common knowledge that application of a norm to a concrete case always requires appropriate interpretative work. But this is not to say that there is any sharp division into general statements and statements which are defined by context. We have to deal rather with a gradual transition from the former to the latter. One cannot speak about reality without an implied reference to the context because reality is this context. On the other hand, one cannot speak at all about anything in a manner that would be comprehensible to another if one's statements are separated from the concrete context of reality. The opposition between reality and reference to reality is based precisely upon this hiatus. If one is directly immersed in the reality here and now, one can only live and at best stammer. Comprehensible conversation assumes a certain distance from reality.

We have suggested that whoever rejects the role of the normative in human conduct would have to use a detailed theory of agency, and secondly, that such a rejection cannot be based on a stress on the a-contextual nature of normative statements. If anyone dislikes the triviality of the above statement I can do no more than point out that this reminder has been necessary as a reaction to those who attack the normativism that is involved in humanistic interpretation. However original the formulation that norms are at best a post-factual legitimation of behaviour might seem, it is in open contradiction with common sense and with private experience of sound conscience.

We have thus come to the point at which we can begin to discuss the relationship between norms and human conduct without risking misunderstandings. One cannot speak at all about human agency without referring to some concept of responsibility. That responsibility is contained in definite normative material, whether verbalized or not. Only a naïve division of life into opposing spheres of value 'ought'-judgements and descriptive 'is' statements, which is both valid and essential in the specific domain of logical investigations, can explain the very construction of the problem in the form of a hypothetical causal chain in which a norm causes the conduct that follows. If we are to separate these spheres from one another, this is done only in order to state that they parallel each other. The correct formulation of the problem seems different: a given norm defines the responsibility of the agent for his or her conduct. A norm is not the cause of conduct (such a way of thinking is absent even among those jurists who devotedly study law only in books); but it defines the cause and the effect, the agent, his or her responsibility and conduct.

This line of reasoning enables us to define a little more clearly the naturalness of social facts. That naturalness is understood here to indicate that conditioning by the existence of human community lends itself to interpretation in terms of agency and the normative interpretation described above. This fact in its rise, process, and result differs from its conceivable rise, process, and result if the human community did not exist, or if its existence were different. This means that the human community is made responsible for the particular shape of that fact in its various phases, whatever that fact may be.

At this point these principles are best illustrated with a concrete piece of research, and I shall use the study of the rationing of goods which I began with my friends in the autumn of 1981. In those turbulent days the growing disintegration of the national economy was clearly visible. It was apparent through the ever-growing list of commodities sold only on presentation of the official coupons which were distributed among the population. The queues at every shop were growing, so that people regularly had to stand in them day and night. Queuing was not, however, a new phenomenon. In 1979 I left a farewell party for a colleague departing to the United States and installed myself at the end of an outdoor queue for a traditional Christmas live carp. I discovered, when I got the fish, my colleague was already half-way from Warsaw to New York. Coming to the United States myself I discovered that pictures of the Christmas queues in Poland adorned American newspapers. By 1981, however, it was happening on a much larger scale and far beyond the usual practice in the communist economy up till then. Rationing, which was originally to include only meat, was extended to other kinds of food, toiletries, and various industrial goods from glass to nails. All this was accompanied by the continuing practice of selling motor cars and agricultural machinery for coupons, which had been introduced decades earlier.

Rampant rationing was accompanied by the process which it was intended to prevent, namely the long queues which formed not only when goods were on sale, but also when people were expecting that goods were to be delivered to the shop. The queues, though one of the most conspicuous elements of everyday life under Communism, never became a legitimate subject of sociological interest, except for an MA thesis supervised by Professor Andrzej Kwilecki in Poznań. My personal experience of encouraging students to study queuing, if not as the subject of MA theses then at least as a seminar paper, was disappointing, while other topics were quite willingly accepted. My impression was that queuing seemed to Polish students so self-evident, common, and non-problematic that they found it difficult to treat it in a systematic fashion as an object of scientific interest. It seems that there are certain stereotypes of the proper and legitimate objects of study, deserving of a thesis or paper, and of what is ridiculous, compromising, and failing to meet the standards of sociological and academic propriety. Justice obliges me to add that these stereotypes functioned among the faculty as well. I have never succeeded in convincing otherwise diligent younger researchers to make systematic records of the prices of goods sold on the black market, or exempted from rationing (petrol sold clandestinely without coupons, meat similarly traded, and the like). Even amongst sociologists, carnivorousness is so natural that it precludes looking at the problem of meat rationing from a distance and with proper scientific detachment and curiosity.

I failed in 1980 and 1981, as I had failed earlier, to collect systematic data on queuing. But when watching queues I became more and more fascinated by the mechanisms which pattern the behaviour of people standing in them. My opinion until 1981 was that the introduction of the form of rationing which I later termed situational rationing (that is, specification by the sales staff on the spot of how much of a given product one client could buy at a time), was a glaring infringement of the sense of justice and legal order. If a given commodity is available in the shop, I thought, then it should be sold in any quantity to any customer who wants to buy it and can afford to pay. Every restriction resulting in a specific rationing decision should be treated as a transgression of individual freedom, not to say the fundamental principles of civil law. At any rate, I myself have ground my teeth if a person standing before me bought the last amount of a given commodity available at that time in the shop.

I mention this without blushing because I think that the investigative attitude must be based upon *sui generis* emotional innocence. Of course, any one in his senses must get furious when he is deprived of the opportunity to buy some commodity for his children. But I believed it equally self-evident that people in the queue watching from afar how some attractive commodity was being sold out would nevertheless pay attention to what was obvious to me, namely, that the principle of free trade was indispensable for an improvement of our national economy.

My original viewpoint had already failed to find support when, during the mild economic crisis of 1977, I carried out, with students from the University of Warsaw, a survey of 211 adult inhabitants of the same small town in the sub-Carpathian region of Poland where our research on dispute patterns had been conducted. One of the questions asked was whether sales staff are entitled to limit the sale of various goods by fixing the quota for customers. I was struck then by the fact that as many as 72 per cent of the sample supported such practices. This suggested that, in view of the shortage of goods, public opinion was in favour of this extraordinary prerogative being exercised by sales staff, and of limiting the freedom of the consumers. This is what I recorded at that time. But I also recorded the various arguments offered by customers in support of situational rationing. The principle of equality was mentioned most often: 'Everyone must have an opportunity to buy.' The majority view was perhaps best expressed by someone who said: 'There must be some form of distribution. Otherwise one person would have a lot while another would have nothing. One person must understand another's needs if there is such a situation.' Many criticized the causes: 'This is the trouble with the Polish economy.' Others, while rejecting situational rationing, postulated a universal rationing system resembling the one that functioned under the Stalinism of the early 1950s.

It would be untrue if I said that I paid attention then to these opinions. I recorded them as yet more evidence of the fact that the existing system made people forget the principle of the free market.

But the results of that study came to my mind again in the summer of 1980 when I read the demands made by the strikers. The list of twenty-one demands raised by the Inter-Factory Strike Committee in Gdansk included Point 13: 'Introduce rationing of meat and meat products.' The problem was forgotten at first because the authorities were under the illusion for several months after signing the Gdansk Agreements with the strikers that it would be possible to avoid rationing. Nevertheless, in February

1981 the Cabinet had to introduce meat rationing, for the period 1 April to 30 June of that year. This began an avalanche of rationing. The intriguing fact for me was that rationing was not imposed by the authorities, as had seemed to happen in the past, but that it was forced on the authorities by the strikers.

At that moment the interpretation of rationing had to change for a second time. I first changed it when what I took to be illegal interference by sales staff with the rights of the customers proved to be accepted by almost everybody. I thought at that time that this was a manifestation of authoritarian attitudes, consisting in the abandonment by the holders of rights of their freedom in favour of a temporarily accepted authority to distribute goods in short supply. This time it appeared that a strange authoritarianism had been forced upon those in power.

It is assumed that from the natural point of view of a member of a socialist society that redistribution is something abnormal, the normal being the possibility of free purchase and sale of goods and services in the market. We also assume that the mechanism of redistribution is abnormal from the economic point of view, the market mechanism being the norm. The second assumption is historically incorrect, while the first has never been the subject-matter of reliable empirical studies. By treating rationing and, redistribution generally as something abnormal and temporary we have not paid it the attention it deserves. Under the socialist system redistribution is intended to be the foundation of social life, planning being only an instrument, and the defects in its functioning are everyday problems for most inhabitants. Free prices, treated as a defect in a centralized system, are a logical element of a system based upon redistribution. Under socialism, social conflicts focus on the struggle for a share in redistribution that would be most favourable for a given group or social category.

The above passage is the next signpost towards arriving at a specific cognitive equilibrium which may be disturbed by successive failures in interpretation. This time rationing is seen in a different context. On abandoning the ideal of the free market and the autonomy of the individual, a context in which rationing is deviant, we turn to a positive image of the socialist economy as a system based, unlike free-market capitalism, on redistribution. Rationing, whether situational or universal, changes from deviance into normality, almost paradigmatic under socialism. In this case it is not the rationing of bread by sales staff and the rationing of meat by the state throughout the country, but a *lack* of such rationing in some places, some circumstances, and in some periods which calls for an explanation.

But this explanation, too proves unsatisfactory in view of subsequent events. The gap can be seen already in the question which concluded the redistributive interpretation quoted above. Research grounded in what is happening around us will always tend to disclose gaps of this kind.

But what does a sociological interpretation mean? May we speak about a sociological interpretation of facts? If it is true that there are no facts without theories within which one could speak about those facts, then, self-evidently, there are no sociological facts without sociological theories. And there are plenty of the latter, as may be seen by consulting any textbook. But matters look worse when we come to a sociological fact as such, a sociological fact in general. Can one speak about it other than as a fact which forms the domain of facts constructed by specific theories, a model of those theories? Is there anything other than collections of facts, which are the model for the Marxist theory of society, facts which satisfy symbolic interactionism, ethnomethodological facts? Are there as many collections of facts as there are theories, whether already formulated or conceivable?

Ronald Dworkin[2] observed that a constructive interpretation of a fact is one which best makes this fact a representative of a definite species. If we stick to this definition, we would say that sociological interpretation of a fact would consist in making it a representative of a definite theoretical category.

A moment go we made rationing a representative of the theoretical category, system of economic redistribution. In Karl Polanyi's great historical *panneau*[3] this is one of the four basic types of economic order, next to reciprocity, the free market, and the household economy based on interdependence. It would be an abuse to say that by referring to that typology we have used the procedure of deductive or inductive reasoning. Comprehension consisted in placing the social fact under consideration in a definite categorial context. The small role ascribed to that process by the positivistically oriented philosophy of science is common knowledge. Suffice it to say that, in a usual interpretation, the

[2] R. Dworkin, *Law's Empire* (London, 1986).
[3] K. Polanyi, *Personal Knowledge* (London, 1973).

whole thing is either completely disregarded or at most appears as a preliminary stage compared with the extended explanatory work. At best one would refer to the useful role of typology and classification in those cases in which more advanced theoretical work is not possible. In this way the procedure which is fundamental in humanistic operations, intended to secure mutual understanding, becomes a necessary evil, barely tolerated on the margin of true science.

In fact the real research process is precisely the opposite. By this I mean that recognition of a social fact being studied passes discretely from one interpretation to another, activated by categories belonging to different contexts. The object of interest for the positivistically oriented philosophy of science, namely explanation carried out according to this or that schema, if they take place at all, find that place within each interpretation. On having assumed in a given phase of the research process that the phenomenon of rationing can at best be understood in terms of the four basic types of economic order, we can, if we are at all interested in explanation, try to carry out hypothetically deductive reasoning, or any other reasoning, so as to arrive at those aspects of rationing in which we are interested. Some statements on redistribution could help us to make deductions from these same statements on rationing; by acting as it were in reverse order from the real order of cognition, we would finally arrive at the desired explanation. But before a thing is explained it must be clarified. Before we make use of one or another operation, we must somehow carry out a constructive interpretation of a given sociological fact.

This is so because the research process when applied to the natural social fact has no end, unlike the finite nature of the logical operations of inference, referred to in which it is called the philosophy of scientific explanation. In the latter case we work with a finite number of steps which must be made in the process of inference, but in the former we participate in a creative process which does not lend itself to any counting at all.

Let us revert to our example. The interpretation of rationing in terms of redistribution ceases to be convincing if we consider the resistance of the authorities. Such resistance is a real force. In the course of further research I have, thanks to the hospitality of the Centre for Socio-Legal Studies at Wolfson College in Oxford, had an opportunity to study historical data pertaining to rationing in Great Britain during the Second World War. The systems differed in many respects, were introduced in different circumstances, and were based on different social grounds. But in spite of those differences we find sufficient similarities to make a controlled comparison in several respects. In making that comparison I was struck by the resistance of the British administration to the introduction of the various rationing schemes. R. J. Hammond, who made a detailed examination of the problem, saw the causes of that resistance in a specific feature of the British system of rationing, namely the administrative safeguarding of individual rations. According to Lord Beveridge, the British nation was to be fed during the war as an army, and the Ministry of Food would, in its own eyes, be doomed to disaster if the rations were not guaranteed. That allegedly British feature turned out to bear a surprising resemblance to the Polish case, which was described more fully in the previous chapter. To sum up here:

the pressure of public opinion for the introduction of rationing may be treated as striving to subject the administrative authorities to individual supervision by society. The resistance of the authorities may be due to unwillingness to be subjected to such supervision under unfavourable economic circumstances. The rationing contract implies not only the transfer by individual consumers of the prerogative to determine the purchases made, but also the transfer to the administrative authorities of the responsibility for availability of necessary supplies. This responsibility, in a situation that only seemingly resembles a free market, is in fact carried by the consumer.[4]

This kind of successive, contractual, interpretation of rationing is, from the professional viewpoint of the sociologist, obviously linked with elements of the theory of social exchange. Within that theory one can try to deduce the 'contract on rationing' with which we deal here from the various assumptions made about exchange. One can try to do it, but one need not. The interpretative clarification at which we have arrived in a given stage of the research may be sufficient without additional logical exercises in explanation. *De gustibus non est disputandum.*

But there is still one aspect of cognition which so far has

---

[4] R. J. Hammond, *Food Agriculture in Britain 1939–1945: Aspects of War Control* (Stanford, Calif., 1954).

escaped us whenever we have opposed interpretation to explanatory procedures. This is the work on the comprehension of social
facts, which consists of the reconstruction of certain material
sequences of events in which those facts are involved. Reference
is made to only certain relatively isolated systems of events,
which, for training purposes, we try to reduce in practice to
sketch causal sequences, more or less literally genetic in character. In this preliminary formulation we notice already the importance of the opposition of natural facts to other, abstract facts,
about which, as linguistic intuition suggests, one cannot meaningfully say that some develop from others. That linguistic intuition must be observed. It enables us to reconstruct the process
whereby a certain fact comes into existence; that reconstruction is
also carried out in abstract terms, but only those which are the
conceptual generalization of real events.

At this point we will return to the first assumption of the
'Memoirs of Everyday Life'. The reality of the referents of the
categories used in interpretation are treated intuitively by reference to the concept of responsibility. However advanced our soci-
ologism may be, we would not ascribe such responsibility to, say,
'networks of interaction', 'social classes', or 'societies'. Whatever
position we might take in the controversy between sociological
nominalists and realists, these categories become abstract in character just because no responsibility is attached to them, and
behind them are neither real constellations of human individuals,
nor really active communities, nor even the collective soul. It
would be otherwise with 'Jacek's peers' or 'Polish gentry', and
even with 'British Society', although nominalists would argue
with realists about whether it is legitimate to speak about collective responsibility at all.

In the study of rationing the question about responsibility is
repeated on several occasions. From this point of view one of the
premisses underlying the questionnaire applied in the small town
emerges as absurd. As I have said, that premiss consisted of per-
ceiving the customers as responsible for agreeing to various limitations on their freedom of action whenever they agree to
situational rationing. Hence, the question was asked with the
intention of defining the level of their abandonment of that freedom. But such a premiss was spontaneously rejected when, while
commenting of the situation described in the questionnaire,

respondents used to say that 'everybody must have something'. Situational rationing was taking place in an interpretively different situation from that which I had assumed as a researcher. I was thinking in terms of the hypothetical plenty in which it is problematic that a customer may abandon the right to buy as much as he likes. The respondents were thinking in terms of the actual shortage in which there is no freedom to be surrendered. In such a situation the acceptance of rationing means the abandonment of the privileges enjoyed by some at the cost of others. This is confirmed in practice on a small scale when those standing in the queue, such as a pregnant woman or a disabled person, enters the shop, even if such a privilege is accepted by the crowd, and on a large scale whenever mass organizations such as trade unions, political parties, and the public administration negotiate the allocation of rations. The responsibility for rationing in no case rests on the consumers. That fact is self-evident for them, and the comprehension of their attitudes and action must take that into consideration from the very beginning.

Thus we have, almost without recognizing it, found ourselves in the domain of the second rule of the 'Memoirs of Everyday Life', which has been termed the pluralism of sources. Methodological pluralism of this kind is directly linked with the image of facts that must be accepted by a reality-friendly researcher. The radical opposition between theory and experience, the world of imagined concepts and that of full-blooded experience, the world of the 'ought' and of the 'is', cannot be afforded. Such radical oppositions are permitted only in research work that is deliberately dissociated from experience. But the everyday life of society requires that both its stratification and the variety of shades of reality are taken into account. Thus, behind the methodological pluralism we discover an ontological one as well.

The question on situational rationing which we posed to the inhabitants of the small town in 1977 was self-discrediting. It has accredited the investigator and his co-workers with the status of ignorance. Such a procedure in the context of the cross-cultural gap assumed from the outset is, for the cultural anthropologist, the most obvious step towards understanding and comprehension. In case of the sociologist it is considered to be risky because it infringes upon the assumed superior professional competence of the latter. Hence such a question, radically posed, has the honourable status of ethnomethodological provocation. From that point of view, to doubt the sales-person's right to limit the amount of goods to be sold to a single customer, so that everybody could buy a certain amount of these, was as provocative as Garfinkel's question 'When?' to the ritual farewell formula: 'See you later!'

Hence the point is not that absurd questions should be avoided. The point is: like questions produce like answers. This seemingly self-evident truth becomes sometimes quite dramatic in character, as when everybody, including the authors of the questions authorized by General Jaruzelski close to the end of Communist rule, were unable to find an unequivocal interpretation of the national referendum on the need for political transformation in the country. To vague questions one gets vague answers. To an absurd question one gets an answer which is absurd, unless other circumstances are taken into consideration. At the time when we asked the question about situational rationing, sugar had already been rationed for one year for the purpose of increasing exports. But nobody was then facing as a real possibility the rationing of other food items for coupons. The authorities were responding to the increasing pressure of the consumers by selling meat of lower quality or at higher prices. Universal rationing of meat and its products had not yet existed as a social fact. From the perspective of methodological dualism it emerged as a *deus ex machina* in the form of the thirteenth item on the list of demands made by Gdansk strikers in summer 1980. It would be possible perhaps to identify the person who explicitly formulated such a demand when the list was under preparation. Does it mean that meat rationing really commenced at this moment, rather than at the moment when the agreement between the authorities and the strikers was solemnly signed?

My answer to the question is negative. I think that such a dualistic interpretation of social facts differs too much from reality to be useful in comprehending everyday life. At each moment answers exist to questions which will only be posed in the future. If we agree that reality is cognitively never given to us in full, there are not only certain facts not enacted in the collective action, but also certain facts which have not been verbalized, and even certain facts which have not been thought of. Pinpointing them is possible, but it requires either luck or a really admirable degree of intuition. I can boast of neither.

I do not think that in this context we should revert to such obvious things as the need to keep a balance in making use of the various cognitive sources. If skilful questioning and evoking spontaneous answers, well guided by appropriate triggering stimuli, can help in discovering various unconscious psychological processes, then there is no reason why such work on verbalized data should not help in discovering collective unconsciousness on a larger scale. Let us state once again that no conversation takes place without a context, and reference to context is necessary in the case of questionnaire studies as well as in other enquiries. Perhaps the point here is to remember that in such a cognitive activity all sources have the same initial value: unintended statements and gestures, statements and gestures provoked by the investigator, collective action (that is, all the factors which, combined, form the biography of the individual and the history of a society). In the course of an investigation intended, as we have stressed, to determine responsibility, one should not disregard any circumstantial evidence nor evidence of any other kind: leaflets, curses, utterances, silence, action, and non-action. In that laborious task every indexical sign should also be taken as a genuine sign, so that one could put together all the cognitive aspects at one's disposal.

Everyday life is as it is, and therefore one cannot reflect upon it without doing violence to it. The violence done sometimes takes the form of an educative experiment, as in those twentieth-century plays whose authors break up, step by step the ordinary course of events, leading us to doubt the most fundamental premisses of our lives. It is essential to believe that the uniformed people who sit at the wheel of public buses are not obsessed by suicidal ideas, or ordered to drive passengers to a place of execution. Violence can be brought about also through the direct use of force. A killer driving a few dozen or several hundred thousand victims to their deaths is exploiting the sense of everyday normalness in order to achieve at least the minimum of unwilling co-operation. We assume that if we are arrested it is in order to imprison us and not to shoot us in the corridor. If they force us to compulsory labour, it is certainly in order to produce something. If they make us form a queue this is certainly in order to offer us something. Who will assume that these, apparently everyday, actions aim at the ultimate settlement of the Jewish, the Gypsy, or the class question, or the question of our individual existence? But this is negation of everyday life. Just as in Ionescu's play the setting-out of chairs on the stage doesn't end up in the usual way, so in the world that negates everyday life, interrogation is just another form of torture, and is not aimed at forcing the truth out of the tortured, and labour becomes yet another method of killing, for which one has to line up in a well-ordered queue. The orderly march to death cannot be explained without reference to manipulation of everyday life, and this is why the study of everyday life is of such importance.

How do we arrive at the basic components of everyday life? How do we know that such principles are really hidden in the surrounding world? Research until today has accumulated details that by no means come together into a consistent whole. 'one needs to acknowledge that it is difficult to imagine a procedure that would efficiently lead to the systematic disclosure of common assumptions. How can we study something which is basically characterized by "transparency" and which cannot be apprehended in its entirety?'[5] Imagine that I have just entered everyday life and stood in a queue: for a newspaper, in the food store, for wine, for a bus, in the dentist's waiting room. Should one make any effort to study such trivial social facts? But each queue, apart from its individual features, also has some universal ones. Moreover, it is a universal social event and as such should attract our professional interest. As is appropriate for an elementary social fact it cannot be dismembered into its components. Take any queue and try to eliminate its participants one after the other. The queue will remain a queue until two persons remain: the first and the last. Such an ordered pair embody the queue that is dreamt of at night by neurotic sales staff and customers.

The concept of 'everyday life' has a rather unclear relationship with the concept of 'normalness'. Ferdinand Gonseth has devoted some beautiful pages to the concept of normalness, commencing with the statement that this is one of those elementary concepts that any normal person has at his disposal. It is interesting because it is an elementary concept and so may illustrate some basic thought processes. Let us discover what 'normalness' is. If we open a dictionary we are told that normalness means

[5] Teresa Hołówka, *Myślenie potoczne* (Common Thinking) (Warsaw, 1986), 172.

'fitting the norm'. Under 'norm' we will find references to 'principle' and 'rule'. Behind both the idea of some law is hidden. But if we move on to the law, we shall again discover the idea of rule and regularity. As usual in all definitional enterprises, we have come full circle. If one were, however, more persistent then one could think of the relationship between what is normal and what is usual and repetitive. Such a definition would, nevertheless, betray the concept under definition. In the concept of normalness there is an undisputed normative element. When we say that something is 'abnormal' we are expressing a pejorative judgement, while familiarity and repetitiveness are descriptive terms. Gonseth warns us not to pursue a futile course. 'Normalness' is undefined, it is an elementary concept that cannot be reduced to others. Moreover, it is complex. It is both necessary and undefinable, elementary and complex.[6]

Chaim Perelman and L. Olbrechts-Tyteca, in the theory of argument, link normalness with probability. Reflecting upon the premisses of common thinking, they point out that the most common of these is, that each category of facts has its normal aspect that makes possible reasoning and application in language in order to express the normal aspect, though in general we do not make a detailed calculus in concrete circumstances. We say that 'normal' is what is most frequent, having in mind sometimes the average, sometimes the median, and sometimes the modal value of a given distribution. Moreover, normalness is always related to a reference group which is usually undefined, and which, moreover, might change as a human group in which normal beliefs are those of the majority, and dissenters are eliminated. At worse the reference group may be limited to one ideal person.[7] This common lack of detail in operating with a seemingly very strict, or at least easy to restrict, concept of normalness seems to justify the stand taken by Piotr Łukasiewicz who, after considering the classic distinction between the practical and normative concepts of normalness, returned to the notion that homogeneity of normalness is normal.[8]

---

[6] F. Gonseth, 'La notion du normal', in *Dialectica*, I, 3 (1947).

[7] C. Perelman and L. Oblrechts-Tyteca, *La Nouvelle rhetorique: traité de l'argumentation* (Paris, 1958), i, 95 ff.

[8] P. Łukasiewicz, 'Życie codzienne, system społeczny a poczucie normalności' (Everyday Life, Social System, and Sense of Normalcy), in *Kultura i Społeczeństwo*, 2 (1985).

Łukasiewicz follows the concept of 'social normalness' as introduced by another Polish writer, Tadeusz Szawiel, who refers to the 'the activities of everyday life being performed within organizations and institutions subordinated in a new or another way to the System', and also to 'a set of habits, patterns of reaction at work, for propaganda, in face of the troubles of everyday life'.[9] The interest Polish sociologists displayed in the notion of 'normalness' was no accident. Polish reality under Communism was characterized by the discrepancy between practical and normative normalness. Gonseth had probably not experienced himself the situation where what is (that is, what is 'normal'), is exactly what one needs to escape from. But such an experience points toward further complexities which one had to consider concerning the concept of normalness.

Polish authors would prefer to state that normalness has a normative load, but that there are different concepts of normalness. Łukasiewicz observed that the expression 'here it is normal' usually applied to facts that arouse laughter, amazement, or condemnation, and in modern Polish is pejorative. So, 'normal', as in the modern Polish expression 'abnormal normalness', is used to hide negative evaluation of Communist reality made through comparative reference to norms. Some of those reference norms according to Łukasiewicz are norms of meaningfulness, credibility, aspiration, imaginability, and similarity to other societies. This enumeration leads, however, to the conclusion that the common concept of normalness is construed through negation of the observed and sensed abnormality. So where do we go from here?

Things will become clearer if we agree first that the same facts may be subject to different assessments, made by reference to different groups; secondly, that evaluations may be positive and negative. When a Polish worker under Communism used to say: 'That's what our Polish construction works are like and there is no reason for it', two convictions were expressed at once in that statement: first, that badly organized construction works are normal in the here and now; second, that it is abnormal from the perspective of another, Polish but pre-Communist, foreign, or ideal and non-existent reality. The division into practical and normative normalness, that seems so evident and useful in the

[9] T. Szawiel, 'Struktura społeczna i postawy a grupy ethosowe' (Social Structure, Attitudes and Ethos Groups), *Studia Socjologiczne*, 1–2 (1982).

positivist perspective, neglects a trait that is common to both apparently different concepts of normalness. In both cases one needs, however, to refer to a norm.

Let us recollect the probabilistic interpretation of normalness. In order to say 'that is what our Polish construction works are like' one needs to think that it is so 'often', 'usually', or 'almost always'. Behind this statement there is an idea of a typical 'Polish construction works', that would hold even if detailed studies were to reveal numerous cases of well-organized construction works. A good illustration would be the Polish state construction company 'Budimex', active in the foreign market context, and in 1990 ranked as fiftieth in the world list of the 250 largest construction firms. But there is a pattern, or norm, which when applied in reality allows us to tell how normal or abnormal something is. Even in the purely non-judgemental statement that a given woman has measurements like Venus de Milo, a normative procedure is involved. A statue of a female serves here as the norm to make it possible to characterize another female. The latter is 'normal' if she has the measurements of Venus. What should one think, however, of the apparent ease with which the descriptive and the normative characterizations are both made? Is not 'practical' normalness at the same time 'normative'? Venus de Milo and Communist construction works—both provide certain normative standards that permit a decision to be made on whether something is 'with the norm', that is, normal or not.

Judgements on whether a thing fits a standard or not may be devoid of additional judgements. If they are supplemented by additional evaluations, the division into normative and practical normalness is supported. Those labels are invalid, as practical normalness involves the normative aspect as well. This is why Gonseth rejected the equation of normalness with regularity. Normal is not what is repeated but what is expected when one knows the norm. Such a definition encompasses the normative burden of normalness. If the normality of something is established by reference to pattern P1, it might still be discovered that the same thing is abnormal in reference to another pattern, P2. Some construction works are normal in relation to the standards of Communist Poland and abnormal with reference to the standards of the non-Communist world. Durkheim realized that even among virtuous monks deviance emerges as in the monastery the reference-frame changes. The slightest misdemeanour that would escape attention among 'normal' sinners gains immediately in importance among the saints. This is the complexity to be encountered by anybody who would like to develop absolute standards and normalness.

Additional evaluations of normalness are positive or negative. A woman fitting the Venus de Milo 'norm' may be disqualified when choosing fashion models for the present day, when a slimmer body is assumed to be more 'normal'. There is a set of 'normal' traits expected from a criminal as well as a set of 'normal' traits for a saint. It seems that a 'normal' criminal should not, for instance, be a 'normal' person in his or her everyday life. Those who agree must accept also that a reality, or more exactly some image of the reality, provide the negative pattern in making a decision as to what is normal. It is then that statements like 'This is normal here' become negative judgements. More interesting, however, are the ambivalent situations. Someone is beginning a job and is surprised that deadlines are not kept, clients are cheated, and extra fees are charged that are not recorded. 'It is normal here', would be the most likely answer from a boss or older colleague introducing a greenhorn into the reality of the job.

*Normalka* is the colloquial Polish term for this experience, and should be of interest to the student of everyday life. It would be wonderful if the concept of 'abnormal normalness' and the negative evaluation of what there is were simply hidden. I am afraid, though, that something else was hidden, namely the simultaneous positive assessment of actions of a kind linked to the not-fully neutralized feeling that such actions should be evaluated negatively. There is a border between the normalness rejected by its participants and the normalness to which they refer when judging the reality they encounter in everyday life. This border also goes through the human conscience, and this means that instead of normalness imposed as confronting the normalness experienced, one deals instead with the confrontation between higher and at the same time deeper strata of what Americans have called 'countermores'.

It could be answered, and usually was in public debates, that some frames imposed from above by the Communist system resulted in various countermores flourishing that would not appear in the daylight of commonly accepted principles of ethics and human propriety. Countermores would thus be a by-product of the normalness imposed from the outside and practical normalness in the sense of pragmatic adjustment of individuals to external limitations. 'It is not me who is crazy, it is the System that is abnormal!' would be the most adequate explanation of those countermores.

Taking it seriously: if what there is is contrary to the norm of what should be, still what there is remains as it is. I am myself part of what is there and thus I must fit it. This formula when expressed in a nicer way would mean: to live is to be in accordance with reality. This is what on the one hand is called conformism, and on the other realism. We dislike conformism, and on the other hand we cannot take away the right to realism. A way out of the dilemma may be found if the classic distinction between phenomenon and disposition is considered. Conformism to countermores may coexist together with a disposition to act in an ethically proper way. If reality is created collectively, then realism means the attempt at its collective transformation, not the momentary solipsistic negation of reality as it is then.

At this point I would like to refer to a concept of normative according to which the notion of 'ought' belongs to certain elementary notions which, like the previously discussed notion of normalness cannot be defined. The ought is expressed in various ways, not only in normative expressions. Not surprisingly, as has been observed, facts that result from the interaction of subject and object by themselves achieve normative power, and even the most trivial 'reality' may have such a normative burden independent of the assessment to which it will be subjected. Normativity is both elementary and complex. It comprises the whole complex of events of which only some arrive at the level of expressed, verbalized, and publicly agreed ethical principles.

Whoever believes in the simple division into what is and what ought to be, into what people do and what people think they do, would certainly not accept the incessantly recurring transition of human hopes and decisions, the polymorphism of human nature about which Stanisław Ossowski wrote, together with many other contradictions among which the well-known psychometric paradox that the more important the object, the more flexible are the attitudes towards it may serve as illustration. An approach to reality is still possible that would take into account exactly this flexibility and changeability, multi-sidedness and multi-stratification. The essential danger would then still be the perception of social reality as flat, without paying attention to the depth.

According to this concept of social reality the normative is one of its dimensions, and therefore it would be artificial and futile to attempt to sublimate its normative aspects. Besides, it is impossible to think consistently of social reality so as to exclude thought as a component. Various patterns appear with varying degree of clarity in life, in social thought, and in social action. Patterns differ also as to the degree to which they are put into effect. What people say differs according to the circumstances. People often say, think, and feel several different things at once, and are often ready to do still other things.

The concept of the normativity of social reality may be of assistance in another task, that is, when the principle of responsibility is to be discussed in the context of queuing or any other fragment of everyday life.

Ferdinand Gonseth presided in Neuchâtel in 1944 over philosophical debates on free will and determinism.[10] The cast of characters in the debate included the President, the Host, a Mathematician, an Astronomer, a Physicist, a Physician, a Sociologist, a Psychiatrist, an Engineer, a Philosopher, and Individualist, and a Sceptic. Gonseth began by urging the representatives of the various 'disciplines' to express their deterministic creed, and later allowed for some doubts that lead towards more detailed resolutions. After agreeing that both ideal and real science, sciences and the humanities, theoretical and practical disciplines construct the deterministic image of the world, the participants in the symposium began to discover a place for free will. The President, recollecting the Cartesian *cogito ergo sum*, asked for attention to be paid to the fact that one needs to live before thinking. Are there not, therefore, initial conditions that need to be satisfied before objective cognition of a deterministic character is possible? The mathematician, speaking first, added that though one assumes at the beginning the falsity of the thesis, one wants to argue for the freedom to assume the thesis to be

---

[10] *Determinisme et libre arbitre*, presided by Ferdinand Gonseth and edited by H.-S. Sagnebin, 2nd revd. edn. (Neuchâtel, 1947).

true or false. The very possibility of mathematical reasoning assumes, therefore, a certain freedom. The Host reminds us that freedom is implied by the very idea of truth. If the falsity or verity of our statements were determined by preceding or parallel facts, then there would be no truth or falsehood. There would be no autonomy of the mind either. The Physicist adds that he must have freedom of decision whenever he begins to experiment, while under the principle of absolute determinism his errors would be as inevitable as the appropriate observations. The Sociologist, embarrassed by the backward state of his discipline, prefers to rely on political economy, saying: 'If absolute determinism ruled the play of economic factors, then in each situation there would be a specific economically appropriate solution determined causally.'

Many economists allude to such a solution when speaking about the liberal economy, free of any disturbing intervention. But how can we make a distinction between what is economically normal and everything that is artificial, between free play and systematic intervention? Do not economists paradoxically, when calling upon the state to intervene (for instance, against trusts) in order to re-establish the normal functioning of the economy, link the idea of the normal economy with the idea of a certain equality of rights for economic units of the same character? The idea of pure economics is thus conceivable only under the aegis of the idea of justice. There is no normal functioning of the economy without securing some social justice. Invoking pure causality demands putting it into frames set by some ethics.

Finally, towards the end of the symposium, the principle of complementarity as formulated by Niels Bohr is brought to their attention. Light presents itself under two forms that both complement and exclude each other, in the case of corpuscular and undulatory theories of light. The Psychiatrist advocates considering the whole of human activity on two planes, one in which determinism and chance are important and the second in which free will plays a role. The President warns that perhaps there are not two planes but rather a double thread in the reality of our existence. The Host ends by saying that the deterministic order of events and the volitional order of morality approach each other. Determinism applies to the domain of observation, through categories that result from the autonomy of mind, while

our free will is expressed in choice on the basis of the consequences predicted with the help of determinism.

Today, more than half a century after the dialectical symposium held in Neuchâtel, we see some issues more clearly than
the participants, but one may doubt whether we have better solutions than those then suggested. A sociologist today would not
risk a determinist confession of faith that would lead to the realization of the Comtian ideal of social physics. Nevertheless, the
urge to document things as they happen demands description if
not causal explanation of events. And even in describing, one
encounters the fundamental obstacles that illustrate the basic
issues in social cognition.

We have also experienced these troubles when attempting,
with students from the then Institute of Social Prevention and
Resocialization at the University of Warsaw, to describe queuing
in Warsaw. Queues start, however, in situations which are varied
and difficult to describe. To describe something one must set
some limits. For instance, one needs to select a particular zone in
the city and a particular time. Each investigation needs to be
related to this particular area and time, and the limits of generalization remain arbitrary. It took a dozen people a whole day's
work to attempt an approximation of what happened on Friday,
15 November 1985, the day before 'free Sunday'. In Poland since
the 1970s Sundays were 'free' except one a month; this meant
that shops of all kinds were closed in the heart of Warsaw, the
West side of the Nowy Swiat Street—which is the equivalent to
Oxford Street in London. Over a few dozen metres there we
established twenty-seven points at which a queue for something—meat, books, or a seat in the coffee-shop—could start.
This was by no means the same as the total number of shops, as
queues form at the individual 'openings' for goods made by the
individual sales people, or through automats. The number of
such points also changes, as openings are closed and opened
according to the influx of goods and customers. The flexibility
between such 'openings' is apparent when, for instance, a lady
who sells dairy products is called to help another person who is
selling sweets, and establishes a new 'opening' by starting the sale
of some newly arrived chocolates. It is by no means easy to establish what is offered at particular points, and at which moment
the highly conventional queue of those who wish to enter the

coffee-shop changes into the really smart group waiting for the cabaret which will start on the coffee-shop premises at a fixed time, and for which tickets are required.

It is thus not true that counting people waiting in a queue is a time-consuming but non-problematic step in research procedure. Observations repeated, as ours were, every fifteen minutes may neglect groupings and disappearances which occurred in-between. It demands arbitrary decisions over whether to count someone who is talking to a sales-person as a friend or as a customer. It also demands an arbitrary decision to count as customers those who are physically present at a given moment without interviewing them, if someone has left the queue just for a while and will return later. But even such detailed interviewing will not lead us to the ideal of objective information about the queue, as from our own experience and other observations we know that each such queue, apart from its hard core of participants, has places subject to negotiation, fighting and bargaining. The following quotation comes from research notes taken by my student J. Arcimowicz on 9 November 1985:

Sunday; 6.15 a.m. I arrive at the shop. Inside a large group of people are standing or sitting on heaters close to the separate meat stand. I am No. 16. All the time people enter and stand behind me. Some ladies ask for their turn to be served and go to the grocery. We are waiting. The queue is composed of middle-aged people. At the beginning there are two old ladies, one behind me and one close to the heaters. I observe that each newcomer moves according to the same pattern: first he goes to the counter, looks at the shelves, and asks: 'Will there by anything?', and then takes a place in the queue. Only the ladies at the beginning know what has been brought in, and they patiently inform the newcomers: smoked shoulders, sausages, krakauer. The woman behind me comments loudly one cannot count on anything else here. Movement started behind the counter as the meat products are brought in. Everybody from the back moves to the front, everybody takes a look, and asks if there is enough. The answers are always the same: 'As always', 'As usual', 'Some now, and the rest at 4 p.m.' Two women form the sales staff, one stands at the cash register, the second weighs the meat. There is a crowd at the counter. Ladies arrive who had arranged their turn and had to leave for a while. One hears the explanations: 'I stood behind you, yes.' Someone objects loudly: 'I did not see you.' 'This lady was first, only she had to leave', explains a woman behind me. Finally the lady with the pigtail remains. Others have worse luck. In front they don't want to allow anybody in, there are no pregnant women or handicapped people, so every-day can stay. It is noteworthy that not far behind me an old woman is standing with a daughter who looks mentally ill. Nobody pays attention to them. It is 6.45 a.m. Ladies from the end of the queue are getting nervous, and ask for faster service, they say that they are in a hurry to get to work. Nobody answers from the queue, and turns are taken. Some women look nervously at watches, two leave while others ask if those who must work today may be served—'Others may buy later.' Somebody answers that everybody is working and working hard. Nobody gives up their place, the admonition is heard incessantly that coupons should be registered. I am moving to the counter at the speed of a tortoise. The ladies close to the cash-register fuss, one calls the meat scraps, and asks for better pieces to be selected. The sales lady throws the basket upon the counter and selection of the better pieces starts. The queue explodes: 'How is this possible? The sales lady should give out the goods, one should not select, how would the meat look if everybody were picking it up themselves, what an idea!'—everybody talks at once. The sales lady throws the meat back on the shelf, the woman remains with quite a good piece in her hand. Comments continue, but the work and turns are not interrupted. I bought what remained after the selection. I am leaving the shop at 7.20 a.m. and the remaining 27 persons are attacking the counter.

This short note documents typical events in queuing life: initial tension when the pool of goods to be distributed is yet unknown, queue-crime of the kind manifested in disputes about the legitimacy of the turns, and the right to buy goods. There is routine in it, but each performance involves some specific moments, as for instance the sudden attack here by customers upon the rule that the sales staff serve the meat. One can focus on the description of the routine elements in order to immortalize the queue as a specific form of social life. Here the description will be treated as a precise document and point of empirical reference.

In this description of the queue we find all the elements of everyday normalness and the normative that were discussed earlier. The element of determination is so clear that even the participant is able to observe certain traits that recur in queuing behaviour like this: 'each newcomer moves according to the same pattern: first he goes to the counter, looks at shelves, and asks: 'Will there be something?', then takes a place in the queue. Each person who performs this act is performing at the same time an act of free will comprised of the decision to place oneself in the queue in order to do shopping. The queue is also the situation in which the principle of normalness is realized. When seeing somebody standing by the counter I silently take my place or ask: 'Are you the last?', 'Is that the end of the queue?', or 'Is there a queue?' As in the field-notes: 'I am No. 16. All the time people enter and stand behind me.' All the four possibilities listed assume that a queue is something normal and recognizable as such. There is the common experience of shame that we feel when entering a waiting-room, when we do not realize that others are waiting before us and somebody says: 'There is a queue already!' Such transgressions of the micro-social order so colourfully described by Erving Goffman, validate that there is normalness in queuing, that a norm can be detected and that there is a norm in reference to which our action can be classified as conforming or not. We are not dealing here with trivial matters. Sometimes police are called in to re-establish to order of a queue. If we say that one can get killed because of a quarrel about turns in a queue, we should add that one can also die because the queue as such was rejected. What does it mean? Perhaps that, apart from various detailed norms such as the norm of honesty that need not be linked with the norm of the queue, a certainly collectivity of people interested in the same good that cannot be appropriated by them simultaneously get access to this good in strict order of succession.

It is by no means the case that a queue will emerge if the good of interest to participants is not visible. It is not necessary for the amount of goods in supply to be smaller than the amount of goods in demand. When the doors are narrow we queue to enter the concert hall even if it will soon be clear that is only one-quarter full. Strict order does not mean order by the sequence in which we came to be the 'opening'. It was the Polish custom in the crisis, for those officially privileged, to buy without waiting in a separate queue. A queue for a lifeboat is composed of children, then women, and afterwards men, independent of the time of arrival. Therefore debate may develop about the principles of ordering: 'In front they don't want to allow anybody in, there are no pregnant women or handicapped people, so everybody can stay . . . Ladies from the end of the queue are getting nervous, and ask for faster service, they say that they are in hurry to get to work. Nobody answers from the queue, and turns are taken.'

This means that there was a silent refusal to admit a change of the rule of the sequence. The norm of the queue is thus the norm of succession.

A queue does not need to exist physically. Even a physical queue is only an approximation to the normative model. 'Some ladies ask for their turn to be saved and go to the grocery', so physically they are absent from the queue, but they still hold their rights. A queue for cars or housing may not exist at all in the physical sense. Somewhere a list is made on which everybody takes a specific place. Let us observe that in the queue individuality is preserved to the largest degree. Everybody in it has a different number, nobody is in the same situation. Of course, until a particular moment the interests of No. 117 and No. 116 will be felt as identical, but a moment will always come when one is first and the other is last.

Normalness in a queue is thus not factual normalness. The pattern is not the physically existing group but a certain supposed ideal principle. A queue may even be redefined in order to do justice to this fact. A queue signifies strict ordering of the rights to participate in a pool of goods according to the accepted principle of sequence. Moreover, it is not just any possible ordering but just ordering, even if the principle *prior tempore potior iure* is not necessarily the only and highest principle of justice, and does not necessarily fit well with the principles of succession applied in the queue situation.

Rationing in its specific and everyday form of queuing is not ethically indifferent as its appearance in reality is not ethically neutral. The principle 'first come first served' that seems to determine the justice of queuing under normal conditions is well justified due to its arbitrariness. Although it is not listed in Chaim Perelman's *Justice*, it fits very well his ideal of justice as a certain principle that helps to make decisions independent of changing circumstances. The objective principle is pre-established. Whenever the elementary problem of dividing goods between those who are interested arises there are immediately three possibilities: (1) the good in question is indivisible; (2) it may be easily divided among those interested; (3) resources at least for practical purposes may be taken as infinite, and thus may be allotted to all who are interested on condition that each will invest a different amount of time in waiting for his respective share. The last is the assumption of the classical queue in which everybody has invested his or her time, knowing that in due time the investment will pay off.

Under Communism, with the general shortages such a queue is Utopia. Either those who are waiting in the queue do not know if there will be enough goods for them when their turn arrives (not to speak of frequent situations when it is not even known whether there will be any goods at all), or they do not know if, in the face of a possible shortage, it is necessary to decide to buy. Sales staff face the basic dilemma: to allot the good according to need or to satisfy needs only partially? The last choice is taken as the best under the circumstances of permanent crisis. In our survey of a representative sample in Warsaw in 1981, we asked what people thought about a situation in which there is a queue for a suddenly popular miraculous Hungarian remedy for baldness. It was advertised that the full therapy required four bottles to be applied. But in face of the queue, the majority of our sample agreed that situational rationing should be applied and only one bottle per capita should be sold. However absurd it is, everyday life under the redistributive economy offered thousands of everyday illustrations of the general principle that in the face of disaster equality is to be applied, equality which, in fact, involves arbitrariness. It is not that the need for goods is satisfied in this way, but rather the more fundamental need to be put on equal footing in the face of disaster. This is the meaning of egalitarian justice in real socialism.

Perhaps the principle 'whoever is first has priority' would better describe the idea of justice in force in the queue. It is essential, however, that the queue escapes from the phenomenal sphere and step by step moves into the moral, as Gonseth and his interlocutors say, or into the normative, as we prefer to say here. The freedom of choice mentioned already in connection with a decision to join a queue is thus not only a decision to join the group of people standing one behind another like geese, or to become the last on the list. Free choice also encompasses the decision that exactly such a system of executing one's rights to a good is a just one, or that we agree to treat it as just. Joining a queue may not only give us a right to the given good that we have not had before, and give us the right to apply for this good in established sequence, but it also imposes upon us the duty to abide by the situationally established system of system with respect to ourselves and to the others. 'Someone objects loudly: "I did not see you." "This lady was first, only she had to leave", explains a woman behind me. Finally the lady with the pigtail remains.' With accusation and defence, this summary trial taking place in an instant may both amuse and irritate us. If we do not intervene it is because the respective rights and duties will be adjudicated by those closer and therefore better informed. It is, however, an illusion to imagine that one may remain in the queue and be totally alienated from these actions. The existence of the queue as an empirical grouping of people striving in a humanly imperfect way to achieve the ideal of justice demands our participation also unless, in spite of our passivity, we enjoy the queue as a movement towards the ideal sustained by the actions of others. Yet another moment so characteristic of human normativity appears here. People have to act various roles that complement each other, even if this is not their vocation. Someone declares: 'I stood behind you, yes.' Another person objects. Even silence will be treated as a voice in the debate. Indifference cannot be assumed before the others, even if it can be assumed before our inner selves. Actions taken by individual participants, including attempts to move beyond the place that belongs to us, and which function as the indirect validation of the norm, all these make sense if and only if they are parts of the same composition called society. The internal accord may be checked if to an accusation: 'You did not stand here!' one answers with 'There is no queue here, sir!'

This remark will allow me to go back to the earlier question of the relationship between the fundamentals of everyday life and queuing: is not the queue also an example of the trap of everyday life, in which the executioner may catch the victims? A queue to the gas chamber, for instance?

Taking the matter from the phenomenal side, even such an ultimate queue is a queue, and the investigator lost in analysis of behaviour may become interested in the continuation of such patterns even in such an extreme case. But is it really a queue in the light of the analysis we have just concluded? Is it really the strict ordering of rights to some good according to the just principle of succession? In everyday life queues are just because to some degree they approximate to the ideal of justice. Such is the queue to the lifeboat. Boats or bread are in extreme situations truly desired goods, and queues for these are always just, even if the longer the turn the more likely the death. The cruel sophist might not have realized the difference between a queue for life and a queue for death. But there is at least one formal difference. In the latter it is better to be at the end because a miracle may always happen. In this sense it is an inverted queue. If everybody were at the end the executioner could not perform his task, so he works laboriously toward creating the appearance of everyday life as if the queue were approaching some good. There is, therefore, also a deeper difference. This queue, despite external appearances, is not a queue, as it does not move towards the fulfilment of an ethical ideal. In this it is false and betrays the norms of everyday life.

# 12

# *The Constitution of the Heart*

Why should matters like the queue be studied, apart from the natural duty of the sociologist to document all social reality? I think it is because in the processes of this 'economy of everyday life' one can find explanations of other processes. When long go with Kazimierz Frieske, we studied the web of relationships between the socialist enterprises in Poland, we realized that, contrary to what all textbooks on the socialist economy and economic law say about the so-called 'second economy', it is in reality the most normal part of life without which economic life would be impossible. Independent of the legal duty of co-operation between state enterprises according to laboriously prepared plans, the economic relations between enterprises in the socialist economy were closest to the functioning of the Melanesian economy based upon the reciprocity principle, as described by Bronisław Malinowski, and Richard Thurnwald. Managers of socialist industry themselves explained to us how reciprocity of goods, services, and sanctions may result in efficient functioning, though this differs from that assumed by the official plans for the economy of the country.[1]

The real economic relations in Polish society were, then, based upon various mechanisms of exchange most often written about as informal relations. Informality, though, consisted in the fact that those relations were contrary to the officially upheld image of reality. Here planning, there exchange; here production, there stagnation; here market, there rationing. The social evil was hidden not so much in those mechanisms of exchange as in their 'informality'.

This was accompanied by the specific state of public morality which Polish sociologists since 1970s described using various

[1] Jacek Kurczewski and Kazimierz Frieske, 'Some Problems in the Legal Regulation of the Activities of Economic Institutions', *Law and Society Review*, 11: 3 (1977), 489–505.

terms like 'social void' (Stefan Nowak), 'dirty business community' (Adam Podgórecki), and 'crisis of the moral infrastructure' (Andrzej Tymowski).

Anomie, which in fact is diagnosed by all those mentioned, was not related to transformations in the concept of good and evil. Even our surveys from the 1970s and 1980s seem to counter such claim. The durability of some basic ethical components made it possible to speak about ethical continuity in the society, something that led me to propose the idea of the stability of the hidden normative structure of that society.

It is time, however, to ask if the assumption of a hidden normative structure is not, in fact, a way to white wash society? Do we not have enough data at our disposal that point to a fault, if not in this structure then at least in the social structure in which the normative structure should express itself?

Let us look, for instance, at the results of a study by Wojciech Pawlik, who in 1982 observed the everyday economy in the local community of a small town of a dozen or so thousand inhabitants.[2] Most of his subjects had vocational or high-school education, the men usually worked in production, the women in administration, services, or at home. These average Poles agreed that there is, in every state firm, co-operative, or office, a zone of things to be arranged in an informal way between the people acting in private, though making use of their formal roles. The American anthropologist Janine Wedel, studying Poles, introduced the Polish word for such deals, *kombinować*, as the technical term for interaction of that kind.[3] One of Pawlik's respondents summed it up by saying that: 'I start from the assumption that today nothing can be arranged without gifts, money, etc. and this is the general principle in Poland.' When looking for a new job, most people first make the most detailed possible investigation of the opportunities that a given job offers of additional gratifications and benefits of an informal kind. Sometimes employees rejected offers of promotion which looked advantageous from the perspective of official earnings, but which would have meant being cut off from informal opportunities. All

---

[2] Wojciech Pawlik, *Prawo. Moralność. Gospodarka alternatywna* (Law. Morality. Alternative Economy) (Warsaw, 1988).

[3] Janine Wedel, *Private Poland: An Anthropologists' Look at Everyday Life* (New York and Oxford, 1988).

those extra gratuities and fringe benefits that were neither acknowledged officially nor recorded for, say, taxation purposes were included in the earnings as permanent extras, and one could not escape being asked about these 'supplementary' earnings in private conversation between relatives and friends. However, the most important aspect was, was Pawlik wrote, that:

Daily contact with such activity favours not only the dissemination of opinion about the prevalence of corruption and other pathologies but is also accompanied by the weakening of the legal ethical assessment of such conduct, especially in reference to one's own activity. While in the awareness of the inhabitants kombinowanie is perceived as the reason to complain about the general regularities of social life in Poland (stereotype: 'We all steal in this country'), at the same time assessment of one's own conduct is made more in the pragmatic-conformist terms ('One cannot live on the wages alone' or 'One needs to be a good person and keep with the others'). Such conduct is accompanied by language tricks of various kinds that make possible the negative assessment of actions in which the individual is involved. Thus idioms emerge like 'to arrange something', 'to talk with someone', 'to bring something', 'to pay back', 'to have a drink over something', and so on. These euphemisms alleviate the legal ethical assessment of the particular deeds and are used in reference to actions that bring gratification to the subject; when the subject is on the losing side the same actions are referred to as a 'swindling' or 'tricking' of something out of the subject.[4]

This is the essence of the disorders in the functioning of the normative structures in Polish society under Communism. If everybody commits a sin except the speaker, everybody sins. Everybody is also free from guilt, as the responsibility is moved on to 'them'. 'They' are responsible. This stereotype is usually either supported in a more or less theoretical way or is criticized as the way to take the burden of responsibility from the shoulders of the society. The essence of anomie in real socialism lies not in the permanent dissatisfaction of the ever-growing needs, and not in sudden changes, but in the durability of the social structure which takes responsibility off individuals, groups, communities, and so on in matters that relate to them directly. Irresponsibility is the immanent feature of this social structure, and nowhere else

[4] Wojciech Pawlik, 'Ekonomia życia codziennego w społeczności lokalnej' (Economy of Everyday Life in a Local Community), in J. Kurczewski (ed.), *Umowa o kartki* (Warsaw, 1985).

is it more visible than in the domain of socialized property for which, according to the written constitution, everybody is responsible and for which in practice nobody cares. Responsibility for individual or collective action is, in such a system, moved on to those who are responsible for the abolition of responsibility in everyday life. And consequently, transition into a free civil society would mean the resurrection of such responsibility at all levels of social reality.

It is time, towards the end of this journey through some chapters of contemporary Polish history, to look at the lessons it suggests. For it was not a peculiar interest in things Polish, however justifiable that might be, which led us into this enterprise but rather an attempt to decipher the more universal meaning of the particular events which, in other manifestations, could and have happened elsewhere and at other times. The investigation that come to an end is anthropological in perspective, grounded in personal experience but with a view towards transcendence of this. To say that such an investigation is ended in such a context is inevitably to claim too much; no such end is a realistic aim. The investigations is unending; though it may be stopped for a time, any other experience may move it further forwards, and in fact each experience does move it forwards if the real anthropological meaning is intended.

Jean-Jacques Rousseau is held to be responsible for the concept of the *constitution du cœur*. To use the concept in the Polish context is by no means original, as the nineteenth-century poet, philosopher, and politician, Adam Mickiewicz made extensive use of it in his writings. For a nation which lost independence his advice was to follow the voice of tradition and of the heart. For him, the Polish constitution was hidden in the home and the heart, preserved there from persecution by occupying forces when the laws of the country, including the constitution proclaimed on 3 May 1791, had been overpowered by alien prescriptions and prohibitions. Mickiewicz was not original in thinking about the constitution of the heart; but he is important at this point in our story as he linked the universal experience with the concrete one. It was a common Polish experience to seek for the laws of the country in the habits of the heart, and this explains why scholars like Leon Petrażycki and Bronisław Malinowski, the first a Pole teaching in St Petersburg, and the second a Pole teaching in Oxford, found it so natural to speak of law as embodied in customs and not necessarily in the will of a sovereign sanctioned with a monopoly of coercive power.

The heart here metaphorically refers to the complex normative structure of the society that may be reduced into the relations between the elementary normative 'ought' components.

This normative structure continues in the habits of the heart and in social relations, though its essence is not in the rules as felt, but in the rules which constitute. The basic normative structure is thus that of the world made possible.

Communism was defective in design, unless a new normative structure could have been created acknowledging the more basic one. The mutual adjustment of the rulers and the ruled resulted in the social order of Communism. This is where crime was functional and legality dysfunctional.

The official law has little relevance for social life unless it relates to the normative base of the society.

The emerging society is by no means devoid of problems. The functional structures of social action are in contrast to the formal structures of capitalism imposed from above.

Empirical sociology of law in Poland until the 1970s had paid little attention to so-called subjective rights, even if the theoretical stance of the Petrażyckian approach to law, so influential here due to the efforts of, especially, Adam Podgórecki, seemed to be particularly well suited to deal with the area, perhaps even better than other, more traditional, standpoints. For if we may assume, after Petrażycki, that the very core of law is the legal experience composed of correlative duties and claim subjectively felt by any human being, then it seems that, at least potentially, each citizen (and this includes adults as well as children and adolescents) is maintaining his or her own legal system in which his or her rights and duties form the central part. Ideally, it is possible that in some social systems these subjectively experienced legal systems are identical, and this includes the systems held by persons acting in official roles as lawgivers, judges, and the like. Presumably, primitive legal systems closely approach this homogeneous model, although even there some divergence probably occurs. In modern societies it would be quite likely that subjective systems differ and that these differences, at least partially, can be structured according to some ethnic, religious, ideological, and occupational differences. Studies that aim at developing the sociology of law along these lines need, however, to take into account not only the attitudes towards official law but also towards one's own and other individuals', groups', and institutions' rights and duties, whatever their legitimation and justification in the social consciousness.

Some critical issues must, however, be raised by anyone who intends to pursue this type of sociology of law. They are:

what are the indicators of the recognition of rights and duties? what are the indicators of the scope of rights and duties? and what are the indicators of the depth of the recognition of these?

It is possible to assume that a feeling of one's rights and duties is an experience that is common to all people in whichever culture, except for some initial period of ethnical development in children, and some intellectually abnormal adult individuals. On the other hand some, for instance the Japanese scholar Masaji Chiba, doubt this assumption of the universality of subjective rights and develop theories that divide legal or ethical cultures into those which lack this experience, as in traditional Asian societies, and those which have developed it as in western civilization. This seems to be a pretty substantial issue which could be empirically tested on condition that some agreement could be achieved as to the concepts and the empirical indicators involved. The importance of the subject is felt not only in relation to such grand issues as typology of human cultures. When involved in the study of law and dispute treatment in Polish urban communities, I have gained the impression that differences in the declared experience of participation in formal or informal disputes may perhaps be explained by personal and social differences in the concepts of one's rights that are held by the people involved. To test this one would need to have some working decisions concerning the three issues listed above, as both the concept of rights, their scope, and their 'depth' may differ from person to person and from group to group. I cannot do more here than simply raise in a sketchy manner some points related to the subject.

It seems obvious that even standard surveys of attitudes towards 'deviance' may be used as a source of information concerning rights and duties; at least, the right to be 'deviant' in the society under study. It is necessary, then, to make a distinction between the moral or aesthetical assessment of conduct, and the advocated ways of reacting to the act or person that is assessed. Various studies in tolerance provide information of this kind as well. In general, the concept of tolerance is used, and may be used very widely, to cover any case in which a person, group, or institution decides not to interfere with the conduct of another actor, even if the assessment made in moral or other terms is negative. To refrain from counter-action seems to be a pretty good indicator of the recognition of a right of an actor to behave in a given way. One must, however, bear in mind that the respective inquiry need not only take into consideration the acceptance of such counter-action or lack of it, but also the positive and negative assessments and relationship between these assessments and the recognition of the right to intervene or lack of it.

That all these things tend to become more complex whenever we come to empirical investigation may be illustrated by an example taken from yet another survey on the ethical attitudes of young Poles (age 16 to 29, a representative sample n = 1,951 persons) conducted in 1973 by the present author and Krzysztof Kiciński in collaboration with the Public Opinion Research Centre at Polish Radio and TV.[5] Among other questions several hypothetical cases were presented, and subjects were asked whether they thought the described individuals should be forced to change their conduct or whether they should be granted freedom of decision, and whether they 'liked or disliked the conduct of the individual described in the survey form[6] (see Table 12.1).

It is remarkable as a historical document that under the appearance of well-established and legitimized Communism—1973 is the year of prosperity for Gierek's regime—the majority of the young generation refused to acknowledge the right of the state or, in general, the collectivity, to intrude in matters that deal with the individual, with one exception, that of health.

Conceptually, equally remarkable is the fact that not only are there tolerant people among those who dislike some way of acting,

[5] Krzysztof Kicinski and Jacek Kurczewski, *Poglądy etyczne młodego pokolenia Polaków* (Ethical Beliefs of Young Poles) (Warsaw, 1977).

[6] In what follows my paper 'On Measurement of Subjective Rights' from *Polish Sociology of Law Newsletter*, Polish Sociological Association, Section on the Sociology of Law (Warsaw, 1978) is reproduced.

TABLE 12.1. *Attitudes towards individual freedom among young Poles in 1973* (%)

| Cases | Coercion | | | % accepting coercion among | |
| --- | --- | --- | --- | --- | --- |
| | Accepted | Rejected | Don't know | those who Dislike | Like |
| Young man after completing studies refuses to work in a place appointed by the state, as this spoils his personal plans | 19 | 68 | 13 | 45 | 10 |
| Young worker refuses to cut his long hair when ordered, as it does not constitute a risk at work | 27 | 64 | 9 | 42 | 21 |
| Someone permanently refuses to take part in the social activities at work, saying he has more important things to do | 36 | 48 | 15 | 53 | 31 |
| Young married couple do not want to have children, though they are well-to-do and have their own flat | 16 | 64 | 20 | 34 | 9 |
| Man in whom doctors have detected a serious (not-contagious) illness should be treated | 63 | 26 | 11 | 76 | 65 |

but at the same time there are people who are in favour of coercion even if they accept the conduct against which the coercion of this or another type is addressed. Possibly these are the people who at the same time recognize the rights of society or a collective to counteract a given type of conduct and at the same time recognize the right to such conduct. Unfortunately, we have not explored this issue more deeply, and we cannot therefore say whether this explanation is true or whether we are dealing here with a genuine conflict between the legal concepts people have and their sympathy towards a person who behaves in a given way.

All this bring to mind the formulation by Leon Petrażycki of the distinction between strictly moral and legal emotions.[7] Whenever a 'free' duty is imposed upon an individual without the correlative right on the part of, say, society—or an individual, and so on—to enforce the fulfilment of such a duty, this is termed by Petrazycki a purely moral emotion, while the legal emotion involves both respective rights and duties. In this way only those duties will be termed 'legal' that are sanctioned or should be sanctioned according to those questioned. Following this way of thinking, the best way of posing our questions would be, first, to ask whether society and so on should use coercion in a given case, and secondly, whether the individual should give in to the pressure. If both questions are answered positively then it may be decided that the legal duty to behave in a certain way has been recognized by someone who answered our questions. The more sophisticated may even go so far as to ask whether society should behave in such a way or should have only a right to choose coercion as a way of counteraction, and then whether this is just a moral duty (if this is the case) on the part of society or whether it is correlated with the respective recognized claims on the part of the citizens. This is obviously related to some philosophical questions which are at the core of jurisprudence, but it seems that it may be settled in a quite empirical way since, at least for some people, those duties of the state or society will be ultimately of a 'moral' character, while for others they will perhaps be justified by the 'legal' rights held by citizens, even if devoid of the instruments of practical enforcement. Following this chain of regression we may end up at some basic ethical concepts on which the everyday philosophy of law is based.

Coming back to our two hypothetical questions, we need to consider three other possible patterns of answers. Would it not often be the case that people have unclear ideas on whether this or another way of conduct is allowed or not? It would have been easy to assume that two negative answers provide the clue for the inference that a right to act in a given way is acknowledged on the part of the person. This right is of a legal character as the duty to refrain from counteraction on the part of society—Petrażycki saw in it a *facere–pati* type of relationship—is recognized. The next possible pattern is that someone acknowledges the right both of

---

[7] Cf. his *Law and Morality*, trans. H. W. Babb (Cambridge, Mass., 1955).

society to coerce and of an individual to oppose it. This would follow either the failure to distinguish between what one feels as one's own views and what one feels as belonging to the official law, to what other people expect or the genuine adequacy of one's views on the legal rights and duties and that of others. Legal dissonance is thus possible in the peculiar social and historical context and could, perhaps, be related to the already-invoked anomy. It seems to me that this refers also to the fourth of the possible situations, that is, to the case when coercion is not allowed but the duty to stop the specific conduct is accepted. Still, one may say that this is perhaps the moral—in the Petrażyckian sense of the term—duty to behave in a certain way, as an obligation is accepted without correlative claims on behalf of others. At this point it would be worthwhile to introduce a simple scheme of these logical possibilities and conceptual divisions (see Table 12.1).

TABLE 12.2. *Rights and duties* simpliciter

| | | Is coercion by others accepted? | |
| --- | --- | --- | --- |
| | | YES | NO |
| Is performance of behaviour by the individual accepted? | YES | Legal dissonance or two 'free', i.e. 'moral' rights | Freedom of individual action accepted as 'legal right' |
| | NO | Freedom of individual action rejected and 'legal right' or 'legal duty' of coercion recognized | Both coercion and individual action rejected, i.e., 'moral duty of individual |

This scheme, obviously, may lead to more questions than answers. Still, it seems that it would be useful to reinterpret some of the already-existing data with its assistance. Simplification is involved not only in that sometimes the distinction between rights and duties is blurred, but also in that it does not take into account the lack of the respective ethical experience. This is in a way similar to 'gaps' in the official positive law. The presence of such gaps in ethical awareness is in fact more likely as there is no corresponding everyday, informal jurisprudence. The researcher is therefore prone to interpret other people's minds and actions in a more consistent way than they would be able to do themselves. This is not necessarily bad—in fact it may be the essence of the humanistic study of the normative in society and of the discovery of hidden normative structures—but it needs to be acknowledged from the very beginning.

A word on the two remaining aspects of 'width' and 'depth' of rights and duties. We need to become better acquainted with the content of various subjective rights which are recognized and activated by the people in their everyday lives. This means that not only the relations between individual freedom and the state or society at large should be studied but also the mutual rights and duties that are accepted or rejected, negotiated and developed within the family, at work, in school, in the street, and in many other social situations should be studied more closely. Let me recall here the example of 'territoriality' brought by the late Erving Goffman into modern sociology. This, however, needs to be further developed in a more systematic way, even if the original poetic beauty of such an approach will be lost. What are the principles which allow for the comparison of various micro-legal systems of mutual rights and duties? There is little work done yet on those issues apart from the dry social psychology of justice. On the other hand, there are a lot of traditional points of reference that may help to enlarge the area of possible comparisons. Is inviolability accepted as the right of the individual in all spheres of interaction, and on what conditions? What factors determine the emergence of legal rights to territorial privacy in some fields and not in others? Such and similar questions should be a focus of attention for sociology of law in the future. Stress on subjective rights and duties as well as observation of the practical use of one's rights and fulfilment of duties in the everyday life of the individual and society are the forces that may hopefully help to move the discipline from its bareness and the dangerous repetitiveness of its topics, methods, and results.

It is, however, one thing to demonstrate that the whole realm of human experience may be interpreted in terms of rights and duties, and another to demonstrate that such an interpretation is universally recognized and practised throughout all cultures. Following a well-established anthropological custom we can start our brief excursus in the swamps and savannah of the Southern Sudan.

The Nuer—according to E. E. Evans-Pritchard[8]—as late as in
the 1940s used to be a remarkably acephalous society of about
200,000 fierce shepherds devoid of any political institution of
power, not only at the national but also at the local of kinsfolk
level. No chiefs or council were in sight. Even the impressive
figure of the so-called 'Leopard Skin Chief', supposedly invested
with the sacred authority enabling him to reconcile the parties to
a dispute unless they wished otherwise, has recently been called
into question as rather a distortion of reality by the scholar looking around in vain for some authority.[9] Evans-Pritchard himself
had declared that during a year spent amongst the Nuer he had
not found a law in the strict sense of the word, as there was
nobody specialized in legislation or adjudication. The customary
compensations that were thought of as due to be paid in cattle to
a man wronged by adultery, on fornication with his daughter, or
by physical injury did not add up to a legal system, as there was
no authority able to decide on the facts or merits of the case, as
well as no authority able to make people abide by its decisions.
Rarely, Evans-Pritchard thought, the wrong could be repaired in
a different way than by the use of force or threat of it. Lack of law
coexisted, accordingly, with a lack of authority. Rarely does an
anthropological description fit so well the image of the original
state as depicted by Thomas Hobbes: 'To this warre of every man
against every man, this also is consequent; that nothing can be
Unjust. The notions of Right and Wrong, Justice and Injustice
have there no place. Where there is no common Power, there is
no Law; where no Law, no Injustice.'[10]

But, strikingly enough, in another work Evans-Pritchard himself cuts the Gordian knot of law, justice, and power. The very
impossibility of justice without law and authority, or of justice
and law without authority and power disappears when one reads
that the Nuer have a distinctive sense of personal rights and dignity and a developed sense of the righteousness of these as
expressed in the concept of *cuong*.[11] It means that authority is not

[8] E. E. Evans-Pritchard, 'The Nuer of the Southern Sudan', in his *African Political Systems* (London, 1961).

[9] Aster Akalu, *Beyond Morals? Experiences of Living the Life of the Ethiopian Nuer* (Malmoe, 1985).

[10] Thomas Hobbes, *Leviathan* (New York 1950), 105.

[11] E. E. Evans-Pritchard, *The Nuer* (Oxford, 1940), 171.

necessary for there to be commonly accepted in a given society concepts of what are legitimate claims, and of the law understood as a socially functioning system of individual and collective rights and duties. On the other hand, however, the practical efficacy of the legal system understood in such a way may be left to the willingness and resources at the disposal of the interested parties. The efficacy of law will thus be determined by such practical considerations as the distance that separates the homesteads of those involved, or the number of people that each party may bring into an alliance with him. Neither law nor justice disappear, as there is still a point of reference which serves as a standard showing who is right and who is wrong. The lack of specialized officers of law and justice by no means prevents the presence of these qualities. In this respect the Nuer attitudes towards legal self-help are very instructive. Anyone to whom a debt or compensation is owed may, for instance, seize the other party's cattle. Here a neat distinction is made between *kwal*, when the cattle are seized without approval of the possessor in order to secure the claim, and *wuan*, when the cattle are seized with no recognized right, that is, when in our terms they have been stolen. In the first case, further developments depend upon the validity of the claims of the one who seized the cattle. If these are in accordance with customary legal standards and there is also an agreement as to the facts of the case, negotiations will follow and the claims will be acknowledged in exchange for the return of the previously appropriated cattle. If there is a normative or factual dissensus, parties attract a dispute that may easily develop into a fight. Negotiation and fight are also the consequences in the case of theft of the cattle. *Kwal*, as normatively proper action, is however approved by neighbours and kinsfolk, while in the case of *wuan* even those forced by duties of kinship to ally with the thief will do it less heartfully and will at least indirectly mitigate him in course of the negotiations and aggressions that follow thus increasing the chances of the prevalence of the law.

Similarly to the Nuer, it was said of the Dinka, their neighbours both in terms of geography and political tastes, by Godfrey Leinhardt that:

They have notions also of what their society ought, ideally, to be like. They have a word, *ciaeng* or *cieng baai*, which used as a verb has the sense of 'to look after' or 'to order', and its noun form means 'the

custom' or 'the rule', and they well know that this rule and custom differ
from one place to another, even in Dinkaland.[12]

So they differ, though they are alike among themselves in many
aspects, as when, for instance:

in general it is the convention that fighting between subtribes should be
with the club only, through subtribes of a large tribe may be so distant
from each other politically that the spear is used. Fighting with the club
reduces the danger of homicide and is the sign of the recognition of the
desirability of peace between subtribes of a single tribe. Fighting between
tribes is not governed by any such conventions, nor do the Dinka think
that peace between them should be the rule.[13]

To end this survey of old Southern Sudanese normative traits, let
me quote extensively a third case, that of the relatively more centralized Mandari, whose local hereditary chief,

[t]he *Mar*, with the backing of his land-owning line and the important
religious powers vested in his person, was a mechanism for maintaining
peaceful relations with the chiefship. It must be remembered that the
*Mar* never initiated litigation, but waited for persons to put their peti-
tions to him for consideration and judgement. The carrying out of pronouncements made by the *toket* [that is, the council] were in most cases
left to the individuals concerned, although where cattle were handed
over following a case, this was done in the presence of the *toket*. Settlement was often, however, dependent on the ability of the injured party to
exercise self-help in getting his dues. If a complainant was persistent in
his demand for help in this respect to the *toket*, the Mandari say that the
*Mar* might instruct his young men, accompanied by the elders, to seize
and hand over the property awarded in compensation. Mandari also say
that many cases were never satisfactorily settled and people would wait
until the Mar was absent to take their own revenge on their enemies.[14]

This series, ranging from the Nuer who totally lack any political offices, through the Dinka, to the small chiefdoms of the
Mandari manifest certain common features. No wonder it was
possible to express the normative ideas of the acephalous and
thus supposedly lawless Nuer in the proper *coutumier* composed

---

[13] Godfrey Lienhardt, 'The Western Dinka', in John Middleton and David
Tait (eds.), *Tribes Without Rulers: Studies in African Segmentary Systems* (London,
1958), 106–7.
[13] Ibid. 116.
[14] Jean Buxton, 'The Mandari of the Southern Sudan' in: Middleton and Tait,
*Tribes Without Rulers*, 88.

by P. P. Howell.[15] And in general, albeit the African data suggests a high degree of local variation and difference in the normative culture, still lawyers and anthropologists who met in 1966 in Addis Ababa to discuss the ideas and procedures in African customary law found little difficulty in using the terms 'rights' and 'duties' in contrast to the much more complex concepts of legal personality and the like. It seems, therefore, proper to recollect here that they established for comparative purposes some conventions on basic jural concepts. They thus distinguished between (a) a person in law as an entity in whom certain rights and duties are vested; (b) status, as a coherent agglomeration of a variety of specified right and duties or capacities and incapacities; (c) capacity, as specific to a given legal or jural relationship; and (d) the legal or jural unit as:

any person, or set of persons, in themselves of acting in institutional position[s], that is the nucleus of a cluster of rights and duties defined by rules which are subject to external constraint, and which, through the backing of the accredited political organs of the social unit involved, are considered to have public legitimacy.[16]

Much more difficulty was encountered a few months later at the Wenner-Gren Foundation Conference at the Burg Wartsenstein, the year when the famous debate involving Max Gluckman, Paul Bohannan, Sally Falk Moore, and Laura Nader on the proper vocabulary and metalanguage of comparative legal anthropology burst out.[17] Although the applicability of the elementary concepts of rights and duties was never openly put in question, some doubts were raised that could ruin even such a shallow foundation of common discourse. Sally Falk Moore criticized, for instance, Hohfeldian vocabulary in order to describe all jural relationships in terms of the various elements encapsulated in the notion of rights and duties.[18] She had found it 'hopelessly clumsy', artificially distorting legal relations into dyads and analytically distorting complex legal relations into meaningless

---

[16] P. P. Howell, A. L. Epstein, and M. Gluckman, 'Introduction' to: Max Gluckman (ed.), *Ideas and Procedures in African Customary Law* (London, 1969), 47.

[17] Cf. Part IV, 'Comparative Studies' in Laura Nader (ed.), *Law in Culture and Society* (Chicago, 1969).

[18] W. N. Hohfeld, *Fundamental Legal Conceptions as Applied in Judicial Reasoning, and Other Legal Essays* (New Haven, Conn., 1923).

particles. Paul Bohannan almost convincingly criticized the very idea of using the Western analytical model that openly refers to rights and duties, though he neither proposed another elementary model nor did he refrain from the use of the terms 'right' and 'duty' in practice (not to mention his classical study in which he makes extensive use of these concepts).[19] In this debate the following line from the concluding preface written by Sally Falk Moore seems to remain still as a valid warning, as guide-line for all further investigations that attempt to escape from the purse conceptualism of jural analysis without refusing to acknowledge the significance of jural relationships in the social reality: 'it may be, in fact, that the role of certain concepts and principles is less one of defining rights and duties than of defining the general ideological framework in terms of which rights and duties are expressed.'[20]

Recent years have witnessed, however, the resurgence of the debate under the heading that is best exemplified by the title of Aster Akalu's book on the Ethiopian Nuer, *Beyond Morals?*:

[A]s far as can be ascertained the Nipnip do not possess linguistic categories which would enable them to express or formulate moral judgments. In the Nipnip encampment 'moral judgments' are as rare as 'icecream cones'. Conduct is not sorted automatically into categories of either 'good' or 'bad'. Unpleasant social manifestations such as manslaughter, promiscuous adultery, and breach of contract are certainly considered inconvenient but they elicit no collective condemnation.[21]

A similar case was also made for a quite different cultural area. In his paper read at the World Congress of Sociology of Law in Aix-en-Provence in 1985, Peter G. Sack summarized the normative ideas of the Tolai of East New Britain by saying that:

Traditional Tolai social order is horizontal rather than vertical— pluralistic instead of hierarchical—and Tolai society is therefore ungovernable. Tolai law, and Melanesian law in general, reflects this and precludes its translation into a normative, sovereign-oriented, legal system. Melanesian law is a way of life. It is neither totally amoral, nor does it lack normative and coercive elements . . . It gives choice by limiting its range, but it does not prescribe what is good or prohibit what is bad; it

[19] Paul Bohannan, *Justice and Judgement among the Tiv* (London, 1957), 130–1
[20] Part IV 'Comparative Studies', introduction by Sally Falk Moore, in Laura Nader (ed.), op. cit. 347.
[21] Review by William Miller, *Tidskrift foer Raettssociologi* 3:1 (1986), 64.

does not tell people to do only the right thing; . . . it does not presume to be an ideal order.[22]

New Britain is so close to the Trobriand Islands that it seems natural to look back at *Crime and Custom in Savage Society* by Bronisław Malinowski. When comparing it with the already-cited work on the Tolai one gets the impression that, though Peter G. Sack certainly adds valuable subtlety into the concept of order accepted by Melanesians, still he does not erase the general tone of the analysis made by Malinowski. This general tone lies in the stress put on the complexity of a traditional corpus of habits, customs, and other rules as well as on the direct interweaving of what are in Western society called social forces and normative regulation. Of course, it is not 'a normative, sovereign-oriented, legal system', though at the same time it does not 'lack normative and coercive elements', especially if we take into account that Dr Sack takes together what Malinowski divided into different normative structures of different content and in mutual tension, as well as in support of each other.

It seems fully appropriate at this moment to recollect the 'anthropological definition of law' defined by Malinowski in a typically Petrażyckian way, that is, without reference to state, power, sovereign, professional lawyers, courts, and codes:

The rules of law stand out from the rest in that they are felt and regarded as the obligations of one person and the rightful claims of another. They are sanctioned not by a mere psychological motive but by a definite social machinery of binding force, based, as we know, upon mutual dependence, and realized in the equivalent arrangement of reciprocal services, as well as in the combination of such claims into strands of multiple relationships.[23]

This is, of course, not an authority-oriented definition of law as the will of the sovereign, and as such it is subject (as is the whole of the Petrażyckian theory) to various criticisms we do not wish to discuss here. It is my opinion that more widespread use of terms like 'normative systems' and 'normative structures' will help us in overriding the terminological habits that lead to endless

---

[22] Peter G. Sack, '*Bobotai* and *Pulu*—Melanesian Law: Normative Order or Way of Life', *Journal des océanistes*, forthcoming.

[23] Bronisław Malinowski, *Crime and Custom in Savage Society* (London, 1951), 55.

definitional debates. It is not the fact that normative structures are felt as obligatory that makes them normative, but the fact that they are themselves built around an experience of the normative. One would look in vain, however, for pure and elementary experience of this kind, as experience of the normative is always expressed and interpreted in the context of a given particular normative structure.

When concluding, in 1977, my investigation into the so-called internal aspect of law, and reflect upon the theories of H. L. A. Hart and A. Ross, I arrived at the following characteristics: a rule as latent exists in normative experience; socially, it exists once the following five conditions are met: (1) a standard that makes the content of a rule is deliberately expressed, transmitted, and received; (2) a rule-sender is convinced that the fulfilment of the standard is the duty of the addressee; (3) the same refers to the convictions of the addressee of a rule; (4) the convictions of the rule-sender are expressed in an action intended to bring about fulfilment of a standard; and (5), if and only if all these said conditions are met, it is reasonable to assume that a rule fully exists in the social context, though less restrictive versions using a modified and limited set of assumptions are possible as paving the way for the various models of the normative structure.[24]

To all this I would like to add today that I think that the historical normative structures in existence in particular social places need not be divided according to one general scheme of classification into law, custom, and so on. On the contrary even, it seems to me that the particular normative structures cross-cut these traditional distinctions in that they include elements from the various categories. Moreover, these historical normative structures may overlap each other and the individual may use, support, attack, or better, participate in several normative structures at once.

I would like today to stress also a different point, that it is the process of collective action, interpretation, and expression in which each stage is subject to subsequent reinterpretation, so that there is not one canonical interpretation that is valid for a given normative structure once and for ever. The interpretative process is a perpetual one, unless nobody is interested in participating in a

[24] Jacek Kurczewski, *O badaniu prawa w naukach społecznych* (A Study of Law by the Social Sciences) (Warsaw, 1977).

given normative structure. What type of interpretation is to be used depends on various considerations, and in this sense I do not envisage the possibility of an external criterion of the validity of interpretation that might be applied to the different normative structures. This may be illustrated with the help of the latest book by Ronald Dworkin.[25] In his *Law's Empire*, arguments are introduced in support of the view that the interpretative is almost a definition of the legal enterprise, though at the same time it is characteristic of all social practice and humanistic research in particular. The recent popularity of hermeneutics and the concept of interpretation undoubtedly left traces on the book. On the other hand, one cannot ignore the biblical studies which served as the foundation of reflection on the interpretative aspect of social life.

Dworkin rejects interpretative nihilism with the help of a distinction between internal and external scepticism. The latter does not force us to resign from the acceptance of a criterion of validity within a given normative structure. This sound approach allows for discussion of various interpretations inside given normative context. This ideal and model of law as integrity comes into play as it serves as a premiss for what Continental lawyers traditionally call the systematic interpretation. The claims for the validity of an interpretation are well founded if the interpretation fits the principles of law as a coherent system. This is why I would prefer to call Dworkin's approach the coherential theory of law in parallel to the coherential theory of truth. According to the Polish philosopher of science, Jerzy Kmita, there are two basic kinds of interpretation as methodological procedure applies in the humanities—the historical and the adaptive interpretations. In this terminology the concept of law advocated by Dworkin clearly belongs to the adaptive interpretation that 'adjusts the results of past, or alien cultural actions to the given present conditions'.[26] This adjustment is made with the help of the liberal and democratic political philosophy that Dworkin accepts simply as given in his reasoning. His concept of law is thus an elaborated version of the liberal-democratic philosophy of law. His critics would certainly say that he advocates a very flexible interpretation of the American constitution that allows for the derivation of normative

[25] Ronald Dworkin, *Law's Empire* (London, 1986).
[26] Jerzy Kmita, *Wykłady z logiki i metodologii nauk* (Lectures in Logic and Methodology of Sciences) (Warsaw, 1973), 219.

statements fitting the tacit philosophy behind the act. I may like the effects of this enterprise but I do not like absolutization of the practice. Dworkin himself is aware of the fact that under different circumstances perhaps the totally opposite procedure might be necessary in order to arrive at precisely the same conclusions. This means that the choice between the loose and strict rules of interpretation is made relative to the given set of political ideals and the normative text under interpretation. The internal criterion of the validity of interpretation in such a case can reside not so much inside the normative system as inside the political culture of both the interpreter and those whom he or she is concerned with.

So, there is no disagreement as to the role of interpretation in the daily life as well as in the legal life of society; there is even no disagreement as to the lack of absolute criteria of valid interpretation. The different normative cultures and structures offer, however, the opportunity to interpret 'themselves' in various ways, and though there is a possibility of rational debate on the choice to be made between various interpretations offered, still there is not a single 'internally objective' criterion which would make the decision instead of the participants themselves.

Coming back to the action aspect of normative structures, let me emphasize again that this active perspective has recently become as popular in the social sciences as the interpretive. Nevertheless, by no means is this an original way of interpreting social events. It is as old as the pragmatist philosophy and indeed, even older than that. In sociology one should recollect here the normativist theory of social action as proposed by Talcott Parsons, in which rights and duties are linked with the concept of social action. Moving a step back we may also cite Florian Znaniecki, who as early as 1925 wrote that:

From the practical social point of view, the important matter is not what the individual may find 'in his consciousness' when he plays the psychologist and instead of acting analyzes his various moods, feelings and ideas, but what axiological significance is ascribed by him to the elements of the situation as such, and how this significance which they possess in his eyes affects his behaviour with regard to them. And since we mean to study social action as a practical system, this point of view is also the one our theory must take.[27]

---

[27] Floran Znaniecki, *The Laws of Social Psychology* (New York, 1967), 93.

We have already cited Malinowski who, starting with the same concept of law as Petrażycki, supplemented it with the living forces of social action. In a sense another supplementary step was made by Znaniecki in his theory, it is not only that the psychological definition of law is insufficient to explain rights and duties when fulfilled. It also needs to be moved beyond simple introspection as providing the immediate data of the normative experience. This is the assumption that enabled Petrazycki to reject the conceptualism of the positivistic jurisprudence of the twentieth century, but the assumption soon turned out to be too simplistic. Social psychology takes action as the whole in which one needs to be able to decipher the meaning that is inherent though not necessarily intended. The complexity behind such formulations leads us back to the issue of interpretation. To be normative, an action needs to be interpreted as expressing the normative 'ought'. We need to look at actions as wholes in order to discover the rights and duties as these exist in the social interaction. We cannot agree, therefore, with those who, like MacCormick, assume a contrast between the legitimacy of hermeneutics within jurisprudence and the 'approach of psychology of sociology conceived as natural, causal or behavioural sciences'.[28] It would be difficult to find a sociology or psychology that deals with human action not taking an interpretative stand. Whatever the merits of ethnomethodology, it has at least proved beyond doubt that neither professional psychologists nor sociologists are free from the burden of interpretation, nor can everyday interpretation be liberated from the task of permanently reconstructed mutual interpretation.

To make myself more clear: I feel the need to move our way of thinking and talking about the normative away from the static approach that still dominates professional discourse. To give one eminent example: Joseph Raz, while discussing the relationship between ethics and politics, uses the language of rights. According to his view: ' "X has a right" if and only if X can have rights, and, other things being equal, an aspect of X's well-being (his interest) is a sufficient reason for holding some other person(s) to be under a duty.'[29] This is—needless to say—a very interesting

---

[28] Neil MacCormick and Ota Weinberger, *Institutional Theory of Law: New Approaches to Legal Positivism* (Deventer, 1986), 105.
[29] Joseph Raz, *The Morality of Freedom* (Oxford, 1986), 166.

definition that rightly links the otherwise meaningless technical term with the core of ethical issues. I do not wish to discuss this aspect of Raz's theory here. What I doubt, however, is the continued assumption that 'rights' and 'duties' are somewhat like separate entities, instead of taking the respective terms as shorthand signs for complex schemes of social action in which people engage according to their normative experience. This active aspect is difficult to discuss at the individual level—everyday life banalities might hide it from our sight—so perhaps it is necessary to consider the collective experience, that recounted in this book.

I have cited above the experience of archaic societies like those warlike shepherds from Southern Sudan, the almost biblical Nuer, who, as if just emerging from the flood in their postdiluvial simpleness already demonstrate the sense of 'ought' coded in rightful claims. This and similar cases are important as demonstrating that rights and duties are not necessarily dependent upon the centralized authority of the state. In a sense the Polish case illustrates the opposite side of the picture. Here, as in any other Communist totalitarian country, the Party State was of the measure of a real Leviathan. This is exactly where the distinction between right and wrong, justice and injustice was blurred; in societies like this, rights survived among the people *in resistance* to the common power.

I have not claimed that rights and duties exist apart from society and culture. The claim of naturalness is different and, I hope, it may be deciphered throughout this book. Rights and duties are natural in so far as they are part of the structure of reality. For decades, Communist society might have been seen as one in which rights were conditional upon the will of the sovereign party, and duties were absolute and reduced to obedience. The point is that, while until the 1950s the normative had disappeared, after 1956 it started to be resurrected, step by step and explosion after explosion, as if the normative infrastructure were so strong that it could be effectively suppressed for only few years. Pareto writes somewhere about the social order that it is when a pressure is removed and the *status quo ante* reappears that static equilibrium is demonstrated. With all its metaphoric value I think that this gives us a clue to the problem of human nature. Concentration camps, extraordinary revolutionary commissions, and institutionalized corruption may be seen as pressures which force mankind to waver like the reed in the wind, but whenever freedom prevails the claims to basic rights and duties are made again.

Perhaps it is not freedom but the struggle for freedom which removes the oppressive cover from society and makes the normative infrastructure visible again. Adam Podgórecki, when analysing rights from the sociological point of view, supports, wrongly in my opinion, traditional sociological conventionalism as to rights.[30] He reiterates that human natures are different according to different normative cultures, and that therefore there is no ground for the concept of universal human nature. There is nothing new in this remark, which has been made repeatedly by critics of dogmatic concepts of the law of nature for centuries. This argument does not take into account, however, the fact that there are some basics of the human condition that may be analysed as universals—psychology and even sociology are built upon such an assumption—although these may be so obvious for us as to be almost unperceivable. Monsieur Jourdain speaks in prose, native speakers are unaware of the rules of grammar, perhaps it will be always impossible for mankind to realize its own nature for the same close circuit of cognition. The Ethiopian Nuer whom Aster Akalu met may be totally unaware of the distinction between right and wrong, as between right and duty, however impossible such a social world may seem for us. It does not mean that they do not follow rules. If they have no rules of sexual or neighbourly conduct, they have at least some rules of grammar which they must follow in order to communicate with each other. The minimum of the normative is hidden already in the structure of communication, the structure of discourse that makes mankind human. In the same way, there is always an 'ought', even if it is not necessarily felt. And contrary to radical relativism, one may hold that however different normative cultures are there is also a basic normative structure of mankind that is never clear, but that is, nevertheless, built into the existence of the human being as its constitution. Century after century, one cultural type after another, mankind is concerned with some basics which are similar though never identical in shape. There is

[30] Adam Podgórecki, 'Toward a Sociology of Human Rights', paper presented at 1988 World Congress of Sociology of Law in Bologna.

a law of nature, but it will never be fully explicated and put in the open. It is under the permanent process of reconstruction and reinterpretation, the discovery that in fact is the resurrection. No new rights are discovered in this sense, but the same dimensions of the human condition are under the permanent process of reinterpretation that takes the form of new rights superseding or supplementing the old ones.

Podgórecki points, however, to a very important social fact when he attempts an explanation of the emergence of rights. He introduces the distinction between crippled and complete human rights. The notion of crippled rights take on a Paretian colour in his theory.

In social reality, as a rule, human rights are mainly abstract, meaning that they are pronounced, but not necessarily practised. Abstract human rights become crippled when they do not provide realistic conditions for the operation of these rights. Sometimes a crippled human right expresses only an indirect promise of obligatory force. Under certain conditions, this abstract norm may transform itself into a motivational impulse to the concerned parties. It may also be a source of constant frustration, since state agencies, in fact, may not be willing to observe it. Crippled human rights may appear not only in the form of an abstract message which may or may not be accepted into social practice; they may surface also in the form of dormant human rights.[31]

Inequality, according to Podgórecki, is the starting point for the genesis of a human right:

As a rule, human rights do not appear to be mature. It is true that a gap between ought (abstract norms) and is (people's attitudes) can cause them to operate, in some instances, even more vehemently than when there is no gap at all. This is because the drive to link them together would play a subsidiary role. Strange though it may seem, crippled human rights can produce more social effects than their complete counterparts—certainly they invoke more social noise.[32]

This theory seems to fit the Polish case, and perhaps it developed out of it as well. Let us observe that Podgórecki speaks of 'dormant' rights in a sense similar to the 'hidden' rights I discuss. But there is no 'empirical sociology' able to wake up the 'dormant' or exhibit the 'hidden' normative structures, unless the

---

[31] 'Toward a Sociology of Human Rights'. 3.          [32] Ibid. 9.

multiplicity of the layers of social reality is accepted, of which the 'dream', 'unconscious', or 'infrastructure' are part. So, certainly, the gap between ideal and practice, experienced as dissonance, makes people more aware of the respective normative components, but if the punishment is too harsh and chances of success too slim the same dissonance may be subdued and repressed from awareness. This seems to have been the state of Polish society under the climax of Stalinism in the early 1950s, with the empire of Communism seemingly invincible. Certainly it is when the repressive power of the regime weakened and the international military and economic situation of Communism proved to be less prosperous, that the experience of the gap led to awareness and recaptured its motivational force. The relativity of human nature may mean that this nature reveals itself in relation to the particular set of circumstances, and only in this version we can find it acceptable. I do not consider natural anything that occurs in life. To be a dirty, illiterate cannibal is by no means more natural than to be the educated author of modern genocide. Under favourable circumstances both could have been more open to the suffering of others. Permanent killing of one another is inimical to social co-operation, and the continuous presence of wars in human history proves only that the areas of order and co-operation may be isolated from each other by barriers of hate and indifference. By saying all this one does not necessarily mean to imply the existence of a separate layer in the physical or biological sense, but the special situation of potentiality of resurgence of the experience that is for convenience only labelled as the special mode of being. Once again one needs to stress the danger of psychologism. There is no need to postulate the internal aspect as the mirror-like mental experience of rights and duties, of 'ought' in its various modalities. Experienced or not, the normative remains as the structure that needs to be considered in order to account for the individual and collective actions observed when the pressure is removed. Conscience is manifested in the biography of the individual as well as in the history of the nation. There is thus a hidden normative structure, in that it can be activated under friendly circumstances. These circumstances are somewhere between the despair that leads to loss of heart and stagnant satisfaction. One can imagine that the fulfilment of rights is equal to the disappearance of the normative. In this sense rights and duties as driving human conduct are always 'crippled', in that they always result from the discrepancy between the claim and the actual reality. The latter brings us to the question of the future of rights under the new political conditions.

# 13

# *Personal Freedoms: Religion, Personality, and the Privatization of the Body*

If one looks at the 1988 survey, the concern with issues of religious doctrine and religiosity might seem obsessive. But religion was for decades the main source of ethical judgement for most people, and this function was finally recognized even by the atheist regime. In the last and most tense days of the strikes in the summer of 1980, the primate, Cardinal Wyszyński, who had been for decades the enemy of the Communist establishment, was televised across the country preaching the need to return to work. This move was immediately discounted, however, by the opposition as Communist propaganda manipulation. One may, however, think that the Church, through the primate, was willing to speak on behalf of fundamental social order, of which the Communist authorities were inefficient instruments and not masters in their own right. Since this unexpected move the Church has been continually invited to join the political scene as the major repository of the values promoting social solidarity. A high order of political skill was demonstrated in the way that it accepted some of these invitations—the massive construction programme of hundreds of churches throughout the country was the main concession accepted—but also took care not to lose its moral position of independent and superior judgement. So, to understand the political position of the Roman Catholic Church in the 1980s, one ought to think in terms of comparison with the Church of England and the monarchy.

The Roman Catholic Church, in a country where something like 90 per cent of the nation are Roman Catholics (the others belonging to the Orthodox, Greek Catholic, Jehovah's Witnesses, and declared atheist milieux), is in fact something like a national church. It has always been closely linked with the history of the nation, as the state's Church through centuries of independence. It was involved in the protection of national culture and identity in the nineteenth century under foreign domination, and in two parts of Poland—Russian and Prussian—played a different role as a denomination religiously alien to the main bulk of the populace. The Roman Catholic Church of Poland is the Polish Church for Poles, where Polish songs have been sung since the Middle Ages, where the liturgy has been in Polish since the Second Vatican Council, whose bishops as Polish, and where the shepherd, now residing in Rome, speaks Polish as well. One had good reasons to doubt the patriotism of the Polish United Workers Party that claimed allegiance to the world Communist movement, with its capital in Moscow, and whose leaders were often people who had served in the Red Army and NKVD against Poland. But one could not cast any doubt on the patriotism of the Church, which had been throughout the post-war period the only official institution that had remained independent from the party.

It was in the churches that the great deeds of the Polish kings, Polish saints, and Polish intellectuals of the past were commemorated. When one enters St John's Cathedral in Warsaw one sees to the right various plaques commemorating the fight of the Home Army against the Germans, the tragedy of Lvov, the third largest Polish city annexed by the Soviet Union since 1939, and the Polish airmen who took part in the Battle of Britain. Further up the southern aisle one sees the images of Roman Dmowski, the fervent Polish nationalist, and of Wincenty Witos, the leader of the agrarian party, both foes of Marshal Piłsudski and of Stefan Stanunski, who had been appointed by Piłsudski's political camp to run the Warsaw government and who led the defence of the city, to be killed by the Germans in a concentration camp. None of these was a saint in his life, all were often anti-clerical, and they were political enemies, but still they stay peacefully together in the cathedral. The main point is, however, that this was the only place where, until the 1980s, such a display of the great figures of the Polish past was at all possible. All statues of Piłsudski, who led the Polish victory over the Red Army in 1920 and who ruled the country in the years 1926–35, were destroyed by the Communists, and streets called after him were renamed, while in Cracow's cathedral on the Waivel castle hill his tombstone was venerated by thousands of visitors. The story is similar for all the other pre-Communist politicians as well as pre-Communist political events, erased from the public space and taken into the Church. The Church thus provided the real public space for the nation. Within it asylum the nation could commemorate events, such as the 1791 Constitution Day on 3 May 1918, Independence Day on 11 November 1920, Battle of Warsaw Day on 10 August, and 1944 Warsaw Insurrection Day on 1 August. Only powerful bishops could protect such gatherings, but the feeling of a common patriotic heritage spread into the smallest church in the countryside. The Communist authorities, though recognizing the freedom of religious service in the churches, were not willing to accept the extension of it into overtly political freedom of expression. The construction of new churches was not allowed; taxes on the Church were levied; the numbers of the priesthood were controlled; the sermons to the faithful were recorded; those priests who were politically outspoken in their critique of Communism were prosecuted; and at the peak of the Stalinist regime early in the 1950s the head of the Polish Church, Primate Wyszyński, was himself arrested and interned without any due legal warrant in a small monastery on the Polish–Russian border.

The internment and release in 1956 of the primate were very symbolic events. Throughout Polish history the tradition developed that the head of the Church in Poland was an interrex between the death of the old and the election of the new monarch. After the war some continued to see the role of the primate of Poland in the same way, though this time the people were not awaiting the election of a monarch but a representative government and parliament. This is why the Polish Church has some affinity to the institution of the monarchy. It has a certain unwritten right to be exempted from the hardships of Communist government. The Church has a special place in the life of the nation—and this was acknowledged practically and also, in contrast to all other churches and denominations, in that the Roman Catholic Church was not subject to legal statute. It did not exist under Polish Law in the Communist period. One might add that the Church shared this legal non-existence with the Communist party itself, as that also was never registered under the public law of corporation or association, and did not have a legal personality awarded in the way that others were required to seek. So, both were above the laws of the country. The Church distanced itself from political issues, but understood its role as the moral censor of political life. It was more active than the monarchy is allowed to be in Britain, but a tradition of veneration lay behind it too as the only legitimatizing force.

In the author's nation-wide survey a majority (59 per cent) of the population declared a high level of religious affiliation, that is, believing and practising; 29 per cent said that they believed and practised on an irregular basis; and 8 per cent believed but did not practise at all, making altogether 96 per cent believing compared with 3 per cent who declared themselves non-believers, and 1 per cent who found the question difficult to answer.

Further questions give more meaning to those results. The first deals with the various elements of the Judaeo-Christian tradition that are upheld in the Catholic world-view (see Table 13.1). If one compares the proportion of those who say they believe in God and those who believe though do not necessarily practise, it is clear that few of the latter have not included belief in God among their beliefs. In general it might be said, however, that in Polish society an overwhelming majority believes in God, and to a slightly lesser extent in sin. (The latter result will be discussed in the last chapter.) This makes analysis of normative attitudes in terms of sin not only necessary to satisfy curiosity but also justified in terms of its importance for the people. The remaining elements on the list have been reported as part of their world-view by a majority, between 62 per cent and 76 per cent of those interviewed. All the elements were accepted by the majority of the sample, and when the complexity of the matter is considered, the fact that only 13 per cent found it difficult to give an answer to

TABLE 13.1. *Belief in main precepts of faith, 1988* (%, n = 926)

| Do you believe in | Yes | No | Difficult to say |
|---|---|---|---|
| God | 93 | 4 | 3 |
| Life after death | 68 | 21 | 11 |
| Heaven | 71 | 17 | 12 |
| Hell | 62 | 25 | 13 |
| Last Judgement | 76 | 13 | 11 |
| Sin | 86 | 8 | 6 |
| Satan | 63 | 24 | 13 |

some of the questions is surprising. Priests will find it difficult to understand that Satan is conceivable without Hell as his territory, or that one can believe in Heaven while not believing in life after death. But those inconsistencies mark the much deeper underlying tension, that is, between the modern-day view of the world around us and the supernatural perspective offered by the faith. This tension we must leave unanswered, but one needs to note that, so far, the results indicate that Poles not only attach themselves to organized religion but also that they uphold its basic tenets.

Nor is this the case only in basic theology; but concerning moral aspects as well. In a society where belief is so widely spread, it is hardly surprising to find that the overwhelming majority take the Ten Commandments as binding for them personally, and this is valid not only for social ethics—91 per cent feel bound by the ninth commandment and 92 per cent feel the same about the sixth, but also 97 per cent feel bound by the fourth and the fifth—the religious commandments. Also, 88 per cent of Poles feel bound to observe the Lord's Day, 87 per cent feel that no other gods should be taken, and 86 per cent that God's name should not be taken in vain.

If we turn now to the link between social class and religious affiliation, measured crudely by asking whether one is a practising believer, we need to remind ourselves first that frequency of regular practice of believers systematically decreased with the level of education, from 76.6 per cent among class A (that is, the self-employed with no more than elementary education) to 47.19 per cent among class F (white-collar workers with more than a high-school education). Level of education alone does not explain the differences, however, as the workers with elementary education declare intensive religious affiliation in 64.6 per cent of cases. So we are left with a need to speculate on the quality of education received, or we need to accept the fact that there are occupational and other factors playing an important role here as well. Most interesting in this context is the fact that workers with high-school education (class D), of whom 48.8 per cent are regularly practising, are close to class F, and less affiliated than white-collars at the same level of education. High school educated (class D) and the intelligentsia of today (class F), as well as workers, have in common a relatively high percentage of those who believe but do not practise at all (14.6 per cent of D and 10.6 per cent of F). In general, therefore, the 'new middle class' of skilled workers and of skilled white-collar workers—as is generally the case in Polish society—does not lose its faith, but it does loosen its link with the organized religious life more often than other categories.

TABLE 13.2. *Social class and religious belief*

| Social class | Relative frequency of belief in | | | | | | |
|---|---|---|---|---|---|---|---|
| | God | Life after death | Heaven | Hell | Last Judgement | Sin | Satan |
| A | 1 | 1 | 1 | 1 | 1 | 1 | 1 |
| B | 2 | 3 | 4 | 3 | 3 | 3 | 3 |
| C | 4 | 5 | 3 | 4 | 4 | 4 | 4 |
| D | 3 | 2 | 2 | 2 | 2 | 2 | 2 |
| E | 5 | 4 | 5 | 5 | 5 | 6 | 5 |
| F | 6 | 6 | 6 | 6 | 6 | 5 | 6 |
| % believing in sample | 93 | 68 | 71 | 62 | 76 | 86 | 63 |

This similarity of the 'new middle classes' may be paired with quite substantial dissimilarity, though. Table 13.2 gives the rankings for the particular classes for the frequency with which they profess belief in some basic tenets of the Judaeo-Christian religion—belief in God, life after death, Heaven, Hell, Last Judgment, sin, and devil. The striking thing about this table is that the simple gradation of education levels does not coincide with differences in degree to which a given element of the faith is supported. What intervenes most clearly in this relationship is the peculiarity of high-school educated workers (D) who are most likely, after the self-employed (mostly farmers) with elementary education to continue to believe in the basic elements of the Judaeo-Christian faith. In this they offer a contrast with the white-collar workers, especially those with higher education, who manifested the lowest degree of faith. Taking into account the previously discussed relationship between social class and religious affiliation, we are in a good position to suspect that, while educated workers refrain from institutionalized religious life, they continue to be religious in their world-view. Among the intelligentsia, however, the disconnection from institutionalized religious life accompanies secularization of the world-view. The further consequences, if there are any, may be investigated by looking into those items from the questionnaire which deal with the relationship between morality and religion, and with the attitude towards religious precepts.

As to the fundamental frame of reference for the evaluation of personal conduct, education seems to be the decisive factor. The better the level of education the more often the general good of society is cited as the reference-point in evaluative decision, and the percentage of those mentioning God and the precepts of religion decreases. This becomes more complex, though, when we move to two other issues covered by the questionnaire, religious conformism and the link between religion and morality.

When it comes to moral theology, the allegedly traditional religious view is expressed in agreement with the statement that: 'It is difficult to imagine moral convictions not based upon a faith in God.' The wording of this question replicates the question asked by Kiciński in surveys of moral opinion among the inhabitants of Warsaw.[1] This view was upheld by 46 per cent of Poles, while 26 per cent agreed with the modern view that: 'There is no relationship, believers need not to be moral people, and moral persons may not believe.' The 'traditional' view was supported by 54 per cent of those with elementary education, but only by 35.3 per cent of white-collar workers with higher education (class F) and 34.1 per cent of class D. Again, educated workers are more similar in their attitudes to the intelligentsia proper (43.3 per cent in class E). For all those with high-school education, however, the 'modern' view dominates over the 'traditional', and all these, workers, intelligentsia, or just white-collar workers, differ from the more numerous, less-educated classes.

This pattern reappears when it comes to the issue of religious conformity. It is not the 'white-collar workers' in general, but again the 'new middle classes' of educated workers and intelligentsia who are closest to each other on the issue. They are least likely to think that the 'precepts of religion should be obeyed even if they are wrong according to our opinion' (17.1 per cent of D and 18.8 per cent of F, in contrast to 25.2 per cent of C, 29.9 per cent of E, 38.6 per cent of B, and 47.6 per cent of A'. They are

[1] Krzysztof Kiciński and Jacek Kurczewski, *Poglądy etyczne młodego pokolenia Polaków* (Ethical Beliefs of Young Poles) (Warsaw, 1977).

the most likely to think that 'one should not follow precepts that one thinks are wrong' (51.2 per cent of D and 52.9 per cent of F, in contrast to 47.8 per cent of E, 42.5 per cent of C, 37.7 per cent of B, and 34.7 per cent of A). It is interesting to note that this religious nonconformism—not to be confused with the Nonconformist religion itself—is not replicated in the case of attitudes towards the law. There the educated workers remain the most nonconformist class—as in social reality, we might add—while the intelligentsia proper most often advocates strict legalism even against political reason.

Two points emerge from the analysis of this survey data so far. First, there is a clear similarity between educated workers and educated white-collar workers (with levels of education being different in both cases) concerning attitudes towards institutionalized religion. More often, members of what I call the 'new middle classes' in socialist society feel themselves personally free moral agents, in that it is up to them to decide their own conduct even if this contradicts the teachings of the Church. This, in a way, could provide a bridge between their attitude towards religion and their political engagement. The militants of Solidarity are recruited from both milieux. There is a strong feeling of both agency and subjectivity that, after a deeper analysis, may serve as the explanation for both. It does not imply, however, a secularized 'world-view', which, as we remember, is distinctively religious for the workers. Secondly, there is evidence of the better-known link between 'secularization' of the world-view and level of education. The majority believe in God and in other elements of the Judaeo-Christian world-view, but basically less often with more education.

Taking into account all that has been said in chapter 5 on Polish society, it is interesting to see whether the classification applied here will produce a similar characterization for the lower strata of workers. When asked about confidence in other people (Question 43), Poles most often answered that one can trust only those whom one knows well (47 per cent), with the more trusting ('one should trust everybody until this confidence has been let down'—27 per cent) and those who declare absolute lack of confidence in others (23 per cent) almost equally represented. This is an interesting question, as in previous studies of public opinion it was the only attitude where responses correlated with attitude towards the death penalty, those who were suspicious being more likely to favour it. The three social classes most often expressing full, unconditional trust in others were those composed of people with at least secondary education—D (36.6 per cent), E (38.1 per cent), and F (34.1 per cent)—independent of their occupation (see Table 13.3). There was a slight decrease associated with higher levels of education amongst workers but, still, the workers with elementary education (B) were more often open to others than the self-employed (A) with the same level of education (21.8 per cent and 17.7 per cent respectively). On the other hand, the workers with elementary education only were more often unconditionally distrustful of others than the remaining classes. Another related question previously used by Podgórecki in his pioneer studies on knowledge and opinion about law in Poland, asked the sample whether they knew many people outside the family who were sympathetic towards them, or none at all. The question asked was 'Do you know many people outside your family who wish you well?' and the answers were: 1. Nobody; 2. Few; 3. Many; and 4. Don't know. The answer is, of course, subjective. One person might feel quite alone among a dozen friends, while another will be happy with one. But this question was found to be related to the earlier question on trust, as well as to attitudes towards the death penalty. Judging by answers to this question Poles are quite widely socialized, the majority (52 per cent) answering that they knew many such people, while only 4 per cent answered that they knew nobody sympathetic. The workers with elementary education again included by a small margin the lowest percentage of those who believe they have wide social support (48.2 per cent), and the highest percentage by a small margin of those who felt isolated (5 per cent); the workers with secondary education, whom we take as being the most

TABLE 13.3. *Social class and trust in other*

| Trust in Others: | Social Class | | | | | |
|---|---|---|---|---|---|---|
| | A | B | C | D | E | F |
| Trust everybody | 17.7 | 21.8 | 23.4 | 36.6 | 38.1 | 34.1 |
| Trust only those already well known | 57.3 | 44.1 | 47.7 | 36.6 | 43.3 | 58.8 |
| Trust nobody | 22.6 | 38.1 | 23.8 | 24.4 | 16.4 | 10.6 |

politically mobilized in Polish society, evidently felt the widest social support and involvement (61 per cent), as compared even with the intelligentsia (54 per cent), farmers (52.4 per cent), and non-manual workers (52.2 per cent).

The question on satisfaction with life showed again the highest percentage of the unhappy to be among workers with elementary education. But here those with at least secondary education differ, the intelligentsia being happy more often than workers, and giving similar answers to the farmers.

It is common knowledge in Polish sociology that education is thought to be the major predictor for various social attitudes in Polish society, stronger than any other factors such as class, place of residence, gender, wealth, or age. So let us look briefly into the links between education and attitudes.

Religiosity decreased with level of education, with the more-educated not only more likely to describe themselves as non-believers or non-practising believers, but also more willing to give a clear answer to questions about the relativity of moral values and more likely to accept this view. Taking views on the lack of absolute criteria for defining evil and belief in its existence together, it seems that moral absolutism is more likely to be found among people with secondary education. When considering religion and morality, the better-educated are more likely to think that there is a relationship between the two, and less likely to think that morality must be governed by belief in God. After years of official atheism, only a small minority favoured an atheistic foundation for morality, regardless of their level of education.

Unconditional acceptance of religious rules decreased and willingness to support open disobedience increased with level of education. But a different pattern emerged in answers to the question of conflict between law and individual conscience. On this point, the most legalistic group were those with secondary education. The less-educated were more likely to advocate simple rejection of official law, while the best-educated proposed implicit circumvention. When asked about pressing for one's own interests the level of education had little impact, with only a slight tendency for the better-educated to be more outspoken in presenting their own claims.

There was no linear relationship between level of education and feelings of personal security, which were at their highest in the group of people with secondary education. And feelings of personal happiness and social integration were unrelated to levels of education or to gender.

Psychological security was highest among those aged 30 and 45, and this perhaps rightly point to the importance of the age factor. The relative security of this age-group as compared with others may, however, be related to the political biography of its members, who spent most of their school years under Gomułka and Gierek, and passed their youth in the period of relative prosperity and freedom of the early 1970s. This is not borne out, however, in the replies given to another question from the same psychological set, which could indicate the extent of social isolation as well as trust in others. By this indicator the young generation describe living within small circles of friends, whose support may be taken into consideration whenever a problem arises. The response to the question on happiness may be useful in shedding some light on the results so far. The question asked was 'In general do you consider yourself happy with life?' 1. Yes, definitely; 2. Yes, mainly; 3. No, mainly; 4. No, definitely; and 5. Difficult to answer. The results are, however, ambiguous. On the one hand, there is the edifying tendency of the elderly to strongly declare happiness. This might be explained by the homeostatic urge in the face of approaching death. But on the other hand the low position of the middle-aged groups is hard to explain with conventional wisdom. In view of this it seems that the initial explanation made in terms of political context in which those aged 30 to 40 were brought up cannot be dismissed.

It is interesting to note that the same age group (30–40) is least likely to express full allegiance to religion, though the overall religiousness of all those aged under 60 is in marked contrast to the higher degree of practice among the oldest. It was surprising to find that the relationships between level of religiosity and gender differs in the various age-groups under examination. In the young and upper-middle age-groups the differences are negligible, while in the middle-aged group as well as among the elderly, the females out weigh the males in declared religiosity. The youngest age-group is clearly very religious, with fewer agnostics than among the older groups. One may wonder about the nature of this religiosity among the young and how long it may continue, and whether this may be last generation of Poles who, having passed through the Church of the Underground and Resistance against Communism, will be able to tolerate the Church of the Establishment.

The question asked was 'Which opinion do you adhere to?' 1. There are clear principles of good and evil valid for everybody independent of circumstances; 2. There are no such unconditional principles of good and evil independent of circumstances; and 3. Don't know. But leaving aside religiosity, perhaps belief in absolute moral principles may be taken as the more fundamental element in the individual view. On this point, however, there was no relationship with age. It is not unimportant, though, to note that the differences in practice and frequency of religious allegiance observed between the age-groups do not correspond with differences in belief in absolute ethical principles, and that the ratio of absolutists to relativists remains the same across the generations.

Elderly women reported relying on a small circle of friends far more often than elderly men, who had many contacts outside the family. Do men develop a large social circle that survives and becomes stronger throughout their lives? Or do they develop a large network for mutual support in old age? We cannot say. The men reported a constant level of happiness into old age, when they reported an increase in their feelings of wellbeing. A small number of women aged 45–60, however, said they were not so happy, perhaps for health reasons.

The main aim of this part of the study was to reveal the relationship between actual beliefs and the official normative teachings of the Roman Catholic Church, which at the time of the survey was the main public institution in the country independent of the Communist Party State. It was also important to document the consciousness of various individual rights, such as the right to political expression or the right to economic entrepreneurship. The importance of the survey was both practical and theoretical. The last issue leads us back to previous statements about normativity. Throughout the book it has been assumed that there is a heart to society, a normative deep structure that is responsible for these or other political or cultural reactions and movements, a Polish ethos in confrontation with history seen as dominated by the *nomoi* of freedom and rights. Whether this could be detected at the level of attitudes and through the conventional medium of the questionnaire was the problem. Then there is the question of the normative regulation of the body—the problems of abortion, of new technologies of reproduction through transplantation, of naturism, and of sexual freedom: what are these about if not control of the body? With the strengthening of the role of the Church in the political life of the country and the return of institutionalized religion in the public domain, it was interesting to check how the freedom- and political rights-oriented ethos of Solidarity's Poland coexisted with the liberation and privatization of the body, that is, the impact of modern civilization.

The human body is of course involved in every social transaction, and lies behind all the cultural veils we use. Culture might have been defined just as the covering of the body, its various movements, events, and postures; and even more, as filling the body with the socially negotiated interpretation that becomes our personality. The culture once formed and acquired is of so solid an appearance that one needs to wait for an unusual occurrence to happen before the fragility of this cultural life-world is experienced. The intimacy of the sexual act, catastrophe and sudden death, an illness that unexpectedly turns us aside from our well-organized plans for tomorrow—these are just examples of situations in which the body is caught in its functioning as if *in flagrante*, and reminds us about the frame within which our life goes on.

From what has been said it may be predicted that in attitudes to the body, Judaeo-Christian tradition as filtered through the teachings of the Roman Catholic Church will find its way; that education will slightly decrease the strength of this tradition; that the 'new middle classes' will more often apply the not-necessarily consciously elaborated concept of the free moral agency of man to this area; and that, even so, the attitudes of educated workers might differ from those of the intelligentsia.

To this we may add the common sociological model of culture lag according to which the working class milieu lags behind the white-collar workers in terms of the speed with which ideas enter into the world-views of the people, as, for example, farmers lag behind urban customs.

Armed with this not-very sophisticated theory, we discovered that in the case of attitudes towards the body studied with the help of a questionnaire, all the points raised above apply, though it is impossible to predict why exactly this or another one is in force here or there. There is also a new point to be added.

Concerning body-organ transplantation, there is a clear trace of education plus culture lag acting in the case of responses that express the sacredness and untouchability of the body. This statistically marginal attitude is most frequent among the elementary-educated self-employed (26.6 per cent) and least common among white-collar workers with higher education (5.9 per cent). The latter are slightly more often in favour of a purely individualistic approach, according to which the body belongs to the individual and can be sold, used, and abused as one wishes. The high-school educated workers, on the other hand, represent more often the dominant Polish attitude that body organs can be exchanged, for instance as a gift when there is a need, though there should not be commercial traffic.

In respect to the new technologies of human reproduction, the effect of education and culture lag is seen in the frequency with which the dominant answer that this is justified only for the purpose of helping infertile couples appears. It is less frequent among the self-employed with elementary education (57.3 per cent) and then rises to 67.1 per cent among white-collar workers with higher education. The peak is, however, in class E (white-collar workers with high-school education only), with 73.1 per cent, which could suggest that on some issues the dominant or new trend of opinion might be represented by this particular class of people more often than by others. Also, workers with high-school education demonstrate their peculiarity here, as they more often then others (14.6 per cent) support unlimited progress at the expense of the sacredness attitude.

All these points emerge even more clearly in the case of attitudes towards public nakedness (see Table 13.4). We cite this table to give a good example of the pattern we have been speaking about. As to the dominant attitude, its frequency diminishes as we move from elementary education at the left to higher education at the right of the table, and from the farmers at the left to white-collar workers on the right. This clear pattern is, however, contradicted by the high-school workers (class D) as being closer to the best-educated white-collar workers (class F) than to their

TABLE 13.4. *Attitudes towards nakedness*

| | Social class: | | | | | |
|---|---|---|---|---|---|---|
| | A | B | C | D | E | F |
| 1. A naked body (independent of age and gender) is something normal so there is no need to hide it | 7.3 | 9.1 | 17.8 | 19.5 | 26.1 | 22.3 |
| 2. Some human bodies are beautiful and therefore may be shown publicly | 4.8 | 10.9 | 15.4 | 29.3 | 24.6 | 31.8 |
| 3. Beautiful or not, nakedness ought to remain covered before strangers | 86.3 | 73.6 | 59.8 | 43.9 | 47.8 | 42.3 |

*Note*: figures are column percentages, don't knows are omitted.

own school peers who work as white-collar workers or to work colleagues with lower educational achievement! This occurs agin when we look at the middle row, in which figures are shown on the frequency of what might be called a hedonistic approach to nakedness. Education, culture lag, and the 'new middle classes': in the top row we see these factors in action again, raising the frequency of what might be described as dogmatic naturism from 7.3 per cent to 22.3 per cent. But the peak is reached among the white-collar workers with high-school education only. It is difficult not to use here a rather untheoretical description of this as an example of low-style modernity most often represented not among the real vanguard of the sociological forces of culture, but amongst those who wear a low-cost, 'trendy' style of dress, and so on, those who are, on these issues, more Catholic than the Pope himself.

It may come as a surprise to the reader to find that attitudes to sexual activities are not determined by social class in Poland. The percentage distributions of particular answers to the question about the necessity for moral regulation of sexual life, do not differ in practice across the social classes.

Finally, a related matter concerning the approach to marriage and family life. When asked about solubility of marriage, Polish public opinion demonstrated here for the first time a pure pattern of education and culture lag. With increased education, and moving from the countryside to the town, through workers to white-collar workers, the frequency of answers suggesting the permanent character of marriage and family decreases from 48.4 per cent to 10.6 per cent, and the frequency of answers leaving the matter to the discretion of those involved increased from 35.5 per cent to 77.6 per cent. Age and gender are not discussed separately, for two reasons. First, the meaning of gender changes with the stage in life-development: it is a different experience to be a woman in a nursery, or in the university as a student, or as a teacher. Even the physiological characteristics of gender change, so a social definition may provide only very apparent signs of permanence, as one is not 'a woman' all through life except for the convenience of bureaucracy. The same is true for men. We need to divert our attention from the fiction of gender as something permanent and biological in its totality. All this does not mean that some peculiarities of gender, like some peculiarities of age-stages in life, cannot be pointed out when it comes to questions of attitudes. (The question of nature or nurture is not considered here.)

For instance, women always seem to be more religious, particularly elderly women. I do not think that there is anything innate in women that makes them more vulnerable to the teachings of religion, and it is even more difficult to imagine an innate factor that would make it emerge in its fullness after the age of 60; nevertheless, this is the fact. Out of twenty-eight possible cases for comparison concerning belief in the basic items of the Judaeo-Christian faith, women express their faith more often (in twenty-seven instances), that is, in 96 per cent of cases. (The excess on average is 5.9 per cent in the 16–29 years age-bracket, 3.7 per cent in the 30–45 years age-bracket, 5.3 per cent between 46 and 59 years, and then suddenly 13.5 per cent among those aged 60 or more.) It is noteworthy that elderly women differ not only from their male peers, but also from women in younger age-brackets. This holds not only for faith in the elements of the religious world-view, but also for religious affiliation.

As to organ-transplantations, gender and age have no clear relationship with the various attitudes. Suffice it to say that neither the simple theory that women see the human body as sacrosanct, nor another simple theory such as an attitude-change with age or following the pattern of religiosity described above, holds true.

In the case of the new technologies of human reproduction, age comes to the fore. The older groups in our sample more often supported the idea of the natural boundaries of experimentation and biological conservatism, so to speak, in these matters. It is noteworthy that the relationship we speak about is by no means clear, but there is a contrast between those aged under 45 years and those who are older. The younger generation of Poles are more inclined than their elders to accept experimentation, but only if it aims to help infertile couples.

In the case of public nakedness, women, independent of age, are less inclined to accept dogmatic naturism and more inclined to reject public nakedness than men, the difference being largest in the middle age-bracket. Age relates in a pretty linear mono-tonical way, the younger respondents, independent of gender, more often accept dogmatic naturism, while with increase in age the general rejection of public nakedness increases in frequency, with the important exception of middle-aged men, who are the least enthusiastic about such a rejection and more likely than other categories to support what we have termed hedonistic naturism, that is, they support nakedness when it is beautiful, possibly erotic.

Strikingly, but as in the case of social classes, gender and age do not relate meaningfully in any way to attitudes towards the moral regulation of sexual activities. As to marriage and the family, the permanent and dissoluble character of the union is stressed more by men among the youngest and more by women among the oldest in our sample.

*The Body in Particular Situations* The first part of our questionnaire included twenty-five situations which the subject was asked to evaluate from the legal, religious, and his own point of view. Situations were introduced in the following way:

We begin by presenting you with a variety of behaviours. With reference to each of them we would like to learn:

first, whether according to your opinion such behaviour is proper or not?

secondly, whether according to your knowledge such behaviour is prohibited by the law in force in our country;

thirdly, whether according to you one has a right to behave so even if this is improper?

After each of the situations was presented each of these questions was asked, this time in a shortened form, for example: 'Is this sinful?, with the options: 1. It is sinful; 2. It isn't sinful; 3. Difficult to say.' I quote the original formulation here, as even a layman will realize how much in the area of survey research depends upon the precise wording of questions and answers. We know that there is no ideal wording, though this does not mean that one could not find a better wording than the one used. The context of other questions is of importance. The context of the micro- and macro-situation in which the survey was made is important. All this means that, although the questionnaire was meant, as in the good old days, to treat different people with one and the same verbal stimulus, in fact this identity of stimuli is illusory in practice. This illusion is, however, a matter of degree. Responses to the same statement in the questionnaire might be treated as responses to more similar questions than responses to two different questionnaire statements.

In the heterogeneous collection of situations dealing with sex, work, family life, and political relations it is striking, first, that in all situations the majority of subjects were able to say whether they considered a given behaviour to be sinful or not. The average of 'don't know's was 16.8 per cent, and above-average levels were given in those situations that deal with labour relations, public policy, and new technologies of reproduction. It should be added, however, that even in the purely political area using the category of sin was not difficult, especially in the case of food rationing or anti-nuclear protest. From the religious point of view the most ambiguous situation was, therefore, not the political one but the newest reproductive experiment, in which a South African woman had offered her womb in order to bear a child for her daughter. The almost equal division of answers to this question among those who thought it sinful, not sinful, and don't knows is so natural that it strengthens our confidence in the survey. It reflected exactly where consternation had been expressed in public opinion. As expected we have achieved the random distribution: 1—1—1.

If we correct the data for the differences in 'don't know' answers by taking into account only the answers of those who define a behaviour as sinful or not sinful, the following categorization might be made:

1. political behaviour is for the majority beyond sin;
2. behaviour such as abortion, sexual cohabitation without marriage, not maintaining an old parent, stealing from the factory, and divorce are seen by an overwhelming majority as sinful;
3. behaviour seen as sinful by between 60 per cent and 75 per cent included drinking, concealment of one's political beliefs, and contraception in marriage;
4. behaviour seen as sinful by a slight majority included naturism, resale of goods, and accounts for employees benefit; and
5. behaviour seen as not sinful by a slight majority included surrogate parenthood.

We turn now to focus attention on several questions that dealt with attitudes towards the body and the use of it. These included questions on sexual cohabitation without marriage, on public sunbathing, on marital contraception, on abortion, on surrogate motherhood, on teaching contraception in schools, and on dispersing anti-government demonstrations by force. Although the latter case is evidently different in character and focuses on political rights of freedom of expression and on political violence, it nevertheless deals with the body because an abuse is implied, and it therefore serves as a good reminder of the other dimensions of the attitude towards the body that are present in social life.

## Sex without Marriage
Question 5. *People cohabit sexually without being married*

| | | | |
|---|---|---|---|
| 1. Is it sinful or not? | sinful, 81% | not, 12% | don't know, 6% |
| 2. Is it lawful or not? | forbidden, 9% | not, 85% | don't know, 6% |
| 3. Has one a right to do so? | yes, 44% | not, 43% | don't know, 13% |
| 4. Is it proper or not? | proper, 32% | not, 58% | don't know, 10% |

This behaviour is evidently felt by the majority to be forbidden by religion, and not by the law. The majority also feels that it is improper, but public opinion is quite evenly divided as to whether one has a right to do so or not.

Parental status is of interest when studying the relationship of this question with social and personal attributes. People who have dependent children are most likely to find sexual freedom proper. In this they oppose—as might have been expected—maritally experienced parents of adult offspring. The latter group is the only one to differ from others on the remaining two dimensions, being more likely to call the behaviour in question sinful, and to refuse a respective right.

The contrast between the views of those from the countryside versus the views of those from a metropolitan milieu appears strongest here. The right to engage in sexual activities without marital ties is afforded by the majority of inhabitants of large cities, and refused by the majority of villagers.

Gender is related to attitudes on this issue, independently of age, in a fairly systematic way. Women more often see relationships as sinful and improper. When it comes to the respective right, generation has a dramatic impact. Amongst the youngest (16–29 years), women are more likely to grant a right to non-marital sex, while in the middle-aged and especially among the elderly generation it is just the opposite.

As to social class, the already familiar pattern of education plus culture lag reappears, with the self-employed elementary educated being least likely to accept propriety of sexual behaviour and the higher-educated white-collar workers being for the most part of the same view. As to the sinfulness of the act, no marked differences between the social classes are observed, and the likelihood of greater tension between perceived religious duties and one's own moral concepts increases with the rise up the social ladder. Here, as well as in some other similar situations further on, the difference between the number of those who think one has a right to sexual freedom is thus greater among the better-educated and culturally more advanced milieux. On the other hand, the decrease in the strength of religious affiliation follows the same pattern. It might be said for the purpose of this model that tension is removed by the last fact—people believe less and so they care less about the difference between their views and religion. This does not work so well in our special case, that of the high-school educated workers who, though weakly affiliated, retain the faith. We may suspect that to cope with the problem they develop their own concept of sin as a hypothesis to be tested in future. Here they have become trapped. They do not think, as often as white-collar workers that sexual freedom is permissible; in fact, they think so even less often than workers who had not completed high school. But they also do not think that this is improper. In terms of tolerance as expressed by granting people the right to sexual freedom, they follow their place in the order determined by the education plus culture-lag pattern. So what finally happens is that they are then over-represented among the 'don't know' answers (26.8 per cent as compared with a 14.1 per cent–8.1 per cent range for other social classes on the propriety dimension).

*Naturism* In the years leading up to 1989 naturism grew in Poland as quite a new phenomenon, getting high visibility with the help of a mass media censored in its political content. There were fights with local people, and considerable television coverage of the naturist movement, especially the mass Miss Nature contests on Polish beaches.

Question 6. *People of both genders and different ages sunbathe naked on beaches*

| | | | |
|---|---|---|---|
| 1. Is it sinful? | yes, 56% | no, 31% | don't know, 13% |
| 2. It is forbidden by law? | yes, 18% | no, 72% | don't know, 10% |
| 3. Is it right to do so? | yes, 48% | no, 40% | don't know, 12% |
| 4. Is it proper? | yes, 30% | no, 62% | don't know, 8% |

Naturism has not found approval from the majority of Poles, where nevertheless, in view of the stereotype of hypocrisy, it is remarkable that naturists, by a small majority, won their right to behave as they like even if potential participation does not exceed a third of the population. In this connection religious ambiguity concerning behaviour is important. Only a small majority this time considered the behaviour sinful. One could say that acceptance of nudity suddenly won over this society to a much larger degree.

Is this victory evenly distributed over the population? Of course not, and as we might have supposed, women irrespective of age more often than men found it improper and were less tolerant towards it. The first great age-divide is at 45 years, after which people of both genders are less often approving and tolerant; the next is at 60 years, after which women become much more anti-naturism than men. But as to religious evaluation of naturism, it is important to note that for both genders it changes step by step, with from 50.9 per cent of the youngest generation of women seeing it as sinful, up to 80.6 per cent of elderly women.

Attitudes towards sinfulness and tolerance of naked sunbathing in public show a somewhat different pattern from simple approval of it as proper behaviour. The latter view is expressed most often, for example, inhabitants of small towns of under 50,000 inhabitants and not by people from the larger cities. Also, if parental status is considered, both the unmarried (that is the youngest) and parents of dependent children are more in favour of naturism, while childless people with marital experience and parents of adult children are less so. When social class is considered, the attitudes towards naturism seem to be related purely to the education plus culture-lag factor. As our special case does not appear as deviant from the pattern, we might suspect that naturism does not function as a problem of conscience for the otherwise principled high-school educated workers.

*Contraception*  The Polish Pope's firm stand against the use of contraceptives has not been directly challenged in Poland's media, and this is a serious matter. On the other hand, the sale of contraceptives is often harassed by militant Catholics, while the popular youth and women's magazines continue to advise on the choice and use of them. As almost all weddings are religious as well as civic, each Polish couple is reminded that the use of contraceptives is morally wrong from the religious point of view, and that within marriage sexuality is only for procreation, and only natural birth control is allowed. Whether Polish Catholicism extends so far remains in doubt, however.

Question 7. *A married couple uses contraceptives in order to prevent a pregnancy*

1. Is it sinful?              yes, 67%    no, 24%    don't know, 9%
2. Is it forbidden by law?    yes, 5%     no, 89%    don't know, 6%
3. Is there a right to do so?  yes, 65%    no, 25%    don't know, 10%
4. Is it proper?              yes, 60%    no, 32%    don't know, 8%

The majority of Poles see contraception as sinful, proper, and rightful behaviour on part of the married couple. This combination gives us a very important hint as to the degree to which the current Polish ethos reflects the Catholic *nomos* as professed and taught and—let us not forget—enforced by the Church. Already in the research on rights conducted with Krzysztof Kiciński in the early 1970s, we were able to document firm support for the privacy of procreative decisions, and this right is granted against the state's authority as well as against the Church's. This right is supported most often by people who still have dependent children and rejected by those who already have adult offspring. The first group also see contraception in marriage more often as proper, while the second more often as sinful behaviour.

In addition, moving from village to a larger city increases the percentage of those who see contraception as improper, and the percentage of those who grant the respective right increases as well. On the question of sin, the large cities are more liberal than other milieux.

Gender affects attitudes towards contraception only among the elderly on questions of propriety and right—men are more approving. But middle-aged women more often see the behaviour as sinful. For both genders, 45 years of age is the border after which positive evaluation becomes less frequent.

Positive evaluation as to propriety and right increases with the education plus culture-lag factor. No difference is seen on this dimension as to religious evaluation of the behaviour.

The data convinced us that conformism with religion on this issue is related to gender, age, education, and milieu, and forms a part of the traditionalist complex of ideas not being supported by the more active elements in the social structure.

*Abortion* One might wonder if something similar will not happen in the case of abortion. Abortion has been legal since 1956, and then as well as now it has been under attack from the Church. We have selected the most pro-choice formulation of the issue in our questionnaire:

Question 8. *A woman aborted simply because she did not wish to have a child*

| | | | |
|---|---|---|---|
| 1. Is it sinful? | yes, 90% | no, 6%, | don't know, 4% |
| 2. Is it forbidden by law? | yes, 17% | no, 75% | don't know, 8% |
| 3. Does one have the right to do so? | yes, 37% | no, 54%, | don't know, 9% |
| 4. Is it proper? | yes, 23% | no, 70% | don't know, 9% |

In contrast to the matter of contraception, the Church's position on abortion seems to be accepted by the majority of Poles, though one needs to remember that, against the Church's stand, a majority grants the right to abort in some circumstances with additional justification. The fact that it is found improper most often by the youngest men and women, just after the elderly ones, as well as by yet-unmarried people, suggests that on this issue the voice of the new generation is more in line with the Church's teaching than that of the preceding generation (30–45 years), who, independent of gender, most often find it proper. The same is true concerning the respective right that is granted by as many as 50 per cent of men and 41.1 per cent of women in that age-bracket.

Looking at the distribution of answers by social class we see the role of high-school educated workers as important. On the issue of abortion, they contrast dramatically with the white-collar workers with higher education. The former have adopted the sanctity of human life as their point of faith, independent of their severed link with institutionalized religious life, and see abortion as improper and sinful almost with the same frequency as people from the countryside. On the issue of right, however, they almost follow the order expected on the basis of the education plus culture-lag factor.

*Surrogate motherhood* Experiments on human reproduction are not conducted in Poland, but the South African case received wide publicity in the Polish media at the time of this research:

Question 9. *A mother allowed an embryo to be transplanted from her sick daughter's womb into her own in order to bear the child for her*

1. Is it sinful?					yes, 30%		no, 36%		don't know, 34%
2. Is it forbidden by law?		yes, 7%		no, 56%		don't know, 37%
3. Does one have the			yes, 48%		no, 27%		don't know, 25%
   right to do so?
4. Is it proper?					yes, 42%		no, 33%		don't know, 25%

The ethical ambiguity of the situation due to its novelty is evident in this data. People under 45 years of age are in general more affirmative towards surrogate motherhood. No clear difference between genders are visible on this issue except among those aged over 45, men being less often tolerant and, unusually, more likely to describe the act as sinful. There is also an untypical finding in that village-dwellers most often find surrogate motherhood proper and not sinful, compared with the other categories in the first case and the inhabitants of large cities in the second case. One is prompted to say that perhaps direct contact with animal reproduction under human control lies at the base of this closer-to-earth approach.

In the network of social classes the classical pattern of education seems to prevail with two changes, one resulting from the specific position of the country people we have just mentioned, and secondly, the high-school educated workers being this time again slightly less enthusiastic than their rank in the educational hierarchy would lead us to expect. Also they are slightly less likely to support the right, though not against it. In sum, the educated workers seem rather uneasy morally about the issue in comparison with the intelligentsia or other people with high-school education.

*Teaching Contraception* In 1987 a heated debate was aroused when a new school textbook on family life was introduced by the national Ministry of Education. First the Catholic press and then the Church itself criticized the textbook because of three things: an instrumental and technical approach to sex; too explicit material; suggestions concerning the sexual life of school youth; and the teaching of various contraceptive techniques. The Communist government then in power thought it better to surrender on the issue and the handbook was finally withdrawn.

Question 20. *School authorities have decided to teach pupils in high school how to use contraceptives to prevent unwanted pregnancies*
1. Is it sinful?          yes, 35%     no, 53%     don't know, 12%
2. Is it forbidden by law?   yes, 7%      no, 79%     don't know, 14%
3. Does one have the      yes, 68%     no, 23%     don't know, 9%
    right to do so?
4. Is it proper?          yes, 70%     no, 25%     don't know, 14%

We might have deduced from earlier results concerning the approval of contraception by a married couple that the teaching of contraception would be approved by the majority of Poles as well. Interestingly, it is not found sinful, though for an individual teacher of Catholic persuasion this might present a crisis of conscience. Some people find it sinful already. Gender and age come in here in an interesting combination of forces acting in different directions. After 45 years of age women more often than men see the teaching of contraception as sinful, and after 60 women more often than men also see it as improper and not rightful. Among the youngest, however, there is a slight difference in the opposite direction, this time young women being more often for such teaching. The relationship of the attitude with age as such is by no means clear.

A suspicion that attitudes towards the teaching of contraception in schools is related to the vague traditionalism complex is reinforced when we learn that approval of the teaching in question increases when we move from the village to the larger cities. Education and culture lag explain the difference in ranking the social classes on the issue.

*Summary*   There is no better way to start our general review of the observations collected above than to go back to the general questions related to some aspects of the body in our questionnaire. First it is important to note that for a majority of the Poles (57 per cent) collective utility—however difficult it might be to establish it—remains the basic point of reference in evaluation of the situation (Question 26) and not God's precepts or religion (25 per cent). If it cannot be said that the Polish ethos is religious, it is nevertheless rather pro-socially oriented at the normative level. One may suspect in this the effects of post Second World War exposure to socialist doctrines and Communist propaganda, but one can also say that the name of the old Polish state—the Res Publica—epitomizes the importance of the *nomum communum* in the normative sphere. Almost one in two of Poles (46 per cent) find it hardly possible to imagine moral beliefs that were not based upon faith in God, but nevertheless one in three (36 per cent) see no relationship. Moreover, the religious foundation might here refer to the Ten Commandments and the fact that basic moral teaching for both children and adults comes through the Church and through the religious context of prayer, first communion, and so on. This does not mean that the nation is ready to accept everything in the moral teaching of the Church. On the contrary, 44 per cent answered our question on religious conformism (Question 32) by saying that one ought not to follow religious precepts contrary to one's own view, and only 31 per cent were ready to accept the precepts of religion even if they ran contrary to one's view. Thus, the Poles are religious and pious but they reserve to themselves the right to decide in case of uneasiness what is the proper conduct. They are, in other words, Catholic but not a well-disciplined body of followers. The Pole more often than not assumes the Protestant attitude in his or her Catholicism, by deciding for him- or herself what will suit God.

Through detailed study of the various situations we could see how this works. On some issues people are simply deaf to the voice of their Church, as is the case with contraception, which is approved even though its sinfulness from the religious point of view is well known. There are also at least two currents in Polish religiousness. One is older, conveniently labelled as 'traditional' and related to old age, lower education, a more backward social and ecological milieu, and to a slight degree of femininity. Old Polish peasant women chanting their monotonous religious songs for hours embody this strand. But there is also the strong religiousness of the young generation, as well as the more Protestant-like personal religiousness of the relatively well-educated younger workers who do not necessarily practise but who are sometimes strong believers. Those people possibly feel a stronger affinity with Pope John Paul II than with their local clergy. Those people feel strongly on the abortion issue, and see it as wrong for choice to be restricted not only by moral persuasion but possibly also by legal means. But never at the price of human rights! This seems to be the unspoken premiss of their moral views.

Most Poles think that 'man may offer to his fellow man in need a part of his body as a gift, but this ought not to be a matter of commerce' (61 per cent). Only 16 per cent accept unconditional privatization of the body ('The body belongs to an individual and it is a private matter for that individual what is done with the body for money or for free'), and only 17 per cent also profess the idea of the sacredness of the body ('given to a man as an integral totality which one cannot dispose of freely'). From this and from my earlier surveys conducted in Warsaw in 1987 I know that people quite readily accept various transplantations, sperm donation, and so on, but with the idea that this is not just an ordinary transaction. It does not follow from this that transactions of this kind need to be forbidden, and those on the individualistic fringe are able to develop such a market, if they have not yet done so, by serving foreign consumers.

Also, a degree of experimentation in the area of human pro-creation will generally find a tolerant welcome, and might even be embraced if justified in terms of some good. People are, however, rather afraid of unpredictable consequences—one feels obliged here to add, quite rightly so—and majority (65 per cent) agrees that 'experiments in this area should be allowed only if they help otherwise infertile married couples to have offspring'. The idea of helping lesbian couples to have babies, for instance, would—I guess—be rejected, not necessarily out of lack of tolerance but because of the shock of something unknown and unheard of.

The ambiguity and lack of strong reactions can be illustrated by the issue of nakedness. The majority (62 per cent) think that 'beautiful or not, nakedness ought to remain hidden from strangers'. Such an answer in an Islamic society could mean the idea of women being entirely covered except for their eyes. But this is a society where tens of thousands gather, sometimes wholly naked on a beach, to applaud a Miss Nature contest organized by witty entrepreneurial characters, and where normal, everyday movies include doses of nakedness that make Americans blush. Seen in this context the question perhaps is taken more seriously by the respondents than a corrupted sociologist might have suspected. It always impressed me how quickly nude calendars became standard equipment in Polish grocery stores. Those who know how grey those shops are and how grey the women who work there look, may not be surprised at the suggestion that, in contrast to the classical pornography issue and to the issue of commercial exploitation of human nakedness, we are dealing here rather with the way the women prefer to ornament their dark and gloomy milieu with something as attractive as a woman's body is supposed to be. So, again, a mixture of curiosity and hypocrisy may be the frame within which the new (because all that is new for Polish culture) approach to human nakedness emerges under Western influence, despite the Church's reservations.

In common with the Americans and the Irish, however, Poles like to see the sexual functioning of the body subjected to some moral rules valid for everybody (74 per cent). I have not studied sexual ethics and mores, but in this context it is important to stress that in our survey the validity of the Ten Commandments was acknowledged by more than 90 per cent of respondents in this area too. Some sins are seemingly felt as adding a pinch of salt to everyday life.

Finally, in regard to the second element of our title, throughout the survey people were asked whether they thought that this or another behaviour was sinful or not. It was established that, outside politics, the situations described have the connotation of sin. A lot of people think in terms of sin, and almost everybody is able to do so. People were also asked about whether one has a right to behave in such and such a way, even if we find it improper and, of course, even if it is sinful. We have established the readiness to tolerate many cases of behaviour that people themselves find improper and which they know are wrong from the point of view of official normative standards as embodied in the teachings of the Roman Catholic Church. This readiness might be illustrated by the average percentage of those who consider the seven types of behaviour discussed in this paper sinful (55.7 per cent); improper (49.1 per cent); and as not being a right of a subject (37.9 per cent). The difference between two first figures and the last shows the degree to which moral evaluation became privatized by the educated workers. The more often people think that one has the right to use the body in this or another way, even if they themselves find it improper or even disgusting, the more evident is the privatization of the body that for centuries had been under the direct control of the rulers, the masters of the state or the masters of the family or the house. As society (a metaphor to be used for people and agencies in power) grows willing to remove the controls from the expression of the political soul of the citizens, and the privatization of political views becomes a fact, so the same thing happens in the sphere of social controls over the body—it becomes privatized too.

# 14

# *The Rule of Law: Democracy and Freedoms*

The social history of rights described so far has dealt with the decisive forces and events of the post-war period. But to learn how the processes leading up to the resurrection of freedom related to Polish society in general it will be helpful to look at data from public-opinion surveys. There are difficulties with using such data. Some rights and freedoms may have lain dormant, so that only particularly sensitive individuals would have been aware of their significance. Other rights and duties, though reaching public awareness, may not have been fully appreciated. It looks as if the majority of Poles were aware of the lack of free elections. But it does not follow from that that people were aware of the conditions under which such freedom can be enjoyed, that is, the need for a plurality of political parties between which choices can be made. Freedom of speech might have been perceived as frustrated freedom of one's own speech, but this was not necessarily accompanied by awareness of the need for freedom of speech for others. The context also changed. The same people who were not interested in thinking about freedom of religion or of the press, simply because they were unable to see any possibility of these existing in the actual conditions then present, might express vivid interest in such freedoms once the basic political conditions changed. In other words, public-opinion polls gain in significance when public opinion is more significant. The Marxist sociologist Jerzy J. Wiatr suggested once that, in contrast to bourgeois democracy, in a socialist society it is more appropriate to talk about 'social' rather than 'public' opinion. He may be right in that the only way to make society's attitudes public was to make a sample survey and publish it in social-scientific language. There was no other way for public opinion to become public. In this sense no public opinion was really possible under

Communism at all. Not surprisingly, when Soviet sociologists were discussing the possibility of the democratization of their society in the 1970s, they suggested the development of a new science of 'opinionology' which would present results of surveys to the Communist management as a kind of feedback.

In Poland the Catholic Church and a few independent and heavily censored publications (of which the most important was the Catholic *Tygodnik Powszechny* weekly edited by Jerzy Turow-icz, with a circulation of about 50,000 copies) were the only channels for the expression of opinions which differed from the official ones. To this one may add the closed milieux of writers, artists, and sociologists joined in their professional organizations, with their own publications censored and limited in scope, under permanent political scrutiny and financially dependent upon the goodwill of the authorities. The 'Voice of America' and Radio 'Free Europe' acted as substitutes for an independent media, but being located outside Poland had a legitimacy problem among wide sections of the population, especially during the periods of internal stabilization. Informal talk developed as the most important form of public communication. This communication was made in private. If a representative of the regime felt offended about the content of a message, he or she could always make a formal charge against the author. The penal code continually included provisions against those who disseminate false information that could damage the interests of the People's Republic, its political system, and economic interests. It was rarely used in practice but it was always possible that it could have been activated. Also, in order to discipline the society, an interlocutor could ask: 'Do you mean this privately, or officially?' Such a question was standard practice, making double-talk into a commonly accepted and normal societal routine. Only during the short-lived periods of liberalization, such as 1956 or 1980/1, was this double-talk removed. On the other hand, one needs to remember that the Solidarity revolution of 1980/1 lasted long enough to develop resistance against the reintroduction of standard Communist communicative dualism. Conformity had been maintained by allowing free speech in whispers. But suddenly it was no longer acceptable to leave the stage to Communist professionals. Polish actors, who in the 1970s or earlier had been quite relaxed about the discrepancy between the message of their public performance on the stage and the private feelings which they expressed backstage, began to boycott state television. Attempts at ritual mobilization of the masses through institutions such as the National Front, named after 13 December 1981 the Patriotic Front of National Salvation (PRON), and the mandatory meetings of employees ceased to work. Under these circumstances, survey questions that twenty or thirty years ago would have been discarded as frivolous, if not dangerous for a respondent, now seemed quite appropriate and deserving of an answer.

The questionnaire which I prepared for the national opinion poll conducted in October 1988 by the professional Centre for Public Opinion Research (OBOP) at Polish Radio and TV contained several items dealing directly with rights and civil liberties. On the eve of the Round Table negotiations it was important to know how, after decades of Communism and the last seven years of the Jaruzelski's administration, society was thinking about freedom. Censorship, however, was still active. Questions about the ideal state, such as 'What would you like society to be like if there were to be changes?' seemed to be too abstract. After several pilot studies, which included two surveys of the sample of Warsaw inhabitants interviewed in 1987, I felt compelled to focus the questions on issues directly related to the experience of those interviewed. In November 1990 I had an opportunity to repeat the survey, so public opinion in Poland was surveyed on the issue of political rights and obligations at the crucial moment of change in the political system.

One needs to remember how different the situation was when the first and second surveys were conducted. In October 1988 the paramilitary units were still ready to disperse with force supporters of the illegal trade union Solidarity, and the country was ruled by Communists from the Polish United Workers Party. Two years later the nation was engaged in the electoral campaign preceding free election of the president, and the totalitarian organization of society had already become past history. While the first of those surveys aimed to check, after decades of Communism, how widely basic freedoms and civil rights were accepted in Polish society, the second was designed as a control for the previous results, to test whether these were not just a reaction to the political and economic crisis of the old system. Society could have rejected various limitations on individual autonomy only because those were the work of the hated system, and the same limitations might be acceptable once the Communists had lost power. It could have been that freedom of speech was accepted in the case of a speech against Communist power, but rejected in the case of a speech against the Church, Solidarity, or the democratically elected president. The research aimed, therefore, to check how deep and principled acceptance of freedom in Polish society was, and to what degree it was independent of political circumstances. The future of democracy in Poland, as well as in other post-Communist countries, depends upon the moral capital. One technique of assessment of the volume of this capital is to ask how many Poles support various rights. The state of public opinion need not be reflected in the opinions of the politicians precisely, but interest in elections seems to be a factor that would secure the minimum influence of society on public decisions, a minimum that would make it impossible for a democratic government to neglect society. This society, as mentioned in earlier chapters, differs from the society of established democracies. Polish society entered the Communist period still predominantly agricultural, with a minority of the work-force employed in industry and administration; it left Communism with the majority engaged in industry, urbanized, and educated at elementary and trade-vocational level. In 1990 it is a workers' society, with the upper classes composed of skilled or better-educated workers and various shades of intelligentsia. The majority, 76 per cent, count themselves as middle class, but this is neither the nineteenth-century class of artisans, small businessmen, and shopkeepers, to whom the leaders of the economy seem to trust the future, nor the modern middle class of those engaged in services such as social work or education. It seems to me that in Poland the feeling of relative autonomy of the socialist 'new middle class' of skilled workers and white-collar workers which developed under socialism still persists. Both the proletarianized unskilled workers and the office clerk are outside this category. The political careers of electricians and journalists were startling; now, however, this 'new middle class' of socialism is likely to fall apart, while capitalism threatens the mass proletarianization of those who until now were employed by the state, whether in an industrial enterprise, an office, or a service industry. Changes are, nevertheless, just beginning, and the directions as well as the pace are by no means as clear as it might seem from the political declarations of the national political élites.


## THE STATE AND THE CITIZEN

When we speak of these issues it seems worthwhile to learn how people in Poland approach the state as authority and what expectations they have of it. I have asked on two occasions about the various duties of public authorities towards the citizen. In 1988 the state was the Communist state, and one might think that the answers are related to the discrepancy between the official vocation of the socialist state and its real functioning. It was hardly surprising, then, that an absolute majority of 91 per cent thought that the state had a duty to secure permanent employment for everyone in accordance with his or her skills. Two years later the percentage was lower, but 71 per cent of Poles still think this to be a duty of the state. One could not today refer to the relationship between doctrine and practice; it is evident that in the national consciousness there is a deeply rooted conviction that to provide adequate opportunities for citizens to fulfil their aspirations is the vocation of public authorities. It is, therefore, no wonder that almost every Pole—95 per cent in 1990 and 93 per cent in 1988—think that it is a duty of the state authorities to safeguard for everybody a minimum survival income, pension, or benefit. A clear majority of those surveyed in 1990—66 per cent—think that the state also has a duty to provide housing for everybody if they are poor and homeless. No changes occurred either in the views on rationing that led in 1980 to Solidarity enforcement on the state authorities of universal rationing coupons for various goods; 70 per cent in 1988 and 74 per cent in 1990 were of the opinion that, when faced with shortage of certain goods, the state has a right to introduce rationing coupons. The belief that it is a duty of the state to 'safeguard the welfare of each citizen' decreased dramatically from 56 per cent to 33 per cent over the two years. The majority surveyed—77 per cent in 1990 and 84 per cent in 1988—thought that the relationship between the citizen and the state was based upon the principle of reciprocity, and that 'the citizen should fulfil his obligations towards the state if the latter takes care of the citizen's rights and interests'. In this matter I observed a slight increase from 10 per cent in 1988 to 17 per cent in 1990 in those who think that 'the citizen should always fulfil his obligations towards the state independent of whether the state takes care of the citizen's rights interests'. This change may have resulted from increased affiliation to the state following its de-politicization and de-Communization. In both cases, however, we saw a small minority of citizens who would like to be, for instance, ready for some sacrifices on behalf of the state, unless a basic threat such as loss of independence is in question. I did not ask directly about these matters, but some indirect data is available from answers to the questions about whether a young man has a right to refuse military service for political reasons. Such a right was afforded in 1990 by 46 per cent of those interviewed, and enjoyment of such a right was approved by 36 per cent. One may not think these percentages large, but for the fact that two years earlier, when under pressure from the conscientious objectors' Freedom and Peace movement (WIP), the still-Communist army removed from the military oath any reference to socialism and alliance with the USSR. The respective percentages then were smaller and amounted to 33 per cent and 23 per cent respectively. The change to democracy also, as we see, further decreased acceptance of the duty of loyalty to the state authorities. At the same time, acceptance of the right to emigrate from Poland because of the bad economic conditions increased from 74 per cent in 1988 to 86 per cent in 1990. Those figures suggest that during democratization the sense of civil obligation towards the state weakens, that it is present only amongst a minority, and that Polish public opinion is now characterized by acknowledgement of the priority of private interests over the public, and of the duty of the public authorities to serve the private interests of the citizens.

It is important to check whether those attitudes are predominant in specific sectors of society or are evenly distributed. The latter is evident in the case of the duty of the state to safeguard a minimum standard of living for each citizen, as this is acknowledged by practically everybody. On other issues tackled by the survey some differentiation of opinions may be observed. Gender, however, was not significant. Age appeared to be of great importance in the case of the attitude towards military service. While half of the generation under 30 accepted a politically motivated

objection to the military oath, among older people such acceptance becomes more rare, falling to one-fourth of those over 60
years old. The right to politically motivated objection is accepted
by the majority of the young and rejected by the majority of the
older generation. The eldest group were also more likely to support unconditional loyalty of the citizen towards the state, though
even among this group this view is held by only 27 per cent. On
the other hand, when the obligations of the state towards the
individual are discussed, the young recognize more often the duty
of public authorities to safeguard employment for everybody,
while older people are more ready to accept any employment.

Education, like age, bears no relation to attitudes towards emigration. With education, however, the frequency of approval for
politically motivated objection to military service increases, and
acceptance of the duty of the state to provide employment—
appropriate to the skills of the individual or not—and welfare
decreases. It is important to note that it is among those with
higher education that one finds the largest proportion of those
who support unconditional loyalty towards the state. Below university education level, making loyalty towards the state conditional upon performance by the state respecting individual's
rights and interests increases with the educational level (from elementary incomplete through intermediary levels to higher complete). This seems to reflect the peculiar attitude towards the
Polish state amongst the intelligentsia. The same result appears
when type of job is taken into consideration, though the unskilled
workers are usually in opposition to the white-collar workers with
higher education, who are least likely to accept emigration.

The data cited above suggests that in Poland the majority
expect the public authorities to safeguard not only a subsistence
minimum standard of living but also properly paid work fit for
their skills; and their loyalty towards the state is conditional upon
the fulfilment of their rights, interests, and aspirations. This
social and political fact needs to be taken into account by the
intelligentsia who took responsibility for the state, and who are
ready to accept loyalty towards the state even if this would not
safeguard for a citizen anything except subsistence. Economic
reality may force us to consider the concept of the welfare state as
unrealistic, but it would also be unrealistic to neglect the political
reality of contemporary Poland. The reality includes the expecta-

tion of the masses in a society undergoing acute economic transformation of protection and assistance from the state.


## FREEDOM AND EQUALITY

It is clear that Polish society is attached to basic political freedoms. In 1990, 68 per cent, and in 1988 70 per cent of those
interviewed regarded it as a duty of the state to safeguard the citizen's right to public expression of political opinions. Is, however,
the question of freedom paramount, especially in the face of a
permanently malfunctioning economy and low standard of living?
Socialists for two centuries stressed that true freedom is impossible without social equality. The right has stressed, on the other
hand, that individual freedom is impossible if equality restricts
human aspirations, achievements, and entrepreneurship. Poles
are divided equally into those who put freedom and those who
put equality first. In 1988 a majority of 51 per cent thought that
in Poland there was too little freedom, while 29 per cent thought
that there was enough, 10 per cent that there was too little, and
10 per cent had no opinion. After Communism, in Autumn
1990, feelings of a lack of freedom were reported by 30 per cent,
40 per cent were satisfied, 20 per cent thought there was too
much freedom, and 10 per cent as before had no opinion. As a
sociologist I feel ashamed to present such a quantitative assessment of such dramatic political change. Freedom led to a
decrease of 21 points in the frequency of dissatisfied liberals, and
an increase of 10 points of the dissatisfied anti-liberals. The net
increase in social satisfaction was 11 per cent.

'And what about equality, is there too much or too little of it?'
I asked in both surveys. In 1988, the last year of real socialism 74
per cent answered that there was too little equality in Poland, and
11 per cent did not answer the question. Dissatisfaction with the
degree of equality under Communism was even larger than dissatisfaction with the degree of freedom, an apparent paradox only
if we take into account both the real social differentiation, and the
stress on equality as both reality and as a promise for future. In
Autumn 1990 a slightly smaller majority were dissatisfied with
the level of equality—71 per cent—while 13 per cent found the
level appropriate, 13 per cent too large, and 9 per cent refrained

from expressing an opinion. To assess these results properly one needs to add that between Autumn 1988 and Autumn 1990 the frequency of those who answered that they felt satisfied with their life increased from 74 per cent to 78 per cent. One feels entitled to suspect various individual factors apart from politics behind those answers. When Adam Podgórecki asked the question for the first time in a national Polish survey[1] in 1964, 65 per cent of the urban population and 72 per cent in the countryside were satisfied with life. Who knows if the gentle course of the 'velvet revolution' in Poland as well as in other Communist countries resulted from the ability to adjust one's way of life to the environment to such a degree that a decisive majority in society were satisfied with life? The frequency of satisfaction has increased by 4 points over the last two years and, though small, the increase should be noted. It is insignificant, though, when compared with the increase in satisfaction with freedom. How all this will affect the political attitudes of society in the future is difficult to say. One cannot, however, neglect the high degree of dissatisfaction with inequality in Poland. Capitalism under other circumstances offered equal opportunities, more equal than feudal or socialist society had offered, and one should take this egalitarian component of capitalism into account instead of judging it as a relic of the Communist mentality or the threat of populism now widespread in the Polish media and political establishment.

How are freedom and equality judged by people who differ by age, gender, education, or job? Age was unrelated to the choice between those two values, though younger respondents often complained about insufficient freedom in Poland, while the majority of the elderly thought that there was too much freedom, as well as too little equality, today. Women and men did not differ on those issues. With education, however, the frequency of those who chose freedom as the more important increases.

To be more specific, among those who did not complete their elementary education in 1990 41 per cent opted for freedom and 47 per cent for equality. Among those with full elementary education the respective figures were 44 per cent and 46 per cent; among those with trade-vocational education and full middle education, 45 per cent and 50 per cent; among those with some

---

[1] Adam Podgórecki, *Prestiż prawa* (Prestige of Law) (Warsaw, 1966).

middle education, 64 per cent and 33 per cent; and among those with full higher education, 80 per cent and 15 per cent. The choice between freedom and equality as the more important was not unequivocally related to assessment of society on other criterion. The low value the intelligentsia in Poland attaches to equality is shown by this group's difference from all others in their opinion that there is too much equality in Poland today. Such an anti-egalitarian attitude is characteristic of only a minority of Polish public opinion and prevails only in the minority category of the intelligentsia. One cannot refrain here from the observation that this may result from the fact that the intelligentsia in Poland felt levelled down to the level of the 'new middle classes' of socialist society, and that freedom, democracy, and capitalism seem to offer to the intelligentsia the promise of a better social position than in the past.

## POLITICAL FREEDOMS

But what political freedoms are we talking about? In the questionnaire several issues were raised that are related to the traditional catalogue of political liberties. But the political context changed radically between the two surveys. The general liberal stance of Polish public opinion, nevertheless, remained unchanged. This is shown by several items from the 1988 and 1990 studies. In 1988, 50 per cent acknowledged the right to ridicule public figures by caricature, with 32 per cent opposing and 18 per cent of no opinion. In 1990 the acknowledgement of such a right increased to 58 per cent, with 28 per cent opposing and 14 per cent not expressing an opinion. In both surveys the distribution of answers to the question concerning the dispersal of illegal anti-government street demonstrations, discussed in detail in the preceding chapter, is the same—32 per cent recognizing the right of state authorities to disperse demonstrations with force, 53 per cent not granting such a right to the authorities, and 15 per cent not having an opinion. One must observe, however, that in 1988 the question would most probably be answered with Solidarity demonstrations against the Communist government in mind, while in 1990 the Solidarity-based government would be the object of protest by illegal street demonstrations, not necessarily by Communists, but by the both right-wing and left-wing radical groups.

The continued dominance of the liberal trend in Polish public opinion is perhaps best illustrated, however, not by the same question asked both in 1988 and in 1990, but from a question which had to be drastically changed following the change in the political context. In Autumn 1988 when asked whether authorities had the right to de-legalize Solidarity, 28 per cent granted the authorities such a right, 51 per cent refused it, and 21 per cent expressed no opinion. Granting a right and approval might be two different things. When asked whether they approved the de-legalization, 20 per cent said yes, 62 per cent said no, and 18 per cent did not give an answer. In Autumn 1990 the closest equivalent of this item in the questionnaire was the question about whether the authorities have the right to forbid the activities of organizations that continue the Communist tradition and that of the Polish United Workers Party. The right of the authorities to ban Communist activities was acknowledged by 32 per cent, opposed by 46 per cent, and 22 per cent expressed no opinion. This is impossible to check, but it seems likely that some of the 1988 opponents to the legality of Solidarity are the same people who today support a ban on Communist activities. Such a ban would be supported by 21 per cent and opposed by 68 per cent, while 11 per cent gave no answer. The distribution of answers was strikingly similar over time. The majority consistently support freedom of expression, association, and assembly independent of ideological content. This suggests strong political tolerance. Are the enemies of freedom to be found together in one of the various social categories?

Age seems to play some part here. The elderly are more likely to refuse the right to publish political caricatures, and more likely to approve the right to disperse anti-government demonstrations. Women (the stereotype of feminine mildness may be of influence here) are somewhat less often inclined to accept the right of the police to disperse street demonstrations, and the right to caricature political leaders. Skilled workers, people with middle-school education, and especially people with higher education are more likely to recognize the right to political satire, though education and skills were not related to attitudes towards freedom of assembly. Neither age nor gender were related to the attitudes towards Communist activities. Here education seems to play the crucial role. Amongst those with partial elementary education, 31 per cent rejected the right of the authorities to ban Communist activities, while 37 per cent would accept such a ban. Among those with only elementary education the figures are respectively 39 per cent and 48 per cent; among those with trade or vocational and partial middle-school education, 44 per cent and 53 per cent, among those with completed middle-level education, 53 and 62 per cent; and among those with a partial higher education, 55 per cent and 64 per cent. One needs to stress here, however, that the positive relationship between liberalism and education is brought about mainly through a decrease in the 'don't knows', who represent 38 per cent among the least-educated and less than 10 per cent among the best-educated. That is, although the frequency of those who openly support political tolerance increases with education, the proportion of the intolerant remains unchanged.

## FAITH AND POLITICS

The preceding chapter raised the question of the complexity of Polish moral and religious attitudes. The transition from Communism to democracy in Poland was linked to the strengthening of the public role of the Catholic Church, which emerged as the strongest institution in the country, one that even Solidarity, much weakened after martial law, could not rival, not to mention the compromised public authorities. Polish public opinion becomes of direct political importance in these circumstances.

For instance, the most heated political debate at the turning-point for the political system turned out to be the debate over the future of abortion. Abortion had been legalized in 1956 as part of the liberalization package, but the Church had never been able to accept this, and with passage of time in the Catholic opposition media the legality of abortion was moved gradually further back in time and labelled as genuinely Stalinist legislation. Both the last days of the Communist parliament and the new 1989 parliament were divided on the issue, as Catholic deputies drafted laws aiming not only to ban abortion but also to punish aborting women and their helpers in the medical profession.[2] The signs from public-opinion studies, including my own, were not, however, supportive to those 'pro-life' attempts at legislation. Catholic public opinion and politicians found themselves suddenly in conflict with general public opinion which until then they had been willing to represent. Not surprisingly, in view of this, the pro-lifers started to stress the basic and indisputable character of the right to life, that could not be compromised by submission to a national referendum. The results of such a referendum would, most probably, oppose an unconditional ban on abortion. In 1990, when the specific question was included in my questionnaire, only 13 per cent supported a total ban and punishment for abortion, while 33 per cent were in favour of abortion when medical considerations indicated such a decision, 26 per cent were for the right to abortion under difficult living conditions and in large families, and finally 23 per cent thought that an abortion should be performed whenever a pregnant woman wishes. Polish public opinion, which is predominantly Catholic, wants children to be taught religion in public schools if their parents wish it (79 per cent); but also (70 per cent in 1988 and 77 per cent in 1990) that children should learn about contraception in order to prevent the necessity to consider abortion. In public opinion the dominant model differs from that propagated by the Church and subject to controversy in the media and parliament. The popularity of the Church started to decrease for the first time. Primate Cardinal Józef Glemp stated that the Church was not competing in a popularity contest. But democracy cannot accept the imposition in the name of Catholicism, of laws to which society is opposed. When asked directly about the relationship between religion and public life, Poles explicitly supported separation. In Autumn 1990 only 9 per cent chose the answer that 'the majority of Poles are Catholics and therefore Catholicism should become the state religion and the Catholic Church should influence public decisions'. The majority, (61 per cent of the sample) thought that the 'state should be separate from religious issues which should remain private for every citizen', and 27 per cent chose the opinion that 'Catholicism should be sup-

---

[2] See M. Fuszara, 'Legal Regulation of Abortion in Poland', *Signs* (1991), or 'Will the abortion issue give birth to feminism in Poland', in *Women's Issues in Social Policy*, ed. M. Maclean and D. Groves (London, 1991), 205–29.

ported by the state, but with safeguards for the rights of other religions and non-believers to public expression of their beliefs and freedom of conscience'. In view of the very high percentage of those without opinion on other issues it is noticeable that here only 3 per cent gave no answer. It is clear that the majority explicitly reject the involvement of the Church in public life as well as the establishment of religion.

In 1990 the Ministry of Education reintroduced teaching of religion in public schools for children whose parents wished it. This has resulted in an upheaval among the more agnostic who were irritated both by the administrative character of the decision that involved an important constitutional matter, as well as by the fact that the decision was made by the government of Tadeusz Mazowiecki, who was considered to be less prone to Catholic bigotry than other politicians. The constitutionality of the administrative act has since been upheld by the Constitutional Court, acting in response to a question posed by the Ombudswoman Professor Ewa Letowska. The controversy tempted me to ask in the 1990 questionnaire if people would accept the introduction of religious teaching in schools as obligatory if such was the decision of the majority of the parents. It is interesting to note that as many as 41 per cent would support the compulsory teaching of religion introduced in a democratic way, with 53 per cent opposed and 6 per cent expressing no opinion. Support for such democratically introduced compulsory religious education in the public schools increased with age, from 28 per cent in favour and 68 per cent opposed among those under 30, up to 58 per cent in favour and 36 per cent opposed among those at least 60 years old. Education was also of related significance, as support for compulsory religious education increased from 69 per cent among those with partial elementary education to 23 per cent in favour among those with completed higher education, while the figures for those opposing compulsory religious education were respectively 28 per cent and 72 per cent. Education, skilled work, and younger age were related to less support for unconditional protection of the unborn child. Gender made no difference on this issue! Support for the idea of making Catholicism the state religion in Poland also slightly increased with age and decreased with education, but in all social categories remained marginal, achieving a maximum of 17 per cent supporters among farmers, and 15 per cent among those with incomplete elementary education. The relation between the opinion of the constituency and that of the elected representative remains the most mysterious aspect of modern democracy, but certainly the idea of making Poland a Catholic state raised by some politicians seems, in the context of this data, to show either ignorance or total disregard for their own society, or even a challenge to the majority that may lead to mass anti-clericalism and the departure of Polish society from the Church which protected it for decades against totalitarian nihilism and disregard for human rights.

## The Machinery of Democracy

If I had known the direction that the abortion debate would take later, I would have included in the 1990 questionnaire the issue of a referendum, and whether such mechanisms for democratic government are supported by Polish public opinion. It seems to me, nevertheless, quite obvious that the concepts of freedom and democracy that function in Polish society assume the direct participation of those interested in making decisions on matters which they are involved in.

This participatory concept of direct democracy had been detected already by M. Fuszara in her 1989 research on a representative sample in Warsaw.[3] She asked people who should decide whether a troublesome child should be sent to an institution—whether it should be the parents or some other persons acting in a formal role such as the police, the school, or the court. Parental authority being her main interest, it was interesting to see whether the collectivistic ideology has resulted in overturning the rights of parents and the autonomy of family. The answer was no, as 66 per cent held that the parents should decide, though the court was next in popularity with 40 per cent, 25 per cent pointed to the school, and 6 per cent to the police. More than one answer could have been given. In the next set of questions (see Table 14.1), various public issues were presented, and respondents were asked who should be involved in the decision-making process: the people themselves, organizations, representa-

---

[3] Unpublished survey on 'Parental Authority and Law'.

TABLE 14.1. *Opinions on responsibility for decision-making* (%)

Who should decide on important local issues, e.g. about construction of a nuclear power plant, a large industrial plan, establishment of a nature reservation, or construction of an expensive sewage cleaning system in the area?

| | |
|---|---|
| Local residents through a ballot | 75 |
| Head of region | 6 |
| Local council | 11 |
| Government | 5 |
| Seym | 13 |
| Court | 2 |
| Someone else | 3 |

Who should decide about the existence of an organization, e.g. a trade union, political party, or association?

| | |
|---|---|
| Only people who want to establish the group | 89 |
| Police | 1 |
| Government | 6 |
| Seym | 7 |
| Court | 6 |
| Someone else | 1 |

Who should decide what is published in a newspaper or book?

| | |
|---|---|
| Content should be decided by the author and nobody else | 67 |
| Editor and publisher should decide | 31 |
| State censorship | 11 |
| Court | 1 |
| Someone else | 2 |

Who should decide on the closing down of a place of work?

| | |
|---|---|
| Employees in a ballot | 33 |
| Employees' self-management | 31 |
| Director of the management | 18 |
| Government minister | 19 |
| Local council | 7 |
| Regional head | 2 |
| Court | 5 |
| Someone else | 8 |

Who should decide which and how many trade unions should function in a work-place?

| | |
|---|---|
| Employees in a ballot | 78 |
| Employees' self-management | 17 |
| Government | 2 |
| Seym | 2 |
| Court | 2 |
| Director | 5 |
| Someone else | 1 |

Who should have the right to put forward candidates for the Seym and local councils?

| | |
|---|---|
| Each adult citizen | 50 |
| Citizens, but only if the candidate is supported by a group of e.g. 3,000 people | 40 |
| Trade union | 24 |
| Polish United Workers Party | 10 |
| Agrarian Party | 10 |
| Democratic Party | 12 |
| Solidarity | 23 |
| High organizations | 8 |

tives (in 1989 that would still be a rather dubious notion as democracy was just beginning), or the authorities.

It is clear that in all the listed areas of public life, and the workplace as a socialist state's employing establishment, whether enterprise or office (public as well), that public opinion was suspicious of representative bodies and organizations, and supported direct decision-making by the citizens themselves. The citizens are to put forward candidates to the representative bodies, the author is to decide about publication, and the residents about what is to be constructed in that area. Even Solidarity, as is clear from the last question in Table 14.1, has not been invested with unconditional confidence by the majority.

In my research this dimension had already emerged when I asked about the compulsory teaching of religion if such was the will of the majority of the parents. This is supported only slightly less frequently than the opposite position. In fact we are dealing here with two models of democracy: a liberal one, which safeguards the rights of the losing minority, and the 'majoritarian', according to which Huguenots or Catholics are to surrender to the winning side. This is related to another dilemma of democratic theory, that is, whether a direct model of democracy is to be applied in which the will of the people is directly expressed through referendum or plebiscite, or an indirect one, in which the enlightened will of the people is expressed by its elected representative even in conflict with the directly expressed public opinion of the constituency. This question is touched upon in another question from the national surveys in which I asked whether the authorities have the right to construct a nuclear power plant without asking local residents their opinion. Both in 1988 and in 1990 only 16 per cent acknowledge such a right for the authorities, while 71 per cent in 1988 and 77 per cent in 1990 forbade the authorities to act. In 1990 I added another question of more actual significance, that is, whether the authorities have a right to sell the state's enterprise to a private buyer without asking the employees their opinion. Here, and under the new democratic government, direct participation in decision-making was acknowledged by a substantial majority: 70 per cent thought that the authorities have no right to do so, 20 per cent gave the authorities the right to do so, and 10 per cent gave no answer. In my surveys this particular item seemed best to illustrate the proclivity to direct participatory democracy. It is interesting that it was only in this case that the generation under 30 differed from all the preceding ones in that it gave the authorities the right to make decisions on their own without consulting the employees concerned. The intelligentsia, who are the least exposed to such situations, are the most prone to reject the duty to consult employees, while skilled workers, the politically crucial category, most often supported obligatory consultation. But even among those with higher education, the concept of participatory democracy dominates, and the idea of delegating the decision to the authorities was accepted by only about one-third.

Attachment to the mechanisms of direct decision-making is something that the politicians shaping the public institutions of Poland need to take into account. It could be a manifestation of the distrust for those who rule, resulting from decades of bad experience. The widely observed critique of the functioning of the 1989 parliament may also result from such mistrust and unwillingness to leave matters in the hands of even the most freely elected representatives.

The mistrust of representative democracy need not be related to the willingness to be actively involved in public life. I asked in 1990 whether in the last, politically cumbersome year, people had been directly involved in any public activities. According to their answers it looks as if even at such a historically important moment direct public activity remains a minority experience: 16 per cent had appeared publicly at a meeting; 6 per cent had written to a newspaper or called the radio or television; 7 per cent had taken part in a strike or strike alert; 4 per cent had taken part in a demonstration; 7 per cent were on the list of candidates to some elected body; and as many as 59 per cent declared taking part in local-government elections. As the latter figure was lower in reality, so the other manifestations of public involvement may also have been over-reported. Attachment to the idea of direct democracy lies not so much in active participation as in the willingness to have nothing decided without the agreement of those directly involved. Polish democracy at the turning-point is thus ideally not so much representative parliamentary democracy as the self-governing society that was idealized by Solidarity in its Programme of 1981, ridiculed by the technocratically minded Communist ruling élite of the 1980s, and today more and more often neglected by the equally technocratic politicians who came from Solidarity to power.

New power, as the elections and public-opinion polls prove, is under permanent critical assessment by a society that is neither inclined to praise an individual nor a movement, even one with such a meritous history as Solidarity. In Autumn 1990 a relative majority was convinced that changes in Poland were too slow, and some acceleration as well as a total change of the system was needed, while 33 per cent opted for gradual changes, and 10 per cent gave no opinion. Those three tendencies—radical, moderate, and conservative in relation to real socialism—are not equally distributed in Polish society. Contrary to common belief, age is irrelevant here, and men are only slightly more often in favour of radical changes than women, and less often conservative. The major factor seems to be education. Only among those who have completed the middle level of education did the moderates (44 per cent) prevail over the radicals (39 per cent), and among those with higher education there were 51 per cent of moderates as opposed to 31 per cent of radicals. For comparison, amongst those with partial elementary education the respective figures were 41 per cent radicals and 16 per cent moderates; among those with full elementary education 45 per cent and 26 per cent; among those with trade-vocational and partial middle education 46 per cent and 33 per cent; among farmers 45 per cent and 16 per cent; among unskilled workers 37 per cent and 32 per cent; and among skilled workers 47 per cent and 33 per cent. These differences, which should be considered together with the differential size of the particular groups in society (those with higher education are 7 per cent, while those with full middle-level education 32 percent of the electorate), have been manifest during the duel between Wałęsa and Mazowiecki. The majority of society expected quick changes that would result in positive outcomes for their lives.

Politicians who would like, however, to develop social demogoguery in the long run should take care as the above-mentioned mistrust that accompanies attachment to the idea of direct democracy results in high moral expectations of politicians. It does not mean that everybody is necessarily in favour of the public transparency of office, but it is important that 79 per cent of public opinion in Autumn 1990 thought that a parliamentarian or member of a local council has no right to introduce regulations that would effect his or her private business. An absolute majority—83 per cent—also thought that a politician has no right to promise during the electoral campaign something that he or she knows it would not be possible to implement afterwards. The latter needs to be made clear to all who decide to enter public life in the new post-Communist Poland. The fate of parliamentary democracy is in their hands, as it is extremely easy in such conditions and in the context of such expectations to break the trust of society. Such a failure would most probably lead in the direction of the more direct, though at the same more anarchic democracy which Poland enjoyed in the sixteenth to eighteenth centuries. But who knows? Europe is full of debates between the proponents of the more participatory models of democracy and those who defend the classical model of representative government. At a time when the idea of state as owner is a bad memory of the socio-technical barbarian era, this debate preserves and seems to be the legacy of the debate between the Left and Right. It might emerge, though, that the apparently Left concept of direct democracy would be best met if a Swiss referendum were to be linked with Belgian compulsory voting, American rotation on the jury panels . . . and the Polish model of the political rights of employees and their trade unions.

The thesis of this book is that throughout the post-war history of Communist rule in Central Europe—and this includes Poland, Czechoslovakia, and Hungary—the internal standard brought in by the victorious Soviet Union coincided with another that was present both in the indigenous culture as the hidden constitution of heart and in the message arriving from the free world. Both patterns were external to the system, but the system was also alien and external to them, so it was prone to collapse when the opportunity arose.

One may tend to think that the phenomenon is geographically, culturally, and historically limited. But after all, what was the Tiananmen Square demonstration about, even if its details in apparent insulation remind us of the early nineteenth-century Russian dissidents, the Decembrists. Here and there one can blame events on foreign influence. The Russian Army that visited the West brought back constitutional ideas, while foreign media and studies abroad may have done the same for a new generation of Chinese intelligentsia. In both cases the peasant army is used by a tyrannical government to crush the hopes expressed in a disarmingly peaceful way. This implies that the ultimate leadership will listen to and change its mind. But it means also that there is a ground in each human soul that makes it ready to accept the message.

Totalitarianism can flourish on the green hills of Tuscany as well as in the steppes of Eurasia. The liberation movement in Mongolia has proved to be more successful until now than in China or Russia. The second thesis is, thus, that the Rule of Law meant as the Rule of Rights is founded in human nature and belongs to the universal constitution of the heart even if hidden very deep in this structure. One can explain events in Poland by reference to the Polish tradition of individual freedoms, as one can try to explain events in Albania by reference to Italian television commercials. But to neglect the universality of the phenomenon is to miss the basic message about mankind and its proclivity for freedom, evidenced in the doctrine of Original Sin.

The third point I wish to make here is that, while to understand the institutions of a given society one needs to investigate and clarify the standards by which they can be assessed, to understand both the potential for change and the actual pace of it one needs to look into another comparative frame of reference. In our case those two frames interrelate. What was the model yesterday became the negative frame of reference today, past patterns of aspiration and reference became the model of today.

In what follows I would like to focus on how the present performance and the present model are related; in other words, what is the present state of the Rule of Law in Poland. I will also try to hint at some of the critical points in which the legacy of the past permeates the present and shapes the future.

It happens that 1991 was a bicentennial of the first Polish Constitution proclaimed by the Polish Parliament on 3 May 1791. This was the second constitution in the world, passed after the American Constitution and inspired by it as well as by the common spirit of enlightenment and freedom that gave rise to the founders of the American as well as the Polish Constitution. In those days, however, as well as later, the fire of freedom was better preserved across the ocean than in Europe. Poland lost its independence a few years after the Constitution was passed. In fact it was the Constitution itself that provoked the outburst of aggression on behalf of the absolute monarchies that bordered on Poland, with the result that the once-great power was divided between Russia, Prussia, and Austria. The idea of constitutional government was not extinct, and even the Treaty of Vienna provided that in part of the territories taken by Russia, where the Kingdom of Poland was created and ruled by the Russian tsar, the regime was constitutional. This experiment with a Russian autocrat in charge of a constitutional state could not flourish. After the Poles lost the war against Russia in 1831 both Polish autonomy and their constitution were dismantled in this part of Europe, and one needed to wait until the Spring of Nations (the Year of Revolutions in 1848) to see the emergence of constitutional monarchies in Prussia and Austria, a still-convulsive process that continued into the last years of the nineteenth century, and was joined by Russia after 1905. In 1918 Poland was resurrected as an independent state with new frontiers, and with a legacy of Prussian, Austrian, and Russian law. In 1923 the new Constitution was passed that guaranteed several basic freedoms as well as social rights. The geopolitical environment was again hostile to democracy. International Communism, after attempts to spread throughout Europe, failed when the Polish army defeated the Red army in 1920, and turned to the construction of a totalitarian Soviet state to the east of Poland. From the south the ideology of Italian fascism was spreading, and in the west National Socialism gained power in Germany. The parliamentary democracy was frustrating the expectations of major sectors of politically active public opinion, and an anti-constitutional coup was executed in 1926 by Piłsudski, the man who established independence at the end of the First World War. In a multi-ethnic and multi-denominational society the dominant Polish majority felt threatened in the attempt to reconstruct the Polish state. Polish nationalists in the 1930s were in opposition, inciting anti-Semitic attitudes, and the ruling political camp, though co-operating with Zionists, was trying to assimilate by all possible means the Byelorussian, Ruthenian, and Ukrainian minorities. Politicians from the extreme right and extreme left were interned. The new Constitution of 1930 centralized power in the hands of the president and limited the division of power. The anti-liberal character of this constitution was severely criticized by the right and the left. Soon it was revealed, however, that it was still a far cry from the abuse of human nature as practiced by Brown or Red totalitarianism, when Poland lost independence again in 1939 at the beginning of the Second World War and emerged from it in 1945 as a state ruled, at first *de facto* and then *de iure*, by the Communists.

The new democratic Poland that started to emerge, first in 1980/1 under the aegis of the independent and self-governing trade union Solidarity, that united 10 million members (almost one-fourth of the population of the country), and then again since the 1989 Round Table agreements between the opposition and the Communist administration, has inherited the Constitution that was imposed in 1952 by the Communists on the model of Stalin's (in fact Bukharin's) Soviet Constitution from the 1930s. One of the first moves of the new Parliament in 1989 was to amend this Constitution and to initiate work on the new Constitution, setting the Bicentennial as the deadline. Such deadlines are sure to be dangerous. There were many reasons why the task proved to be difficult. First of all, the 1989 Parliament that functioned until 1991 was composed of two houses elected in different ways. The Senate, limited in power, had been elected in a freely contested way, while the lower house, the Seym, had been elected in a way that guaranteed the Communists one-third and their political allies another one-third of the seats, with the remaining third open to free contest. The effect was that, though Poland ceased to be a Communist country, and even the Communist party itself dissolved, giving birth to two competing small Social-Democratic, parties, the representatives elected on the Communist party ticket played a critical role in the legislature. It was understood from the beginning by the anti-Communist political groups not running the Solidarity ticket that this was not a parliament which represented the people, and thus had no right to proclaim the new Constitution. This critique did not apply in the literal sense to the Senate. The lower house was, nevertheless, drafting a new constitution, while the Senate drafted its own. The extra-parliamentary representation of the anti-Communist political opposition started to draft its own proposal. Not surprisingly, the attempts to pass the new Polish Constitution by the Bicentennial failed. The lower house and the Senate agreed on a new preamble to the Constitution of 1952 which, with amendments, is still in power after the new, this time fully democratic, elections of late 1991, and on a series of new amendments that would eliminate the remnants of Communist terminology. This has not been made effective yet, and the country lives under the Constitution of the Republic of Poland as amended on 29 December 1989.

The Constitution as amended, and with all these amendments declared temporary in 1992, then starts with the proclamation that: 'The Republic of Poland is a democratic legal state [*demokratyczne państwo prawne*] implementing the principles of social justice.' This Article 1 epitomizes the compromise between past and present. There was controversy over the 'social justice' clause, as some of the parliamentarians from the Solidarity ticket thought it a relic of totalitarian rhetoric.

Controversial compromise further permeates the text of the document. This Constitution includes, as always, a long chapter (chapter 8) on Fundamental Civic Rights and Duties. I will list the rights explicitly mentioned: equality independent of gender, birth, education, profession, nationality, race, denomination, social background, and social position; the right to employment for pay according to amount and quality of work; the right to leisure; the right to health-protection and to care in case of illness or work disability, including free medical care to all employees and their families; the right to use the natural environment; the right to free education; the right to participate in culture and its creative development; freedom of conscience and of religion; the right to participate in public life and to raise grievances against all state agencies; the right to personal immunity, privacy of home and mail, those rights to be surrendered only in cases provided for by act of parliament; the right to protection abroad and freedom of political asylum. Some of those rights are more specific, such as gender equality (Article 78), protection of the family (Article 79), racial, national, and denominational equality (Article 81). Article 83 guarantees citizens 'freedom of speech, print, assemblies and meetings, demonstrations and parades', and Article 84, freedom of association. Freedom of association is, however, constitutionally limited by Paragraph 3: 'Creation and participation in associations that in their purpose or functioning contravene the political and social system or the legal order of the Republic of Poland is forbidden.' Duties of the citizens are also listed, some of which correlate to the previously listed rights, supplemented with independent ones such as the duty to protect the natural environment; the duty of parents to raise their offspring as duty-conscious citizens; the duty to protect and strengthen the national (social) property as the immutable foundation of the development of the state; safeguarding state secrets; sensitivity to threats from enemies of the nation; and the defence of the country.

The list shows the coexistence of concepts of various origins, such as the liberal tradition (for example, the separation of state and religion), and the totalitarian legacy of Communism (the last-mentioned duties to protect the state against the enemies of the nation). This coexistence is not peaceful, however, if we take into account, first, that overall control of public life by the Communist party has been abolished; second, that this list is accompanied by the division of powers and explicit judicial procedures that safeguards constitutional rights and duties. Let it suffice to point out that the constitutional powers are at the moment busy subverting the duty to strengthen nationalized state property through a programme of accelerated privatization and re-privatization. The Democratic state cannot continue with such internal contradictions and certainly those are the alterations that will 'cleanse' the Constitution. The problem is, however, what is to be cleansed. For some cleansing involves erasing such totalitarian duties as cited above, for others, abolition the right to free schooling, for yet others, the abolition of the separation of state from religion. This is the area where the ideological battle about the future shape of the society is fought. This is, of course, also the area of the major battle between the actors in the pluralist political life of contemporary democratic Poland.

The role of international standards needs to be stressed at this point. They have helped all the time, especially since the Helsinki Agreements. Poland, with free elections to the lower house, has joined the Council of Europe. This brings the opportunity to have the European Court of Human Rights hear cases brought by citizens against the detailed European covenants which serve as the fundamental constitution. That should serve as an example for other regions and for the global community, including the

United States. But let us have no illusions. Cases brought against member governments of the European Community show that the problem with human rights is perennial. The change of the political system is a necessary, but not a sufficient condition for improvement, and the role of independent civic bodies that watch the local situation is of great importance.

Speaking of political institutions, one would not realize how different the Constitution is today without knowledge of the prior provisions. The shameful preamble which in 1976 elevated the 'leading role' of the Communist party to an explicitly acknowledged constitutional principle disappeared with the Polish United Workers Party itself. According to Article 2, supreme power resides in the nation and is executed through elected representatives and referenda. This is narrowed down in Article 20, which makes the Seym, the lower house, the 'supreme agency of the state power' that 'realizes sovereign rights', being 'the supreme agent of expression of the will of the Nation'. This amounts to the sovereignty of the lower house, members of which enjoy immunity and are irrevocable.

Three comments seem necessary at this point. First, the role of the lower house was distinguished because of the political agreements made in 1989 that secured a majority for the Communists and their allies. Secondly, this makes political life full of competition between the lower house and the Senate, which developed its earlier image as both more legitimate as elected in fully open electoral contest and nevertheless relegated to secondary importance. As if the competition between Senate and Seym were not enough, the position of the executive is by no means clear. The president is the 'highest representative' of the state. The role of the president was, however, construed with the political representative of the old regime, General Jaruzelski, in mind. Not surprisingly, apart from representative functions, supreme military command, and appointment of the prime minister, the president supervises local self-government, introduces on his or her own martial law, mobilization, and a state of emergency in case of external or internal threats, to the state's security. Finally, to counterbalance the prime minister and the government, who *in corpore* as well as individually may be revoked by the lower house, the president may appoint ministers of state without any intervention of parliament and take over the presidency of the Council of Ministers in 'matters of extreme importance'. As we see the subtle political contract made at the Round Table between the Communists and Solidarity resulted in the complex power arrangement whereby there are four basic elements: Seym, Senate, government, and president. The Senate in this model serves as an advisory body to the lower house—it has the legislative initiative though it can neither legislate on its own nor effectively veto the lower-house legislation. The government is responsible before the sovereign lower house, so it is parliamentary government. The president can, however, limit the role of both the parliament and its government through extraordinary constitutional measures. The position of the president in this system was strengthened further after the end of Communism due to the amendment that provided for direct election of the president by the nation.

The Rule of Law is directly introduced at this point both through the constitutional duties imposed upon the incumbents of power and through the system of constitutional responsibility and judicial control. 'All agencies of power and state administration act according to the provisions of law' (Article 3.2). The principle of the sovereignty of the lower house is, however, not waived. Although parliamentary legislation may be sent to the Constitutional Tribunal by the president, the verdict on unconstitutionality is still not binding unless the Seym itself agrees. We have already stressed that members of the parliament individually are also not responsible before the constituency. In a situation where the political parties have not yet fully evolved and are often composed only of the parliamentarians themselves, the political responsibility of the representatives is also a fiction. Government is responsible both politically before the lower house and constitutionally before the Tribunal of the Republic. The latter serves also as a special court for the president in case the parliament as the whole—this detail strengthens the position of the president— decide to put him or her under accusation. The tribunal of the Republic (*Trybunal Stanu*) is composed of twenty-two judges appointed by the lower house, and is the special impeachment court which makes decisions on the responsibility of persons who occupy 'the highest state positions for abuse of constitution and laws'.

To summarize: signatories of the Round Table Agreements

and the parliament elected on the basis of this accord have created a system not so much of the Rule of Law as of the Rule of the Seym. Sovereignty resides with the lower house, fragmented after the 1991 elections into eighteen parliamentary factions of from sixty-two to three MPs. The president is an autonomous political force who may constitutionally overpower the parliamentary government, but not sovereign in as much as he or she is under the judicial control of the politically appointed Tribunal of the Republic.

The situation in which Polish society finds itself in the last decade of the twentieth century is that suddenly, under conditions of political democracy, the construction of a capitalist economy is initiated with the approval of the numerically dominant hired-labour force that struggles for the preservation, if not for improvement, of the safe life, and which has at its disposal trade unions that are in reality the strongest mass organizations in the country. Decades of Communism compromised socialism in Poland. A political philosophy that manifests itself in the speech and in the deeds of a society makes it possible to presume that we will not be dealing here with simple approval of the free market without state intervention. A Darwinian model of social development has come to the fore in post-Communist Europe and seems to serve as a more or less explicit philosophy of the new political class, and often includes converts to this way of thinking from those who previously thought in terms of class struggle. This is not far from the truth. The problem is that, however important the spirit of entrepreneurship is, the Darwinian model of capitalism applies neither to the realities of modern capitalism, nor to the Polish ethos.

One can complain that Polish society is uneducated, afraid of capitalist promises, and that it had been thoroughly indoctrinated by decades of socialist teaching at school and in the media, but all this would not change the reality. In a democracy a politician who complains about the electorate should be advised to emigrate, a right Poles very willingly grant each other. It is of course possible, and quite often the case, that politicians hide the truth from the electorate, especially when speaking about economic policies. It is hardly surprising that someone who thinks he or she knows best what is good for the country will try to implement the recipe even when aware that the electorate would reject the offer if told the costs of the procedure. It is hardly surprising also that the electorate will listen more and more cautiously to promises. Sooner or later it will emerge that in order to survive in politics, democratic politicians need to build up a capital of trust with the help of truthfulness, personal integrity, and a readiness to acknowledge past mistakes.

There is another possible scenario. Poland, as well as other post-Communist countries, may develop the old political culture with which several Western democracies have been struggling recently. The vicinities of national assemblies will mushroom with little cafés where representatives of various lobbies and business firms will deal with the representatives of the people, the press will report daily on scandals related to payments taken by this or that politician for state contracts on 'consulting', while the surprised public will read the honourable names on the lists of boards of trustees of the former state enterprises now changed into holding companies. Society, through its 10 per cent representation, will attend the election, while the majority will continue to be busy in developing entrepreneurship in struggles with the revenue office, customs, and with the state generally. In Europe prior to the Second World War, and in Latin America today, there are institutions of democracy such as free elections, parliament, and responsible government, but neither society nor state are democratic. The reason is the social void that separates the political cells from the social masses. The great totalitarian movements of the twentieth century were a response to such social architecture. By abolishing parliamentarism, these movements have widened the social void even more and left the human individual uprooted, atomized, and defenceless before the System. The only preventative measure that comes to mind is the permanent struggle for giving more depth to democracy through wider participation and the richness of its forms. The classroom opposition between representative and participatory democracy takes a different shape in practice. In a developed modern democracy, representatives, the executive power, the judiciary, and political parties are of importance. Americans may complain about low participation in elections and low interest in local government, but in American public life there are still thousands of active associations, from notorious American Rifle Association to the Congress of American Poles and the Congress of American

Jews. Forms, institutions, and rules may change from country to country but the essence is the same from the United States to the United Kingdom to Japan. The political class needs to be under the direct pressure and control of the various associations that represent the specific interests and values of various social categories and groups. The unaffiliated citizen is exposed in a democracy to the same threat as in totalitarianism. Live democracy is necessary in order to prevent corruption, nepotism, parliamentary oligarchy, and manipulation.

The third stage in the construction of a democracy, after the abolition of Communism and the introduction of parliamentary pluralistic representation, is to fill the social void between state and citizen through thousands of openly and legally active voluntary associations that would in daily life, in-between parliamentary elections, control the representatives and precede the assumption into political Heaven that, as the beginnings of the new democracies show, seems to be miraculously easy to attain. Pluralism in public life, apart from pluralism in the market and party pluralism in political life, also seems the only way out of the dilemmas that arise out of the aforementioned expectations which the former subjects of Communism address towards the liberated state. Free competition of pluralistic interest-groups is the only way in which, under public control, the common interest might be shaped. In fact, as we all suspected, there is nothing new in that; the novelty is only that we may again enter the imperfect world of democracy and undertake the unending task of its continuation.

# *Index*